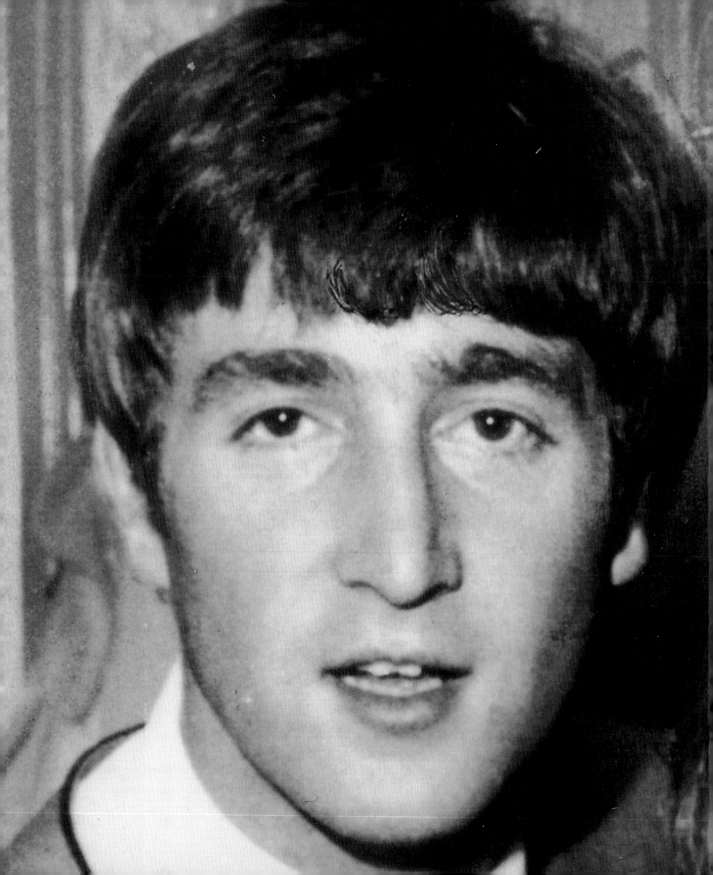

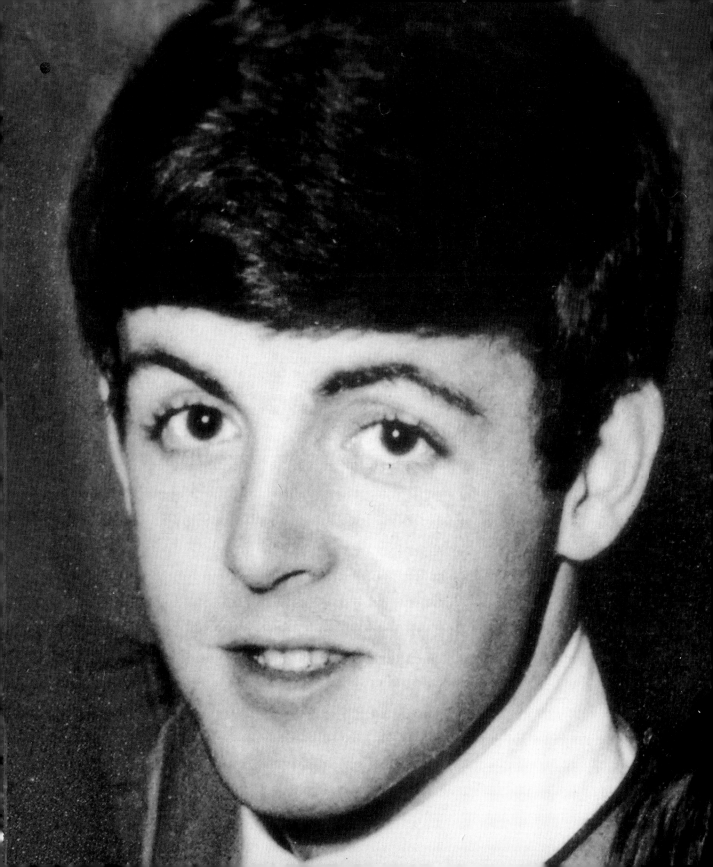

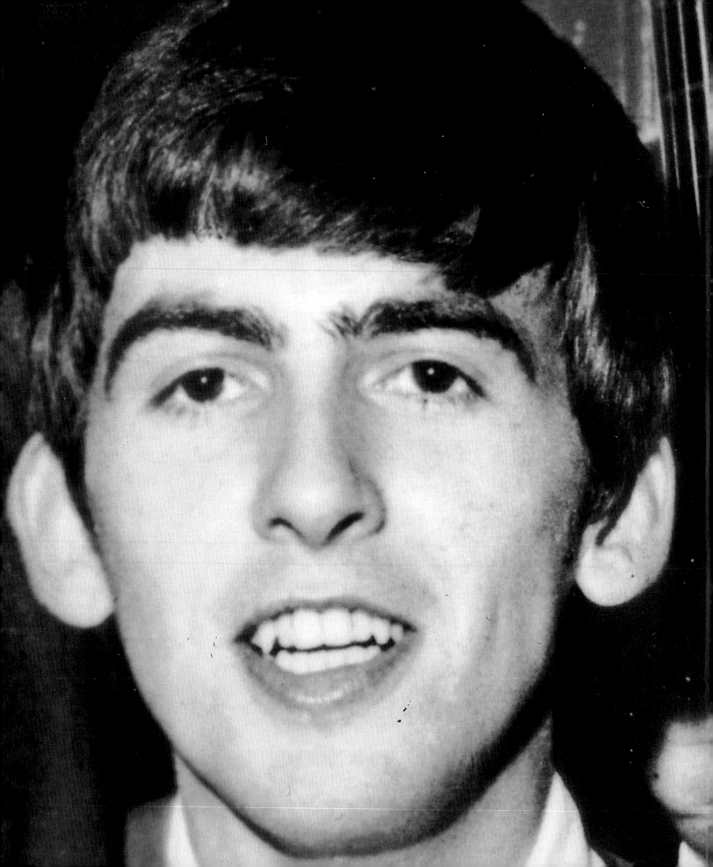

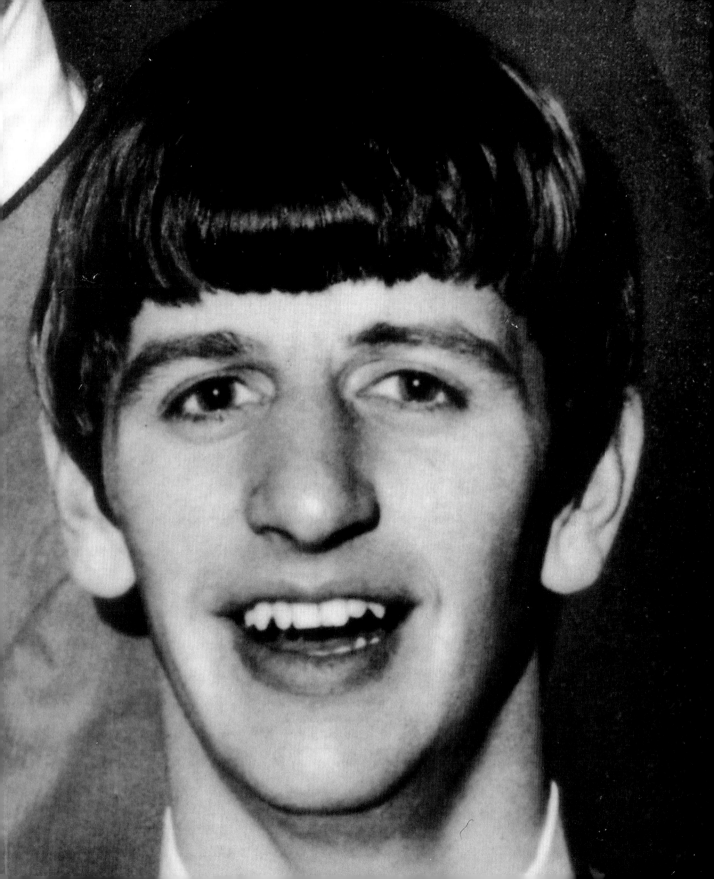

Photos on pp. i, ii, iii,1,10, 26, 58, 60, 71, 73, 78, 93, 102, 103, 119, 123, 168, 171,177, 184, 197, 203, 206, 217, 232, 237, 277, 289, 295, 303, 312-315 courtesy of Photofest; p. 15 courtesy of Getty Images; pp. 32, 57 courtesy of Central Press/Hulton Archives/Getty Images; pp. 54, 129 courtesy of Hulton Archives/Getty Images; pp.107, 180 courtesy of Bob Gomel/TimeLife Pictures/Getty Images; pp. 72, 110, 117, 292, 298 courtesy of Bettmann/Corbis; p. 117 courtesy of Underwood & Underwood/Corbis; p.139 courtesy of Harry Benson/Hulton-Deutsch Collection/Corbis; p. 269 courtesy of Herb Schmitz/Corbis. All other photos courtesy of the authors.

ISBN 1-57912-369-4

Library of Congress Cataloging-in-Publication Data

Spignesi, Stephen J.
Here, there, and everywhere : the 100 best Beatles songs / Stephen J. Spignesi and Michael Lewis.
    p. cm.
 Includes index.
 ISBN 1-57912-369-4
1. Beatles. 2. Rock music—History and criticism. I. Lewis, Michael (Michael D.), 1962- II. Title.

ML421.B4S662 2004
782.42166'092'2—dc22
                                    2004002394

Book design: Scot Covey

Manufactured in the United States of America

Published by
Black Dog & Leventhal Publishers, Inc.
151 West 19th Street
New York, New York 10011

Distributed by
Workman Publishing Company
708 Broadway
New York, New York 10003

g f e d c b a

To the memories of John and George

*I do not know what I may appear to the world, but to myself I
seem to have been only a boy playing on the seashore,
and diverting myself in now and then finding a smoother
pebble or a prettier shell than ordinary. Whilst the great
ocean of truth lay all undiscovered before me.*
—Isaac Newton

For those who are awake the cosmos is one.
—Heraclitus

STEPHEN J. SPIGNESI

• • •

**To the memories of my mother Catherine
and grandmother Sophie**

*When I find myself in times of trouble,
mother Catherine comes to me…*

MICHAEL LEWIS

Here, There and Everywhere

The 100 Best Beatles Songs

Stephen J. Spignesi and Michael Lewis

BLACK DOG
& LEVENTHAL
PUBLISHERS
NEW YORK

Contents

One, two, three, FOUR!

Dear Sir or Madam, Won't You Read Our Book?

"Guitar groups are on their way out, Mr. Epstein."

—Dick Rowe
Decca Records

"'Strawberry Fields Forever' and 'Penny Lane' are what I always imagined when I made a vow with John Lennon to make Liverpool famous, to promote our own experiences and environment."

—Bill Harry

"The importance of the Beatles cannot be overstated."

—Paul Evans
The Rolling Stone Album Guide

Ask a Beatles fan which of the Beatles 206 songs are his or her favorites and the answer will probably be, "All of them!"

Here, There and Everywhere: The 100 Best Beatles Songs is, admittedly, an unusual addition to the library of books about the Beatles, but it is a book that we passionately believe in, and one that we greatly enjoyed writing. Yes, fellow Beatlefans, with boldness and unabashed love for the Fabs, we rank the 100 best Beatles songs. But what is "best" anyway, right? The *American Heritage Dictionary* defines "best" as "surpassing all others in excellence, achievement, or quality; most excellent," and we kept those standards in mind as we were selecting, evaluating, and ranking the songs.

That question begs another question, however: What *is* excellence in art, perhaps the most subjective of all human endeavors? Have you ever seen a painting that consisted of nothing but a yellow canvas, but which art "critics" described as brilliant? Have you ever heard a popular song that you thought was trite, boring, repetitive, and unoriginal, yet it was Number One on the charts and selling by the boatload? Have you ever sat through a movie that was so slow, so depressing, and so mind-numbing that you trudged from the theater seriously thinking about what color stationery you should use for your suicide note—while the rave reviews for the flick echoed through your addled brain?

Art is subjective on two levels: excellence and popularity. Great art is not always the most popular art. And the most popular art is not always the artist's finest work.

This brings us to a discussion of the criteria we used for ranking the 100 best Beatles songs, and the process of culling down to 100 the 206 Beatles songs on our master list.

If a song was written by a Beatle and it appeared on a Beatles record, it became part of the master list. *We did not include covers*, since, even at their best ("Twist and Shout," "Please Mr. Postman," "Money," etc.), these tracks were the Beatles rocking out with *somebody else's* song.) Also, there are a couple of songs on the Master List that are better known as solo Beatles songs, specifically Paul's "Junk" and George's "All Things Must Pass." Yes, they first appeared in final form on Paul and George solo album, but since they were written when the Beatles were together, and since they were originally considered for inclusion on a Beatles album, and since they did, ultimately, *appear* on a Beatles album (*Anthology*), we went ahead and included them on the list. (Neither made the top 100 here, though. However, they do make the top 100 in another book we'd like to write, *John, Paul, George & Ringo: The 100 Best Beatles Solo Songs*.)

To start with, each of us reviewed the master list of 206 and picked the ones we felt definitely deserved inclusion in the top 100. We each came up with close to 150 songs. Next, we created a list of the songs common to both our lists. This totaled around 125 songs. Then we started cutting. We each cut separately and then compared our lists. Eventually, we had a master list of what we both agreed were the 100 best songs.

Our first pass at a Number One included "Strawberry Fields Forever," "A Day In The Life," "Let It Be," "Hey Jude," "Yesterday," and "All You Need Is Love." We both quickly agreed that it should be either "Strawberry Fields Forever" or "A Day In The Life," and we ultimately decided on "A Day

In The Life," with "Strawberry Fields" taking the Number Two spot. "A Day In The Life," the definitive Lennon/McCartney collaboration, emerged as the obvious choice. We then worked on the remainder of the top 10, which was actually pretty easy since we had already selected several of the Beatles' all-time best songs.

The remaining 90 songs were much more difficult to rank. (We're still arguing about "Martha My Dear" being, at once, both too high and too low!) The first thing we did was come up with a "recipe" of the elements that made up a Beatles recording. This resulted in four artistic criteria:

1. **Songwriting**: The further away the song moved from rock's classic (and, truth be told, by now, cliched) three-chord progression (I-IV-V), the higher this rating.
2. **Musicianship**: This covered the Fabs' performance on a given track, both individually and as a group, and included both the playing of the instruments and the quality of the vocals and harmonies.
3. **Production**: we evaluated the use of groundbreaking studio techniques on the track and ranked the song higher if the Fabs and George Martin pushed the technological envelope for the time in which the song was recorded.
4. **Lyrics**: The closer the words were to pure poetry, the higher this rating. Evocative imagery, poignant themes, and meaningful messages all factored into our evaluation of the lyrics.

We hope that our research, our attention to detail, and our explanations as to why we put a song where we did will entertain and enlighten you. We want you to have fun with this book, and possibly learn something new about the Beatles' music.

We have both been listening to, studying, and writing about the Beatles for years, and yet we still learned a lot about their music while researching and writing this book. In acknowledgment of the dilemma of liking a Beatles song but not considering it one of their best, we do include a "fans' favorites" poll at the back. We asked dozens of people—serious and casual Fab fans—for their five favorites. Eventually we had a list of the songs the fans we talked to like the best.

Acknowledgments

Five Things We Want You To Know About How We Compiled This Ranking

1. We wish not to offend, we wish not to blaspheme.
2. The absence of a song from this list in no way demeans it or suggests that it is not a great song. The concept of the book from the get-go was 100 songs so there were a limited number of slots available.
3. Picking the 100 best Beatles songs was a ridiculously difficult task. We were re-evaluating and rearranging songs up until we turned in the final pages of the manuscript, even to the point of nudging a song only a couple of notches up or down. The 106 songs that did not make the list are an extraordinary collection of musical brilliance. That said, you can imagine how we feel about the top 100!
4. We consistently tried to look at each Beatles song as an individual work of art and then evaluate it based on the lyrics, music, production, performances, and overall mojo.
5. Once again, for purposes of this book, and because we're obsessive-compulsive, hardcore completists, we followed one specific rule regarding the eligibility of a song. If it was *written* by a Beatle and it *appeared* on a Beatles album, then it was a candidate for the top 100.

We hope you enjoy our magical mystery trip through the Beatles octopus's garden of songs. And if you come together with anything at all from this book, it should be one simple thing: all you need is love.

Stephen Spignesi
Michael Lewis

June, 2004

As a team, we would like to thank Marilyn Allen, Laura Ross, John White, Bob Diforio, J.P. Leventhal and the entire team at Black Dog & Leventhal, Marisa D'Agosto, Scot Covey, Ron and Howard Mandelbaum and all the fine folks at Photofest, Bill Harry, Donovan, Christopher Clause, Lee Pfeiffer, Stephen Teller, Michael Pye, Kristin Turberville, Tommy Thayer, the Raspyni Brothers, and everyone who voted in our fan's favorites poll.

Steve would like to thank Pam, Lee and Frank, Dolores, Carter, Mike Streeto, Bill Savo, Sheryl and Vinny, Linda and Steve, Paul Hickman, Janet and Jerry and Amanda, Alyse and Rob, Gina and John, Emily Resnik-Conn, Angelyn, John and Barbara White, Dr. Michael Luchini, Dr. Ed and Tonya, Mary Toler, Charlie Fried, Laura and Josh, Lois Pellegrino, and Aida Cupo.

Mike would like to thank Amy, Samantha and Sydney for cheerfully enduring endless hours of hearing the same songs played over and over again; Betty Hamilton; Marilyn Allen; Dr. Chuck Berg; Pastor George Hanssen; Barbara Hetlyn; Juan Valdez for the coffee; the South Beach Diet; family and friends for their opinions, encouragement, and support ... and especially to Catherine and Sophie, my guardian angels.

Note: We welcome your thoughts on what your favorite Beatle songs are, and we will include a new, expanded Fans' Faves poll in future editions of this book. You can contact us through Steve's website, www.stephenspignesi.com, or through our publisher. Thanks!

A Day in the Life

*We could go anywhere with this song;
it was definitely going to go big places.*
—Paul McCartney
The Beatles Anthology

Throughout his career, Woody Allen has frequently admitted that not a single one of his movies fulfilled the vision he originally had for it. In *The Beatles Anthology*, John acknowledged a similar sentiment: "I like 'A Day in the Life,' but it's still not half as nice as I thought it was when we were doing it." We Woody and Beatlefans can only marvel at what the movies and songs might have been if the artists had achieved their initial vision.

"A Day in the Life" changed popular music, especially rock, for all time. Yes, the Fabs had been groundbreakers and musical innovators prior to *Sgt. Pepper* and this track but, coming as it did at the end of the definitive rock album, in the waning days of a turbulent and pivotal decade, the song quickly attained legendary status as an artistic milestone.

Why it is the number-one song

"A Day in the Life" has long been heralded as the Beatles' most accomplished musical achievement. It has been compared to T. S. Eliot's epic poem "The Waste Land," and it was quickly perceived to be one of those unique (and infrequent) works of art that served as a bridge between decades, generations, and cultures. High praise, indeed, and it's reasonable to wonder how much of it is warranted. The answer is, "All of it."

We can also ponder the question, Would "A Day in the Life" have had the impact it did if it had *not* been used to close the *Sgt. Pepper* album? The answer is yes. And if it *had* been dropped into another album outside the context of the *Pepper* concept, the likely unanimous consensus would be, to put it crudely, that the song was slumming. *That's* how good "A Day in the Life" is.

We gave it the top slot for another reason, too: It's a true, pure collaboration. Granted, we can identify the "John" sections and the "Paul" sections, but it took artistic openness, purpose, and creativity to meld the individual elements into a song that is musically seamless.

What the song is about

The narrator of "A Day in the Life" is a rueful Everyman wandering alone in an eerie landscape of abstract, existential terror.

He reads the news—a hoped-for link with reality—but it does not ground him: His weary and offhanded "oh boy" in the first line speaks of the irrelevance of such information and its meaninglessness to him.

And what, precisely, is in this news? First, the story of a man who died in a car accident because he "didn't notice that the lights had changed." But hang on a moment. This poor chap "blew his mind out in a car." Isn't "blew his mind out" another way of saying "blew his brains out," a common term for committing suicide by a bullet to the head?

And who is this man? We are told he was a "lucky man who made the grade"—another euphemism, this time for someone who has achieved a particular standard. Thus, he was accomplished, and he may have been famous—"nobody was really sure if he was from the House of Lords"—but so what? Our hero is unmoved by this tragedy, and the waste of a valuable life: "Well I just had to laugh."

In the next verse, we learn that he saw a film whose conclusion showed the English army winning the war. The next line, though, reveals that the reaction to this victory was not cheers and glory: "A crowd of people turned away…" Why would people turn away at the end of a war? Because the slaughter, mayhem, and destruction were too much to bear. Our wanderer does not look away, however—he "just had to look"—because he "read the book," yet another euphemism, this time for the willing self-exposure to the horrors of war and, by extension, to the nightmare of life itself.

His reaction to all this? "I'd love to turn you on"—a sentiment that begs the question, Turn us on to *what*? Angst and pain? Or numbing intoxicants that inure us to the misery? Either way, our hero is aching for an escape.

After a cacophony of sound and noise—the externalized shrieks of our boy's confusion and woe—a steady, structured, confident repeated piano note announces the possibility of a return to normalcy and perhaps even redemption. Another voice enters the tale, steps onstage, and begins to sing of the daily routine of his life: "Woke up, got out of bed, dragged a comb across my head…" He continues recounting his hurried trek to work, and we are lulled into thinking that perhaps everything will be all right. But in the end, this bloke, too, is lost: "Somebody spoke and I went into a dream." The orchestra returns, summoning images of swirling demons and Armageddon, voices in the dark, and the angst of the void, its sounds rising in crescendo until we think we can bear it no longer.

And then suddenly we're back to our narrator, who is still reading the news and still trying to hold on—to sanity, to reality, to life itself. There are four thousand holes in Blackburn, Lancashire, and someone counted them all. What, after all, are holes? Areas of nothingness. Someone, somewhere, is counting *nothing*—perhaps the ultimate pointless, meaningless endeavor.

This proves to be the last straw, and he once again tells us desperately that he'd love to turn us on. This time, however, we *know* it's not his pain he wishes to share with us, but respite.

Alas, this is not to be. The cacophony returns, rising ceaselessly into the void, until the final eternal chord ends it all—and all existence fades away into an infinity of nothingness.

• • • ✵ • • •

- The working title of the song was "In the Life Of…"
- On January 17, 1967, John read a news story in the "Far and Near" column of the *Daily Mail* that began, "There are 4,000 holes in the road in Blackburn, Lancashire, or one twenty-sixth of a hole per person, according to a council survey."
- John's lines "I saw a film today oh boy/The English army had just won the war…" were a reference to his cameo in the film *How I Won the War*. People knew about the film and that John was in it, but it would not premiere until October 1967.
- One of the influences on John as he was writing the song was the December 18, 1966, fatal automobile accident of Guinness heir Tara Brown, a friend of the Beatles. Brown went through red lights driving his Lotus at 110 mph and smashed into a parked van while swerving to avoid a car that had pulled out. John told Hunter Davies, "I didn't copy the accident. Tara didn't blow his mind out. But it was in my mind when I was writing that verse."[1]
- In a 1984 interview with *Playboy*, Paul noted, "The orchestral crescendo and that was based on some of the ideas I'd been getting from Stockhausen and people like that, which is more abstract."
- During the recording of the song, the Beatles wandered around the studio with expensive cameras, taking pictures of everything and everybody.
- Toward the end of the final, ringing E major chord, you can hear a piano stool squeaking and the hum of the studio air conditioner. These sounds were picked up because engineer Geoff Emerick slowly turned the volume up as high as possible as the chord faded so as to make it last as long as possible.
- BBC executives banned both "A Day in the Life" and its promotional video because of the line "Went upstairs and had a smoke," which they interpreted as a reference to marijuana. (The "love to turn you on" line probably didn't help, either!)
- In a recent poll conducted by the U.K. magazine *Uncut*, a panel of celebrity judges that included members of R.E.M., Radiohead, and Travis voted "A Day in the Life" the Fab Four's best song ever.
- In 1982, composer-conductor Leonard Bernstein (*West Side Story*) said that fifteen years after first hearing it, "A Day in the Life" "still sustained and rejuvenated me."
- The song has been covered by Charlie Daniels, Eric Burdon and War, José Feliciano, Lighthouse, Neil Young and Crazy Horse, Robyn Hitchcock, Shirley Bassey, Sting, the Beach Boys, the London Symphony Orchestra, and Wes Montgomery.

Did you know?

The recording

Location: **Abbey Road Studios, London.**

Dates: **January 19, 1967,** 7:30 p.m.–2:30 a.m. – The first four takes of the song were recorded. John sang and played guitar; Paul played piano. Take 1 used only two of the four available tracks. At this time, they knew that something would go in the center of the song, but did not yet know what. The echoing voice of Mal Evans counted out the bars, from 1 to 24, accompanied by a tinkling piano with notes ascending in pitch in tandem with the numbers. An alarm clock sounded at the end, and this was ultimately kept in because, according to George Martin, they couldn't remove it! Take 4 consisted of John's vocal overdubs onto two tracks. By the end of the night, three of the four tracks available were replete with John's heavily echoed vocal.

January 20, 1967, 7:00 p.m.–1:10 a.m. – Reduction mixdowns, vacating tracks for more overdubbing. Take 6 was marked "best" and was augmented with another John lead vocal, Paul's bass, and Ringo's drums. This day also marked the first appearance of Paul's vocal in the middle section. (It was a happy coincidence that the section began right after the alarm went off.) Paul would re-record his vocal on February 3 because this day's work was only a rough guide, and he cursed at the end as he flubbed his line.

January 30, 1967 – George Martin worked at EMI Studios from 7:00 to 8:30 p.m. producing a rough mono mix so acetate discs could be cut. (The boys were out filming the "Penny Lane"/"Strawberry Fields Forever" promotional video.)

February 3, 1967, 7:00 p.m.–1:15 a.m. – More overdubs onto Take 6. Paul re-recorded his middle vocal and also a new bass part. Ringo decided to wipe his original drum track in favor of a new and distinctive tom-tom sound. George Martin commented, "That was entirely his own idea. Ringo has a tremendous feel for a song and he always helped us hit the right tempo first time. He was rock solid and this made the recording of all the Beatles songs so much easier."[2]

February 10, 1967 – This was one of the most auspicious days in Beatles history, the day the orchestra was brought in to play the instrumental buildup to fill the twenty-four-bar gap between the John and Paul sections of the song. Forty musicians (the Fabs had originally wanted ninety) were instructed to play from a preselected low note to the highest note their instrument could reach. George Martin sketched out a chart with a squiggly line to suggest the ascent to the high note, and he was paid eighteen pounds for his arrangement. The musicians were given somewhat unusual instructions: Start quietly and end loud; start low in pitch and end high; make your way up the scale independent of the other musicians around you. The orchestra cost EMI 367 pounds, 10 shillings. Martin and Paul took turns conducting, leaving Geoff Emerick in the control room to monitor the controls and capture the crescendo. The segment was recorded manipulating the acoustics of the room using "ambiophony," a rudimentary precursor of surround sound.

The recording session, which ran from 8:00 p.m. to 1:00 a.m., was an *event*. The musicians all wore formal evening attire, but they also donned novelty items such as clown noses, fake nipples, and gorilla-paw gloves. Recording was filmed with seven handheld cameras and edited, along with stock (non-Beatles) footage, into an early music video, but it was never broadcast. (It can be seen on the *Anthology* DVD.) Also on hand were Patti Boyd, Mick Jagger, Marianne Faithfull, Keith Richards, and Mike Nesmith.

Everyone in the studio broke into spontaneous applause after the last orchestral crescendo. When the orchestra left, the Beatles and friends stayed to record the final chord, a long "hummm," which would remain the song's ending until February 22.

February 13, 1967 – Four new mono mixes were prepared.

February 22, 1967 – The Beatles decided that the choir of humming voices was not a powerful enough way to end the song. John, Paul, Ringo, and Mal Evans, sharing three pianos, simultaneously struck an E major chord to replace the choir. The recording went nine takes before they all hit the chord at the right time. Take 9 was overdubbed three times, and then George Martin added a harmonium until all four tracks were filled. The concluding wall of sound lasted fifty-three seconds, although it faded about ten seconds earlier on the record, because the speakers of the time could not handle the last supersoft sound. (The ending of the 1987 *Sgt. Pepper* CD also concludes in forty-three seconds.)

February 23, 1967 – Geoff Emerick prepared a stereo master.

March 1, 1967 – A new piano track was added to Take 6. This overdub was never used.

April 21, 1967 – Recording of the inner groove chatter. The Fabs recorded gibberish and funny noises, chopped up the tape, put it back together, and threw it onto the track. (After the album was released, people of course played the chatter backward, and claims surfaced that it says something naughty. This is not true, according to engineer Geoff Emerick, who swears there is no hidden meaning in the words.) They also recorded the high-frequency sound that only dogs can hear.

June 1, 1967 – First released on the U.K. LP *Sgt. Pepper's Lonely Hearts Club Band*.

Players/Instruments:

- **John Lennon:** Acoustic guitar, lead guitar, lead vocal, piano
- **Paul McCartney:** Piano, bass, lead vocal
- **George Harrison:** *
- **Ringo Starr:** Drums, piano, bongos, maracas, timpani
- **George Martin:** Harmonium, piano
- **Mal Evans:** Alarm clock, piano
- **Session musicians:** Twelve violins, four violas, four cellos, two double bass, a harp, an oboe, two flutes, three trumpets, three trombones, a tuba, two clarinets, two bassoons, two horns, and a percussionist

* Did George Harrison participate in the "A Day in the Life" recording sessions? There is no mention in *The Beatles Recording Session* of him *playing* on the track, although there are photos of him in the studio at the time. Mark Lewisohn also stated that after the orchestra left, "*the Beatles*" remained to work on the coda.

What we really like about this song

Steve: After being dazzled by a dozen tracks of the *Sgt. Pepper* album, I arrived at "A Day in the Life," the last cut on the record and the ballad I had been trying to write my entire life. John's chord changes were beloved to me. I had been working with the G–B minor–F-sharp–E minor–D–C sequence for years, looking for the perfect melody and the perfect lyrics to go with what I had always felt was one of the most poignant and melodic sequences in music. (Even Bach loved it! His Air on a G String, and other works, begins with the same sequence as the John section of "A Day in the Life.") Lately, after years of hearing musicians using the same chords for ballads clearly inferior to John's, I've been trying to work with it again. Wish me luck.

Mike: How can I adequately describe my appreciation for the most important record from my favorite band? The track has all the elements of a great Beatles song—power, drama, and uniqueness—and it is offered in a groundbreaking collaboration. Every instrument is played to perfection, each fitting the varying moods of the song. It amazes me the sounds they were able to get out of the antiquated production facilities. Beginning with the stark opening, and the introduction of John's eerily detached voice, it's a blend of reality and dream, and the song ebbs and flows, taking us on a very strange roller-coaster ride. When the orchestra first starts to come in, shivers still creep up my spine. When it reaches its crescendo, I want to pump my fist in the air. And when the final chord bangs across three keyboards, I always listen to the whole thing, probably—no, definitely—because I don't want the song to end.

[1] *The Beatles*.

[2] *The Beatles Recording Sessions*.

Strawberry Fields Forever

Before the very first recording of "Strawberry Fields Forever" John stood opposite me in the studio and played me the song on his acoustic guitar. It was absolutely lovely.

—George Martin
The Beatles Recording Sessions

One of the most

compelling moments in *The Beatles Anthology* was when Paul played the opening of "Strawberry Fields Forever" on a Mellotron and then sang a few bars of the song. He could have played *anything*, but he played a John song. The line "Let me take you down…"—which *so* belongs to John Lennon, and which we will likely always hear sung in his voice—was sung by Paul, and it sent collective chills up and down the collective spines of Beatlefans everywhere. As Paul said later in the *Anthology*, "I was a big fan of John's."

A few months after completing "Strawberry Fields Forever," perhaps John's greatest song, he would write the line, "Nothing you can do that can't be done" (for his anthem, "All You Need Is Love"). We cannot help but wonder if his experience *creating* (and that word is used deliberately; we could also describe the process as *building*) the "Strawberry Fields Forever" track had something to do with inspiring this line.

After recording several versions of his lovely new song, John went to George Martin with a request: He wanted Martin to do something that could not be done. Or so it seemed. John liked the beginning of one take of the song, and the second half of another. The problem? The two segments were in different keys and different time signatures. *It can't be done, John,* said George Martin, to which John replied, with the confidence, enthusiasm, and naïveté of the technically unskilled: "Well, you can fix it!"

Why it made the top 10

"Strawberry Fields Forever" is the Beatles' most classically inspired recording. The lyrics are poetry, the melody is gorgeous, and George Martin's production, with input from the Beatles, was groundbreaking at the time and still sounds fresh after all these decades. (And that aforementioned edit appears at 1:00 on your digital counter!) Simply breathtaking.

"Strawberry Fields Forever" defines everything the Beatles were about: introspection, experimentation, and, above all, beautiful music. One of the key tests of a song's excellence and timelessness is how it sounds when all the production effects are stripped away. If a song is as lovely and moving when performed on an acoustic guitar or solo piano as it is with a full band, an orchestra, harmonies, and all the other elements that go into a pop recording, then it's a song for the ages, and the songwriter has done his or her job.

"Strawberry Fields Forever" sounds as glorious on an acoustic guitar, or performed as a piano ballad, as it does in the final Beatles recording. It is an ethereal marriage of the perfect lyrics with the perfect melody.

What the song is about

John wrote "Strawberry Fields Forever" in Spain during the six lonely weeks he spent filming the movie *How I Won the War*. The song evokes nostalgia, loneliness, existential angst, and the search for identity, while at the same time being a harsh critique of life in a world that embodies the diametrical opposite of John's mission statement, "All you need is love."

He tells us that "living is easy with eyes closed, misunderstanding all you see." The strawberry fields become a metaphor for the earthly plane of human existence. And how does John perceive this reality? "Nothing is real."

John has admitted that the "my tree" line referred to his own personal feelings of alienation, or at least of being outside the norm. The next line, in which he addresses critics of his "outsider" persona—"you can't… tune in but it's all right… it's not too bad"—is a plea for tolerance, while also an acknowledgment that those who don't fit in are often quite aware of their "outlander" status.

While all this is going on, the song also evokes John's childhood in much the way "Penny Lane" evokes Paul's memory of Liverpool, but "Strawberry Fields Forever" is much more sophisticated in both tone and purpose.

• • • ❧ • • •

- John's original opening line for the song was "Let me take you back," not "Let me take you down." (His acoustic demo of the song can be heard on *Anthology 2*.)
- In the January 1981 issue of *Playboy*, John revealed what he thought about the lyrics of the song: "The awareness apparently trying to be expressed is—let's say in one way I was always hip. I was hip in kindergarten. I was different from the others. I was different all my life. The second verse goes, 'No one I think is in my tree.' Well I was too shy and self-doubting. Nobody seems to be as hip as me is what I was saying. Therefore, I must be crazy or a genius—'I mean it must be high or low,' the next line. There was something wrong with me, I thought, because I seemed to see things other people didn't see. I thought I was crazy or an egomaniac for claiming to see things other people didn't see."
- In the 1996 "Free as a Bird" video created to accompany the release of the single (see song number 25), a bird is seen flying over the Strawberry Field (no final -s) Salvation Army orphanage, a well-known Liverpool landmark and one of John's inspirations for the song. Strawberry Field is located at Beaconsfield Road, Woolton, Liverpool. It has been a children's home since 1936.
- We know it's a crushing blow to "Paul is Dead" conspiracy theorists, but John does not say "I buried Paul" at the end of "Strawberry Fields Forever." He says "cranberry sauce." His words can be heard clearly on *Anthology 2*.
- On April 20, 1982, an area in New York's Central Park was christened "Strawberry Fields" and dedicated to John's memory. It features a mosaic circle of tiles, spelling out

Imagine, and is in sight of the Dakota apartments, where John lived and died.
- On June 28, 1990, for the first time, Paul McCartney performed, at a concert at King's Dock in Liverpool, what ultimately became known as his "Lennon Medley." This was the first time that Paul publicly performed John's songs. The medley consisted of "Strawberry Fields Forever," "Help!," and "Give Peace a Chance."
- "Strawberry Fields Forever" has been covered by the Ventures, Richie Havens, Debbie Harry, the King's Singers, the Bobs, Sylvia McNair, Christopher Clause (a stunning acoustic guitar version), Todd Rundgren and Utopia, the Hollyridge Strings, Sandy Farina (in the *Sgt. Pepper* movie), and Cyndi Lauper (performed live at the 9/11 tribute concert "Come Together: A Night for John Lennon's Words and Music").

The recording

Location: **Abbey Road Studios, London.**

Dates: **November 24, 1966,** 7:00 p.m.–2:30 a.m. – Take 1 of the song, very different from the final version, was recorded. The opening was played on the then-new instrument, the Mellotron. The rhythm track plus many overdubs were recorded, including Paul's Mellotron part, John's vocal, George's guitar, Ringo's drums, plus maracas, a slide guitar part, and scat harmonies by John, Paul, and George. This version of the song ended with the Mellotron. The track was recorded slower so it would sound faster on replay.

November 28, 1966, 7:00 p.m.–1:30 a.m. – Three takes were recorded, plus one false start (Take 2). Take 4 was considered the best: It was given John's speeded-up vocal and three rough mono remixes.

November 29, 1966, 2:30–8:00 p.m. – Takes 5 and 6 were recorded, with more attempts at recording the rhythm track, which was becoming progressively faster in tempo. Onto Take 6, John overdubbed another experimental vocal. Tape reduction, then Artificial Double Tracking (ADT) was done to the vocal. Piano and bass were overdubbed. Three rough mono mixes.

December 8, 1966, 7:00 p.m.–3:40 a.m. – A complete remake of the song. Fourteen complete takes of a new rhythm track were recorded before the orchestra would be overdubbed on December 15. Technical engineer Dave Harries had to start the session as producer and engineer because Emerick and Martin were late. He recalled, "Soon after I had lined up the microphones and instruments in the studio that night, ready for the session, the Beatles arrived, hot to record. There was nobody else there but me, so I became producer/engineer. We recorded Ringo's cymbals, played them backwards, Paul and George were on timps [timpani] and bongos, Mal Evans played tambourine, we overdubbed the guitars, everything. It sounded great. When George and Geoff came back I scuttled upstairs because I shouldn't really have been recording them."[1] Ultimately, Martin and Emerick edited together the first three-quarters of Take 15 with the last quarter of Take 24. A reduction mix was begun, but would continue the following day.

December 9, 1966, 2:30–10:00 p.m. – Tape reduction, mono mixing, and then overdubbing of some heavy drum sounds and backward cymbals, recorded similarly to the backward guitars in "I'm Only Sleeping." George Harrison added his swordmandel part.

December 15, 1966, 2:30 p.m.–midnight – Overdubbing of the orchestra part, which was scored by George Martin. A reduction mix was made, and then two separate lead vocals. (Onto the second overdub, John said "cranberry sauce.") Mono mixing.

December 21, 1966, 10:00–11:45 p.m. – Overdubbing of more John vocals and another piano track.

December 22, 1966, 7:00–11:30 p.m. – This is the session in which George Martin "fixed" the song, as per John's wishes. They did mono mixing, and then edited together the speeded-up remix of the first version and the slowed-down remix of the second. Geoff Emerick recalled, "We gradually decreased the pitch of the first version at the join to make them weld together." The edit happens at sixty seconds into the released version, although most people can't hear it. George Martin commented, "That's funny. I can hear it every time. It sticks out like a sore thumb to me!"[2]

December 29, 1966 – Tape copy made for the North American market. Mono mixing, then stereo mixing. (The individual segments were each mixed separately and then mixed together.)

December 30, 1966 – Tape copying for the U.S. release.

January 2, 1967 – Tape copying for the U.S. release.

February 13, 1967 – First released in the United States as a double-A-side single, with "Penny Lane."

Players/Instruments:

- **John Lennon:** Lead vocal, lead guitar, harpsichord
- **Paul McCartney:** Electric bass, piano, flute, bongos, timpani, Mellotron
- **George Harrison:** Lead guitar, timpani, bongos, swordmandel
- **Ringo Starr:** Drums, electric drum track, backward cymbal
- **Mal Evans:** Tambourine
- **Session musicians:** Four trumpets, three cellos, and an alto trumpet

What we really like about this song

Steve: If Martians landed and asked, "What are these Beatles everyone so lovingly speaks of?" all you would need to do is play them "Strawberry Fields Forever" and they would immediately understand all. The song has gravitas and is, ironically, both a simple ballad and a complex, multilayered work of musical art. Even now, after all these years, there are still little things to hear. Did you know that at 2:01, you can hear somebody counting from one to four? Or that the best way to hear the legendary edit at 1:00 is to listen carefully to the drums and Mellotron on the left track? No matter who covers it (and, admittedly, there have been some superb versions of the song), "Strawberry Fields Forever" is so identified with the Beatles that no other artist can do it justice.

Mike: I love "A Day in the Life," but "Strawberry Fields" is my favorite *John* song—and it truly was a John song, not only about the magical place he remembered, but about his alienated state of mind; his feeling slightly out of place because he thought differently than most people. As a kid, I could relate. I have a feeling that if John had lived, he would have made several more attempts at recording this song. It's interesting to hear the earlier versions on *Anthology 2* and various bootlegs, but there's so much to like about the released version, including the opening strains of the Mellotron, Ringo's distinctive drumming and backward cymbals, the moment the orchestra rises up, the fade/return, the "cranberry sauce," and, of course, the lyrics. I could listen to this song every day (and often do).

[1] *The Beatles Recording Sessions.*

[2] Ibid.

Let It Be

I had a dream one night about my mother. She died when I was 14, so I hadn't heard from her in quite a while and it was very good. It gave me some strength. In my darkest hour, mother Mary had come to me.

—Paul McCartney

"Let It Be" begins like a hymn, reads like a prayer, and sounds like an anthem.

Its ringing opening piano chords are now instantly recognizable, and the song's simple structure has allowed many an amateur pianist to impress fellow partygoers and spur an impromptu sing-along. The song is as well known around the world as "Hey Jude," perhaps more so, and it is probably the best thing to come out of the contentious *Let It Be* film project.

Why it made the top 10

"Let It Be"—in all its variations and incarnations—is a straightforward rock ballad with very few bells and whistles. But it isn't in the top 10 for its production values. It's one of the most beautiful songs Paul ever wrote, and one of the most emotionally powerful tracks the Beatles recorded. Some have described it as the definitive Beatles song. Although we bestow that honor on "A Day in the Life," it's likely that "Let It Be" is better known: Even those who may not know the entire Fabs catalog can sing along. Its message is uplifting, its sound nonthreatening (that orchestral crescendo in "A Day in the Life" has been known to freak out some people), and its beloved status well deserved.

What the song is about

For all its religious imagery and obvious spiritual theme, "Let It Be" can also be described as "You Never Give Me Your Money," Part 2. Paul himself has admitted as much. He said, "I wrote ["Let It Be"] when all those business problems started to get me down. I really was passing through my 'hour of darkness' and writing the song was my way of exorcising the ghosts."[1]

Some of Paul's most notable earlier works were about *other* people's troubles: "Eleanor Rigby" comes to mind, as does "She's Leaving Home," "The Fool on the Hill," and even "Blackbird." "Let It Be," however, is determinedly first person.

Paul's mother's name was Mary, and he has said that it was she he was writing about in the song, but the accidental, secondary association with the Virgin Mary, the Mother of Jesus, adds a dimension to the words that elevate them to a type of devotional.

Mother Mary comes to Paul in his hour of darkness, and also when the night is cloudy. But in the second verse, the song goes beyond the personal when he speaks of reuniting the "broken-hearted people." How will this occur? When they "agree," which is code for the elimination of intolerance and hatred—and a restating of the song's title and chorus: If everyone would just let everyone else "be," then there will be an answer. And that answer is? Peace and love.

Amen.

• • • 🐞 • • •

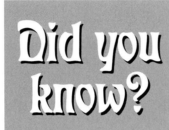

- John had his own ideas as to Paul's inspiration for "Let It Be": "I think it was inspired by 'Bridge Over Troubled Waters.' That's my feeling, although I have nothing to go on."[2]
- The line "I wake up to the sound of music…" may have referred to Paul's experience awakening with "Yesterday" in his head.
- Paul admitted imagining Aretha Franklin singing it when he wrote the song. She later covered it. (We can't help but wonder if her recording sounded like what Paul had heard in his head.)
- EMI would not allow George Martin's name to appear on the original record: "EMI came to me and said, 'You made this record originally but we can't have your name on it.' I asked them why not and they said: 'Well, you didn't produce the final thing.' I said, 'I produced the original and what you should do is have a credit saying: "Produced by George Martin, over-produced by Phil Spector." They didn't think that was a good idea."[3]
- In 1984, ATV Music sued Sesame Street Records for recording a parody of "Let It Be" called "Letter B," performed by the Sesame Street Beetles.
- "Let It Be" was re-recorded March 14, 1987, to benefit the families of victims of the ferry disaster off the coast of Zeebrugge, Belgium. The new recording featured Boy George, Kim Wilde, Bananarama, and the Alarm, along with Paul's original vocal.
- The song has been covered by Aretha Franklin, Arthur Fiedler, Bill Withers, Chevy Chase, Dion, Gary and Randy Scruggs, Gladys Knight and the Pips, Ike and Tina Turner, Joan Baez, Joe Cocker, John Davidson, John Denver, José Feliciano, King Curtis, Darlene Love, Leo Sayer, Richie Havens, Tennessee Ernie Ford, the Everly Brothers, the Ray Coniff Singers, and Wes Montgomery.

The recording

Location: **Abbey Road Studios, London.**

Dates: **January 25, 1969** – As with many songs of the *Get Back* period, very few recording details exist for "Let It Be." The logs simply say that recording was begun on this day. This track is on *Anthology 3*, but the song was incomplete: The "And when the night is cloudy" and "I wake up to the sound of music" verses were not yet written.

January 26, 1969 – The song was recorded during a day of playing and recording many old-time rock classics, in addition to "The Long and Winding Road" and George's "Isn't It a Pity?"

January 31, 1969 – Nine takes of the song were recorded. The sarcastic opinion of the song by the other Beatles is evident: John is heard saying "Are we supposed to giggle in the solo?"

March 10, 1969 – Stereo mixing by Glyn Johns, who was handed a stack of tapes and asked to make a record.

April 30, 1969 – A lead guitar solo was overdubbed onto the best take from January 31. This was to be the solo featured on the single and the planned *Get Back* album.

May 28, 1969 – Stereo mixing.

January 4, 1970 – Today was the last Beatles recording session. Several overdubs of the song, including George and Paul's harmonized backing vocal, were recorded onto the January 31, 1969, recording. Three tape reductions were made, all with a simultaneous overdub of brass, scored by George Martin: two trumpets, two trombones, and a tenor sax. On top of the best tape reduction and brass overdub they added more singing, a Leslied lead guitar solo by George, Ringo on drums, and Paul on maracas. The cellos at the end were scored by George Martin. Glyn Johns, however, was committed to releasing *Get Back* with *no* overdubs whatsoever, so he refused to even consider this new version.

March 6, 1970 – The single was released in the United Kingdom, backed with "You Know My Name (Look Up the Number)." (Both guitar solos can be heard in the middle eight, although the Leslied solo is more prominent in the mix.)

March 26, 1970 – Editing. Phil Spector added some echo to Ringo's high hat, added a repeat verse to the end of song, and omitted the April 30 overdub.

May 8, 1970 – The album version of the song was first released on *Let It Be*. (The Leslied guitar solo is not heard.)

November 18, 2003 – *Let It Be… Naked* was released worldwide. Unlike the single and album version, the same master tape of the song was not used. The organ is different, and the piano is more prominent during George's Leslied guitar solo. (This "naked" version quickly became a favorite of many fans around the world, including your humble authors.)

Players/Instruments:
- **Paul McCartney:** Piano, lead vocal
- **John Lennon:** Bass, harmony vocal
- **George Harrison:** Lead guitar, harmony vocal
- **Ringo Starr:** Drums
- **Billy Preston:** Organ

Note: These details are for the single version of the song. For the album version, George played a Leslied guitar, Preston didn't play, and an orchestral backing was dubbed in. George played different guitar solos: The solo overdubbed April 30, 1969, was for the single; the January 4, 1970, overdub was for the album. The brass and cello were lower in the mix in the single.

What we really like about this song

Steve: "Let It Be" has always been on my list of top 10 favorite Beatles songs, and the years have not diminished my affection for this gorgeous ballad. I recall first hearing it on a friend's bootleg (anyone remember *The Silver Album*?) when I was seventeen. I asked to borrow the LP and got into trouble when I, uh, forgot to return it. (He made his mother call and yell at me.) Everything about the song appeals to me. If I had one gripe, it would be that sometimes the chorus seems to go on a tad too long, but this is a small complaint about what can justifiably be considered a masterpiece.

Mike: This song has grown on me over the years. I've come to appreciate its message more as I get gray around the temples and raise children. As both my mother and grandmother died while I was writing this book, this song—and all the Beatles' music—has helped to ease the pain. "Let It Be" says to me, *Peace be with you*, and it sounds so much like a hymn that I'm surprised no contemporary church has adapted it and added it to their book of worship. May it continue to bring us comfort and peace in our hours of darkness.

[1] *A Hard Day's Write*.

[2] *Playboy*.

[3] *The Beatles Anthology*.

Yesterday

It was my most successful song. It's amazing that it just came to me in a dream. That's why I don't profess to know anything; I think music is all very mystical. You hear people saying, "I'm a vehicle; it just passes through me." Well, you're dead lucky if something like that passes through you.

—Paul McCartney
The Beatles Anthology

A man, a guitar, and a string quartet.

These simple elements combined (in a stunning example of the sum being greater than the individual parts) to create an achingly beautiful, iconic ballad that has, since 1965, become Paul McCartney's most beloved, most recognized, and most often covered song. (Yes, it's officially a "Beatles song," but that's in name only. Let's face it: "Yesterday" is a solo McCartney track if there ever was one.)

Why it made the top 10

"Yesterday" came to Paul in a dream: "I woke up one morning with a tune in my head and I thought 'Hey, I don't know this tune—or do I?' It was like a jazz melody. My dad used to know a lot of old jazz tunes, I thought maybe I'd just remembered it from the past. I went to the piano and found the chords to it (a G, F# minor 7 and a B), made sure I remembered it…"[1]

"Yesterday" changed the world's perception of the Beatles. The live version on *Anthology 2* (and on the *Anthology* video) is interesting for one very important reason: The Fabs themselves almost didn't know what to make of this new venture. George introduces Paul, joking that the lad from Liverpool is finally a success; and when the song is over,

John mockingly thanks "Ringo" for the performance. The audience is likewise a tad puzzled. The nonstop screaming of the fans does diminish for most of the song, but one gets a powerful sense of audience confusion as Paul begins singing and strumming his acoustic; even more so when the taped string quartet comes in.

But, as has been said, nothing ventured, nothing gained, and Paul, for all his initial embarrassment over his unconventional ballad, did the Fabs' fans—and the world of popular music—a favor by writing, performing, and recording what he heard in his dreams.

What the song is about

Our hero said something stupid ("I said something wrong"), it aggravated his lady love to the point that she dumped him ("she had to go"), and now he's sad ("I long for yesterday").

That is the essence of "Yesterday." In terms of a time line, the singer is telling us his troubles the day after he committed his *"What did you say!"* gaffe.

He's melancholic and regretful, and he realizes that he might have been taking his relationship a little too much for granted ("love was such an easy game to play"). Interestingly, nowhere in the song does he say he would like to make amends and win back his love. Instead, he mopes and withdraws ("I need a place to hide away").

No wonder he believes in yesterday: He had self-esteem and a girlfriend who put up with what was apparently recurrent

nonsense from him. Now he has been called on the carpet, but he doesn't seem to have the emotional wherewithal to do anything beyond acknowledging his mistake. Did he learn from this experience? Probably not, since he repeatedly tells us that he believes in and longs for yesterday.

Those who cannot remember the past are condemned to repeat it, right?

• • • 🐞 • • •

- At first, Paul had only the melody for "Yesterday": In *The Beatles Anthology*, he said, "It didn't have any words at first so I blocked it out with 'Scrambled eggs, oh my baby, how I love your legs—diddle diddle—I believe in scrambled eggs.'" John was quoted as regretting they found words for it: "I was sorry in a way, we'd had so many laughs about it."

- Paul worked on "Yesterday" while the Fabs were filming *Help!* Director Richard Lester later recalled, "At some time during that period, we had a piano on one of the stages and he was playing this 'Scrambled Eggs' all the time. It got to the point where I said to him, 'If you play that bloody song any longer I'll have the piano taken off stage. Either finish it or give it up!'"[1]

- After first hearing Paul play and sing "Yesterday," Ringo proclaimed that the song had no need for drums, and John and George likewise agreed that it did not need more guitars. It was then a short hop to the decision to release the Beatles' first *solo* song.

- John was regularly approached by people who believed that he wrote "Yesterday." One story appeared in *The Beatles Anthology*: "I sat in a restaurant in Spain and the violinist insisted on playing 'Yesterday' right in my ear. Then he asked me to sign the violin. I didn't know what to say so I said, 'OK,' and I signed it, and Yoko signed it. One day he's going to find out that Paul wrote it. But I guess he couldn't have gone from table to table playing 'I Am the Walrus.'"

- The four members of the string quartet George Martin hired to record "Yesterday" had never played together as an ensemble before the session.

- "Yesterday" was released as a single in the United States and quickly reached Number One. It was not, however, released as a single in the United Kingdom until February 1976 (although it was included on the *Help!* soundtrack and on the *Yesterday* EP). In *The Beatles Anthology*, Paul

talked about the fears the Fabs had for the song: "We didn't even put it out as a single, in England. We were kind of a little embarrassed by it. We were a rock 'n' roll band. We thought we were like a little R&B combo."

- Paul sings "Yesterday" in his movie *Give My Regards to Broad Street* dressed as a busker outside the Leicester Square subway station. He had to ask permission to use the song since he doesn't own the publishing rights anymore.

- In 1996, Paul asked Yoko Ono to agree to officially reverse the credit on "Yesterday" to "McCartney/Lennon" for the *Anthology 2* release. She refused. Since then, Paul has released a compilation of live tracks, *Back in the U.S.*, on which the song is credited to Paul McCartney and John Lennon. Yoko has yet to initiate legal action.

- "Yesterday" has been covered more than any other song—over twenty-five hundred times. Here are fifty of the artists who have recorded their own version of this classic: Al Martino, Andy Williams, Anita Bryant, Arthur Fiedler and the Boston Pops, Benny Goodman, Bob Dylan, Boyz II Men, Charlie Byrd, Chet Atkins, Dino, Desi and Billy, Dionne Warwick, Don Ho, Dr. John, Elvis Presley, En Vogue, Enzo Stuarti, Ferrante and Teicher, Frank Sinatra, George Martin (as "Scrambled Eggs"), Gladys Knight and the Pips, Henry Mancini, Herbie Mann, Jack Jones, Jan and Dean, Johnny Mathis, José Feliciano, Kate Smith, Liberace, Lou Rawls, Marianne Faithfull, Marvin Gaye, Merle Haggard with Willie Nelson, Michael Bolton, Nelson Riddle, Patty Duke, Percy Faith, Perry Como, Peter Nero, Placido Domingo and John Denver, Ray Charles, Sergio Franchi, Smokey Robinson and the Miracles, Tammy Wynette, the Smothers Brothers, the Supremes, the Temptations, Tom Jones, Wes Montgomery, Willie Nelson, and Zamfir (and his Magic Flute). (FYI, George Gershwin's "Summertime" supposedly has been covered more than twenty-*six* hundred times.)

The recording

Location: **Abbey Road Studios, London.**

Dates: **June 14, 1965,** 7:00–10:30 p.m. – Paul recorded two takes of "Yesterday" after recording six takes of "I've Just Seen a Face" and seven shrieking takes of "I'm Down." (Take 1, with Paul on acoustic calling out chord changes to George Harrison—who does not appear on the track, but who *was* in the studio—appears on *Anthology 2*.) George Martin, in *The Beatles Recording Sessions*, recalled the decision to add strings to the track: "I suggested a classical string quartet. That appealed to him but he insisted 'No vibrato, I don't want any vibrato!' If you're a good violin player it's very difficult to play without vibrato. Paul told the musicians he wanted it pure. But although they did cut down the vibrato they couldn't do it pure because they would have sounded like schoolboys. I think Paul realized in later years that what he got was right… There is one particular bit which is very much his—and I wish I'd thought of it!—where the cello groans onto the seventh the second time around."

June 17, 1965 – Mono mixing.

June 18, 1965 – Stereo mixing.

August 6, 1965 – First issued on the U.K. LP *Help!*

Players/Instruments:

- **Paul McCartney:** Acoustic guitar, vocal
- **Tony Gilbert:** First violin
- **Sidney Sax:** Second violin
- **Francisco Gabarro:** Cello
- **Kenneth Essex:** Viola

What we really like about this song

Steve: This beautiful ballad is the kind of song I wish I could write. (Who wouldn't?) It's simple, and clear, and honest, and the arrangement serves the music and lyrics. Paul's guitar playing is perfect for this tune and I, for one, am extremely grateful that he realized that the rapid, flamenco-style strumming he used in Take 1 of the song on *Anthology 2* just didn't fit.

Mike: It's a simple yet elegant song but, after hearing it hundreds of times, it may be a bit played out for me. I realize its importance, though, and thus its deservedly high ranking. It's interesting when you consider that John's "Help!" and Paul's "Yesterday" were similarly themed (disillusionment with current events, longing for the simplicity of the past) but their execution was vastly different, and both songs appear on the same album. I think it's cool that Paul was reluctant to record the song—he seemed to be concerned that it might be too wimpy to attribute to the band—but the song became his obsession: It wouldn't go away; it *had* to be recorded!

[1] *The Beatles Anthology.*

[2] *A Hard Day's Write.*

All You Need Is Love

This is an inspired song, because they wrote it for a worldwide program and they really wanted to give the world a message. It could hardly have been a better message. It is a wonderful, beautiful, spine-chilling record.

—Brian Epstein
The Beatles Anthology

On Sunday, June 25, 1967, the Beatles and a bunch of their friends attempted to elevate the world's consciousness. Four hundred million people on the planet tuned in to the Beatles' live performance of "All You Need Is Love" on the *Our World* TV show.

So did the Fabs' message of love change the world? Even briefly? Around the globe, were there small moments of kindness, gestures of forgiveness, overtures toward peace? Did enemies lay down their arms? Did criminals abandon their plans? Did we give peace a chance?

Yes… and no. Certainly, the Beatles' effort made a difference in some places, for some people. Their performance—and this song—was a baby step toward world peace. Lest we forget, though… baby steps are how we learn to walk.

Why it made the top 10

This stunning anthem of peace and love is gloriously uplifting—and a beautiful song to boot. The phrase *All you need is love* became a totemic motto for the second half of the twentieth century before transforming into a rallying cry for the twenty-first.

Plus, "All You Need Is Love" is just plain great music, performed with style and passion. It endures as one of the Beatles' signature creations.

What the song is about

The chorus of "All You Need Is Love" is simple and straightforward, the verses less so.

"There's nothing you can do that can't be done." What does this mean? Pared down to its essence, it means anything is possible. This is authentic positive visualization, and the philosophy is almost George-like. Using that as a thematic jumping-off point, the rest of the verses fulfill this mandate—this *creed*—in a series of poetic statements that are quintessential Lennon.

You can sing anything, you can say what needs to be said, you can make anything, you can save anything—all these affirmations are rattled off by John, culminating in the definitive message of the song itself, as well as of John's artistic raison d'être: "You can learn how to be you in time."

Be yourself and anything is possible… and love is the key.

• • • 🎶 • • •

- The opening fanfare of "All You Need Is Love" is the "Marseillaise," the French national anthem. It was George Martin's idea to begin the song this way, and it was there from the earliest versions on.
- In the long, chaotic outro of the single, five specific pieces of music are played or referred to: Bach's Two Part Invention in F Major (trumpet duet), "In the Mood" (played by the brass), "Yesterday" (shouted by John), "Greensleeves" (played by the strings), and "She Loves You" (sung by John). (Mark Lewisohn stated in *The Beatles Recording Sessions* that the trumpet duet is from Bach's Brandenburg Concerto no. 2. 'Tisn't.) During rehearsals, John also sang snippets of "She'll Be Comin' Round the Mountain," but this did not make it into the final mix.
- For the broadcast, George played a Stratocaster that he had painted by hand. Paul wore a shirt that he had painted. The shirt was stolen immediately after the broadcast, and Paul suspects it will show up for auction at Sotheby's one day. (The studio and its visitors were

beautifully—and *colorfully*—decorated. Too bad the broadcast was transmitted in black and white!)

- John used three different time signatures to compose "All You Need Is Love": 4/4, 3/4, and 2/4. George once commented on John's innate songwriting ability: "John has an amazing thing with his timing—he always comes across with very different time signatures, you know. For example, on 'All You Need Is Love' it just sort of skips a beat here and there and changes time. But when you question him as to what it is he's actually doing, he really doesn't know. He just does it naturally."
- The Beatles were sued by the Glenn Miller estate for using a bit of "In the Mood" without permission. (George Martin thought it was in the public domain.) EMI settled the suit.
- Al and Tipper Gore played the song as their wedding recessional.
- The song has been covered by Anita Kerr, Echo and the Bunnymen, Ferrante and Teicher, the Fifth Dimension, Tears for Fears, and Tom Jones.

The recording

Locations: **Olympic Sound Studios, Barnes; Abbey Road Studios, London.**

Dates: **June 14, 1967**, 10:30 p.m.–3:00 a.m. (Olympic Sound Studios) – The Beatles recorded thirty-three takes of the song's ten-minute-long backing track. John played harpsichord, George played violin, Paul played double bass, Ringo was on drums. Rough mono mix.

June 19, 1967, 7:00 p.m.–1:45 a.m. (Abbey Road) – Overdubbing of the lead and backing vocals, drums, piano (played by George Martin), and banjo (John).

June 21, 1967 – Mono mixing. Acetate copy given to the *Our World* director.

June 23, 1967, 8:00–11:00 p.m. – The orchestra performed for the first time, recording a number of takes as overdubs. Tape reduction.

June 24, 1967, 5:00–8:00 p.m. – One hundred

journalists and photographers were in the studio as the Beatles and the orchestra made some additions to the rhythm track.

June 25, 1967, 2:00 p.m.–1:00 a.m. – Ten rehearsal takes of the song were recorded, and the final one—Take 58—was the broadcast version. The only elements of the performance that were live were the vocals, bass, lead guitar solo in the middle eight, drums, and the orchestra. Accompanying the lads for the performance were Eric Clapton, Graham Nash, Mick Jagger, Keith Richards, Marianne Faithfull, Keith Moon, Jane Asher, Patti Harrison, Gary Leeds, Mike McGear (aka Mike McCartney, Paul's brother), Hunter Davies, Brian Epstein, and other notables of the music world. Their performance was seen by an estimated four hundred million people worldwide. According to tape operator Richard Lush, John was quite nervous. Manfred Mann instrumentalist Mike Vickers conducted the orchestra. A copy of the broadcast is stored at the United Nations.

June 26, 1967, 2:00–5:00 p.m. – Mono mixing for the single.

July 7, 1967 – First released as a single in the United Kingdom, backed with "Baby You're a Rich Man."

November 1, 1967 – Mono mixing for the *Yellow Submarine* soundtrack.

October 29, 1968 – Stereo mixing for the *Yellow Submarine* soundtrack.

Players/Instruments:

Backing track:
- **John Lennon:** Harpsichord (rented from Olympic Studios for ten guineas; one source says it's a clavichord)
- **Paul McCartney:** String bass played with a bow (one source says it was an Arco bass guitar with a bow drawn across)
- **George Harrison:** Violin
- **Ringo Starr:** Drums

Abbey Road track:
- **John Lennon:** Vocal
- **Paul McCartney:** Bass guitar
- **George Harrison:** Guitar
- **Ringo Starr:** Drums
- **George Martin:** Piano
- **Session musicians:** Two trumpets, two trombones, two saxes, one accordion, four violins, and two cellos

Live performance:
- **John Lennon:** Lead vocal
- **Paul McCartney:** Backing vocal
- **George Harrison:** Backing vocal
- **Studio orchestra**
- **Chorus:** Friends and relatives

What we really like about this song

Steve: This song still gives me the chills when I listen to it; it captures an era, and a mood, and, of course, the heart and soul of the Beatles themselves in that 1967 summer of love. The writing is John at his best. The orchestration is a quantum leap beyond anything they had attempted thus far. The chorus is transcendent. Groundbreaking and optimistic, fearless and fun, "All You Need Is Love" was a milestone moment in Beatles history.

Mike: It's a simple (albeit musically sophisticated) song, with a no-nonsense message, and one that I never tire of. It still holds up melodically, and the message is just as important today as it was in 1967—perhaps even more so. It was reported that during the Beatles' first appearance on the *Ed Sullivan Show* there was virtually no crime in America. I'd like to think that the same was true worldwide when "All You Need Is Love" first aired. When I think of the song, sadly, I remember the crowds holding vigil outside the Dakota in December 1980, sorrowfully singing it. If the song could have touched that one deranged individual, maybe John's life would have been spared.

Hey Jude

It's hard to imagine this man was thinking about me and my life so much that he wrote a song about me... If I'm in a bar and the song comes on the radio, I still get goose pimples.

—Julian Lennon
www.julianlennon.com

Prior to its release, there had never been a ballad like "Hey Jude": a seven-minute-plus production in which the ending is longer than the song itself, and that travels from an a cappella "Hey" all the way to an orchestra and dozens of chanting voices.

None of the Beatles' prior singles had prepared the way for this record—it was a masterpiece unto itself—and we think it's fair to say that the song has become the model for every rock anthem released since.

29

Why it made the top 10

"Hey Jude" may be the most beloved Beatles song of all time.

Yes, there were dozens of other songs named when we asked fans for their favorites, but throughout our polling process, fans singled out "Hey Jude" as something so special and unique that they felt it deserved an honored place of its own. (Many fans would have ranked it in the Number One spot on this list.)

We are comfortable with the song at Number Six (look at the five above it, for Lordy's sake!) but we agree that there is something… *transcendent* about its appeal.

What the song is about

Beatlefans know that Paul wrote "Hey Jude" as a consolation message for then five-year-old Julian Lennon, who was upset that his father and mother were divorcing. The opening sentiments—"don't make it bad" and "take a sad song and make it better"—are a kindly and concerned uncle offering valuable advice. The next line, though, is more pointed: "Remember to let her into your heart." Let *who* into his heart? Why, Yoko, of course. Paul was telling Julian that the sooner he accepted his father's new love, the better things would be—for everyone.

The second verse continues the guidance, but explodes metaphorically, with Paul seemingly using the pronoun *her* to mean tolerance and open-mindedness, not only to Yoko, but to the new life in the offing. Within this context, "the minute you let her under your skin" becomes a plea for self-control and resolution.

The first bridge is cautionary: Don't give in to the pain, and don't be a fool by withdrawing from the new circumstances of your life ("it's a fool who plays it cool…"). This is followed by the third verse in which Uncle Paul exhorts Julian not to let him down (hmm… didn't Julian's father once express a similar message?). He reinforces his earlier advice to let "her" into his heart and reassures him that "then you can start to make it better." (Interestingly, John had his own ideas about the song: "I always heard it as a song to me. If you think about it… Yoko's just come into the picture. He's saying, 'Hey Jude—hey, John.' I know I'm sounding like one of those fans who reads things into it, but you can hear it as a song to me. The words 'go out and get her'—subconsciously he was saying, Go ahead, leave me. On a conscious level, he didn't want me to go ahead. The angel in him was saying, 'Bless you.' The devil in him didn't like it at all, because he didn't want to lose his partner."[1])

The second bridge begins with a simple plea to breathe through the pain:—"let it out and let it in…"—then acknowledges that Julian might want to act out because of the ongoing turmoil: "you're waiting for someone to perform with…" But, again, Paul offers wisdom. Look within: "don't you know that it's just you" is followed by the line Paul thought he should cut, but that John insisted made the song: "the movement you need is on your shoulder." What movement is on our shoulders? Why, a *nod*, of course. Another positive affirmation.

The final verse is a repeat of previous counsel and sets up the coda, a chanting refrain that could easily mesmerize a five-year-old by its repetition, making him susceptible to the suggestions expressed in the rest of the song.

• • • ❧ • • •

- The legendary final "na-na-na" refrain begins at precisely 3:09, the phrase is repeated eighteen times, and it fades to silence after the beginning of the nineteenth. The syllable *na* is repeated 198 times within the eighteen complete refrains. Each individual "na-na-na" refrain lasts approximately thirteen seconds.
- Paul's original lyric/title for the song was "Hey Jules."
- "Hey Jude" was always intended to be a single. It was never considered for *The White Album*.
- In the January 31, 1974, issue of *Rolling Stone*, Paul talked about a demo tape he had made of the song: "I remember I played it to John and Yoko, and I was

saying, 'These words won't be on the finished version.' Some of the words were, 'The movement you need is on your shoulder,' and John was saying, 'It's great!' I'm saying, 'It's crazy, it doesn't make any sense at all.'… So when I play that song, that's the line when I think of John; and I sometimes get a little emotional during that moment."

- In December 1996, Julian Lennon paid $39,030 at a London auction for Paul's recording notes for the song. His manager, John Cousins, told the *London Times* that Julian was collecting for personal reasons. "These are family heirlooms if you like."
- In a recent interview, Paul talked about performing "Hey

Jude": "A couple months ago, I was playing with Elton John and we were doing 'Hey Jude.' And he was going to take one of the verses… And he said, 'What key is it in?' I said, 'Don't ask me. How the hell do I know?' So we got the record out and tried to figure it out." (It's in F, by the way.)

- In 1984, ATV Music sued Sesame Street Records for recording a parody of the song called "Hey Food" performed by the Sesame Street Beetles.
- The song has been covered by Arthur Fiedler and the Boston Pops, Bing Crosby, Boots Randolph, Charlie Byrd, Diana Ross and the Supremes, Ella Fitzgerald, Elvis Presley, Frank Sinatra, the Grateful Dead, José Feliciano, Junior Walker and the All-Stars, Laurindo Almeida, Lawrence Welk, the Lettermen, the London Symphony Orchestra, Maynard Ferguson, the New Christy Minstrels, Paul Mauriat, Peter Nero, Petula Clark, the Ray Charles Singers, Ray Stevens, Roger Williams, Smokey Robinson and the Miracles, Sonny and Cher, Soundgarden, Stan Kenton and His Orchestra, the Temptations, Tiny Tim and Brave Combo, Tom Jones, the University of Nebraska Marching Band, Wilson Pickett, and Yusef Lateef.

The recording

Locations: **Abbey Road Studios; Trident Studios, London.**

Dates: **July 29, 1968**, 8:30 p.m.–4:00 a.m. – Six takes of the song were recorded at Trident Studios (with its eight-track equipment), but only three were complete. (The three were all different times: 6:21, 4:30, and 5:25.) Paul played piano and sang the main vocal, John played acoustic guitar, George played electric guitar, and Ringo was on the drums. George Martin had the night off.

July 30, 1968, 7:30 p.m.–3:30 a.m. – Seventeen takes of the song were recorded while the Fabs were filmed for a feature about the music of Britain called *Music!* The final film included about six minutes of finished Beatles footage, mainly from Take 9 of the song. They only recorded piano, drums, and acoustic guitar, so there was nothing for George Harrison to do. He was shown in the control room with George Martin. Tape reduction and a rough stereo remix were completed, and George Martin took them to use in arranging the score.

July 31, 1968, 2:00 p.m.–4:00 a.m. – Re-recording of four takes of the rhythm track.

August 1, 1968, 5:00 p.m.–3:00 a.m. – From 5:00 to 8:00 p.m., they overdubbed Paul's bass and lead vocal, and George and John's backing vocals. From 8:00 to 11:00 p.m., they recorded the thirty-six-piece orchestra. (Paul had wanted a full symphony orchestra—usually around a hundred musicians—but George Martin had told him he wouldn't have been able to book one so quickly.) In *All You Need Is Ears*, George Martin recalled the session: "I wanted them to sing and clap their hands as well as play, and one man walked out. 'I'm not going to clap my hands and sing Paul McCartney's bloody song,' he said, in spite of the fact that he was getting double rates for his trouble."

August 2, 1968, 2:00 p.m.–1:30 a.m. (Trident) – Three stereo remixes.

August 6, 1968, 5:30–7:30 p.m. (Trident) – Mono mixing.

August 7, 1968, 3:00–7:45 p.m. (Abbey Road) – Tape copying.

August 8, 1968 (Abbey Road) – Mono mixing. Tape copying.

August 26, 1968 – First released as a single in the U.S., backed with "Revolution."

Players/Instruments:
- **Paul McCartney:** Piano, bass, lead vocal
- **John Lennon:** Acoustic guitar, backing vocal
- **George Harrison:** Lead guitar, backing vocal
- **Ringo Starr:** Drums, tambourine
- **Thirty-six-piece orchestra:** Ten violins, three violas, three cellos, two flutes, a contra bassoon, a bassoon, two clarinets, a contra bass clarinet, four trumpets, four trombones, two horns, one "percussion," and two string bass

What we really like about this song

Steve: I love the chord changes, the harmonies, the piano part, the lyrics, the ending, Ringo's drumming, Paul's vocal, and everything else about this song. It is, without question, one of my all-time personal favorites.

Mike: This song would rank higher on my list if the fade-out was maybe half as long. As it stands, it seems a bit...excessive? But I know many people consider this their favorite Beatles song. Length notwithstanding, it's got a lot going for it, including a message of hope—not only for Julian, but for the turbulent world of 1968 and beyond. Listening today, the song sounds like a hymn, and you can picture the congregation standing, holding hands, swaying, and chanting the "na-na-na"s.

Paul lets loose

This is the complete text of Paul's exclamatory vocal riffing from approximately 3:58 in the song through the end. Go ahead and read along as you listen to it. A perfect transcription![2]

"Jude Judy Judy Judy Judy Judy... ow, wahow!"
"Ow hoo, my my my"
"Jude Jude Jude Jude Joooo…"
"Na na na na na, yeh yeh yeh"
"Yeah you know you can make it, yeah Jude, you not gotta break it"
"Don't make it bad Jude"
"Take a sad song and make it better"
"Oh Jude, Jude, hey Jude, wooooow"
"Ooo, Joooode"

"Yeah"
"Hey, hey, hey-yay"
"Hey, hey, hey"
"Now Jude Jude Jude Jude Jude Jude, yeah yeah yeah yeah"
"Woh yeah yeah"
"Ah nanananananana cause I wanna"
"Nanananana… nanalalal ow ow ow"
"Oh God"
"The pain won't come back Jude"
"Yeah, eh hehe heh"
"Make it through"
"Yeyeye Yeah .. yeah y-yeah… yeah-hahahaha…"
"Goodeveningladiesandgentlemen mymymymy mahhhh"
"Oooo"
"Woooh"
"Well then a na-nanan"

[1] *Playboy.*

[2] Thanks to Mike Brown of www.stevesbeatles.com for chronicling these epic exhortations for Beatlefans everywhere.

In My Life

I remember that he had the words written out like a long poem and I went off and worked something out on the Mellotron. The tune, if I remember rightly, was inspired by the Miracles.

—*Paul McCartney*

When John Lennon wrote

"In My Life," he was going on twenty-five years old. This is a simple fact with extraordinary import.

Why? Because the song comes off as a reminiscence of a man much older. When John sings "there are places I remember, *all my life…* ," the "life" he is referring to (assuming a normal life expectancy, of course) is a mere third completed. Tragically, John would die at forty, so when he wrote "In My Life," ironically, and unknowingly, more than half of his life was over. The melancholy "looking back" sentiment of the song is astonishingly mature for someone so young. (The same has been said about Paul's "Yesterday." See song number 4.)

Why it made the top 10

"In My Life" is the song that heralded the awakening of John Lennon as an autobiographical songwriter. In his lengthy 1981 *Playboy* interview, John admitted as much: "It was the first song I wrote that was consciously about my life…Before, we were just writing songs à la Everly Brothers, Buddy Holly, pop songs with no more thought to them than that—to create a sound. The words were almost irrelevant…[I]t was, I think, my first real major piece of work."[1]

The lyrics and melody are truly beautiful. Its appeal is evident in the many singers and musicians who have covered the song. (See below.)

What the song is about

On first hearing, "In My Life" sounds like a somewhat melancholy man singing about lost friends and remembered places. Some of his friends have died, some are still alive, and we get the sense that while he still "loves them all," he may not see many of them as often as he he'd like.

But then we get to the second verse and come to the surprising realization that "In My Life" is a love song, not for lost friends and places, but one in which the singer is assuring his current love that few of the things he just longed for matter. No one or nothing from his past "compares with you." He admits to her that he will always have affectionate feelings toward the people and places from his past, but that many of his memories "lose their meaning" when he thinks about his new love; in the end, he loves her more.

A seemingly autobiographical reminiscence is instantly transformed into a mature rejection of the past in favor of an optimistic present—and future—filled with new love and *new* memories.

- Longtime friend Pete Shotton said that John told him that "some are dead and some are living" referred specifically to Stu Sutcliffe and Pete.
- The baroque harpsichord-like instrumental break in the song was played by George Martin, only it wasn't a harpsichord. Martin played the break on a piano, then played it back and re-recorded it at double speed to get the sound he wanted.
- After John's tragic assassination in 1980, Yoko hired Elliot Mintz to compile an inventory of John's personal possessions. Mintz, quoted in *A Hard Day's Write*, remembered coming upon the first handwritten draft of the lyrics to "In My Life": "It was part of a large book in which he kept all his original Beatles compositions. He had already told me about how the song was written and that he considered it a significant turning point in his writing."
- John wrote some lyrics for "In My Life" that were not used. One verse went, "Penny Lane is one I'm missing/ Up Church Road to the clock tower/In the circle of the Abbey/I have seen some happy hours." At the time, John

Did you know?

considered it a "most boring sort of 'what I did on my holidays bus trip' song."
- The source of the song's melody is disputed. Paul has stated publicly that he remembers writing all the music to the song by himself. He claimed to have gone off with John's lyrics and worked out a melody on a Mellotron. He said "his" melody was probably inspired by "You Really Got a Hold on Me" by the Miracles. John's position was that "[Paul's] contribution melodically was the harmony and the middle eight itself."
- Artists who have covered "In My Life" include Judy Collins, José Feliciano, Keith Moon, Rod Stewart, Stephen Stills, Bette Midler, Crosby, Stills and Nash, Lena Horne, and Joel Grey.
- "In My Life" was one of George Harrison's favorite Lennon/McCartney songs. He once caused an uproar by rearranging the music and lyrics when performing the song live in concert in 1974. In place of "I love you more," George sang either "I love God more" or "I love him more."

The recording

Location: **Abbey Road Studios, London.**

Dates: **October 18, 1965** – After a rehearsal period, three takes were recorded, the last being the best. At this point, the middle eight bars were left open because they didn't know yet what to put in it.
October 22, 1965 – George Martin recommended putting a keyboard in the middle eight. Martin initially played a Hammond organ, but no one liked it. (They wanted the sound of a baroque piano, but Martin couldn't play it at the tempo he wanted.)
October 25, 1965 – Mono mixing.
October 26, 1965 – Stereo mixing.

Players/Instruments:

- **John Lennon:** Lead vocal
- **Paul McCartney:** Bass, harmony vocal
- **George Harrison:** Lead guitar
- **Ringo Starr:** Drums
- **George Martin:** Piano

What we really like about this song

Steve: I do like "In My Life," but it isn't one of my all-time personal favorite Beatles songs. That said, I do consider it a beautiful ballad and almost the perfect song to offer up to people who think all the Beatles did was yell "yeah, yeah, yeah."

Mike: I'm always a sucker for a melancholy tune, an ode to loves lost, the time that is fleeting, and our lost youth. But John's passing made this song even sadder for me. Fortunately, the song ultimately puts forth a message of hope—love lives on—and that's all that really matters. The vibe is similar to that of "Julia," although perhaps not as sad. The liveliest part of the song is the piano solo. Give George Martin his due for hearing the perfect sounds in his head for the middle eight and then knowing how to create them. I'm glad John changed the tune and removed the specific references to the literal places he remembered. By making it less specific, he made it less autobiographical and more universal.

[1] *Playboy*, January 1981.

Penny Lane

The song itself was generated by a kind of "I can do just as well as you can, John," because we'd just recorded "Strawberry Fields"... And they were both significant. They were both about their childhood.

—George Martin
Rolling Stone, *March 1, 2001*

Barber, banker, fireman, nurse.

And don't forget the children and the queen, of course! Within weeks of its release, "Penny Lane" was in *all* our ears, and the world's Beatlefans all became honorary Liverpudlians.

Why it made the top 10

Back in the days when singles were a big deal, the Beatles were under a lot of pressure to provide material for top 40 radio. Their first single in 1967 was the extraordinary double-A 45 "Penny Lane" and "Strawberry Fields Forever."

This boggles the mind when we consider the fact that some artists would have probably built an entire album around *one* of those songs and padded the rest with filler. The Fabs were dynamos of creativity, and they put as much effort into songs not slated for a particular album as they did tracks specifically intended for an LP. A song was a song, and "Penny Lane" was one of their all-time finest creations—a pop song that did not sound like any that had yet been released.

They had hoped to include it on *Sgt. Pepper,* but they agreed to release it as a single—which, let's face it, was (still is?) a more disposable format than an album. Didn't matter. A song was a song.

What the song is about

There is nothing ambiguous about the meaning of "Penny Lane": It's a nostalgic reminiscence of one Liverpudlian's childhood.

The barber in the song is based on Mr. Bioletti's Barber Shop (still there on Penny Lane); the nurse was a real nurse Paul saw selling poppies for Remembrance Day; and it's likely the banker and fireman were similarly based on real people.

The story is recounted in straight narrative form, seasoned with little tidbits and anecdotes about the individual personalities. The banker never wears a raincoat "in the pouring rain," and, whether it's raining or not, the local children laugh at him behind his back. Poor bloke.

One of the local firemen uses, of all things, an *hourglass* to tell time. He also keeps a picture of the queen with him, and, in the first of the two mischievous sexual jokes in the song, he apparently is quite attentive to his, er, "machine."

The nurse selling poppies feels like she's in a play. What does this mean? Does she feel as if she's constantly on stage, constantly being watched? Is there some undercurrent of insecurity in her that makes her feel self-conscious? Perhaps. But we are then told "she is anyway" (in a play), and that the essence of this image (as Paul told us in *The Beatles Anthology*) is that it was just "one of those trippy little ideas that we were trying to get in."

The chorus of the song presents a lad sitting on a bench watching the goings-on ("Penny Lane is in my ears and in my eyes…"), happy to be there.

The second chorus, though, boasts the other naughty sexual reference in the song—"a four of fish and finger pie…"—which was Liverpool slang for the female private parts. In *The Beatles in Their Own Words*, Paul said, "We put in a joke or two: 'Four of fish and finger pie.' The women would never dare say that, except to themselves. Most people wouldn't hear it, but 'finger pie' is just a nice little joke for the Liverpool lads who like a bit of smut."

• • • ❦ • • •

- In *The Compleat Beatles* video, George Martin talked about the use of the Bach trumpet[1] in the song: "Paul on one evening watched on television the Bach Brandenburg Concerto [no. 2, in F major], and he came to me the following day and said, 'Great sound I heard last night. A tremendously high trumpet.' And I said, 'Yes, sure, it was a Bach trumpet.' And he said, 'Can't we use it?' I said, 'Of course we can.' It never occurred to me, but it occurred to him. So we got the guy from the LSO to play piccolo trumpet, and that was the result." (The player they used, David Mason, actually played for the New Philharmonia Orchestra, not the London Symphony Orchestra.)
- Penny Lane was a big bus terminal that all the Beatles knew very well. Paul sang in the choir at St. Barnabas Church across the street from it.
- "Penny Lane" may have been inspired by the poem "Fern Hill" by Dylan Thomas, which Paul had been reading around the time he wrote the song. The poem begins, "Now as I was young and easy under the apple boughs…"
- John Lennon was the only Beatle who actually lived in Penny Lane, which was, in addition to being a street, also a district. (He lived on Newcastle Road during his early years, when his dad was still in town.)
- After the song became a hit, the "Penny Lane" street signs were stolen so often that the Liverpool city fathers had to paint the street name on the buildings.
- The song originally had a trumpet fanfare at the end, and that version was released for the U.S. single; it's now a rare collectible. The U.S. version can be heard on the *Rarities* LP.
- Mr. Bioletti's Barber Shop is now a unisex salon with a picture of the Beatles in the window. The shelter on the roundabout has been renovated and reopened as Sgt. Pepper's Bistro. The Penny Lane Wine Bar has the song's lyrics painted above its windows.
- "Penny Lane" is one of ten Beatles songs that mention rain. (See the complete list in song number 72, "Hey Bulldog.")
- The song has been covered by Count Basie, the 101 Strings Orchestra, Kenny Rankin, and Sting (live performance only).

Did you know?

Location: **Abbey Road Studios, London.**

Dates: **December 29, 1966,** 7:00 p.m.–2:15 a.m. – In a November 1965 interview, Paul said he was toying with the idea of doing a song called "Penny Lane" because he liked the poetry of the name. At this end-of-the-year session, though, the song was yet unnamed. Six takes were recorded of the main piano part, but only the last two were complete. Paul then worked alone in the studio adding a cornucopia of overdubs: two more piano parts, one played through a Vox guitar amplifier with reverb, another played at half speed and then speeded up. He also added a tambourine; two-tone high-pitch whistles from a harmonium fed through a Vox amp; and various percussion, including something sounding like machine gun, as well as a cymbal being played fast and then drawn out. Two mono remixes.

December 30, 1966 – The song now had a title. A reduction mix was made, bringing the song down to one track. Paul overdubbed a lead vocal; John sang backing vocal. Two mono remixes.

January 4, 1967, 7:00 p.m.–2:45 a.m. – Overdub of yet another piano part (this one played by John), a lead guitar part by George, and another Paul vocal.

January 5, 1967 – An overdub of a new Paul vocal replaced the overdub of the previous evening.

January 6, 1967, 7:00 p.m.–1:00 a.m. – Overdubs of Paul on bass, John on rhythm guitar and conga drums, and Ringo on drums; all sounds recorded were put through a limiter. A reduction mix was made, and then an overdub of the John and George Martin piano parts; handclaps; and John, Paul, and George Martin singing scat guide vocals where the brass would later be.

January 9, 1967, 7:00 p.m.–1:45 a.m. – An overdub of four flutes, two trumpets, two piccolos, and a flügelhorn. (Some musicians played more than one instrument.) Two mono remixes.

January 10, 1967, 7:00 p.m.–1:40 a.m. – An overdub of scat harmonies and hand bell for the "fireman" lyrics.

January 12, 1967, 2:30–11:00 p.m. – An overdub of two trumpets, two oboes, two *cor anglais*, and a double bass. Bassist Frank Clarke recalled, "They wanted me to play one note, over and over, for hours."[2] Mono remixing.

January 17, 1967, 7:00 p.m.–12:30 a.m. – Two overdubs of a piccolo (Bach) trumpet by David Mason, his solo in the middle eight and the flourish toward the end. Mason recalled: "We spent three hours working it out. Paul sang the parts he wanted, George Martin wrote them down, I tried them. But the actual recording was done quite quickly. They were jolly high notes, quite taxing, but with the tapes rolling we did two takes as overdubs on top of the existing song. I read in books that the trumpet sound was later speeded up but that isn't true because I can still play those same notes on the instrument along with the record… Although Paul seemed to be in charge, and I was the only one playing, the other three Beatles were there, too. They all had funny clothes on, candy-striped trousers, floppy yellow bow ties, etc. I asked Paul if they'd been filming because it really looked like they had just come off a film set. John Lennon interjected 'Oh no mate, we always dress like this!'"[3] Three mono mixes were made, the best sent to Capitol for American pressing.

January 25, 1967, 6:30–8:30 p.m. – The Beatles decided they were dissatisfied with the January 17 mix, so three more mono mixes were done, and Mason's trumpet was removed from the end. The original American edition with the trumpet at the end is now considered a rare collectible.

February 13, 1967 – Released as a double-A-side single with "Strawberry Fields Forever" in both the United States and United Kingdom.

September 30, 1971 – Stereo mixing.

Players/Instruments:
- **Paul McCartney:** Piano, bass, harmonium, lead and backing vocal, tambourine, percussion
- **John Lennon:** Piano, rhythm guitar, harmony vocal, conga drum
- **George Harrison:** Lead guitar
- **Ringo Starr:** Drums, hand bell
- **George Martin:** Piano
- **David Mason:** Piccolo trumpet (Bach trumpet)
- **Session musicians:** Four flutes, four trumpets, two oboes, and two bass violins

What we really like about this song

Steve: "Penny Lane" is a splendid song and a splendid recording. The song itself is one of Paul's best, and it's revealing what he was able to produce when his competitive streak reared its head. The writing is superior—both lyrics and music. And the production, complete with piccolo trumpet and fire bell, is ceaselessly interesting. An irrefutable Beatles classic.

Mike: It's interesting how Paul and John could write a song about the same subject, but the finished projects could sound so different—and both sound so excellent. Via the vivid imagery of the Paul's words, we reminisce along with him about this special neighborhood, and we even learn something about the characters he's celebrating. Every instrument is played and recorded brilliantly—there are so many layers to the instrumental wash (on only four tracks!) that, recently, listening to the song on headphones, I heard a flute that I swear I had never heard before.

[1] Vincent Bach (Shrottenbach) made the first Bach trumpet in 1924, notable for its high range. The Vincent Bach Corporation was bought by the Selmer musical instrument company in 1961.

[2] *The Beatles Recording Sessions*.

[3] Ibid.

Revolution

(With a few words about "Revolution 9")

> *If you want peace, you won't get it with violence. Please tell me one militant revolution that worked. Sure, a few of them took over, but what happened? Status quo... What I said in "Revolution"—in all the versions—is "change your head."*
>
> —John Lennon
> The Beatles Anthology

John would always get a little angry when people referred to the two versions of "Revolution." There are three, you know, he would say. When we look at the lyrics of the two musical versions, and then ask ourselves why he titled his sound collage "Revolution 9," we get a glimpse at John Lennon's definition of revolution. And it ain't just rallies, protest marches, and sit-ins. It was more like an ever-changing kaleidoscope of ideas, deeds, reflections, and questions. And, in the end, it seemed to be more about meaning than sounds.

Why it made the top 10

This is one of those Beatles songs that have become iconic over the decades. It was their first politically themed song, and the single, with its unexpected, raunchy, buzz-saw guitar intro, widened eyes and provoked smiles the moment we flipped over the "Hey Jude" 45 and heard it for the first time. Bands still cover it live, and it always elicits enormous applause and screams of approval. "Revolution" is as relevant today as it was when John wrote it more than thirty years ago, perhaps more so.

What the song is about

"Revolution" and "Revolution 1"

John directly addresses revolutionaries in this song, and his words are, perhaps, the bluntest and most honest message radicals had ever been given. It can be boiled down to this: Yes, change is good, but unless you guys can come up with a system to replace the one you want to tear down, then "you can count me out."

This is one of John's finest, most on-the-nose set of lyrics, and he offers his message as a dialogue in which he speaks to the militants and then counters their rhetoric with logic and common sense. "You say you want a revolution?" he begins, and then agrees that, yes, "we all want to change the world." But he then cautions them that "when you talk about destruction... you can count me out."

John was adamant that revolution should only be employed to serve a greater good. The destruction of the status quo—with *nothing better* to replace it—was unacceptable. In *Playboy,* John said, "As far as overthrowing something in the name of Marxism or Christianity, I want to know what you're going to do *after* you've knocked it all down. I mean, can't we use *some* of it? What's the point of bombing Wall Street? If you want to change the system, change the system. It's not good shooting people."

39

In the song, does John have any ideas about what to do to achieve positive change? Yes: "You better free your mind instead."

A note about the "out/in," seemingly contradictory message in the album version of the song: On *The White Album*, John sings, "when you talk about destruction, you can count me out… in…" Did John ultimately have a change of heart and decide to embrace violence? No. The "in" addition was an obvious sign of his frustration with the slow pace of world change; he wanted to stir things up a little. He succeeded.

"Revolution 9"

Is "Revolution 9" an autobiographical soundscape; a collage of seemingly unconnected sounds that all reflect a certain time or event in John's life? Or is it a sonic revolution—a revolution set to music? Or is it a random hodgepodge of noises, music, tape-loop sound effects, and spoken-word passages? Or is it all of the above?

There are those who claim the piece is specific and meaningful, and we have seen second-by-second deconstructions of the song that include some intriguing and convincing evidence that everything in it is intentional. For instance, at 2:07, a baby's cry is heard, but also present, buried in the mix, is the final note of "A Day in the Life." Accidental? Hardly. The "life/death" metaphor here is blatant. Also, at 4:02, the actual sounds of an audience screaming for the Beatles are heard.

If John did intend to write (although *create* is actually a better word) his autobiography with "Revolution 9," it seems to begin with the wartime grain rationing in England during the forties when he was a baby ("the shortage of grain…"), and it concludes with John's bonding with Yoko, who is heard in the final seconds of the piece.

Can *you* hear any of this in the track?

Now you have a reason not to skip over it when you listen to *The White Album*.

• • • ❦ • • •

• The boys recorded a promotional video for the song. In it, they lip-synched to the single version, but then added "live" elements so as to not have the British union ban the video. Elements were added from "Revolution 1": John's out/in wordplay, George and Paul singing the shoo-bee-doo-ahh background vocals, a piano solo, John panting, and more harmony vocals. (This version can be seen on the *Anthology* DVD.) In the video, George is seen playing the same Gibson Les Paul that Eric Clapton played on "While My Guitar Gently Weeps."

• The *New Left Review* called "Revolution" "a lamentable petty bourgeois cry of fear." *Time* magazine said the song "criticized radical activists the world over."

• "Revolution" was used in a Nike commercial in 1987 without the Beatles' permission. Apple sued Nike, its ad agency, and EMI/Capitol for fifteen million dollars. In an August 6, 1987, full-page ad in the *Oregonian*, the Beaverton, Oregon–based Nike company said, "Frankly,

Did you know?

we feel we're a publicity pawn in a longstanding legal battle between two record companies." Nike reportedly paid Capitol $250,000 to use the song, and the campaign ran for almost a year. There is some question as to whether Yoko was in on it and insisted they use the Beatles' version instead of a cover.

• John later regretted the "Chairman Mao" reference. In the April 1972 issue of *Hit Parader*, he said, "I should never have put that in about Chairman Mao. I was just finishing off in the studio when I did that." His reversal is puzzling, since the essence of the line continues and expands the message of the song, which is, if you associate yourself with Commies and violent militants, "you ain't gonna make it with anyone anyhow."

• The song has been covered by Mike and the Mechanics, the Grateful Dead, Nina Simone, Butthole Surfers, Stone Temple Pilots, and the Thompson Twins (at Live Aid, and then later on a studio album).

The recording

Location: **Abbey Road Studios, London.**

Dates: **May 30, 1968,** 2:30 p.m.–2:40 a.m. ("Revolution 1") – Although the Beatles had previously recorded twenty-three four-track demos of this song at George's country bungalow in Surrey, this was the first official recording sessions for *The White Album.* Eighteen takes of the rhythm track, comprising piano, acoustic guitar, and drums, were recorded (although none was numbered 11 or 12). The last take was different than the rest and became the basis of the LP version. The last take began so soon after the previous one that Emerick announced "Take 18" over John's vocal. (It was the first take with vocals.) They decided to leave the faux pas on the album. The song ran 10:17, until John shouted to anyone listening, "OK, I've had enough!" The last six minutes featured discordant instruments jamming, feedback, John screaming and repeatedly yelling "All right!," John and Yoko moaning, Yoko saying things like "you become naked," et cetera. This last section became the basis of "Revolution 9." Geoff Emerick recalled the session: "John brought [Yoko] into the control room of number three at the start of *The White Album* sessions. He quickly introduced her to everyone and that was it. She was always by his side after that."[1]

May 31, 1968, 2:30 p.m.–midnight ("Revolution 1") – Overdubbing of two John vocals and Paul's bass, which was followed by a tape reduction, and then overdubbing of Paul and George's backing vocal. Rough mono mix made.

June 4, 1968, 2:30 p.m.–1:00 a.m. ("Revolution 1") – Re-recording of John's lead vocal, in which he sang the "out/in" phrase for the first time. Technical engineer Brian Gibson recalled the session: "John decided he would feel more comfortable on the floor so I had to rig up a microphone which would be suspended on a boom above his mouth. It struck me as somewhat odd, a little eccentric, but they were always looking for a different sound; something new."[2] Paul and George recorded an overdub vocal of them repeatedly singing "mama, dada, mama, dada" at the end of the recording. Another drum track and various percussive clicks were recorded by Ringo, as well as a tone pedal guitar part by John and an organ part by Paul. A rough mono mix of Take 20 was made, and the copy was taken by John.

June 21, 1968 ("Revolution 1") – The song was now called "Revolution 1." Paul was in the United States and Ringo was absent, so only John, Yoko, and George were in the studio. Two more overdubs were made of the brass section and then another reduction mixdown. George provided the second overdub of the day, a lead guitar part. Then they moved on to "Revolution 9," which had been started on the twentieth. Stereo mixing.

June 25, 1968 ("Revolution 1") – Stereo and mono mixing.

July 9, 1968 ("Revolution") – A rehearsal of the faster lead and rhythm guitar parts, bass, drums, and John's lead vocal. Any takes from this session were wiped and re-recorded the next day.

July 10, 1968, 7:00 p.m.–1:30 a.m. ("Revolution") – Ten takes were recorded of two distorted guitars, handclaps, and two separate drum tracks. Tape operator Phil McDonald recalled their work on the distorted guitar sound: "John wanted that sound, a really distorted sound. The guitars were put through the recording console, which was technically not the thing to do. It completely overloaded the channel and produced the fuzz sound. Fortunately the technical people didn't find out. They didn't approve of 'abuse of equipment.'"[3] A reduction mix was made, and then John overdubbed two lead vocal tracks, manually double-tracking the odd word here and there and often making mistakes, which were kept in. In the second overdub, John provided the screaming intro. Another reduction mix, mono mixing.

July 11, 1968 ("Revolution") – Overdubbing of an electric piano part, played by Nicky Hopkins—who was paid six pounds, ten shillings for his work—and bass guitar. Reduction mixing.

July 12, 1968, midnight–4:00 a.m. ("Revolution") – Overdubbing of another lead guitar part by John, and another bass part by Paul. Mono mixing, and tape copies taken away by John and Paul.

July 15, 1968 ("Revolution") – Mono mixing, remixing.

August 26, 1968 – "Revolution" was first released as the B side of the "Hey Jude" single in the United States.

November 22, 1968 – "Revolution 1" and "Revolution 9" first released on the U.K. LP *The Beatles* (*The White Album*).

December 5, 1969 – Stereo mixing for the U.S. album *Hey Jude*.

Players/Instruments:

"Revolution" (single):
- **John Lennon:** Lead guitar, vocal
- **Paul McCartney:** Bass, organ
- **George Harrison:** Lead guitar
- **Ringo Starr:** Drums
- **Nicky Hopkins:** Piano

"Revolution 1" (*The White Album*):
- **John Lennon:** Guitar, lead and harmony vocal
- **Paul McCartney:** Bass, piano, harmony vocal
- **George Harrison:** Guitar, harmony vocal
- **Ringo Starr:** Drums
- **Session musicians:** two trumpets, two trombones

What we really like about this song

Steve: Mike and I decided that, for this chapter, we had to go on the record (ha, ha) as to which version of the song we personally preferred. I toyed with the idea of saying "Revolution 9" to be mysterious and eclectic, but ultimately decided that everyone would know I was goofing on them, and I'd probably get called a wanker. (In Liverpool, anyway.) I like the slower, *White Album* version best. I like the harmonies, the brass, the acoustic feel to the song, and its all-around more elaborate production. I always enjoy the false start and the count-off on the album version. It really makes me feel like I'm a fly on the wall in the studio.

Mike: I love the single version. It's the one I heard first and the version that's most familiar to me. I'm a sucker for a more heavily distorted guitar sound, and John's "Revolution" guitar riffs are arguably a harsher sound than even the chain-saw buzz of the axes on "Helter Skelter." To me, thoughts of a revolution fit better with the single's loud, distorted guitar, the screams, and the thumping drums than with the slower, shuffling version on *The White Album*. Leave it to John to say, *I'm all for change, but let me see what you've got in mind; I don't want mayhem.*

[1] *The Beatles Recording Sessions.*

[2] Ibid.

[3] Ibid.

George Harrison and Eric Clapton.

10 While My Guitar Gently Weeps

It's lovely, plaintive. Only a guitar player could write that; I love that song.

—Mick Jagger
Rolling Stone, *January 2002*

This is arguably George's greatest song. It is unquestionably one of the greatest rock guitar songs of all time, and yet it begins with a piano riff. Perfect, right?

George had been reading the I Ching and was particularly taken by its philosophy that everything in reality is connected to everything else. He tried an experiment: He opened a book randomly, and the first words his eyes fell on were *gently*

weeps. I will write a song, he thought, and one of his greatest artistic achievements was the end result.

Why it made the top 10

We remember hearing a comedian launch into a tirade targeting classic rock radio stations, reminding them that there exist more "classic rock" songs than "Sweet Home Alabama," "Stairway to Heaven," "Layla," and "While My Guitar Gently Weeps." (He had a point, yes?)

That's funny, but it also illustrates the popularity and legendary stature of one of George's finest songs, and it justifies the song's ranking here in the top ten.

"While My Guitar Gently Weeps" was the first Harrison composition we heard on our first listen to The White Album and boy oh boy, did it strike a chord (so to speak). The last two George songs Beatlefans had heard were the Yellow Submarine tracks "Only a Northern Song" and "It's All Too Much," both of which were competent, but no one would go so far as to call them milestone efforts.

All that changed with The White Album. In addition to standing out as one of the best tracks on the two-disc set, it also heralded George as a songwriter who just might be able to hold his own against his teammates. The other George compositions on The White Album—"Piggies," "Long, Long, Long," and "Savoy Truffle"—were likewise George at the peak of his powers. Soon to follow? "Something" and "Here Comes the Sun."

What the song is about

This song can be viewed as the second part of a two-part message from John and George: John told us that all we need is love, and George reminds us that we still haven't come to a full understanding of this principle. In fact, our love is still sleeping.

The singer takes a look around and sees the love that's sleeping, and his guitar weeps in pity. He sees the mundane chores of earthly life (the floor needs sweeping), but he is so distraught that he cannot tend to them, and his guitar continues to cry in pain.

He cannot help himself. He must ask: Why didn't anyone show you how to unfold your love? And the unspoken message here is, Weren't you listening when we told you that all you need is love?

Who is controlling you? he wants to know. Who bought and sold you? he asks, and we the listeners reflexively wonder who let them get away with it.

Is there hope? Perhaps. He tells us that he believes that with every mistake, we must be learning, but still, his guitar weeps in pain.

"While My Guitar Gently Weeps" is a contemplation of blindness and suffering, and it stands as a sad, pessimistic prelude to George's subsequent explosion of optimism in "Here Comes the Sun" (see song number 14).

• • • 🐚 • • •

- Brian Gibson, in *The Beatles Recording Sessions*: "George particularly wanted to get the sound of a crying guitar but he didn't want to use a wah-wah pedal, so he was experimenting with a backwards guitar solo. This meant a lot of time-consuming shuttling back and forth from the studio to the control room. We spent a long night trying to get it to work but in the end the whole thing was scrapped and it was around that time that Eric Clapton started to get involved with the song."
- In George's handwritten lyrics (reproduced in *I Me Mine*), he wrote "*Whilst* My Guitar …"
- In appreciation for Eric Clapton contributing his guitar brilliance to "While My Guitar Gently Weeps," George cowrote Cream's "Badge."
- When performing live, George would often revise the

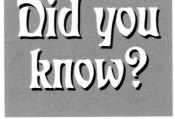

lyrics to "Gently Weeps" to "While my guitar gently smiles."
- There is a sequel to "While My Guitar Gently Weeps" on George's *Extra Texture* (1975) solo album called "This Guitar (Can't Keep from Crying)."
- Eric Clapton's participation in *The White Album* was uncredited. For the session, he used the alias "Eddie Clayton."
- "While My Guitar Gently Weeps" can be heard on the soundtrack for the Handmade Films comedy *Withnail and I*.
- One of the infamous "Paul is Dead" clues had George ostensibly singing "Paul, Paul, Paul" at the end of the song, supposedly lamenting his demise. (Just so we're clear: Paul isn't dead, and George was not singing his name.)

The recording

Location: **Abbey Road Studios, London.**
Dates: **July 25, 1968,** 7:00 p.m.–3:15 a.m. – This session was more of a rehearsal than an attempt to capture the perfect rendition of the song. There exists only one numbered take of George playing acoustic guitar and singing the song. George took with him the tapes of his unnumbered rehearsals for home listening. An overdubbed organ was added at the end. (This is the version on *Anthology 3*.) Brian Gibson, in *The Beatles Recording Sessions*, said, "The song changed considerably by the time they had finished with it. They completed the song on eight-track tape and this gave them the immediate temptation to put more and more stuff on. I personally think it was best left uncluttered."

August 16, 1968 – An electric version of the song was attempted. From 7:00 p.m. to 5:00 a.m., they taped fourteen takes of a rhythm track. The last take was reduced into Take 15 to make space for overdubbing.

September 3, 1968 – After "stealing" an eight-track recorder from the office of EMI technical expert Francis Thompson, George worked alone from 7:00 p.m. to 3:30 a.m., assembling a painstaking backward guitar solo for Track 5, after the existing four-track tape was recorded onto eight-track.

September 5, 1968, 7:00 p.m.–3:45 a.m. – In the first part of this session, George added two separate lead vocals, Ringo added maracas and drums, and another lead guitar track was added, filling a total of six tracks. Compared to the released version, this one had a less prominent vocal, and the backward guitar and organ were brought to the fore. But George didn't like what he heard in playback and recorded a new basic track with Ringo on drums, George on acoustic guitar and guide vocal, John on lead guitar, and Paul on piano and organ. Take 25 was considered the best. (FYI, Take 40 developed into an impromptu jam session with snatches of "While My Guitar Gently Weeps" and "Lady Madonna," both with Paul as vocalist.)

September 6, 1968, 7:00 p.m.–2:00 a.m. – Clapton's guitar solo was one of a number of overdubs recorded. Paul played a fuzz bass, George threw in a few organ notes, Ringo added percussion. George taped his lead vocal with Paul adding harmonies.

October 7, 1968 – Stereo remixing.

October 14, 1968 – Remixes. Chris Thomas, in *The Beatles Recording Sessions*, recalled, "I was given the grand job of waggling the oscillator on the 'Gently Weeps' mixes. Apparently Eric insisted to George [Harrison] that he didn't want the guitar solo so typically Clapton. He said the sound wasn't enough of 'a Beatles sound.' So we did this flanging thing, really wobbling the oscillator in the mix. I did that for hours. What a boring job!"

November 22, 1968 – First released on the U.K. LP *The Beatles*.

Players/Instruments:
- **George Harrison:** Acoustic guitar, lead guitar, lead vocal (occasionally double-tracked)
- **Paul McCartney:** Bass, piano, harmony vocal
- **John Lennon:** Organ
- **Ringo Starr:** Drums, castanets, tambourine
- **Eric Clapton** (uncredited): Lead guitar (George's Gibson Les Paul, not his typical Fender Stratocaster)

What we really like about this song

Steve: I like the fact that it opens with a piano riff; I also like that it is relentless in its rhythm: It chugs along with no worries about becoming plodding and, in fact, it never does. It has an odd rhythm for a rock song, and yet it works perfectly. Plus George's lyrics are some of his best (although, to be fair, his "diverted–perverted–inverted–alerted" rhyme does seem a little forced to me).

Mike: I like its placement on *The White Album*, right after the rowdy hunters of "Bungalow Bill." I also love Clapton's guitar—it is perfect for the song: sad/weeping, soaring/aching. As usual, the Beatles always know what to add, where to add it, and the perfect tone for the song. Clapton adds a soaring exclamation point and high drama to an already beautiful and moving song. I also liked it even more after I learned how George came to write it: He challenged himself. Just imagine if he had decided to go with "While My Ukulele Gently Weeps" or "While My Sitar Gently Weeps" (two instruments he was also very into playing). It would have been quite a different song. I also like that it is one of George's more down-to-earth and relatable songs. Yes, the philosophical/mystical overtones and subtext are there, but it's a fairly straightforward lyric.

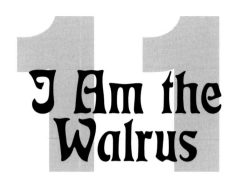

I Am the Walrus

No you're not!

—*Little Nicola*

For all its flaws, the *Magical Mystery Tour* movie holds a special place in Paul McCartney's heart, because the movie includes the *only* performance by the Beatles of "I Am the Walrus." He's got a point, don't you think?

Why it made the top 100

"I Am the Walrus" is one of the Beatles' most significant songs. It was written and recorded at the height of psychedelia, and yet it stood out, even in the sixties, when music lovers did not have the benefit of the forty years of hindsight that we do now. Compared to other "flower power"–era songs—like Strawberry Alarm Clock's 1967 "Incense and Peppermints," or the same year's Doors megahit "Light My Fire"—"Walrus" is so heavily weighted with musical gravitas that it really shouldn't even be on the list of "psychedelic" songs from that period. It was unique, and still is.

What the song is about

Throughout this book, we write about the meaning of the lyrics of the Beatles songs. There are a range of possible meanings even in such apparent nonsense songs as "Come Together," and we always try to interpret lyrics within a broader, universal context—even if one of the composing Fabs commented on the song and revealed the "personal" meaning of the words.

That said, we are making an exception here and will not be delving into in-depth analysis of the lyrics. Why? *Because*

the bloody song doesn't make any sense! (Logical, reality-based sense, that is. If you're tripping on acid while listening to it, it makes all the sense in the world. Or so we've heard.)

To wit: A wheat-coated herring ("semolina pilchard") climbs up the Eiffel Tower. (Singer Marianne Faithfull is on record as saying that she believes that John was referring to Detective Sergeant Norman Pilcher, the London police officer who made a name for himself by targeting pop stars for drug possession. Due respect to Ms. Faithfull, the problem with this theory is that the man's name was *Pilcher* and John sings *"pilchard,"* which is a real word: A pilchard is any of various small marine fishes related to the herring, especially a commercially important edible species, *Sardina pilchardus,* of European waters. Do soundalike references count? We don't think so. By the way, Pilcher served six years in prison for planting dope in people's homes.)

The singer of the song—the eggman, of course—is sitting on a cornflake awaiting a van. (Rumor has it that the "eggman" reference was to Animals lead singer Eric Burdon, who allegedly enjoyed breaking eggs over his female conquests while making love.)

Then there's "Crabalocker fishwife, pornographic priestess": We understand all the words in that phrase, except *crabalocker* (which we think is made up), but do they come together to have meaning? Or were they just strung together for their sounds?

In general, "I Am the Walrus" is a compilation of brief descriptive phrases about odd characters, including flying policemen, choking smokers, texpert experts ("expert texpert"), and, of course, the walrus. We also learn that you can get a tan from standing in the English rain.

Providing the final word on all this is John himself, who commented on the meaning, or lack thereof, of the song's lyrics in *The Beatles Anthology:* "'Walrus' is just saying a dream—the words don't mean a lot. People draw so many conclusions, and it's ridiculous. I've had tongue in cheek all along—all of them had tongue in cheek. Just because other people see depths of whatever in it… What does it really mean, 'I am the eggman'? It could have been the pudding basin for all I care. It's not that serious." (*I am the pudding basin?*)

So, there you have it. But simply because there is no blatant meaning in the song does not mean there weren't *influences* on John when he wrote it. See Did You Know?

- John told *Playboy* that the inspiration for the song came from the "Walrus and the Carpenter" poem of Lewis Carroll's *Through the Looking Glass* (Alice's adventures in Wonderland). He ultimately realized that the walrus was the bad guy in the story: "I thought, 'Oh, shit, I picked the wrong guy. I should have said, "I am the carpenter." But that wouldn't have been the same, would it? [Sings, laughingly] 'I am the carpenter...'"
- Did John get his famous "goo, goo, g'joob" from James Joyce's *Finnegan's Wake*? The phrase "googoo goosth" appears in Joyce's experimental novel, but this seems like a stretch to us. Also, a pervasive Beatles legend is that Humpty Dumpty (the eggman!) supposedly said "goo goo g'joob" just before he fell from the wall, but he doesn't say it in the "Humpty Dumpty" chapter of the aforementioned Lewis Carroll work, nor does he say it in the original nursery rhyme. Apparently, not all legends are true!
- According to John, the words "element'ry penguin" meant that "it's naive to just go around chanting Hare Krishna or just putting your faith in one idol." He admitted he had Allen Ginsberg in mind when he wrote the line.
- John wrote the first line ("I am he as you are he as you are me as we are all together...") while on an acid trip one weekend and the second line ("See how they run like pigs from a gun, see how they fly...") on another acid trip the following weekend. He said he filled in the rest of the lyrics after he met Yoko.
- As he did with "Happiness Is a Warm Gun," John pieced together three song fragments to compose "I Am the Walrus." The first part is the "I am he..."/"Mister City Policemen..." part, and he wrote it to the oscillating sound of a police siren. The second part is about John in his English garden in Weybridge. The third was a nonsense song he had begun about sitting on a cornflake.
- For one line of the lyrics, Lennon friend Pete Shotton reminded John of a rhyme they sang as schoolkids: "Yellow matter custard, green slop pie. All mixed together with a dead dog's eye. Slap it on a butty, ten foot thick. Then wash it all down with a cup of cold sick."
- The song was originally banned by the BBC for the line about the naughty girl who let her knickers down, and because of the suspicion that the choir was chanting "smoke pot" at the end. (They weren't. See the recording info.)
- The U.S. and U.K. versions of the song differ slightly. The U.S. single has a few extra beats in the middle; the U.K. version has the intro riff repeated six times, not four.
- The song has been covered by Oasis, Oingo Boingo, Frank Zappa, Men Without Hats, Crack the Sky, Dead Milkmen, Foetus, Gray Matter, Hash, Chain of Fools, Marc Bonilla, Mike Fab, and Skeleton Crew.

The recording

Location: **Abbey Road Studios, London.**

Dates: **September 5, 1967,** 7:00 p.m.–1:00 a.m. – After Brian Epstein's August 27 death, the Beatles met at Paul's house in St. John's Wood on September 1 and decided to continue the *Magical Mystery Tour* project. In this session four days later, they agreed to continue recording the soundtrack. (Filming of the movie began on September 11.)

George Martin, in *The Beatles Recording Sessions*, commented on the project: "I tended to lay back on *Magical Mystery Tour* and let them have their head. Some of the sounds weren't very good. Some were brilliant but some were bloody awful. 'I Am the Walrus' was organized—it was organized chaos. I'm proud of that. But there was also disorganized chaos that I'm not very proud of." Sixteen takes of the basic rhythm track—consisting of bass, lead guitar, electric piano, drums, plus a Mellotron overdub—were recorded, but only five takes were complete. The first three takes were erased as tape wound back and recorded over them.

September 6, 1967 –A reduction mix of the previous day's Take 16 was made, then an overdub of more bass from Paul, plus Ringo's drums, and a new lead vocal from John. Mono mixing and acetates were made for the review cut.

September 27, 1967 – Two separate overdub sessions of sixteen orchestral instruments in the afternoon, plus a choir of sixteen voices in the evening session. A reduction mix was made, then seven attempts were made at more overdubs, then another reduction mix.

September 28, 1967 – Reduction mix, then superimposition of two prior takes. Mono mixing.

September 29, 1967 – Seventeen mono mixes were made, but only two were complete, and the final version was made by splicing the two. The first was up to the lyric "Sitting in an English garden." The other half was done with a live feed from a radio: a BBC Third Programme's production of *King Lear*, Act IV, Scene VI.

November 6, 1967 – Stereo mixing, which was somewhat challenging since the live Shakespeare radio feed was in mono.

November 17, 1967 – A new remix of the first half of the song for the stereo master.

November 24, 1967 – First released as single in the United Kingdom, as the B side of "Hello Goodbye."

Players/Instruments:
- **John Lennon:** Mellotron, lead vocal
- **Paul McCartney:** Bass, backing vocal
- **George Harrison:** Tambourine, backing vocal
- **Ringo Starr:** Drums
- **Session musicians:** Eight violins, four cellos, a contra bass clarinet, and three horns
- **Choir:** Eight male, eight female
  Note: One source says that the boys sang "Oompah, oompah, stick it up your jumper," and the girls sang "Everybody's got one." In *The Beatles Recording Sessions*, Mark Lewisohn said that what they sang was random, and was not arranged by gender. (We tend to defer to Lewisohn on matters such as these.)

What we really like about this song

Steve: I can't help it, but one of my favorite moments of this song (and perhaps one of my all-time favorite Beatles moments) is John's pronunciation of the *p*'s in the "Mister City, p'liceman sitting pretty little p'licemen in a row" line (beginning at 1:04). He spits out the *p* with snarling deliberateness (you can actually hear him winding up for the *p*, hesitating a millisecond before letting fly), and we can easily imagine him smirking after the line. I love everything else about this song, too—the whole piece is like a surrealistic mini epic that combines rock, classical, and spoken word, and the track can legitimately be considered a genre unto itself. In fact, in *Playboy*, John said that everything ELO did was a continuation of what he began with "Walrus."

Mike: Classic John. Not much melodically to speak of, and the words don't have much meaning, but it wins points for style and nerve. Unlike my coauthor (who counts this as one of his faves), I don't listen to "Walrus" as much as others on *Magical Mystery Tour*, like "All You Need Is Love" and, of course, "Strawberry Fields," but every time I do play it, I hear something I've never heard before. Standouts for me include the relentless, marching tempo, the laughing jokers and sniding (snieding?) pigs, George Martin's great score, and John's final "goo-goo-goo'joob"s to close things out.

Julian's drawing.

Lucy in the Sky with Diamonds

12

Compared with Paul's songs, all of which seemed to keep in some sort of touch with reality, John's had a psychedelic, almost mystical quality. "Lucy in the Sky with Diamonds" was a typical John song in that respect, and a lot of the analysts and psychiatrists were later to describe it as the drug song of all time. They were talking rubbish, but the tag stuck.

—George Martin
All You Need Is Ears

In his autobiography, *All You Need Is Ears*, George Martin described John Lennon as an "aural Salvador Dali." If you're even remotely familiar with the great Spanish painter's surreal dream landscapes and melting clocks, you will understand Martin's comparison and, in all likelihood, agree with him.

49

The problem with treating this song as nothing but a drug-inspired fable is that countless acid trips by countless people have been embarked upon over the decades, and rarely has brilliant art resulted from those mind excursions. "Lucy in the Sky with Diamonds," though, has long been considered one of the Beatles' greatest recordings. If the art is not in the artist, then taking drugs will not result in art.

And the song is not about drugs—it was inspired by a drawing of Julian Lennon's. John said in *Playboy*, "It was purely unconscious that it came out to be LSD... I mean, who would ever bother to look at initials of a title? It's *not* an acid song."

Okay, we'll take John at his word. Acid may not have been the *casus artis* for the song, but the fact that the Fabs were doing a lot of acid at the time had to have inspired the dream imagery and surrealistic panorama of the song. Just a happy coincidence that it spelled out *LSD*.

Why it made the top 100

This *Sgt. Pepper* track is one of the Beatles' most creative efforts, a mélange of great lyrics, innovative production, and a weird vocal track. Appearing as it does on *Pepper* after the relatively straightforward opening rocker and Ringo's "With a Little Help from My Friends," it came as something of a surprise to us that summer of '67. Strangeness was in the wind, and the Beatles were its messengers.

What the song is about

"Lucy" begins with the storyteller speaking directly to us and telling us to "picture yourself in a boat on a river." This realistic image quickly devolves into a sudden rush of surrealism: On the side of the river are "tangerine trees." Are these real fruit trees, or does the word *tangerine* refer to their color? This ambiguous image opens the gates for the full-ahead rush of astonishing imagery. We are told that above this river are marmalade skies. Suddenly we have orange trees and an orange sky, and we realize we're not in Kansas (or Liverpool) anymore.

It is then that Lucy makes her first appearance. She calls out to us, and we "answer quite slowly." The slow motion adds to our sense of detachment and alienation, and the subsequent revelation that this girl has kaleidoscope eyes puts us over the top: Our reality needle is now in the red zone.

The images that follow all emanate from a weird world in which we now find ourselves. *Cellophane flowers, rocking-horse people, newspaper taxis, giant flowers, plasticine porters, looking-glass ties...* all combine to carry us through a landscape of strangeness, a place watched over by Lucy, who is in the sky, with diamonds.

Is there an ultimate meaning to the song? Not empirically: The observation of the song's "reality" does not provide answers. What it does do, though, is take us on a magical mystery tour, which is probably all John intended in the first place.

• • • ❦ • • •

- John and Paul volleyed ideas and images back and forth for the "Lucy" lyrics. Paul came up with "newspaper taxis" and "cellophane flowers"; John thought up "kaleidoscope eyes."

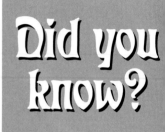

- John told *Playboy*, "The images were from *Alice in Wonderland*. It was Alice in the boat. She is buying an egg and it turns into Humpty Dumpty...There was also the image of the female who would someday come save me—a 'girl with kaleidoscope eyes' who would come out of the sky. It turned out to be Yoko, though I hadn't met Yoko yet. So maybe it should be 'Yoko in the Sky with Diamonds.'"

- John was a fan of the British comedy radio show *The Goon Show*. Spike Milligan, one of the show's writers, recalled, "We used to talk about 'plasticine ties' in *The Goon Show* and this crept up in Lucy as 'plasticine porters with looking-glass ties.' I knew Lennon quite well. He used to talk a lot about comedy. He was a *Goon Show* freak. It all stopped when he married Yoko. Everything stopped."[1]

- "Lucy" was initially banned from airplay by the BBC because of the *LSD* acronym.

- The *Yellow Submarine* film started out as a two-minute pilot film for "Lucy" by Bill Sewell.

- "Lucy" was digitally remixed for the re-release of the *Yellow Submarine* "songtrack." The remix is fuller, with the tracks less obviously separated and the instruments more to the front of the mix. The *Sgt. Pepper* track is the original, but the remix is the superior recording.

- The song "White Lightning" by the Babys tells us that "Lucy in the sky with diamonds" didn't shine like white lightning.

- "Lucy" is one of seventeen Beatles songs that mention the sun. (See song number 82, "Dear Prudence," for the complete list.)

- "Lucy" is one of five Beatles songs that mention the color yellow. The others are "All Together Now," "I Am the

Walrus," "Yellow Submarine," and "You Never Give Me Your Money."

- "Lucy" is one of three Beatles songs with diamond(s) in the lyric. The other two are "Can't Buy Me Love" and "I Feel Fine."
- "Lucy" has been covered by the Grateful Dead, Hugo Montenegro, the Hooters, Bela Fleck and the Flecktones, Bill Murray, Natalie Cole, William Shatner, the University of Nebraska Marching Band, and Elton John. (John Lennon suggested the distinctive reggae break in Elton's version; also, one source says John played rhythm guitar and sang backing vocals, credited as "Featuring Dr. Winston O'Boogie and his Reggae Guitars.")

The recording

Location: **Abbey Road Studios, London.**

Dates: **February 28, 1967**, 7:00 p.m.–3:00 a.m. – For eight hours, the Beatles rehearsed and reworked the song, but no proper recordings of their efforts were made. The Beatles regularly used the studio to work out ideas, and during those periods the crew sat around and waited. EMI's Peter Vince told Mark Lewisohn, "*Sgt. Pepper's Lonely Hearts Club Band* took four months to record and for probably more than half that time all the engineers were doing was sitting around waiting for them to get their ideas together."

March 1, 1967 – Seven takes were recorded, focusing on the rhythm track of piano, acoustic guitar, Hammond organ, drums, and maracas. Paul played the opening passage on a Hammond, which was taped with a special organ stop so it would sound like a celesta. Take 7 introduced a tamboura. Reduction mix.

March 2, 1967, 7:00 p.m.–3:30 a.m. – The speeds of the recording and the mixes were varied. Vocal overdubs (lead and backing vocals) were also recorded at different speeds. A normal speed overdub of the bass and George's fuzzed lead guitar was recorded. Eleven mono remixes.

March 3, 1967 – Four mono remixes.

April 7, 1967 – Five stereo remixes.

June 1, 1967 – First released on the U.K. LP *Sgt. Pepper's Lonely Hearts Club Band*.

Players/Instruments:

- **John Lennon:** Lead guitar, lead vocal
- **Paul McCartney:** Bass, Hammond organ, harmony vocal
- **George Harrison:** Sitar, lead guitar, harmony vocal
- **Ringo Starr:** Drums

Note: The track also features piano, acoustic guitar, and maracas, but the recording logs are silent as to who played what.

What we really like about this song

Steve: I absolutely love the fact that the keyboard beginnings of two of John's most well-known and beloved songs— "Lucy" and "Strawberry Fields"—were both played by Paul. And speaking of Paul, I am especially fond of his bass playing on "Lucy," as well as George's sitar, which drones low in the mix but contributes nicely to the hypnotic, trance-like mojo of the song. The way the guitar mirrors the vocal in the middle eight is groovy, too. I am *not* that big a fan of the clichéd I–IV–V chord progression of the chorus, but that's a small complaint for such an overwhelmingly great song and recording.

Mike: Of John's most surreal songs, including "Tomorrow Never Knows" and "Strawberry Fields Forever," the images in "Lucy" are more vivid to me (although no less unusual). The song boasts a cornucopia of textures and sounds, allowing the listener the pleasure of focusing on the sounds coming from a single instrument and following it all the way through the song. The bass seems to lead the song, and the way it was recorded, it sounds almost like a tuba. The drums seem to shuffle through the track, trying to keep up with the sweeping score—until the three blasts from the bass drum that introduce the chorus. This is a song I can listen to every day and, with all due respect to Sir Elton John, *no one's* version can compare to the original.

Nowhere Man

The hard stuff was the complicated harmonies. It was hard to do them live onstage. Like for instance "Nowhere Man."

—Paul McCartney
The Beatles Anthology

"Nowhere Man," with its opening a cappella harmonies, foreshadowed the similar a cappella opening of the following year's "Paperback Writer." Rock songs did not usually open this way—until the Beatles came along, that is.

Why it made the top 100

"Nowhere Man" is a brilliant blend of Beatles pop and Dylanesque folk that stands as one of the Beatles' simplest and, at the same time, most profound songs. The chord changes in the chorus (back and forth from G-sharp minor to A) are beautiful and poignant, and George's triple-trebled guitar adds a sound that obviously inspired a great many rock groups, including the Byrds. "Nowhere Man" is universally loved by fans and often makes "favorites" lists.

What the song is about

"Nowhere Man" is about existential angst. Existentialism stresses that people are utterly responsible for what they make of themselves, and that—due to human frailty—with this responsibility comes cataclysmic dread, often internalized.

The main character in the song—the "nowhere man"—is living an existential nightmare. He sits in a nowhere land, is making nowhere plans for no one; he doesn't have a point of view, he's aimless and clueless as to where he's going, he's blind, and he's so narrow-minded that he only sees what he wants to see. The singer is trying to redeem the nowhere man—who is consumed by his own depression—telling him the world is at his command and trying to get him to see what he's missing. He reassures the man that there's no need to hurry and that there will always be someone to lend him a hand.

The key line in the song is "Nowhere Man, can you see me at all?" John is taking on two personas in the song, and his ultimate goal—his message to his agonized self—is self-realization and self-redemption.

"Nowhere Man" is a reflection of the social zeitgeist of the sixties, a period of great disillusionment and restlessness; a time of frustration with the establishment and its mores; an era of anger and awareness that resulted in massive social changes still felt today. When John wrote "Nowhere Man," the world had been through the Cuban Missile Crisis, civil rights marches in Washington, the assassination of John F. Kennedy, and the increasingly violent protests against the Vietnam War. It is fair to say that "Nowhere Man" can be looked to as an anthem of a troubled time.

All that, in a two-minute-and-thirty-nine-second pop song.

The recording

Location: **Abbey Road Studios, London.**
Dates: **October 21, 1965** – Recording Takes 1–2. First track incomplete; some experimentation with a higher-register three-part opening, which was scrapped.
October 22, 1965 – Recording Takes 3–5, overdubbing vocals on Take 5.
October 25, 1965 – Mono mix.
October 26, 1965 – Stereo mix.

Players/Instruments:
- **John Lennon:** Acoustic guitar, lead vocal
- **Paul McCartney:** Bass, harmony vocal
- **George Harrison:** Lead guitar, harmony vocal
- **Ringo Starr:** Drums

- "Nowhere Man" was the first Beatles song not about love.
- John spent five hours one morning trying to write a song and finally gave up. As soon as he surrendered and lay down, the song "Nowhere Man" came to him, fully developed with words and music; from there it was only a matter of recording it—almost exactly as John had originally conceived it. The Fabs were under enormous pressure to deliver product—hit singles—on a rigid and unrelenting schedule.
- In early 1966, "Nowhere Man" was one of four Beatles songs (the others were "What Goes On," "If I Needed Someone," and "Drive My Car") that were restricted from airplay in the United States. Why? Because the four songs were not included on the U.S. *Rubber Soul* release, an example of the problems caused by releasing different albums to different markets. "Nowhere Man" was released in the U.S. on *Yesterday and Today* on June 20, 1966.
- Tiny Tim sang "Nowhere Man" on the Beatles' 1968 Christmas record.
- Ironically, John later remarked that he was disappointed by the lyrics of the song. Upon reflection, he thought they were trite.
- "Nowhere Man" was performed live by the Beatles during their 1965 U.K. and 1966 U.S. tours. A clip from one of these performances was shown in *The Beatles Anthology*, and it dramatically illustrates the accomplished musicianship of the Fabs when performing live—and the difficulty of performing a song like "Nowhere Man." As the boys begin singing "He's a real nowhere man, sitting in his nowhere land" in the song's demanding three-part

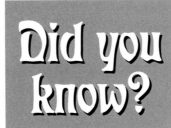

harmony, Paul senses after only a few seconds that their complex harmony is drifting off key. He immediately plays one single note on his bass to give them all a pitch anchor so they can stay together, and they finish the intro without any audible clunkers.
- Covers of "Nowhere Man" include versions by Placido Domingo, Dino, Desi and Billy, the Anti-Nowhere League, Dokken, Hot Rize/Red Knuckles, Mortal, Three Good Reasons, Joe Pass, World Party, Natalie Merchant (performed live at the post-9/11 concert "Come Together: A Night for John Lennon's Words and Music"), and Vikki Carr.
- In *The Beatles Recording Sessions*, Paul talked about how the band always pushed the bounds of recording standards, sometimes even against the wishes of EMI brass. "We were always forcing them into things they didn't want to do. 'Nowhere Man' was one. I remember we wanted very treble-y guitars, which they are, they're among the most treble-y guitars I've ever heard on record. The engineer said, 'All right, I'll put full treble on it' and we said, 'That's not enough' and he said, 'But that's all I've got, I've got one pot and that's it!' and we replied 'Well, put that through another lot of faders and put full treble up on that. And if that's not enough we'll go through another lot of faders and…' so we were always doing that, forcing them. We were always pushing ahead: 'louder, further, longer, more, different.' I always wanted things to be different because we knew that people, generally, always wanted to move on, and if we hadn't pushed them, the guys would have stuck by the rule books and still been wearing ties."

What we really like about this song

Steve: Depending on the mood I'm in, this is often my favorite Beatles song. I absolutely love John's vocal. And the overtrebled guitars. And the ethereal harmonies. And the "listen–missing" rhyme. And the chords of the chorus. I also love that John is singing about this other guy, some loser, a real "nowhere man" who is, in fact, John himself seeking redemption. He shows us how the personal can become the universal in the hands of a true artist.

Mike: I like the fact that John wrote it while suffering from writer's block, but that he worked through the inordinate pressure on himself and the band to produce on deadline, and used the creative block as his muse. I also like that this is a virtual snapshot of John's songwriting at the time, since little was changed from the song John originally envisioned. That was unusual but it speaks to the brilliance of the song.

⑭ Here Comes the Sun

[I]t seems as if winter in England goes on forever; by the time spring comes you really deserve it. So one day I decided—I'm going to "sag off" Apple, and I went over to Eric's [Clapton] house: I was walking in his garden. The relief of not having to go and see all those dopey accountants was wonderful, and I was walking around the garden with one of Eric's acoustic guitars and wrote "Here Comes the Sun."

—George Harrison
I Me Mine

The contrast between the raging ferocity of John's "I Want You (She's So Heavy)" and this lovely pastorale by George can be experienced most viscerally thanks to the invention of the CD.

On the vinyl version of *Abbey Road*, John's song ended Side One and "Here Comes the Sun" began Side Two. There was a moment of respite as we metaphorically pushed the reset button on our internal emotional receptors during the time it took to flip the album over. This pause dampened somewhat the stark differences between the songs. On the CD, "I Want You" ends abruptly (as it is wont to do) and, within a couple of seconds, George's lovely guitar intro begins. We're still reeling from John's shriek of passion and suddenly we're on a walkabout under the new day's sun.

Why it made the top 100

"Here Comes the Sun" is ranked highly because it is the second greatest song George ever wrote as a Beatle. (Our number 10 song—"While My Guitar Gently Weeps"—is his best.) It was a quantum leap in songwriting for George and is without question superior to his other *Abbey Road* contribution, "Something" (although we'll acknowledge that "Something" is definitely the more popular of the two).

George deftly moves through a range of time signatures, never confusing the listener or degenerating into musical gibberish. The song begins in 4/4, but the "it's all right" refrain of the chorus includes the time signatures 2/4, 5/8, and 3/8, before nonchalantly returning to the home time of 4/4. Impressive.

What the song is about

"Here Comes the Sun" is probably George's most straightforward lyric, and it's a bit of a stretch to look for anything more in it than what it appears to be on the surface: a joyous celebration of the end of winter and the reappearance of the sun. That said, though, can we examine the lyrics and try to parse them within a wider context?

Yes. If we interpret winter as symbolizing conflict or trouble, and the sun representing resolution and optimism, then the song becomes a parable of hope. The winter is cold and dark, and your problems may seem insurmountable, but the sun will always return and melt the snow. This, too, will pass.

In fact, all things must pass, right?

• • • ❧ • • •

- At precisely 2:22 in the song, George sings "It *seels* like years since it's been clear." Apparently, he wasn't sure if he wanted to sing "feels" or "seems," and his vocal mangling of the word survived and made it onto the final track.
- Notable live performances by George of "Here Comes the Sun" include the "Concert for Bangla Desh" in 1971; the 1987 Prince's Trust concert at Wembley Stadium (with Eric Clapton and Jeff Lynne), and with Eric Clapton on George's Japan concert tour. George also sang the song with Paul Simon on *Saturday Night Live* in November 1976 when Simon was guest host. (The two dueted on Simon's "Homeward Bound" as well.)
- "Here Comes the Sun" was the first in a quadrilogy of George songs about the sun and moon: "Here Comes the Sun," "New Blue Moon," "Here Comes the Moon," and the poignant song "Rising Sun" on George's postmortem

Did you know?

Brainwashed CD: "In the rising sun, you can feel your life begin/Universe at play, inside your DNA/You're a billion years old today…"

- George had to have the Moog he used for the song specially made for him. He talked about it in *The Beatles Anthology*: "It was enormous, with hundreds of jackplugs and two keyboards. But it was one thing having one, and another trying to make it work. There wasn't an instruction manual, and if there had been it would probably have been a couple of thousand pages long… When you listen to the sounds on songs like 'Here Comes the Sun,' it does some good things, but they're all very kind of infant sounds."
- The song has been covered by Richie Havens, George Benson, Hugo Montenegro, Steve Harley and Cockney Rebel, Robin Crow, Fat Larry's Band, the Disney Babies, Womack and Womack, and Nina Simone.

The recording

Location: **Abbey Road Studios, London.**

Dates: **July 7, 1969**, 2:30–11:45 p.m. (Ringo's twenty-ninth birthday; also, John was not at the session, but was out with an injury from a car accident) – Thirteen takes were recorded, the last being best. George played acoustic guitar and sang a guide vocal, Paul played bass, and Ringo was on the drums. When Take 1 broke down, George said sadly: "One of my best beginnings, that!" The last hour of the session was spent re-recording the acoustic guitar and adding the new performance as an overdub.

July 8, 1969, 2:30–10:45 p.m. – The overdubbing of George's new lead vocal erases his guide vocal. They also recorded overdubs of backing vocals by George and Paul, which were

manually double-tracked. A reduction mix, then a rough mono remix, was made, which George took with him.

July 16, 1969 – Handclaps and harmonium overdubs.

August 4, 1969 – A rough remix was made, and George took it away to assess what else the song needed.

August 6, 1969, 2:30–11:00 p.m. – George overdubbed a guitar part while Paul was recording the Moog piece for "Maxwell's Silver Hammer."

August 11, 1969 – More guitar overdubs by George.

August 15, 1969 – A day of orchestral overdubs for "Here Comes the Sun," "Golden Slumbers,"

"Carry That Weight," "The End," and "Something." They finished all the orchestral overdubs in a marathon day of recording, with two sessions totaling more than nine hours.

August 19, 1969 – Moog overdub. Stereo mixing.

September 26, 1969 – First released on the U.K. LP *Abbey Road*.

Note: One source says "Here Comes the Sun" was worked on at the same time as John's "Sun King," and that they were originally planned to be one combined song. (How happy are we all that *that* didn't happen?)

Players/Instruments:

- **George Harrison:** Acoustic guitar, Moog synthesizer, lead vocal, handclaps
- **John Lennon:** Acoustic guitar, harmony vocal, handclaps
- **Paul McCartney:** Bass, harmony vocal, handclaps
- **Ringo Starr:** Drums, handclaps
- **Session musicians:** Four violas, four cellos, a string bass, two clarinets, two alto flutes, two flutes, and two piccolos

What we really like about this song

Steve: The biggest appeal for me is the song's overall mood, its *sensibility*, and the feeling I get when I listen to it. The guitars are subtle and calm, and yet there is a palpable undercurrent of excitement throughout the tune thanks, in large part, to the Moog and harmonium wash that is always there; neither of which ever hogs center stage, though. Plus the time changes and the lovely harmonies are irresistible. This is one of my favorite *Abbey Road* tracks and, back in the seventies, I made a point of learning how to play it—not on the guitar, though. You should hear how this song sounds on the piano!

Mike: Infighting, the Allen Klein/John Eastman power struggle, the personal intra-Beatles squabbles—it all became too much for "the quiet Beatle," so what did George do? He played hooky at Eric Clapton's house, strumming away in Slowhand's garden on one of Eric's acoustic guitars. Out pops his best Beatles song, as if it had been delivered to him, appropriately enough, via a beam of sunlight. It's a song of optimism, obviously coming from deep within George, given the contention around him. He was seeing his future: that things were definitely looking up for him as a solo artist. It's nice to hear some of George's purest playing, echoed by the weird sounds from the Moog. My favorite part? The repeated lines "Sun, sun, sun, here it comes."

She Loves You

15

There is a scene in a first-season episode of *The Sopranos* in which Christopher's girlfriend Adriana is listening to a band she is managing (called Visiting Day) record a demo. The song sucks, and finally the producer lashes out and shrieks at the band that the song has *no chorus—everything is a verse*, he shouts at them. In exasperation, he cites "She Loves You" as an example of how to write a hit. He was right.

"She Loves You" is more than just one of the most important early songs of the greatest band of all time. With its signature "yeah, yeah, yeah"s and "wooo," it has become a pop culture icon, a sixties touchstone, as well as a primer on how to write a pop song.

Even people who have never bought a Beatles record have heard and know "She Loves You."

Why it made the top 100

"She Loves You" is a tale of ironies.

The "yeah, yeah, yeah"s were at first thought by many to be banal and dumb; they soon became a beloved and respected musical trademark.

The use of "un-pop-like" chords such as major sixths and minor sixths was initially thought to be corny and derivative, or at the very least out of place in a pop song; their use was quickly recognized as groundbreaking and innovative.

The song was, at first, shortsightedly reviewed as terrible. In the August 1980 issue of *Musician* magazine, Paul remarked, "Nearly everything I've ever done or been involved in has received some negative critical response. You'd think the response to something like 'She Loves You' with the Beatles would have been pretty positive. It wasn't. The very first week that came out it was supposed to be the *worst* song the Beatles had ever thought of." But, as is often the case with new ideas, the critics quickly reversed their opinion and admitted their mistake.

Today, the song still *works*, it is a rock classic, and it has found new audiences in each successive generation. Beatles-loving parents are begetting Beatles-loving kids (and grandkids).

Cool.

What the song is about

In *The Beatles Anthology*, Paul talked about the unique point-of-view the Beatles used for the first time in "She Loves You":

> All our early songs had always had "please, please *me*," "from me to *you*," "PS I love *you*." We'd always had this very personal thing. Thank you girl. And we hit on the idea of doing kind of a reported conversation. "I saw her yesterday. She told me what to say. She said *she* loves *you*." So it just gives us another dimension really. It just meant that the song then was something different from what we and other people had written before.

A couple breaks up. A mutual friend of the two runs into the girl, who tells him that she still loves her ex-boyfriend. The mutual friend then tells the guy that his ex knows he didn't deliberately mean to hurt her, and warns him that he may lose her for good if he lets his pride sway his decisions. His advice is to kiss and make up.

But is there a subtler message beneath the surface? Perhaps. Rock critic Dave Marsh, in his book *The Heart of Rock and Roll*, saw "darker nuances" in the lyrics. Marsh suggested that the singer was telling his friend that if he didn't make up with his girlfriend, he might make his own move on her.

Is there an implicit warning in the lyrics? It can't be proven from the lyrics themselves, but it would not be at all far-fetched to imagine someone taking up with one of his friends' ex-girlfriends.

Yes, we're certain that it happens all the time.

• • • ❦ • • •

- The "She Loves You" single sold 1.3 million copies in the United Kingdom by the end of 1963. It was the first Beatles single to sell one-million-plus units in the U.K. alone. It remained the biggest-selling single in the U.K. until Wings' 1978 release, "Mull of Kintyre."
- "She Loves You" was used in a commercial for Schweppes on Spanish TV in 1985.
- On November 4, 1963, the Beatles performed "She Loves You" for the British royal family at a command performance at the Prince of Wales Theatre in London.

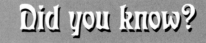
Did you know?

(Yes, this was the show at which John encouraged the people in the cheap seats to applaud and all the others to "rattle their jewelry.")

- On December 20, 1963, Britain's *New Musical Express*'s 12th Annual Popularity Poll ranked the Beatles as the United Kingdom's Number One group, and their single "She Loves You" as Record of the Year.
- Paul sings a chorus of "She Loves You" on the "All You Need Is Love" recording as the song fades out.
- How enduring is "She Loves You"? In 2003, a garage punk

trio that *Playboy* described as "one of the hottest live acts in New York City since the Strokes graduated from the sticky floor circuit" released its first major-label album. The band's name? The Yeah Yeah Yeahs.

- The song has been covered by Peter Sellers, Count Basie, the Chipmunks, Neil Sedaka, Vanilla Fudge, the Everly Brothers, and Funkadelic.

The recording

Location: **Abbey Road Studios, London.**

Dates: **July 1, 1963,** 5:00–10:45 p.m. – A recording log for this day does not exist, so it is not known how many takes of the song were recorded. George Martin, speaking in *The Beatles Recording Sessions*, recalled the day: "I was sitting in my usual place on a high stool in studio two when John and Paul first ran through the song on their acoustic guitars, George joining in the chorus. I thought it was great but was intrigued by the final chord, an odd sort of major sixth, with George doing the sixth and John and Paul the third and fifths, like a Glenn Miller arrangement. They were saying 'It's a great chord! Nobody's ever heard it before!' Of course I knew that wasn't quite true!" Engineer Norman Smith also remembered the day: "I was setting up the microphone when I saw the lyrics on the music stand. I thought I'll just have a quick look. 'She Loves You Yeah Yeah Yeah, She Loves You Yeah Yeah Yeah, She Loves You Yeah Yeah Yeah, Yeah.' I thought Oh my God, what a lyric! This is going to be one that I do not like. But when they started to sing it—bang, wow, terrific, I was up at the mixer jogging around."[1] The B side of the "She Loves You" single, "I'll Get You," was recorded the same night.

July 4, 1963 – Editing, mono mixing.

August 23, 1963 – Released as a single in the United Kingdom, backed with "I'll Get You."

November 8, 1966 – Stereo mixing for *The Beatles 1962–1966* (The Red Album).

Players/Instruments:
- **John Lennon:** Rhythm guitar, lead vocal
- **Paul McCartney:** Bass, lead vocal
- **George Harrison:** Lead guitar
- **Ringo Starr:** Drums

What we really like about this song

Steve: I like the fact that it *begins* with the chorus; I like the fact that John and Paul used harmonies and chords not usually (at the time) found in pop songs; I *love* Ringo's drumming on the track, and I am especially fond of George's nasty little licks that lead off each verse.

Mike: This is an important song for the group—a milestone in their songwriting (writing a song of reportage, rather than personal experience). And it obviously struck a note with fans, as it became their first U.K. million seller. It includes all the elements of classic early Beatles—impeccable harmonies, a toe-tapping beat, catchy instrumentation, and, of course, the trademark "wooos!" (complete with the jubilant shaking of their tousled heads of hair—you *know* they were doing that in the studio!). You can tell they were having fun making this record, and it's always fun to listen to.

[1] *The Beatles Recording Sessions.*

One of my special memories is when we were in Obertauern, Austria, filming Help! *John and I shared a room and we were taking off our heavy ski boots after a day's filming, ready to have a shower and get ready for the nice bit, the evening meal and the drinks. We were playing a cassette of our new recordings and my song "Here, There and Everywhere" was on. And I remember John saying, "You know, I probably like that better than any of my songs on the tape." Coming from John, that was high praise indeed.*

—*Paul McCartney*
The Beatles Anthology

Have you ever listened to a piece by Mozart and gotten the sense that the work *always existed*... that it wasn't actually composed but rather was as much an innate part of reality as the sky or the sun?

Paul McCartney admitted feeling like this when he wrote "Yesterday" (see song number 4). The song had such a presence he couldn't believe that it hadn't been previously written.

"Here, There and Everywhere" elicits that kind of weird existential wonderment. The song is so... what's the word? We want to say *obvious*, but it's more than that.

It may well be the ultimate love ballad, not to mention one of Paul's greatest songwriting achievements.

16 Here, There and Everywhere

Why it made the top 100

There really was no question that "Here, There and Everywhere" would make the top 100; the only debate was where to rank it.

Some of our more intense "HTAE"-loving friends have chastised us for ranking it too low, but one thing is certain:

"Here, There and Everywhere" is one beloved song.

What the song is about

"Here, There and Everywhere" is clearly a heartfelt expression of romantic love, but it is also tinged with the narrator's subtle, yet real feelings of doubt about love's permanence.

This becomes evident in the very first line of the intro when the narrator uses the verb *need*. To lead a better life, he *needs* his love. The choice of *need* over *want* is revealing.

He then admits that the sway his love holds over him is profound: She can change his life with something as trivial as a "wave of her hand." And as he runs his hands through her hair, he says that they are both thinking how good it *can* be—as though this were a possibility, but perhaps not yet a reality. He then tells us that someone is speaking but she doesn't know he's there—who could this be? Is she ignoring

him? Or is there a voice—literal or figurative—in her head trying to lure her away from him? Or, perhaps, is everything in the outside world, everything beyond the two lovers, superfluous?

In the bridge, his message is stated bluntly: "But to love her is to need her."

In the next verse, he is watching her eyes and again he expresses doubt: "*hoping* I'm always there."

The song ends with the narrator avowing he will always be there for her.

"Here, There and Everywhere" is, in the end, a poignant and honest expression of the fear of loving so *much* that it's difficult to know how to survive without that special someone.

• • • 🐦 • • •

- "Here, There and Everywhere" has been covered by José Feliciano, Emmylou Harris, Perry Como, Kenny Loggins, George Benson, Liberace, Johnny Mathis, Petula Clark, Jackie Gleason, Jay and the Americans, Andy Williams, Celine Dion, Claudine Longet, Vince Hill, James Galway, Hugh Masekela, Matt Munro, Bobbie Gentry, and Dick Smothers.
- On VH1's *Greatest Albums of All Time* show, Art Garfunkel called "Here, There and Everywhere" the greatest song of all time.
- Paul said the song was inspired by the Beach Boys' "God Only Knows." (Thus, Beatlefans here, there, and everywhere owe a debt of gratitude to Brian Wilson.)
- Paul also said that when he started writing the song, he wanted a structural challenge, so he constructed each verse of the song around the three adverbs in the title. When he later recorded it, he imagined Marianne Faithfull singing it so he could achieve the effect from his own voice that he wanted.
- Paul covered "Here, There and Everywhere" in the movie *Give My Regards to Broad Street* but he changed the intro from "To lead a better life, I need my love to be here," to "I need a love of my own." There is still debate as to whether or not the change was intentional.

Did you know?

- There are some very interesting alternate takes of this song on several Beatles bootlegs, including one without background vocals that comes off as a lovely solo acoustic ballad performed by Paul.
- "Here, There and Everywhere" is one of several Paul songs in which he uses a particular stylistic musical construct: a declarative word ("Here...") followed by a pause, followed by what musicologist Alan Pollack describes as a "rhythmically active ascent in the tune" ("making each day of the year..."). Other examples of Paul's use of this technique:

"Day after day (pause) alone on a hill..."

"Hey Jude (pause) don't make it bad..."

"Honey Pie (pause) you are making me crazy..."

"Listen (pause) do you want to know a secret..."

"Michelle (pause) ma belle..."

"Oh darling (pause) please believe me..."

"Yesterday (pause) all my troubles seemed so far away..."

The recording

Location: **Abbey Road Studios, London.**

Dates:

June 14, 1966, 7:00 p.m.–2:00 a.m. – Four takes were recorded, but only the last one was complete, and the Beatles only used two of the four tracks available. The lead vocal was not yet recorded, but Paul, John, and George worked on the backing vocal harmony. George Martin worked with them to get harmony right. In *The Beatles Recording Sessions*, Martin recalled, "The harmonies on that are very simple, just basic triads which the boys hummed behind and found very easy to do. There's nothing very clever, no counterpoint, just moving block harmonies. Very simple to do… but very effective." Geoff Emerick, also speaking in *The Beatles Recording Sessions*, commented, "George's real expertise was and still is in vocal harmony work, there's no doubt about that. That is his forte, grooming and working out those great harmonies."

June 16, 1966, 7:00 p.m.–3:30 a.m. – Earlier in the day, the Beatles had appeared on *Top of the Pops*, which was to be their last live musical television appearance. (They lip-synched to "Rain" and "Paperback Writer.") Nine more takes and overdubs were recorded onto the best rhythm track, Take 13. These overdubs included a second set of backing vocal harmonies, plus bass on a separate track. Once these elements were added to the acoustic guitar, finger clicks, drums, and brushed-cymbal playing already recorded, all four tracks were full. The complete recording was then reduced to fit Paul's lead vocal, which was slowed down on the tape to sound speeded up on playback.

June 17, 1966 – Overdubbing of an additional Paul vocal, backing his own lead. Mono mixing.

June 21, 1966 – Stereo mixing.

August 5, 1966 – First released on the U.K. LP *Revolver*.

Players/Instruments:

- **Paul McCartney:** Acoustic guitar, lead vocal
- **John Lennon:** Backing vocal
- **George Harrison:** Lead guitar, backing vocal
- **Ringo Starr:** Drums

What we really like about this song

Steve: The better question would be what *don't* I like about this song and, to that query, the answer is "nothing." I love the chord changes, the melody, the lyrics, the harmonies…every element of the song deserves an unqualified A+. This is one of my favorite Beatle ballads.

Mike: Yet another gem from *Revolver*. I think it's intriguing how the songwriters, on occasion, would challenge themselves to write a song in a certain way. For this song, Paul worked from the adverbs here, there, everywhere. Sure, it's a gimmick, but the lyrics don't seem forced. It's a beautiful song, simple yet poignant, with understated yet compelling instrumentation. The harmonies are first-rate, and hats off to Ringo for always knowing just how to play to suit a song's mood. John numbered this Paul ballad among his favorite Beatles songs. I concur.

17

Blackbird

Art at its most profound works on many levels.

Is Robert Frost's "Stopping by Woods on a Snowy Evening" simply a melancholy and poignant reflection by a solitary traveler heading home? Or is it an imagistic contemplation of the man's own death (or suicide), the snow symbolizing the eternal white sleep awaiting us all?

It is, of course, both.

"Blackbird," a song by Paul on *The Beatles* (*The White Album*), is similarly multileveled and far reaching. Without knowing its creator's specific inspiration, we sense that the song is a tone poem of newfound independence, alienation, and existential searching.

When we learn that Paul wrote the song after reading a newspaper article about a civil rights rally, then the double meaning of the word *blackbird* leaps out at us. In the United Kingdom, the colloquial term for a young woman is *bird*, and, thus, an African American woman is a "black bird."

The song begins with Paul's lovely guitar fingering, a riff in G that quickly zooms up the fret board the way a blackbird takes wing. Chasing the guitar work is Paul's melody, which mimics this flight, ending on a high note with the word *night*.

Throughout the song, the only rhythm accompaniment is the gentle and steady click of a metronome. None of the other Beatles plays on this track, one of the most popular of *The White Album* songs, and a beloved favorite of many fans.

Why it made the top 100

"Blackbird" is, in a sense, a perfect song. The melody is beautiful and perfectly complements the chord changes; the lyrics are poetry; Paul's singing is flawless. (There might be something to the old adage that no one can sing a song like its composer.) John Lennon was right: Paul is good at this stuff, you know.

What the song is about

As noted, "Blackbird" was inspired by media coverage of a civil rights rally. And when interpreted within that framework, the lyrics symbolically reflect the fight for freedom and personal rights. Also, when you consider the deeper meaning of the lyrics, the message stands out in stark contrast to the sunny, "major key" mojo of the song's music. Paul is being encouraging, but he is also acknowledging the long, troubled history ("the dark black night") of the struggle for civil rights.

"Blackbird" is multidimensional and purposely ambivalent. Ponder the adjectives Paul uses: *dead, broken, sunken, dark,* and *black*. Grim, right? And when combined with his choice of nouns, optimism "flies out the window," so to speak: *dead of night, broken wings, sunken eyes,* and *dark black night*.

The verbs, however, are more optimistic: *waiting, singing, take,* and *fly*. And capping off the message are four of the most elevated words in the English language: *light, life, arise,* and *free*.

As in the case of the aforementioned Frost poem, "Blackbird" is art at its most profound. It is encouraging and uplifting, reflective, and sober.

• • • ❦ • • •

- Paul McCartney recorded thirty-two takes of "Blackbird" before settling on the one that appears on *The White Album*.
- "Blackbird" was one of only five Beatles songs Paul performed during his 1976 "Wings Over America" tour. Now, when he tours, his sets are almost 50/50 Beatles/Paul; in the seventies, however, including a particular Beatles song in a Wings set was especially notable.
- At the time Paul was recording "Blackbird," John was in another studio at Abbey Road working on "Revolution 9," a "work" that could justifiably be considered the polar opposite of a song like "Blackbird" (and a track that you will not find included in this ranking). Paul's song was tight, focused, and accessible. John's—a collection of tape loops and sounds—was random, unfocused, and, uh, challenging. This exemplified the distance rapidly growing between the two friends and bandmates.
- Paul would sometimes go off on his own and record a complete track without any contributions from the other Fabs. Reportedly, John and George were often hurt when he did this, yet John did precisely the same thing when he recorded "Julia" (the only completely solo John track appearing on a Beatles record; see song number 80).
- The "This Is How Rumors Start" Department: During a January 1969 recording session at Abbey Road for Mary Hopkins's *Postcard* album, Paul had a conversation with singer/songwriter Donovan about "Blackbird" and made the joke that he played the song *for* Diana Ross and she was offended by it. When Donovan asked him if he was

serious, Paul responded, "Not really," and then stated that civil rights was, however, on his mind when he wrote the song. This exchange prompted the rumor (still alive in some quarters) that Paul originally wrote the song for Diana Ross but that she refused to sing it because she was offended by the "blackbird" reference. Nothing could be farther from the truth. (The Paul/Donovan conversation appears on a bootleg CD called *No. 3 Abbey Road N.W. 8*.)

- On December 3, 1884, BBC2 TV aired a documentary titled *Horizon*, which was about Ivan Vaughn's struggle with Parkinson's disease. Ivan Vaughn, one of the original Quarry Men, was the lad who'd introduced John Lennon to Paul McCartney. Paul allowed the filmmakers the free use of "Blackbird" in the film.
- The version of "Blackbird" included on the *Anthology 3* album is Take 4 of Paul's thirty-two takes of the song. Beatles historian Mark Lewisohn wrote in his notes for the *Anthology* CDs that this take might have been usable if not for excessive background noise. Take 4 is a little different from *The White Album* version: There's no break in the middle with chirping blackbirds, and it's about five seconds shorter.
- "Blackbird" has been covered by Sting, Billy Preston, Bernadette Peters, Kenny Rankin, Dion, Crosby, Stills and Nash, the Barefoot Servants, the Barton Tyler Group, Bobby McFerrin, Sylvester, Nina Simone, the Grateful Dead, Micky Dolenz, and the Chieftains, among others.
- In 2001, Paul McCartney published *Blackbird Singing: Poems and Lyrics, 1965–1999*.

The recording

Location: **Abbey Road Studios, London.**

Dates: **June 11, 1968** – Recording and mixing, Takes 1–32, eleven complete takes.
August 27, 1968 – Copying.
October 13, 1968 – Remixing—locked.

Players/Instruments:

- **Paul McCartney:** Acoustic guitar, vocals (occasionally double-tracked)
- **Blackbirds:** Chirping (from Volume 7: *Birds of Feather* from the Abbey Road sound effects collection)
- **Metronome:** Ticking[1]

What we really like about this song

Steve: I like the guitar work. I once spent a year with a musician friend of mine learning to play it perfectly. I can still play it, too. When I performed a solo piano/vocal act in the early eighties, I did a lot of Beatles songs (even a guitar song like "Here Comes the Sun" worked as a piano song), but I learned very quickly that "Blackbird" was, bang on, a guitar song.

Mike: I like the fact that the song is something of an evolution from Paul's most famous earlier guitar song, "Yesterday," but without the strings. In "Yesterday," Paul basically strums chords; in "Blackbird," he's become a much more facile finger guitarist. Personally, I think John was way off when he said that Paul's guitar work in the song was like John Denver's. That seems unfair and inaccurate.

[1] It has long been written that the timekeeping tapping sound on "Blackbird" was Paul McCartney's foot. In *The Beatles Recording Sessions*, Mark Lewisohn set the record straight and said with certainty that the sound was "a metronome gently ticking away in the background." And for you doubters out there, Lewisohn's book is, after all, subtitled "The Official Abbey Road Studio Session Notes, 1962–1970."

Martha My Dear

18

Don't be fooled: the gracious surface charm of this song is more substantively belied by novel touches in the departments of form, phrasing and harmony than you might ever notice without a closer look.

—*Musicologist Alan Pollack*
Notes on "Martha My Dear"

Every homegrown piano player

immediately knew one thing the moment that Side Two of the first disc of *The White Album* began playing: "I have to learn that!"

We are speaking, of course, of Paul's sophisticated, complicated, and surprising piano intro to "Martha My Dear." (And speaking of complicated, the song routinely switches from 3/2 to 4/4 time in the space of a few measures. Nice.)

This lovely piano sequence introduced what can justifiably be described as a pop concerto and, with this song, the Fabs once again confounded their critics and bedazzled their fans with what may be one of Paul's all-time greatest songs.

Why it made the top 100

A concerto in the classical sense is defined as a composition for an orchestra and one or more solo instruments, typically in three movements. According to those criteria, "Martha My Dear" fits the definition.

The first movement is the "Martha My Dear" verse; the second movement is the "Hold your head up" section; and the final movement is the "Take a good look around you" section.

The range of musicality (writing, production, performance, lyrics, and so forth) presented in this track makes it a must for the top 100 ranking.

What the song is about

Either "Martha My Dear" is about Paul's sheepdog Martha, or it isn't.

For decades, Beatlefans knew that Paul had had a two-year-old sheepdog named Martha when he wrote the song, and everyone believed it was about his beloved canine companion.

Then, in 1988, Mark Lewisohn released the fully authorized *Beatles Recording Sessions* and in it he said, right there on page 159, "Contrary to popular opinion, it was not about Paul's sheepdog of the same name. He may have got the title from his canine friend but that was where the association ended."

So? If "Martha My Dear" is not about Paul scolding a misbehaving sheepdog, then what *is* the song about?

If the song is about a relationship, it is a bit cryptic. Reportedly, Paul and Jane Asher were supposed to be married in 1968. After she went away in July of that year to pursue acting gigs, however, Paul began dating other girls and Jane ultimately called off the engagement. By the time "Martha My Dear" was recorded in October, Paul was dating Linda Eastman.

How does this relate to the singer spending his "days in conversation," telling Martha not to forget him, and advising her to help herself to a bit of what was all around her?

And if it is about Jane, would Paul really address her as "silly girl" and admonish her to hold her hand out, as you might tell a dog to give you her paw so you can tap it in punishment?

Like we said, it's a bit cryptic, and Paul so far has not seen fit to explain it. Until that day comes (if it ever does), we'll have to be content with wondering… and enjoying a terrific song.

• • • ❦ • • •

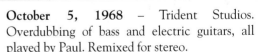

The recording

Location: **Trident Studios, London.**

Dates: **October 4, 1968** – The recording of "Martha My Dear" was essentially a one-man show starring the inimitable Sir Paul McCartney (although he wasn't actually a "Sir" yet). At about 4:00 p.m., Paul recorded one take of the song. Later, session musicians recorded horns and strings for "Honey Pie" and "Martha My Dear," following a tape with piano, drums, and vocal as a guide. George Martin worked off a demo of the song to write the score for the musicians. Paul then replaced his vocal track with a new one (later doubled with Automatic Double Tracking, or ADT), and added handclaps.

October 5, 1968 – Trident Studios. Overdubbing of bass and electric guitars, all played by Paul. Remixed for stereo.

Players/Instruments:
- **Paul McCartney:** Piano, vocal, bass, guitars, drums, handclaps[1]
- **Session musicians:** Four violins, two violas, two cellos, three trumpets, one French horn, one trombone, one tuba, one flügelhorn[2]

What we really like about this song

Steve: Like the homegrown piano player mentioned in the intro to this listing, it took me weeks to learn to play "Martha My Dear" note-perfect and, lemme tell ya, it wasn't easy. (The left hand was particularly tricky, what with the time changes and all.) I can still play it, and I still love the song, perhaps more than any other Paul composition. As for the arrangement (George Martin's handiwork, of course), I think it's one of the finest ever committed to a Beatles record. Listen to the strings, the brass, the gorgeous and poignant solo trumpet line weaving throughout the repeat of the second movement. Listen to Paul's stunning bass line, and the judicious use of drums for a mere fraction of the track. My favorite line in the song is the "that you and me were meant to be" section of the third movement when Paul goes from a C11 chord (B-flat with a C bass) to a B-flat major 7—it's just a strikingly beautiful change. I also like how Paul sings a G-natural note on the phrase "don't forget me" while the accompaniment is an A-flat chord—thus creating an A-flat major 7—again, a really lovely musical effect.

My coauthor and I had several discussions about this song, and I don't think he'd object to my telling you that he wanted it ranked lower. For 99 percent of this book, we were in perfect sync on almost everything, but here I overruled Mike and insisted that it be in the top twenty. I truly believe it is simply *that good.* (Mike gave in, but I had to let him overrule me and include "The Ballad of John and Yoko" in the ranking. Oh well.)

Mike: Steve, you ignorant slut! How could you rank this so high? Seriously, though, I think it's cool that Paul wrote a song to his dog (or at least a song *inspired* by his dog), and it's a damn good song at that. It opens Side Two of *The White Album* while "Julia" closes the side—quite a contrast. The song itself is likewise made up of contrasts—it opens with a ragtime-sounding piano, soon followed by strings and brass, and then a rock feel kicks in as guitar, drums, and bass are introduced. It's a nice arrangement, and it speaks to the possibility of world peace that electronic and symphonic instruments can so perfectly coexist.

[1] Trident Studio session records do not provide conclusive details on who played what during the session, but the consensus (concurred to by Mark Lewisohn) is that Paul played everything. Some sources have the other Fabs at the session, but this does not seem to be the case.

[2] If you're interested, *The Beatles Recording Sessions* provides the names of the session musicians for "Martha My Dear."

I Feel Fine

That's me completely. Including the electric guitar lick and the record with the first feedback anywhere. I defy anybody to find a record—unless it's some old blues record in 1922—that uses feedback that way. I mean, everybody played with feedback on stage, and the Jimi Hendrix stuff was going on long before. In fact, the punk stuff now is only what people were doing in the clubs. So I claim it for the Beatles. Before Hendrix, before the Who, before anybody. The first feedback on any record.

—John Lennon
Playboy

Nineteen sixty-four: What a year it was for the Beatles!

That year included the release of *Meet the Beatles* in the United States; the Beatles' appearance on the cover of *Newsweek*; their arrival in New York and their first appearance on the *Ed Sullivan Show*; the placement of their wax effigies in Madame Tussaud's Wax Museum in London; the publication of John's first book, *In His Own Write*, for which he won the prestigious U.K. Literary Prize (his acceptance speech consisted of the sentence, "Thank you very much, and God bless you"); the release of the Beatles' first feature film, *A Hard Day's Night*; their first Hollywood Bowl concert; and the release of Brian Epstein's memoir, *A Cellarful of Noise*.

This banner year concluded with the single "I Feel Fine" reaching Number One in the United States.

Why it made the top 100

"I Feel Fine" made the top 100 because it is a classic from the Beatles' phenomenal middle period; because it used feedback as *music*; and because it is one of the most beloved Beatles songs.

Yes, the Fabs were churning out singles during this period like "na na na"s at a "Hey Jude" sing-along, but each one was an impeccably written, performed, and produced work of pop-rock art, and "I Feel Fine" deserves a place in this pantheon.

What the song is about

"I Feel Fine" is one of John's most blatant lyrics, and we would be hard-pressed to find much subtext to its sentiments.

The singer is in love and he feels fine. We're told that his girl is happy being his girl, we're told that she *tells* him she is his girl ("all the time"), and that they are both glad that she's "his little girl."

The only clue as to a possible ulterior motive in the girl's adoration of the narrator comes in the line "she's telling all the world that her baby buys her things," including diamond rings. This sounds like our girl could be a little shallow.

For purposes of the singer's total euphoria, however, this issue is irrelevant.

He's in love with her and he feels fine.

- In the fade-out at the end of the song, many people over the years have reported hearing a barking dog. The barking is actually Paul making very realistic barking noises.
- According to George Harrison (speaking in *The Beatles Anthology*), "The guitar riff was actually influenced by a record called 'Watch Your Step' by Bobby Parker. But all riffs in that tempo have a similar sound. John played it, and all I did was play it as well, and it became the double-tracked sound." John confirmed this (also in *The Beatles Anthology*), recalling, "'Watch Your Step' is one of my favorite records. The Beatles have used the lick in various forms. The Allman Brothers used the lick straight as it was."
- There is some dispute as to whether the opening A string feedback was accidental or intentional. Here are the relevant quotes, all from *The Beatles Anthology* DVD. Make up your own mind:

George Martin: "John had knocked around with feedback for a while and yes, it was intentional. He found it quite difficult to get the right amount of feedback. And I think

Did you know?

it was—was it not—the first time that feedback was used on a record. He got things like that. He loved weird kind of effects, and it was his idea. It was great."

Paul McCartney: "John leaned [his guitar] against the amp and then we were just going to go on and talk about the song, and suddenly the A string started feeding back. [makes feedback sound] And we were just 'What?! Can you do that?' 'Oh yes, I can just edit it on the front or something'… I'm sure that's how it happened. It wasn't engineered. It came from the accident and then we made it something we could edit on the front."

George Harrison: "We used to do it onstage then live, so John figured out, you know, you just had to hit the A and buzz it by the amp… he invented Jimi Hendrix!"

- "I Feel Fine" has been covered by Vanilla Fudge, the Ventures, José Feliciano, Nancy Ames, Sweethearts of the Rodeo, Wet Wet Wet, Adrian Baker, Enoch Light, the Iguanas, Mexico 70, Osamu, Penny Dreadfuls, Black Tie, the New Variety Band, the Oriental Spas, and the Sandals.

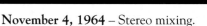

The recording

Location: **Abbey Road Studios, London.**

Dates: **October 6, 1964** – No recording of "I Feel Fine" was done today, but John can be heard fiddling with the riff for this song between takes of "Eight Days a Week."

October 18, 1964 – This day, eight takes were recorded, perfecting the rhythm track of the song. For Take 9, vocals were added. The signature opening feedback was present right from the first track. You can hear Ringo developing the "cha-cha" drumming style as the takes progressed.

October 21, 1964 – Mono mixing. Four remixes; the first two are unreleased.

October 22, 1964 – Mono mixing—this remix also remains unreleased.

November 4, 1964 – Stereo mixing.

November 23, 1964 – First released as a single in the United States, backed with "She's a Woman."

Players/Instruments:
- **John Lennon:** Lead vocal, lead guitar, rhythm guitar
- **Paul McCartney:** Bass, backing vocal
- **George Harrison:** Lead guitar, backing vocal
- **Ringo Starr:** Drums

What we really like about this song

Steve: I love the fact that "I Feel Fine" is in the key of G, yet the opening feedback note is an A, and the first notes of the opening riff are part and parcel a D chord. Thus, the song begins with a D, followed by the notes of a C7 chord, and then they finally settle in on the home key of G. Very tasty. I also love the harmonies. The ethereal, Beatlesque high harmonies stand out in stark contrast to John's rather raw vocal. I also like the little guitar noodlings George sprinkles throughout the verses, playing with the opening riff at will.

Mike: I defy anybody to put this song on and sit still while listening to it. It's the quintessential pop song—nothing strange or unusual (aside from the feedback, of course). The song says to me: summer day, roll down your car window, drive along the beach, crank up the volume. It sounds as fresh as it ever did. Another great John riff on one of his most optimistic songs, which typically include a little pang of nervousness that love is fleeting. There's no doubt that she loves him, he loves her, and he feels fine. So do we all!

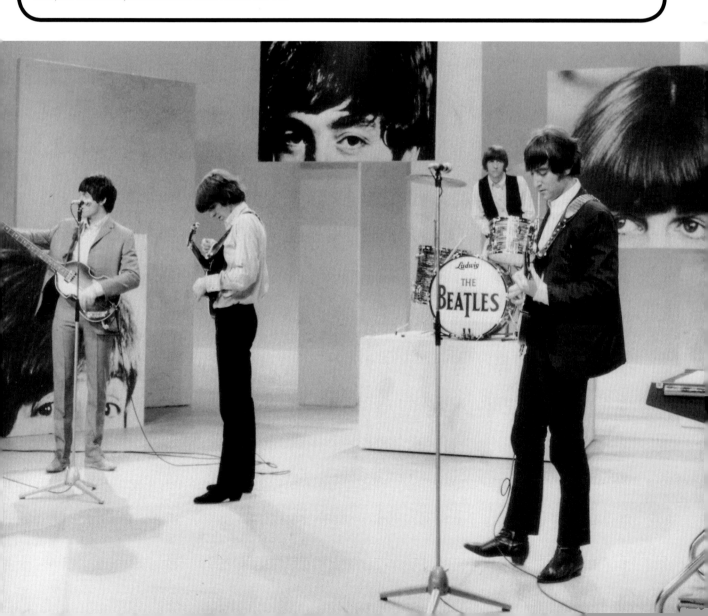

20 I Want To Hold Your Hand

We wrote a lot of stuff together, one-on-one, eyeball to eyeball. Like in "I Want To Hold Your Hand," I remember when we got the chord that made the song. We were in Jane Asher's house, downstairs in the cellar playing on the piano at the same time. And we had, "Oh you-u-u… got that something…" And Paul hits this chord and I turn to him and say, "That's it!" I said, "Do that again!" In those days, we really used to absolutely write like that—both playing into each other's noses. We spent hours and hours and hours.

—John Lennon
Playboy

Another sick thing about the Beatles is they make almost everything the chorus. You'll think you've heard all the hooks, and then some hook that really sells you on the song surfaces in the middle, only lasts a few seconds and disappears, never to return again. That's "I Want to Hold Your Hand" in a nutshell.

—Billy Corgan of the Smashing Pumpkins
Rolling Stone

Do you remember the first time you heard "I Want to Hold Your Hand"?

Even on first listening, the chorus brought a smile to your face, right?

It speaks volumes about the power of the Beatles that even now, forty years later, they can still brighten a dark day with their music. Listen to Ringo's staggered drumroll followed by John and Paul harmonizing on the chorus "I want to hold your hand," and tell us you *don't* play air drums when you hear it.

We don't believe you.

Why it made the top 100

How could "I Want to Hold Your Hand" *not* be ranked as one of the 100 ultimate Beatles songs? It was an enormous blockbuster all over the world, and it signaled the true beginning of the Beatles Era. They had had some modest success before ("Please Please Me," "From Me to You," "She Loves You"), but "I Want to Hold Your Hand" transformed them—almost immediately—from a popular British band to a global phenomenon.

The song has aged gracefully and can justifiably be called a classic.

What the song is about

Bill Cosby does a bit in one of his stand-up concerts about how his adolescent daughters fully understood romance and true love at a very early age, while boys that age were still blowing up frogs with M-80s.

"I Want to Hold Your Hand" is about that type of love: The narrator wants to tell the girl of his dreams that he loves her and he also wants to ask her if he can be her "man" (which is kind of cute when you consider that the singer is probably supposed to be no more than sixteen). There is one condition, though: He wants to hold her hand while he carries out his heartfelt mission.

Of course, the lyrics can be read from a much more mature point of view—"and when I touch you I feel happy" can easily refer to much more than simply holding her hand—but such an interpretation completely betrays the innocence that permeates the song and its message.

No doubt about it: She's got "that something," and the young man is so overwhelmed with his feelings for her that he can't hide, he can't hide, he can't hide his love.

"I Want to Hold Your Hand" is about that time in all our lives when simply holding hands meant *everything*.

• • • 🐞 • • •

- "I Want to Hold Your Hand" was the Number One record in America before the Beatles ever set foot on American soil.

- It was one of five songs the Beatles performed on their second Ed Sullivan appearance on February 16, 1964. They were instructed to clearly sing the phrase "I can't hide," so that it would not sound like "I get high."

- In 1963, a fifteen-year-old Beatles fan named Marsha Albert Thompson wrote to Carroll James, a DJ at radio station WWDC, and asked him to play Beatles music. He obtained a copy of the U.K. single of "I Want to Hold Your Hand" from his girlfriend, who was a flight attendant on British Airways. James began playing the single hourly on December 17, 1963, and other DJs quickly followed suit. Capitol's hand was forced and, ten days later, the single was rush-released in the United States.

- "I Want to Hold Your Hand" was a breakthrough release for the Beatles, and, on a wider scale, for British groups. In *The Beatles Anthology*, John talked about breaking into the U.S. market: "The thing is, in America, it just seemed ridiculous—I mean the idea of having a hit record over there. It was just something you could never do. That's what I thought, anyhow. But then I realized that kids everywhere all go for the same stuff, and seeing we'd done it in England, there's no reason why we couldn't do it in America, too. But the American disc jockeys didn't know about British records; they didn't play them, nobody promoted them, so you didn't have hits. It wasn't until *Time* and *Newsweek* came over and wrote articles and created an interest in us that disc jockeys started playing our records. And Capitol said, 'Well, can we have their

Did you know?

records?' They had been offered our records years ago, and they didn't want them—but when they heard we were big over here they said, 'Can we have them now?' We said, 'As long as you promote them.' So Capitol promoted, and with them and all these articles on us, the records just took off."

- "I Want to Hold Your Hand" was one of only two songs ("She Loves You" was the other) that the Beatles re-recorded in German. The German record company urged them to do records specifically for the German market, telling them that they'd never sell to Germans unless they sang in German. The Beatles acquiesced, but it would be the first and last time they recorded a different version of a song for a specific market.

- At the end of the Beatles' performance of "If I Fell" in *A Hard Day's Night*, Paul exuberantly plays the bass riff from the "I Want to Hold Your Hand" intro while simultaneously dancing a few steps. (Thanks to musicologist Alan Pollack for this delightful Fabs tidbit.)

- In *Lennon Remembers* (1970), John admitted that the melody of "I Want to Hold Your Hand" stayed with him and that he had actually considered recording a new version of the song seven years after its initial release.

- Robert Freeman, the photographer who took the memorable cover shot of the Fabs for the *With the Beatles* album, lived in a flat beneath John at 13 Emperor's Gate in Kensington, England. Freeman educated John in jazz and experimental music, and John tried to turn him on to rock. In *A Hard Day's Write*, Freeman talked about John's interests: "He was intrigued by a contemporary French album of experimental music. There was one track where a musical phrase repeated, as if the record had stuck. This effect was used in 'I Want to Hold Your Hand'—at my suggestion—'that my love, I can't hide, I can't hide, I can't hide.'[1]

- "I Want to Hold Your Hand" has been covered by Diana Ross and the Supremes, Al Green, Arthur Fiedler and the Boston Pops, Bobby Fuller, the Chipmunks, Claude François, the Crickets, Duke Ellington, Enoch Light, Keely Smith, Lakeside, Nelson Riddle, the New Christy Minstrels, Peter Nero, Petula Clark, the Swallows, and Vanilla Fudge.

The recording

Location: **Abbey Road Studios, London.**

Dates: **October 17, 1963,** 7:00–10:00 p.m – Seventeen takes of the song were recorded on Abbey Road's new four-track equipment. The song was perfected before it was put to tape—a practice the Beatles would soon abandon. The takes don't vary all that much, except for Take 2, in which Paul tried hushing the vocal line "and when I touch you"; and Take 4, in which Paul introduced the not uncommon 1963 Beatle *h* into the *s* words, as in "shay that shomething." (You can hear this done on "A Taste of Honey.") The B side of the planned single was to be "This Boy," and that song was recorded immediately after they finished "I Want to Hold Your Hand."

October 21, 1963 – Mono mixing for the single; stereo mixing for unforeseen future use.

November 29, 1963 – The single "I Want to Hold Your Hand"/"This Boy" was released in the United Kingdom on Parlophone.

January 24, 1964 – Tape-to-tape copy of the rhythm track (from Take 17) was made and carried to Paris in George Martin's luggage.

January 29, 1964 – The Beatles had their first EMI recording session outside Abbey Road. They recorded the German vocal for "Komm Gib Mir Deine Hand" at EMI Pathé Marconi Studios in Paris. The group was in France for a nineteen-day concert at the Olympia Theater. The four-track tape was mixed down to two tracks. While in Paris, the Fabs learned that the English version of "I Want to Hold Your Hand" had gone to Number One in the United States.

June 8, 1965 – Norman Smith made a new mix of "I Want to Hold Your Hand" with the vocals placed in the center of the stereo "picture." It was never used. (Mark Lewisohn said in *The Beatles Chronicles* that this mix was intended to be released by EMI affiliates in Australia and the Netherlands.)

November 7, 1966 – A third stereo mix was made.

Players/Instruments:
- **John Lennon:** Rhythm guitar, lead vocal
- **Paul McCartney:** Bass, lead vocal
- **George Harrison:** Lead guitar, harmony vocal
- **Ringo Starr:** Drums

What we really like about this song

Steve: I love everything about "I Want to Hold Your Hand," specifically the guitars, the harmonies, the chorus, the chord changes, Ringo's drumming, and the switch from G to D minor 7 for the bridge. I know John and Paul worked together on the song, but that chord change sounds like something Paul came up with and it really makes the song work. It once again illustrates how "Lennon/McCartney" became a third entity (Lenartney? McCartnon?) when they truly collaborated on every element of a tune.

Mike: "I Want to Hold Your Hand" was the song that jolted America out of the pervading sadness triggered by the Kennedy assassination. It is driven by exuberance, euphoria, hope, joy, and the transfixing and transforming power of music. Although the song is not terribly deep (they were clearly writing for their teenage girl audience), you can't help but get into a good mood when you hear it.

[1]*A Hard Day's Write*.

The Long and Winding Road

It's a sad song, because it's all about the unattainable.

—*Paul McCartney*

There now exist three "official" versions of this song: (1) the strings-and-choir version on the original 1970 *Let It Be* album (which is also on *The Blue Album* and *The Beatles 1*); (2) the same track but without the Phil Spectorization on 1996's *Anthology 3*; and (3) an unadorned Beatles-and-Billy-Preston-only version on 2003's *Let It Be…Naked*.

Is any one of these interpretations *more* definitive than another? If we defer to the intent of the artist, then the *Let It Be…Naked* version is the song the way Paul intended it to be. But many of us can't (and won't) deny that those violins on the Spectorized version sure do give us chills!

Why it made the top 100

This lovely ballad is one of Paul's most sublime musical creations, a subtle, restrained air in E flat that, significantly, begins in that key's achingly sad relative minor of C.

John Lennon himself singled out this song (along with "Let It Be") as one of Paul's final creative "Beatles" masterstrokes. Yes, the song's history is cluttered with the nastiness surrounding Phil Spector adding strings and other unnecessary ornamentation and Paul's subsequent displeasure, but this does not detract from the work's beauty, sincerity, and heartfelt emotion.

What the song is about

Ahhh, look at all the miseries and woes of the lovelorn!

Our hero is still in love with an elusive lady who lives at the end of a long and winding road. The message of our bard is simple: *I repeatedly return to you and you leave me standing at your door.* After he tells us his story, does the song resolve with a reunion and/or reconciliation? No, it does not. He reveals that she left him standing on the road a long time ago, and the song concludes with him pleading to her, "don't leave me waiting here" and a final (rather pathetic) request for her to lead him to her door.

Considering the young lady's silence, the odds are that our poor bloke is *still* standing there.

• • • ❧ • • •

- After hearing the Phil Spectorized version of his song, Paul sent the following note to Allen Klein, dated April 14, 1970. Based on the version of the song released on the original *Let It Be* album two weeks later, Paul's instructions were obviously not followed.

  Dear Sir,

  In future no one will be allowed to add to or subtract from a recording of one of my songs without my permission.

  I had considered orchestrating "The Long and Winding Road" but I decided against it. I therefore want it altered to these specifications:

  1. Strings, horns, voices and all added noises to be reduced in volume.

  2. Vocal and Beatle instrumentation to be brought up in volume.

  3. Harp to be removed completely at the end of the song and original piano notes to be substituted.

  4. Don't ever do it again.

  Signed

  Paul McCartney

- Beatle intimates and colleagues were not pleased with the Spector version of the album. Engineer Geoff Emerick, in the March 1, 2001, issue of *Rolling Stone*, said, "It was an insult to Paul. It was his record. And someone takes it

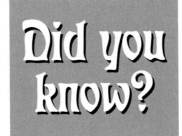

out of the can and starts to overdub things without his permission."

- The title and imagery of the song reportedly come from Paul's experience of staying at High Park, his farm in Scotland. The long and winding road itself is the B842, sixteen miles of twists and turns running down the east coast of Kintyre into Campbeltown, the nearest town to Paul's farm.

- Paul told Barry Miles that when he was writing the song, he was thinking of Ray Charles.

- *The Long and Winding Road* was the name of the project that ultimately became *The Beatles Anthology*.

- "The Long and Winding Road" backed with "For You Blue" was the last Beatles single released in America during the band's existence. (It was not released as a single in the United Kingdom.)

- "The Long and Winding Road" is one of five Beatles songs Paul performed during his 1976 "Wings Over America" tour.

- The song has been covered by Andre Kostelanetz, Aretha Franklin, Billy Ocean, Cher, Cissy Houston, Diana Ross, Gladys Knight and the Pips, Kiri Te Kanawa, Mantovani, Melba Moore, Olivia Newton-John, Richie Havens, the Four Tops, and Tony Bennett.

The recording

Location: **Abbey Road Studios; Olympic Studios, London.**

Dates: **September 19, 1968** – Paul quickly recorded a demo of the song on the grand piano in Studio 1, and then took away the spool of tape.

January 26, 1969 – Rehearsal and recording of an unknown number of takes of the song during a day of recording many rock medleys, as well as version of "Dig It," "Let It Be," and George's "Isn't It a Pity." This version can be heard on *Anthology 3*. It is the same version as on the *Let It Be* album, but without the Spector overdub, and with Paul talking and singing through one of the verses.

January 31, 1969 – Seven takes of the song were recorded live in the studio. The unreleased *Get Back* LP was to include Take 19 of the song.

March 10, 1969 (Olympic Studios) – Stereo mixing by Glyn Johns for the *Get Back* LP.

March 12, 1969 (Olympic Studios) – Stereo mixing.

March 26, 1969 – Stereo mixing.

April 1, 1970 – Technical engineer Brian Gibson recalled Phil Spector's work on the track: "He wanted to overdub orchestra and choir but there weren't the available tracks on the tape, so he wiped one of Paul's two vocal tracks in order to put the orchestra on."[1] (No wonder Paul was pissed!) Strings were dubbed onto Track 6, brass and drums onto Track 7, choir onto Track 8.

April 2, 1970 – Final day of work on *Let It Be*. Stereo mixing.

May 8, 1970 – First released in the United Kingdom on the LP *Let It Be*.

November 18, 2003 – *Let It Be... Naked* was released worldwide. The version of the song on this album is different from the original on *Let It Be*, and is how Paul originally wanted it to sound.

Players/Instruments:

- **Paul McCartney:** Piano, lead vocal
- **John Lennon:** Bass
- **George Harrison:** Guitar
- **Ringo Starr:** Drums
- **Billy Preston:** Organ
- **Session musicians** (*original release only*): Two guitarists, three trombonists, three trumpets, a harp, four cellos, four violas, and eighteen violins
- **Choir** (*original release only*): Fourteen vocalists

What we really like about this song

Steve: This song is deceiving. It starts out slowly, almost solemnly, and it is measured and stately as it progresses through line after line of melancholy poetry. But the overall effect is akin to being shown a beautiful tree, and then stepping back and seeing the glorious forest of which the tree is a single lovely element. The totality of this song creates a depth of emotion and melody that belies its apparent simplicity.

Mike: Paul revisits the theme of loss and despair touched on in "Yesterday," but—with his band virtually disintegrating around him—he offers it as a message of hope. You can understand why Paul was annoyed upon hearing the album version—"Look what they've done to my song!" But, in all fairness, the Spectorized *Let It Be* is not horrible. With the release of *Anthology 3*, and finally *Let It Be... Naked*, we can hear it as Paul intended, as a relatively quiet, simple, peaceful song with a powerful message.

[1] *The Beatles Recording Sessions.*

22

And Your Bird Can Sing

Okay boys, quite brisk, moderato, foxtrot!

—John Lennon

Music polls have often declared

Revolver the greatest rock album of all time, and the presence of "And Your Bird Can Sing" on the record has something to do with those accolades. (Although it should be noted that "And Your Bird Can Sing" only appeared on the U.K. edition of *Revolver*. It had been released in the States two months earlier on *Yesterday… and Today* and was omitted from the U.S. edition of the album.)

In his January 1981 *Playboy* interview, John said that he considered the song a "throwaway." Yet today, the song is rightfully considered a Beatles classic.

Why it made the top 100

"And Your Bird Can Sing" hits the ground running with a two-part guitar riff that is joyfully optimistic and instantly compelling. Try to listen to the beginning of "And Your Bird Can Sing" (preferably loud, although you need not go to eleven) without smiling.

And speaking of this classic riff, is it George double-tracked? George and John playing together? George and Paul playing together? The historical record is ambiguous—even George didn't remember. In the November 1987 issue of *Guitar* magazine, George said of this riff, "I think it was Paul and me, or maybe John and me, playing in harmony…"

What the song is about

Upon first reading, the lyrics of "And Your Bird Can Sing" are rather cryptic—what does a green, singing bird have to do with anything? And how can a bird be "broken"? Wings, maybe. But the *whole bird*?

When we approach the lyrics symbolically, however, the song comes off as a slightly bitter tirade against a woman who either has rejected the singer or is taking him for granted.

This woman apparently has it all, and John reminds her as much: She has everything she wants, she's seen seven wonders, and she's heard every sound. John's response to this abundance? You don't get me, you can't see me, and you can't hear me. Your money can't buy me.

Let's hope that the bird with the bird ultimately accepts the offer of the narrator who is, after all, assuring her, when all the material things are gone, "I'll be round…" Happy ending and all, you know?

• • • 🐞 • • •

- The working title of "And Your Bird Can Sing" was "You Don't Get Me."
- The recording of "And Your Bird Can Sing" on *Anthology 2* is fascinating and important for two reasons: The Fabs can't stop laughing while performing the song, and the track itself is distinctly different from the final version on *Revolver*.
- The song is in the key of E, which is called the dominant. Normally (unless there is a key change during the song), a song ends on the dominant chord (or its relative minor). This gives the song resolution, and the listener a feeling

Did you know?

of closure. Thus, "And Your Bird Can Sing" could have reasonably been expected to end on an E chord. Does it? No, it ends on an A chord, the subdominant chord in the diatonic E scale. The listener experiences unfulfilled expectation, since the song, in a sense, never resolves back to its dominant chord. We—and the narrator—are left hanging.

- "And Your Bird Can Sing" has been covered by the Flamin' Groovies, Guadalcanal Diary, and the Jam.

The recording

Location: **Abbey Road Studios, London**.

Dates: **April 20, 1966** – Two takes were recorded in a twelve-hour session; Take 1 consisted of only the guitars and drums, and Lewisohn noted that the song in this form was "unrecognizable."[1] Take 2 was considered the best and had many overdubs, including three John vocals, two Paul harmonies, and one George harmony, plus the addition of tambourine and bass. John and Paul started laughing during one of the overdubs, and some of this merriment can be heard on *Anthology*. Ultimately the Beatles and George Martin decided to scrap this day's work; they redid the song a week later.

April 26, 1966 – The song was remade in another marathon twelve-hour session. The Beatles recorded eleven takes. The first attempt (Take 3) at a new version consisted of a very heavy rhythm track. Through subsequent takes, though, the song grew progressively lighter, with the guitars always at the front of the song. After Take 13, playback revealed Take 10 to be the best. John's lead vocal was then overdubbed, and Paul and George overdubbed backing vocals. The ending of Take 6—a blend of lead guitar strumming and Paul's bass guitar notes—was added to the final released version.

April 27, 1966 – Mono mixing. The Beatles were in the studio for this session.

May 12, 1966 – Mono mixing.

May 20, 1966 – Stereo mixing.

June 6, 1966 – Tape copying and mono mixing.

June 8, 1966 – Editing together of two mono mixes.

Players/Instruments:

- **John Lennon:** Rhythm guitar, lead vocal, handclaps
- **Paul McCartney:** Bass, harmony vocal, handclaps
- **George Harrison:** Lead guitar, harmony vocal, handclaps
- **Ringo Starr:** Drums, tambourine

What we really like about this song

Steve: There is no question that John was a harsh critic of his own work, but I can't help but wonder why he felt such animosity toward this terrific song. I like everything about it—the dual guitars, the harmony, Ringo's rock-solid bottom, and especially Paul's bass playing, which is very melodic in this song and stands on its own. You can listen to the song and concentrate only on Paul's bass and truly enjoy the experience. I also love the way the Fabs suddenly switch to singing the third verse in harmony—it's surprising and wonderful. The Beatles was greater than the sum of its parts, and "And Your Bird Can Sing" is a classic example of this synthesis.

Mike: I think this is one of the band's most underplayed and underappreciated songs—even by its writer. Contrary to John's harsh criticism, this song is hardly a "throwaway" or a "horror." In fact, it's one of the Beatles most interesting songs, lyrically and melodically. Some of the lyrics may seem nonsensical, until you get to the chorus. Not to wax religious, but the chorus echoes the message Jesus preached throughout his life: When you give up all your possessions, then you can join me. John seems to be saying that bragging about prized possessions—even a trained bird—is not enough to curry favor with him. In addition, the song's melody instantly grabs you, and I never tire of hearing the unusual dual guitar lick that weaves in and out.

[1] *The Beatles Recording Sessions*, page 75.

Paperback Writer

23

Because I had a long drive to get there [to John's house], I would often start thinking away and writing on my way out, and I developed the whole idea in the car. I came in, had my bowl of cornflakes, and said, "How's about if we write a letter: 'Dear Sir or Madam,' next line, next paragraph, etc.?" I wrote it all out and John said, "Yeah, that's good." It just flowed.

—Paul McCartney
The Beatles Anthology

Of the Beatles' eight singles released *before* "Paperback Writer," seven were about relationships ("I Feel Fine," "She's a Woman," "Ticket to Ride," "Yes It Is," "I'm Down," "We Can Work It Out," and "Day Tripper"). Only "Help!" was about something other than romance and love.

Then along came "Paperback Writer," with its a cappella opening, fuzz guitar riff, and story line about a would-be author. And, once again, the Fabs surprised their fans.

Why it made the top 100

"Paperback Writer" is, as John once described it, "son of 'Day Tripper,'" and it took the Beatles' enthusiasm for studio experimentation to the next level. The harmonies were so hot, they were flammable; the sounds of the guitars and bass were dazzling; the rhythm was relentless. Plus, as we have seen, it wasn't a love song.

All this—and the song only has *two chords!*

What the song is about

Every aspiring writer has probably, at one point in his budding career, written the letter that comprises the lyrics of "Paperback Writer."

"Dear Sir or Madam…" is the classic salutation when you don't know anyone at the publishing house, and aren't even sure whether the editor is male or female.

In the first verse, the letter writer tells the editor that his book is based on a "novel by a man named Lear," which is a tad bewildering at first. A novel based on a novel? It seems, though, that the "Lear" referred to is Edward Lear (1812–88), a Victorian painter who also wrote nonsense poems (such as his *Book of Nonsense*, 1846) and songs that John Lennon loved. Although Lear never wrote a *novel*, it is likely that

Paul is using novel as a general term to refer to one of Lear's works upon which a book could be based.

In the second verse, the aspiring author provides details of his book: It's "a dirty story of a dirty man," and this character apparently has a "clinging wife" who doesn't understand. Doesn't understand what? His penchant for lasciviousness? We aren't told. We then learn that the dirty man's son works for the British newspaper *Daily Mail*. Yes, it's a steady job, but this *son* wants to be a paperback writer. Is the letter writer the son, and his book an autobiographical rendering of his miserable life? Are both father *and* son looking for a book deal? You tell us.

In the next verse, the writer describes his book: "It's a thousand pages…" A *thousand* pages? Assuming it's typed out in Courier (a common typewriter font of the time) and double-spaced, the manuscript must be at least 275,000 words. In other words, this paperback writer wannabe has written an enormous epic—probably more than eight hundred book pages in length!—about "a dirty man" with a harridan wife and a malcontent son.

In the final verse, the writer offers the editor the rights, assuring him it'll make a million for him "overnight." Classic "unpublished writer" naïveté.

The song ends with a refrain of his whining "I need a break …," and we are left thinking that his book is, indeed, about himself, and he is desperate to get out of his hopeless existence.

• • • • 🐭 • • • •

- The "Paperback Writer" single was released in the United Kingdom on June 10, 1966, and EMI ran an ad in the June 3, 1966, issue of *New Musical Express* that used the "butcher" photo from *Yesterday… and Today*. In his *Playboy* interviews, John talked about the photo: "The original cover was the Beatles in white coats with figs 'n' dead bits o' meat and dolls cut up. It was inspired by our boredom and resentment at having to do another photo session and another photo thing. We were sick to death of it. Also, the photographer was into Dali and making surreal pictures. That combination produced that cover."
- Paul did not play his beloved Hoffner bass on "Paperback Writer." He played a Rickenbacker and, according to engineer Geoff Emerick, "we boosted it further by using a loudspeaker as a microphone. We positioned it directly in front of the bass speaker and the moving diaphragm of the second speaker

Did you know?

made the electric current."[1] Despite this improvement in sound, though, the developer of this technique, Ken Townsend, was reprimanded by Abbey Road management for incorrectly matching impedances. (There was even fear that the "extra-strength" bass would make the needle skip when fans played the record!) Eventually, the success of "Paperback Writer" forced a revision of the policy and it was allowed—but only for Beatles sessions.
- "Paperback Writer" was completely double-tracked and, thus, was extremely difficult to perform well live. According to George Harrison, though, the Beatles had a solution: "So what we did with it… was get to the point where it was particularly bad, and then we'd do our 'Elvis legs' and wave to the crowd, and they'd all scream and it would cover that. As Paul has said, the screaming did cover a lot of worrying moments."[2]
- Poet Royston Ellis, the first published author the Beatles

had ever met, is convinced that Paul latched on to the phrase *paperback writer* from his conversations with them. In *A Hard Day's Write*, he said: "Although I was writing poetry books then, if they asked me what I wanted to be I would always say 'a paperback writer' because that's what you had to be if you wanted to reach a mass market. My ambition was to be a writer who sold his books and made money out of it. It was my equivalent of their ambition of making a million-selling single." Ellis went on to become a writer of travel books and plantation novels.

- "Paperback Writer" was the first Fabs single since "She Loves You" that failed to enter the charts at Number One. The song went to Number One a week later and stayed there for two weeks.

- The song has been covered by the Cowsills, the Bee Gees, and 10CC.

The recording

Location: **Abbey Road Studios, London.**

Dates: **April 13, 1966,** 8:00 p.m.–2:30 a.m. – Two takes of the rhythm track were recorded, but the first one was a breakdown. Apparently, some overdubs were also recorded, but the log is silent on specifics.

April 14, 1966, 2:30–7:30 p.m. – An overdub of Paul's lead vocal was recorded, as well as George and John singing "Frère Jacques" (which was Paul's idea) as the background vocal. Mono mixing.

May 30, 1966 – First released as a U.S. single, backed with "Rain."

October 31, 1966 – Stereo mixing for *The Beatles 1962–1966* (The Red Album).

Players/Instruments:

- **Paul McCartney:** Bass, lead vocal
- **John Lennon:** Rhythm guitar, backing vocal
- **George Harrison:** Lead guitar, backing vocal
- **Ringo Starr:** Drums

Note: A source says Paul also played Vox organ.

What we really like about this song

Steve: I love the opening harmonies (almost as much as those on "Nowhere Man"); I love the sizzling guitar with its edgy, window-rattling presence, a sound that defined how many rock guitar riffs would play in the coming decades; I love the way Paul plays his bass like a lead guitar, turning it into a force to be reckoned with; and, lastly, I love the song's story line, perhaps because I have been a hapless writer trying desperately to secure a book deal and become a "paperback writer."

Mike: Those who hold down the beat playing bass and drums owe a debt of gratitude to the Beatles and their production team for changing the way their instruments are recorded. I can't help but chuckle at the stodgy suits whose shorts got in a twist at the very thought of the Beatles placing their microphones too close to the amps. The result is a traditional full-on Beatles rocker, a "potboiler," as George Martin is wont to say, but I dare say my stylus didn't jump once. While listening to a bootleg of the song, two things come to mind: (1) The reverb on the "writer" vocal really added a unique touch; (2) much like Led Zeppelin's "Black Dog," which includes the vocals sung a cappella between instrumental blasts, it's up to the drummer to keep things in line. Ringo does so in stellar fashion, miked-up bass drum and all.

[1] *The Beatles Recording Sessions.*

[2] *The Beatles Anthology.*

24 Happiness Is A Warm Gun

They all said it was about drugs but it was more about rock 'n' roll than drugs. It's sort of a history of rock 'n' roll… I don't know why people said it was about the needle in heroin. I've only seen somebody do something with a needle once, and I don't like to see it at all.

—John Lennon
Hit Parader, *April 1972*

The White Album took Beatlefans on a

roller-coaster ride of emotional highs and lows. "Happiness" disconcertingly follows George's stunning "While My Guitar Gently Weeps," and is followed by Paul's jaunty "Martha My Dear."

The first time we heard this trio in order, many of us went from empathizing with George's pain; to being somewhat fearful of what the hell was going on with John; to then smiling with Paul as he walked in the sun with his sheepdog.

"Martha My Dear" is then followed by John's slumberous "I'm So Tired," and his exhaustion mirrored the emotional depletion of we, the Fabs' loyal listeners—who, it must be acknowledged, were loving every second of the tumultuous ride.

Why it made the top 100

"Happiness Is a Warm Gun" is one of John's greatest works and one of the best songs on *The White Album*. It has been one of the Beatles' 100 greatest songs since the day it was released.

What the song is about

"Happiness Is a Warm Gun" is three, three, three songs in one.

The first song runs from the opening line, "She's not a girl…" through "National Trust."

The second song is from "I need a fix…" through the last "Mother Superior jump the gun" (although some Beatles scholars claim that the "Mother Superior" segment should be considered separate from the "fix" section, thus making the song a four-part invention, rather than a three-part suite).

The third song is the old-fashioned "Happiness Is a Warm Gun" refrain, augmented by John's talky "When I hold you…in my arms."

According to John, the song is a history of rock and roll, but John is talking about the *musical styles* of the song, not its lyrical meaning. The first part is a folk-metal prelude; the second, a raunchy, bluesy middle; the final section, a doo-wop, fifties sing-along. If we look at the song that way, then his comment proves correct—because, frankly, the lyrics are arcane and surreal and do not really suggest a summary of the "Story of Rock."

The origin of the title is well-known: A gun magazine belonging to George Martin was lying around the Abbey Road Studio, and when John came across it, the first thing he noticed was a line on the cover that read, happiness is a warm gun in your hand. John was blown away (no pun or disrespect intended, of course) by the line and later commented that he immediately interpreted it as meaning that you had just shot something.

And thus, the song was born. Or should we say the second and third parts of the song were born. Those are the sections John wrote after being inspired by the magazine's cover line.

The first section, with its odd imagery and bewildering message, apparently owes its genesis to LSD.

Derek Taylor, speaking in *A Hard Day's Write*, said that he, John, Neil Aspinall, and Pete Shotton spent the night tripping on acid while staying in a house rented from Peter Asher in Newdigate. John told them about the "half a song" he had written and asked them all to throw out random phrases he might be able to use to finish the piece.

"Not a girl who misses much" was Derek Taylor's contribution. John had wanted a phrase to describe a girl who was really smart. (He was referring, of course, to Yoko.)

Derek then told a story of a guy he and his wife had met who had talked about wearing moleskin gloves while out with his girl, but he wouldn't explain further. That gave John the "velvet hand" imagery.

The man in the crowd with multicolored mirrors on his boots came from a true story about a Manchester City soccer fan who wore mirrors on his boots so he could peek up girls' dresses.

The "hands working overtime" came from a story one of them had heard about a guy who wore fake hands in the arms of his coat. He would rest them on a countertop while he shoplifted things with his real hands, hiding goods behind his coat.

The "donating to the National Trust" line is one of the more repugnant images John was given that night. Apparently, people defecate outdoors in Merseyside. (Or at least they did in the sixties. Please, don't write us with tales of the scenic glories of Merseyside. We're only the messengers.) Thus, locally, to donate something to the National Trust (the agency responsible for the upkeep of the British countryside) meant that you defiled a place by taking a dump there. How John decided that "digested" *soap* would be the "donation" puzzles to this day.

What about the "needing a fix" line? Isn't that about shooting heroin?

Whether or not that was John's intention is, in a sense, irrelevant. The dark lyrics, the disjointed and conflicting meter, the rambling lines about "Mother Superior," the edgy feel to the section all undeniably suggest a junkie wallowing in the filth of his addiction.

The final section of the song is pure parody, but it doesn't bring a smile. How could it when the traditional, cheerful, *expected* background fifties vocal "oooh—ahhhs" are replaced with the violent "bang, bang, shoot, shoot"?

"Happiness Is a Warm Gun" is an extraordinary work of music and poetry, and the depth of its meaning (or meanings) is the hallmark of true art.

85

- The working title of the song was "Happiness Is a Warm Gun in Your Hand," a verbatim lift from the magazine cover that inspired it.
- The "when I hold you" section of the song is in 3/4 (waltz) time, but Ringo continues drumming in 4/4.
- George and Paul *both* said that the song was their favorite on *The White Album*.
- Ronald Reagan Jr., speaking in the February 16, 1984,

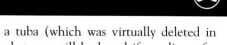
Did you know?

issue of *Rolling Stone*, recalled, "I remember once when I was about 13, I borrowed *The White Album* from [my sister] Patti, and my mother got upset when she heard me listening to 'Happiness Is a Warm Gun.' It really bothered her a lot."
- "Happiness Is a Warm Gun" has been covered by World Party, the Breeders, and U2. (The U2 cover was the B side of the 1997 single "Last Night on Earth.")

The recording

Location: **Abbey Road Studios, London.**

Dates: **September 23, 1968,** 7:00 p.m.–3:00 a.m. – Forty-five takes were recorded, which might be a record for a John song. Unlike Paul, John usually wasn't one to belabor a song. Bass, drums, John's lead guitar, guide vocal, and George's fuzzed lead were all recorded.

September 24, 1968, 7:00 p.m.–2:00 a.m. – Twenty-five more takes of the rhythm track were recorded. On playback, they decided Take 53 was the best of the first half of the song, and Take 65 was the best second half. The two would be edited together the following day.

September 25, 1968, 7:30 p.m.–6:15 a.m. – The two "best" halves were pieced together, then John's lead vocal was added, along with Paul, George, and John's backing vocals, organ,

piano, a tuba (which was virtually deleted in remixes but can still be heard if you listen for it, mostly in the "I need a fix" section), a snare drum beat, tambourine, and bass guitar.

November 22, 1968 – First released on the *The Beatles* (The *White Album*) in the United Kingdom.

Players/Instruments:
- **John Lennon:** Lead guitar, tambourine, lead and backing vocal
- **Paul McCartney:** Bass, backing vocal
- **George Harrison:** Lead guitar, backing vocal
- **Ringo Starr:** Drums

Note: The track also has a piano and an organ, but it is unclear who played them. (We'd bet John played both.)

What we really like about this song

Steve: "Happiness Is a Warm Gun" is one of my all-time favorite Lennon compositions. My favorite section of the suite is the opening, with John's beautiful solo electric guitar work and Ringo's drum crescendo that comes out of nowhere. George's startling guitar chops are the perfect touch.

Mike: Peanuts' Linus Van Pelt once uttered, "Happiness is a warm blanket," but John Lennon had other ideas in this, one of his most startling songs. Is he condoning the type of violence that led to his own death? In fact, he's satirizing the whole *Soldier of Fortune*–reading gun culture. But to me, John's lyrics are still hard to take at times—despite his intention. The song isn't much melodically—just when you latch onto a melody, it changes. But no matter—you gotta love its bizarre lyrical montage. It crams a lot into its 2:43.

Free As A Bird

25

It was real emotional. I mean, just hearing the tape that was sent was pretty emotional. And then we got to the studio and it was difficult for a while. I mean, he's not here. We're all here, where's John? Of course, John's in heaven. We had to get over that.

—*Ringo Starr*
The Beatles Anthology

Two quotations come to mind

when pondering the wonder that is "Free as a Bird," the new Beatles record released twenty-five years after the demise of the band. Both are about the impossible: George Santayana once said, "The difficult is that which can be done immediately; the impossible, that which takes a little longer." And Robert Goddard said, "It is difficult to say what is impossible, for the dream of yesterday is the hope of today and the reality of tomorrow."

A new Beatles record—a *real* Beatles record—years after John's death? Impossible!

Paul, George, Ringo, and Yoko begged to differ.

The nuts-and-bolts reality of "Free as a Bird" isn't all that remarkable. Today, with forty-eight or more digital recording tracks available, and the ability to literally take recordings apart and put them back together, the technical wizardry the Beatles and Jeff Lynne performed to make this single is commonplace. But there is an enormous difference between doing what they did, and doing what they did *well*, and that was the overriding concern among Beatlefans when we heard what the Threetles had in mind for the *Anthology*: Rework a poor-quality cassette of John's into a Beatles-quality single. Also, when we heard that Jeff Lynne, instead of George Martin, would be producing it, we all fretted over the possibility that the new Beatles record

would sound like an ELO record.

From the first two crackling slams of Ringo's snare, though, our concerns vanished into the blue suburban skies. The effort put into making the final track sound like a "real" Beatles record was obvious, and the additions by Paul, George, and Ringo were as Beatlesque as anything they had done when they were Fab.

What would John think of all this? We can't know, of course, but we can't help but suspect he would be pleased. What would "Free as a Bird" sound like if John had lived and recorded it as a solo work? Again, we can't know, but 'tis better to hear a John song than not to, so we have to just enjoy it for the unique creation it is.

Why it made the top 100

John Lennon's musical writing style is instantly recognizable, and "Free as a Bird" is a fine example of his work. It brings to mind other quintessentially Lennonesque ballads (especially *White Album*-era Lennon) such as "I'm So Tired," "Sexy Sadie," and "Cry Baby Cry."

That said, we must also acknowledge the exemplary production of the final version. Jeff Lynne and the surviving Beatles worked diligently to do their fallen mate justice. They wrote new lyrics, created lead guitar riffs, developed harmonies, and made certain that the track was *right*. The loving care put into the song is obvious, and it's clear that they all realized that they

had been entrusted with a monumental, historic task.

Their efforts did John proud.

What the song is about

"Free as a Bird" is a paean to domesticity, with a subtle expression of delight that the ties that bind have been released. Was John speaking specifically of being free of being a Beatle and all that that entailed? Perhaps. Supporting this theory are the first lines of the middle eight (the only lines John wrote of this section) in which he asks, rhetorically, "Whatever happened to the life that we once knew?"

Instinctively, Paul completed this section with more questions about whether or not they could live without each other and when they lost "the touch that seemed to mean so much." Ah, but then, interestingly, after *Paul* talks about that touch (the Beatles magic?) he then admits that it always made *him* feel so *free as a bird*, essentially contradicting the initial message John was communicating!

Whether or not this dual message was intentional on the part of the Threetles, there can be no denying that, irrespective of its Lennon genesis, "Free as a Bird" may be one of most *collaborative* songs the Beatles ever produced.

• • • 🐝 • • •

- Paul and Yoko met up at the January 1992 ceremony inducting John into the Rock and Roll Hall of Fame and discussed the possibility of the Beatles working on some of John's unfinished compositions. Yoko offered Paul tapes of "Free as a Bird," "Real Love," and "Grow Old with Me." Paul received the tapes in early 1994 and soon thereafter began working on "Free as a Bird" with the other Beatles, producer Jeff Lynne, and engineer Geoff Emerick.

- Paul loved the idea that he was once again "cowriting" with John: "I liked 'Free as a Bird' immediately. I liked the melody. It had strong chords and it really appealed to me… The great thing was that John hadn't finished it. On the middle eight he was just blocking out lyrics that he didn't have yet. That meant that we had to come up with something and that now I was actually working with John."[1]
- The surviving Beatles didn't know that "Free as a Bird" had

been heard on bootleg Lennon tapes or that "Real Love" had been heard in the *John Lennon: Imagine* documentary movie and soundtrack. Paul commented, "We didn't know as much as most Lennon fans, because they actually knew all the releases. They knew that 'Free as a Bird' and 'Real Love' had been heard. They'd heard them, we hadn't."[2]

- In an August 1995 interview in *Bass Player* magazine, Paul commented on what it was like to play along with John again: "It was very strange and it was very magic; it was very spooky and it was very wonderful. Before the session we were talking about it, and I was trying to help set it up, because we never even knew if we could be in a room together, never mind make music together after all these years. So I was talking to Ringo about how we'd do it, and he said it may even be *joyous*. And it was—it was really cool."
- On the "Free as a Bird" video made to accompany the single's release, there are specific visual references to well

over a hundred Beatles songs, and an entire subculture immediately sprang up to identify every one of them. (And by the way, the ukulele-playing lad at the end of the video is British music hall star George Formby. Ukulele fan George Harrison had asked to play that part, but the director refused since no other "contemporary" Beatle was shown in the video.)

- George Martin gave the project his cautious blessing but was concerned they wouldn't be able to separate the piano and vocals on the original tape, and thus would be limited to that tempo. "They stretched it and compressed it and put it around until it got to a regular waltz control click and then they were done. The result was that in order to conceal the bad bits they had to plaster it fairly heavily so that what you ended up with was quite a thick homogenous sound that hardly stops."

- This is one of only four Beatles songs bearing the name of all four Beatles as composers. The other three are the instrumental "Flying," the jam "Los Paranoias," and the instrumental "12-Bar Original."

The recording

Location: **The Dakota Arms, New York, New York; McCartney home studio, Sussex, England.**

Dates: **Fall 1977** – John Lennon records a demo of "Free as a Bird" on a portable cassette tape recorder. He sings the lead vocal, accompanying himself on the piano. The song is left incomplete, both musically and lyrically, and the tape goes into the Lennon archive of unfinished songs. We don't know if John ever intended to finish it.

February–March 1994 – Paul, George, and Ringo record the Beatles version of "Free as a Bird" at Paul's home studio.

November 1995 – *The Beatles Anthology* CDs are released. "Free as a Bird" leads off Volume 1.

November 19, 1995 – The "Free as a Bird" song and video debuts on the ABC-TV airing of *The Beatles Anthology*. The single is released.

Spring 1996 – "Free as a Bird" reaches Number Six on the U.S. singles charts.

Players/Instruments:
- **John Lennon:** Piano, lead vocal
- **Paul McCartney:** Bass, five-string bass, piano, acoustic guitar, lead vocal, backing vocals
- **George Harrison:** Acoustic guitar, lead guitar, lead vocal, backing vocals
- **Ringo Starr:** Drums, backing vocals
- **Producers:** John Lennon, Paul McCartney, George Harrison, Richard Starkey, Jeff Lynne
- **Engineer:** Geoff Emerick

What we really like about this song

Steve: This is one of my all-time favorite Beatles songs. What I especially like is John's chord changes for the main verse: He goes from A to F-sharp minor 7 to an F major 7 (or a D minor 7 for the second line) to E7. What a cool move! And the move (albeit briefly) to the key of C in the last line—"free as a bird"—of the verse, and then to a resolving E so he can get back to the main key of A, is breathtaking. Other elements I love are the sound of Ringo's drums, and George's slide guitar. Oh, and there's one other thing. I love my cowriter and soul brother, Mike, with the fire of a thousand flames, but if I hear him use the word *lugubrious* in reference to this song one more time, I will make him bungee jump off the Apple roof without a bungee cord.

Mike: On one hand, the song is lugubrious and the tempo does little to revive me, but I still must give props to Jeff Lynne, who worked his magic with a poor-quality source tape. It was so cool to hear them playing together again, and collaborating on a new song—the classic harmonies and George's stellar guitar work (which I feel fights to add a spark to the song). I especially like the soaring guitar piece after George sings his abbreviated middle eight. And speaking of the newly completed middle eight, it sends a fitting message that no matter what, the lives of John, Paul, George, and Ringo will always be intertwined.

[1] *A Hard Day's Write.*
[2] *The Beatles Anthology.*

26 Help!

When Help! came out, I was actually crying out for help. Most people think it's just a fast rock-'n'-roll song. I didn't realize it at the time; I just wrote the song because I was commissioned to write it for the movie. But later, I knew I really was crying out for help. So it was my fat Elvis period.

—*John Lennon*
Playboy

In their elder-statesmen, post-Beatles decades, Paul, George, and Ringo were all relatively sanguine and stoic about the madness they lived through when they were Beatles. (In the ten years from the breakup of the band to his assassination, John, however, was for the most part either silent or bitter.)

All their standard commentary and pat replies notwithstanding, there is no denying that what they experienced was, indeed, madness with a capital M, and it was of such global enormity, it's hard to fully understand what it was like. As John said in his *Playboy* interviews, "The whole Beatle thing was just beyond comprehension."

In *The Beatles Anthology*, George said that the world had a nervous breakdown when the Beatles were a group, but the four of *them* were the ones who sacrificed their nervous systems. Ringo is on record as saying that there were only four people in the world who *truly* understood what it was like, and that was the Fabs themselves.

Why it made the top 100

Yes, "Help!" was a "commissioned" song, but it is also one of the Beatles' most engaging recordings. The fabulosity of the track belies the dark message of the lyrics and proves that even though the Fabs could "write to order," they never sacrificed artistic merit to do so.

"Help!" is a superior Beatles record, it is the signature song of their hilarious James Bond parody *Help!,* and it is John Lennon at his most personally revealing.

What the song is about

In a 1970 issue of *Rolling Stone,* John Lennon said, "The only true songs I ever wrote were 'Help!' and 'Strawberry Fields Forever.' They were the ones I wrote from experience."

The song opens with a desperate cry for help, and this plea is intended for "not just anybody," but an idealized compadre who will perform an emotional rescue.

The first verse explains our poor wretch's thinking: When I was young and cocky, I didn't need anybody. Those days are gone, though, and my arrogance with it, so I've changed my mind "and opened up the doors," seeking assistance.

The chorus is a rehash of the opening plea, and then the second verse evocatively tells us what it was like to be a Beatle. It begins with the ridiculously understated line, "my life has changed in oh so many ways." He then laments the paradox of the "celebrity prisoner," the person who is so famous, he has literally lost *all* his independence by virtue of being who he is ("my independence seems to vanish in the haze").

Once the second verse is over, the song simply repeats the chorus and the first verse—there is no need for more words: The message is clear. *If you can, help me.*

"Help!" is one of John's most heartfelt and honest songs. It was written at a time when he was, in essence, only a twenty-five-year-old lad from Liverpool, and yet was being treated like royalty and, by some, like a deity.

This took a toll on John. A little less than six months later, he would write what could be considered the other half of a two-song set detailing his emotional state in 1965: "Nowhere Man."

● ● ● ❧ ● ● ●

- "Help!" is the only Beatles song featuring the words *confidence, insecure,* and *self-assured.* (Thanks to Alan Pollack for this Beatlefact.) Aside from their psychiatric overtones, though, John apparently used multisyllabic words for this song specifically to impress journalist Maureen "we're bigger than Jesus" Cleave. In *Playboy,* John said, "I remember Maureen Cleave… asked me, 'why don't you ever write songs with more than one syllable?' So in 'Help!' there are two- and three-syllable words and I very proudly showed them to her and she still didn't like them."
- Longtime Lennon friend Pete Shotton once said, "It may sound presumptuous—and I certainly never queried John on this point—but it was my distinct impression that his song 'Help!,' with lines like 'I do appreciate your bein' 'round,' was directed at me."
- Other names bandied about for the movie *Help!* were *Beatles 2, Beatles Production 2, Eight Arms to Hold You,* and *High-Heeled Knickers.*

Did you know?

- In the mideighties, Lincoln Mercury paid ATV Music a hundred thousand dollars to use "Help!" for six months in a commercial for an SUV-type vehicle that aired only in the United States. The commercial's soundtrack featured a cover version performed by studio musicians and singers.
- The definitive parody version of this song is the Rutles' "Ouch!," which first appeared in the mockumentary *All You Need Is Cash,* and later on several Rutles albums. A cover version (a cover of a parody song—how's *that* for postmodern?) also appeared on the tribute album *Rutles Highway Revisited: A Tribute to the Rutles,* performed by Peter Stampfel and the Bottle Caps.
- The song has been covered by U2, Tina Turner, Deep Purple, the Carpenters, Bananarama, José Feliciano, Count Basie, Al Caiola, Buddy Greco, Peter Sellers, Ray Stevens, Andre Kostelanetz, Mary McCaslin, Peter Nero, Dolly Parton, Alma Cogan, the Damned, David Porter, Jimmy Forrest, and Extreme.

The recording

Location: **Abbey Road Studios, London.**

Dates: **April 13, 1965**, 7:00–11:00 p.m. – Twelve takes were recorded, with the first eight concentrating on the rhythm track. The vocals were introduced in Take 9. Take 10 was a complete rendition of the song. Take 11 was a false start. The last take was best, and it was also the first appearance of George's descending guitar figures.

April 18, 1965 – Three mono mixes; stereo mixing.

June 18, 1965 – Mono and stereo mixing.

July 19, 1965 – First released as a single in the United States, backed with "I'm Down."

Players/Instruments:

- **John Lennon:** Acoustic guitar, lead vocal
- **Paul McCartney:** Bass, backing vocal
- **George Harrison:** Lead guitar, backing vocal
- **Ringo Starr:** Drums, tambourine

What we really like about this song

Steve: I have loved this song from the first time I heard it, and, even now, John's opening "Help!" never fails to surprise me. The backing vocals, in which Paul and George echo John's lead vocal, are quite effective; and Ringo's drumming is, oh, I don't know, *extraordinarily appropriate* might be the way to describe it. I also like that we can hear in the final version the Dylanesque folk song that John had originally intended this tune to be. John's acoustic guitar is not the least bit out of place in this fierce, undeniably electric rocker, and George's little guitar riffs, as always, put the icing on the musical cake.

Mike: This song, on one level, sums up the dilemma facing Ringo as the movie goons try to abscond with his sacrificial ring. Much deeper, though, the song is a cry for help (literally) from John, who was reeling from the pressures of fame and fortune. It seems to begin midsong, going full-bore right from the first notes, and with each subsequent wail of "help!" John's desperation grows. John once said he wished the music better reflected the song's message of frustration and fear. Too bad Nirvana never covered this song—don't you think Kurt Cobain could have done John proud with a droning grunge rendition?

27

Eleanor Rigby

I got the name Rigby from… a shop called Rigby. And I think Eleanor was from Eleanor Bron, the actress we worked with in the film [Help!]. But I just liked the name. I was looking for a name that sounded natural. Eleanor Rigby sounded natural.

—Paul McCartney
Playboy, 1984

"Eleanor Rigby" was Paul's baby, and I helped with the education of the child.

—John Lennon
The Beatles Anthology

Revolver opens with a George song, which in and of itself is unexpected, and then goes into a track that had not only no guitar, piano, or bass, but also no Ringo. Instead, a double string quartet thrums behind the sad and tragic story of a spinster named Eleanor.

Revolver—and the Beatles—were full of surprises, and it's not surprising that the album's influence survives to this day.

Why it made the top 100

"Eleanor Rigby" made the top 100 because it is one of the greatest ballads of the twentieth century and it launched a period of creative exploration by the Fabs that would peak with *Pepper*, *Abbey Road*, and *The White Album* (the almighty trilogy of Beatle greatness).

What the song is about

Eleanor Rigby is a church cleaning woman, and the first time we meet her she is picking up rice after a wedding. We're told she "lives in a dream" and that she "waits at the window." What is she waiting for, standing there forlornly gazing through the glass? We don't know, but it's a safe bet that it's love she's longing for, someone who will take her away from her life of loneliness.

The most surreal line of the first verse is "wearing a face that she keeps in a jar by the door." This can be interpreted literally. Many women describe putting on their makeup as "putting on their face." Thus, the face she keeps in a jar could be makeup she keeps ready in case Mr. Right appears. But the line can also be read metaphorically, with the face symbolizing her alternate identity—perhaps her true self, the person she rarely reveals.

We next meet the second character in the song, Father MacKenzie, another lonely person. He dutifully writes his sermon ("which no one will hear"—the balm of eternal salvation doesn't mean all that much to desperately lonely people mired in an existential limbo), and then darns his socks. "No one comes near." His parishioners ignore him.

Throughout these narrative verses, the refrain underscores the grim state of affairs ("look at all the lonely people"), and sadly asks us all, "where do they all come from?"

The final chapter in the story concerns Eleanor's death and burial. She died in the church (perhaps still waiting at the window?) and was buried "along with her name." She left no family. She left no friends. She left no legacy.

Father MacKenzie was apparently the only one in attendance at her burial, and he symbolically wipes his hands clean of her ("wiping the dirt from his hands") as he walks away from her grave. His obvious, yet unspoken frustration is made clear in the last line of the verse: "No one was saved."

"Eleanor Rigby" is a case study of loneliness and desperation, and shows a keen eye for the sufferings of others. Empathy, thy name is Paul.

• • • ❧ • • •

- The first name Paul tried for the song was Daisy Hawkins.
- There seemed to be some disagreement between John and Paul about how much input John had into the lyrics. In the April 1972 issue of *Hit Parader*, John said, "I wrote a good lot of the lyrics, about 70 percent." In *Playboy*, John said, "The first verse was his and the rest are basically mine." In a 1981 interview with Beatles biographer Hunter Davies, Paul said, "I saw somewhere that [John] says he helped on 'Eleanor Rigby.' Yeah. About half a line."
- Originally, Father MacKenzie was supposed to be Father McCartney, but Paul was worried about upsetting his father, so they changed it to MacKenzie. (John always felt that McCartney sounded better. Father McVicar was also considered.)
- George Martin, in *The Beatles Recording Sessions*, talked about the influences on his score: "I was very much inspired by Bernard Herrmann, in particular a score he did for the [François] Truffaut film *Fahrenheit 451*. That really impressed me, especially the strident string writing. When Paul told me he wanted the strings in 'Eleanor Rigby' to be doing a rhythm it was Herrmann's score which was a particular influence." Martin received a fifteen-pound fee for writing the "Eleanor Rigby" score.
- "Eleanor Rigby" won a 1966 Grammy for Best Contemporary Pop Vocal Performance, Male.
- Paul performed the song in his film *Give My Regards to Broad Street*.
- The song has been covered by the Grateful Dead, the Supremes, Joan Baez, Richie Havens, Wes Montgomery, Blonde on Blonde, Rare Earth, Oscar Peterson, Stanley Jordan, Booker T. and the MG's, the John Tesh Project, Rick Wakeman, Tony Bennett, John Denver, Dick Hyman, the Boston Pops, Paul Mauriat, Paul Anka, Walter Carlos, Frankie Valli, the Standells, the Four Tops, Johnny Mathis, Ray Charles, Vince Guaraldi, Cleo Laine and John Williams, Aretha Franklin, the Mystic Moods Orchestra, Vanilla Fudge, and the Zoot.

The recording

Location: **Abbey Road Studios, London.**

Dates: **April 28, 1966,** 5:00 p.m.–2:00 a.m. – Recording of the musical background with John and Paul in attendance, talking with George Martin through studio talkback system as he conducted a double string quartet. Fourteen takes were recorded. The question of vibrato was raised: They tried recording it with and without, and Paul couldn't tell the difference. The musicians could, though, and they favored playing without. They all wanted a different sound for the strings. Geoff Emerick, in *The Beatles Recording Sessions*, recalled, "We miked very, very close to the strings, almost touching them. No one had really done that before; the musicians were in horror." The eight string instruments took up all four tracks; they were then mixed down to leave room for the vocal.

April 29, 1966 – Overdubbing of the vocals. Then three mono mixes were made, with the third the best.

June 6, 1966, noon–1:30 a.m. – Another vocal overdub by Paul.

June 22, 1966 – Mono and stereo mixing.

August 5, 1966 – First appeared as a single in the United Kingdom, backed with "Yellow Submarine," as well as on the album *Revolver.*

Players/Instruments:
- **Paul McCartney:** Lead vocal
- **John Lennon:** Harmony vocal
- **George Harrison:** Harmony vocal
- **Tony Gilbert:** First violinist
- **Sidney Sax:** Violin
- **John Sharpe:** Violin
- **Jurgen Hess:** Violin
- **Stephen Shingles:** Viola
- **John Underwood:** Viola
- **Derek Simpson:** Cello
- **Norman Jones:** Cello

What we really like about this song

Steve: I really like the lyrics. Regardless of who was ultimately responsible for them (see Did You Know?), they read like poetry and are evocative and imagistic. I also like the strings, and Paul's vocal, and I especially like the counterpoint of the final chorus where "ah, look at all the lonely people" is sung behind "all the lonely people, where do they all come from?" I also admire the way the song ends—no fade-out or big finish. It comes to a pointed close—precisely the way the classical concertos and quartets that inspired it are supposed to.

Mike: This is one of Paul's most poignant songs—so un-Beatle-like and the polar opposite of such Paul *Revolver* tunes as "Got to Get You into My Life" and "Good Day Sunshine." The Beatles were constantly pushing the envelope, testing their fans to see what they could get away with. The fact that this unusual single hit Number One and stayed there reveals that fans were up to the challenge. The song is dramatic, yet not melodramatic. I like the fact that they named it after Eleanor—at least the song's title gives her some dignity—and Paul's singing of the last "ahh, look at all the lonely people" gives the song even more dramatic weight.

28 Something

"Something" was written on the piano while we were making The White Album. I had a break while Paul was doing some overdubbing so I went into an empty studio and began to write. That's really all there is to it, except the middle took some time to sort out! It didn't go on The White Album because we'd already finished all the tracks. I gave it to Joe Cocker a year before I did it.

—George Harrison
I Me Mine

Patti Boyd Harrison in 1969.

John's edgy and odd "Come Together" opens *Abbey Road*, but it is immediately followed by "Something," which acts like balm on a burn.

With its surrealistic lyrics and weird neo-bluesy arrangement, "Come Together" left us a little confused on first hearing. What the hell is *Abbey Road* about anyway? Monkey finger? *Walrus gumboots?*

But then Ringo's gentle drum triplet starts us off, and the soothing strains of what would soon become one of the most covered songs of all time calm us down and assure us that *Abbey Road* is, indeed, a Beatles album, and not a compendium of John's musical experimentations.

Why it made the top 100

"Something" made the top 100—justifiably ranked quite high, too—because it is one of George's finest songs, and a landmark Beatles track.

What the song is about

The message of "Something" is simple: He's in love with her and he feels fine.

If there's any doubt at all expressed, it's in the lines "I don't want to leave her now," and in his later admission that he doesn't know if his love will grow. But this cautionary skepticism is halfhearted at best. It's unequivocally clear that all he has to do is think of her, and he's fulfilled.

With a heartfelt message and beautiful melody, George Harrison gave the world one of the finest love songs of all time.

- "Something" was George Harrison's first A-side single with the Beatles. (His "The Inner Light" had been the B side of the "Lady Madonna" single, released in 1968.) In *Lennon*, by Ray Coleman, we learn that "the single was pulled off *Abbey Road* at the insistence of Allen Klein to bring in some immediate cash." Apple was hemorrhaging money at the time, and this was "the first time a Beatles single had been released solely to make money."
- Even though "Something" was George's first Beatles single and first Number One, he still couldn't seem to get any respect. Frank Sinatra used to introduce it as his favorite Lennon/McCartney song.
- Beatleologists agree that George got his first line from James Taylor's "Something in the Way She Moves" on his debut Apple LP (issued December 1968). The two songs were recorded at same time: Taylor at Trident Studios, George and the Fabs at Abbey Road and Olympic.
- The song had a third verse that was not used. These are the lyrics to that "lost verse" (which can be heard on *Anthology 3*):

    You know I love that woman of mine
    And I need her all of the time
    And you know what I'm telling you
    That woman, that woman don't make me blue.

- George Harrison's favorite cover of the song was the version by James Brown. In *I Me Mine*, George said, "[T]hat was excellent. When I wrote it, in my mind I heard Ray Charles singing it, and he did do it some years later. I like Smokey Robinson's version too."
- In 1987–88, a cover version of "Something" was included in a TV commercial for the Chrysler LeBaron coupe. In the February 1988 issue of *Musician*, Paul commented,

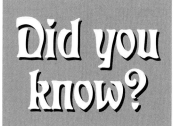

"The other day I saw 'Something'… in a car ad, and I thought, 'Ewww, yuck! That's in bad taste.'"
- A promotional video was made for the release of the single. Each of the Beatles was shown walking with his mate. (This clip can be seen in the *Anthology* series.)
- George first offered the song to Joe Cocker, who recorded and released it (along with the *Abbey Road* song "She Came in Through the Bathroom Window") on his 1969 album *Joe Cocker!* before *Abbey Road*, making it the debut recording of one of George's signature songs.
- "Something" has been covered by many artists, including Al Green, Andy Williams, Barbara Mandrell, Bert Kaempfert, Bloodstone, Bobby Vinton, Booker T. and the MG's, Butthole Surfers, Charlie Byrd, Dhyani Dharma Mas, Dionne Warwick, Don Williams, Ella Fitzgerald, Elvis Presley, Englebert Humperdinck, Erroll Garner, Failure, Fantastic Strings, Ferrante and Teicher, Frank Sinatra, Hugo Montenegro, Jack Jones, James Brown, Jim Nabors, Joe Cocker, John Davidson, Johnny Mathis, Johnny Rodriguez (Tejano), Junior Walker and the All-Stars, Keisuke Doi, Lena Horne and Gabor Szabo, Liberace, Lou Rawls, Maceo and All the King's Men, Martha Reeves and the Vandellas, Mose Allison, Passion, Paul Anka, Peggy Lee, Percy Faith, Perry Como, Peter Nero, Ray Stevens, Rod McKuen, Ronnie Dyson, Sarah Vaughan, Shirley Bassey, Smokey Robinson, Sonny and Cher, Telly Savalas, Crocodile Shop, the Grateful Dead, the Isaac Hayes Movement, the Lettermen, the Mystic Moods Orchestra, the Washington University Pikers, and Tony Bennett. "Something" is second only to "Yesterday" as the Beatles' most covered song.

The recording

Location: **Abbey Road Studios, Olympic Studios, London.**

Dates: **February 25, 1969** – On this day—George's twenty-sixth birthday—he arrived at Abbey Road early and alone to record an eight-track demo of "Something," "Old Brown Shoe," and "All Things Must Pass." "Something" was the last of the three recorded, and he completed only one take, which can be heard on *Anthology 3* (complete with the extra, ultimately unused verse).

April 16, 1969 – Thirteen takes of the basic track were recorded with George on guitar, Paul on bass, Ringo on drums, and George Martin on piano. John was there but didn't participate in the session.

May 2, 1969, 7:00 p.m.–3:40 a.m. – The song was remade again. They recorded thirty-six takes of the basic track, on which George played guitar through a Leslie speaker, Paul played bass, Ringo played drums, John played guitar, and guest Billy Preston played piano. Take 36 was considered best, clocking in at 7:48. (This take included a long, repetitious piano-led four-note instrumental fade-out—a really unnecessary piece of droning music: bass, "Chopsticks"-like piano, a few guitar notes, and drums.)

May 5, 1969, 7:30 p.m.–4:00 a.m. (Olympic Studios) – Overdubbing. Paul improved his bass line; George improved his Leslied guitar part.

July 11, 1969 – Overdubbing of a new lead vocal. A rough stereo remix, a reduction mix. The song was now down to 5:32, consisting of 3:00 for the main song and a 2:32 instrumental ending.

July 16, 1969, 7:00 p.m.–12:30 a.m. – Overdubbing of George's lead vocal, Paul's backing vocal, and Paul, George, and Ringo handclaps. A reduction mix was made.

August 4, 1969 – Stereo remix. It was decided the song needed an orchestral score, and an acetate was given to George Martin.

August 15, 1969 – All the orchestral overdubs for *Abbey Road* were recorded on this day. George Harrison went back and forth between Studio 1 (where he worked with George Martin conducting the orchestral part) and Studio 2, where he oversaw sound recording. Down on the studio floor, George taped a new lead solo for the song's middle eight (which wasn't much different from the song's previous best guitar track).

August 19, 1969 – Stereo remixing—the instrumental piece at the end was excised once and for all.

September 26, 1969 – First released on the U.K. LP *Abbey Road*.

Players/Instruments:

- **George Harrison:** Lead guitar, organ, vocal
- **Paul McCartney:** Bass, handclaps, backing vocal
- **John Lennon:** Lead guitar
- **Ringo Starr:** Drums, handclaps, backing vocal
- **Billy Preston:** Piano
- **Session musicians:** String ensemble consisting of twelve violins, four violas, four cellos, and a string bass

What we really like about this song

Steve: I have long felt that George Harrison's lyrical rhymes sometimes seem forced. Delightfully, this is not the case in "Something." Even seemingly improbable rhymes like "smile"–"style" and "moves"–"woos" completely fulfill the message of the song and fit beautifully. I also love the mellow mojo of the song, and I think Paul's bass part is one of his most creative. "Something" may not be as good as George's "Here Comes the Sun," but it has definitely become his most popular song.

Mike: I agree with the Chairman of the Board: This is the greatest love song of the last fifty years. Its simple six-note guitar lick permeates the entire song, and it features classy instrumental backing of a sweet George lead vocal. The rhythm section particularly shines: I appreciate Ringo's understated yet dramatic drumming (notice his limited use of crashing cymbals), and Paul plays an "active" bass (probably the most energetic performance in the song). The strings come in quietly and don't overwhelm the song like a Phil Spector production might. My favorite part of the song is George's guitar playing in the middle eight, one of his longest and most thoughtful guitar sequences.

Ticket To Ride

I used to like guitars. I didn't want
anything else on the album but guitar
and jangling piano… "Ticket to Ride"
was slightly a new sound at the time. It
was pretty fucking heavy for then, if you
go and look in the charts for what other
music people were making. You hear it
now and it doesn't sound too bad, but
it'd make me cringe. If you give me the A
track and I remix it, I'll show you what
it is really, but you can hear it there. It's
a heavy record and the drums are heavy
too. That's why I like it.

—John Lennon
The Beatles Anthology

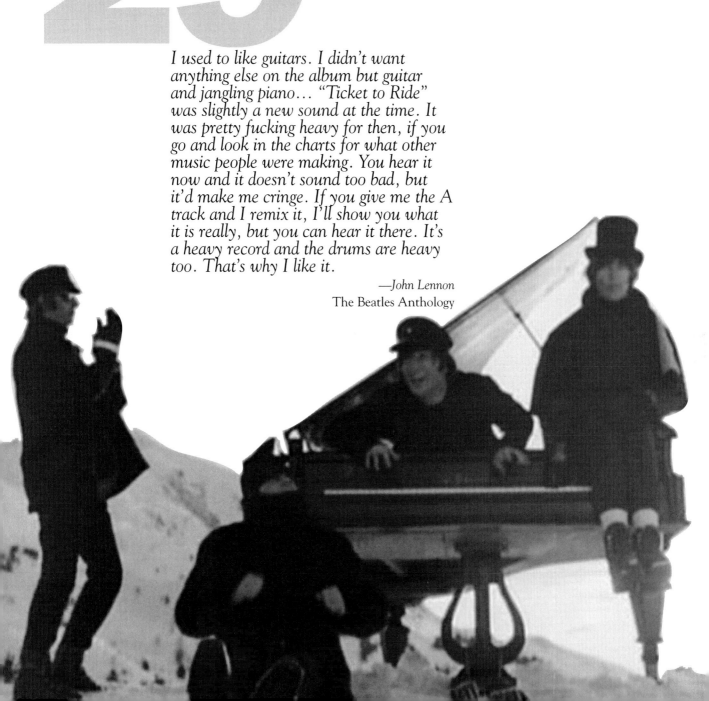

"Ticket to Ride" is a John song, and yet its most recognizable musical signature—the jangly Rickenbacker opening riff—was contributed by Paul. Such was the nature of the Lennon/McCartney creative partnership.

The "all John, all the time" single "Ticket to Ride"/"Yes It Is" was released in the United Kingdom on April 9, 1965, and went to Number One five days later. It was released in the United States on April 19 and went to Number One on May 22, 1965.

Why it made the top 100

As John so eloquently put it, "Ticket to Ride" was heavy before there was heavy. It is an undeniable Beatles classic that broke new ground in pop music. It wasn't, by any stretch or comparison with recordings of the time, *ordinary*, and it foretold to the fan of wondrous things to come, including "Day Tripper," "Paperback Writer," and the industrial-strength *White Album* metal of Paul's "Helter Skelter" and John's "Everybody's Got Something to Hide Except Me and My Monkey."

"Ticket to Ride" was an amalgam of metal, rock, blues, and "Byrdsy" folk—and the smooth assimilation of these styles into one kickass rocker was pure, quintessential *Beatles*.

What the song is about

"Ticket to Ride" takes place on the day the narrator's girlfriend is moving out.

Maybe.

We're told he "*thinks* it's today," a cleverly rendered way of telling us quite a bit about this guy. His girl is driving him "mad" but he can't even be bothered to confirm which day she's leaving him? Not to mention the fact that he's not even certain he'll *be* sad, as he admits in the song's opening line, "I *think* I'm gonna be sad…"

Throughout the song, the narrator's egoistic voice paints a picture. He shamelessly repeats his girlfriend's charges: Living with him is bringing her down, and she'll never be free if he is in her life. Based on these secondhand accusations, the singer sounds like a controlling jerk, which foreshadows John's later autobiographical admissions in "Getting Better," where he acknowledges being cruel to his woman and "keeping her apart." (See song number 35.)

The narrator's shock that his girlfriend would have the nerve to leave him is reinforced by the bridge, in which we're told he can't understand why she is claiming independence ("I don't know why she's riding so high"), and by him again bringing the subject back around to him: According to the narrator, she ought to "do right" by him.

There is also a vague aura of threat in the bridge lyrics, with him repeating four times that "she oughta think twice" before she does anything. As neutral listeners, we cannot help but ask what might happen if she doesn't "think twice"? Perhaps the "angry young man" from "Getting Better" will surface and resort to beating her because his "baby don't care"?

"Ticket to Ride" lends itself to this kind of psychoanalytical interpretation because it is one of the earliest examples of John using his songs to express what was going on inside him. Sometimes he was cryptic (as in "Norwegian Wood"; see song number 42); sometimes he was blatant, as in "Ticket to Ride" and "Getting Better."

It is evidence of the true depth of many Beatles lyrics that we can look back at this midsixties rocker and see in it a reflection of John Lennon, the truly honest artist.

• • • 🐞 • • •

- Clocking in at 3:10, "Ticket to Ride" was the first Beatles single to break the three-minute mark.
- Did John intend the phrase *ticket to ride* to have a more salacious meaning? Don Short, an entertainment journalist who traveled extensively with the Beatles in the sixties, said in *A Hard Day's Write* that John told him the song was about the Hamburg red-light scene: "The girls who worked the streets in Hamburg had to have a clean bill of health and so the medical authorities would give them a card saying that they didn't have a dose of anything. I was with the Beatles when they went back to Hamburg in June 1966 and it was then that John told me that he had coined the phrase 'a ticket to ride' to describe these cards. He could have been joking—you always had to be careful with John like that—but I certainly remember him telling me that."
- Paul told Ringo how he wanted the drums to sound for "Ticket to Ride"—and Ringo delivered admirably.

Did you know?

- The label caption of the first pressing of the "Ticket to Ride" single read, FROM THE UNITED ARTISTS SCREENPLAY, EIGHT ARMS TO HOLD YOU. *Eight Arms to Hold You* was the original working title for the movie *Help!*

- "Ticket to Ride" has been covered by the Carpenters, the Bee Gees, Hüsker Dü, the Fifth Dimension, Vanilla Fudge, the Mystic Moods Orchestra, the Rolls-Royce Coventry Band, the Starliters, and les Bidochons (in French).

The recording

Location: **Abbey Road Studios, London.**

Dates: **February 15, 1965,** 2:30–5:45 p.m. – At this session, the Beatles recorded and/or overdubbed drums, bass, rhythm and lead guitars, lead vocal, tambourine, and backing vocals. Two takes were recorded, but only the second take was complete. Paul played both bass and lead guitar, including the legendary opening riff. (Also, for all you Beatles history completists out there, this is the day John Lennon passed his driving test, at the age of twenty-four.)

February 18, 1965 – Mono mixing.

February 23, 1965 – Stereo mixing. (The Beatles were on location in the Bahamas.)

March 15, 1965 – Mono mixing. (The boys were now in Austria.)

April 9, 1965 – First released as a U.K. single, backed with "Yes It Is."

Players/Instruments:
- **John Lennon:** Rhythm guitar, tambourine, lead vocal
- **Paul McCartney:** Bass, lead guitar, harmony vocal
- **George Harrison:** Lead guitar[1]
- **Ringo Starr:** Drums

What we really like about this song

Steve: I love the jangly opening guitar (love those Rickenbackers!), followed by Ringo's exciting drumroll intro. I also love John's sardonic, world-weary vocal, complemented by a little-too-enthusiastic Paul. In fact, John and Paul's harmony in "Ticket to Ride" is the perfect paradigm of their personalities and writing styles: Paul was relentlessly good-natured and "up"; John was bitter and cynical. "Ticket to Ride" may be a 100 percent John composition, but, as was often the case, the Threetles' contributions transformed a Lennon song into a Beatles record.

Mike: This song instantly reminds me of that great scene in *Help!* when the lads were frolicking and freezing on skis in the snows of Austria. The song had nothing to do with the action, but it worked. This is the sunniest blues song you'll ever hear. Looking at the lyrics, it's a really sad story, but the melody betrays the message—which, as usual for the Beatles, works… big time. (Listen to the Carpenters' cover version and you'll hear the song's bluesy potential.) I especially like the drum playing—it seems to stagger and trip, as Ringo avoids the high hat and seems to be hitting on the off beat (he seems to "trip" less from the second verse on). If Paul did, in fact, suggest this drum styling, he done good.

[1] Some sources say George sang backing vocal; others say he played rhythm guitar, not lead.

The recording

Location: **Abbey Road Studios, London.**

Dates: **September 16, 1968** – An incredible sixty-seven takes were recorded this day, but not all were complete. (The tapes from this session include Paul ad-libbing during the recording: Take 19 of the song included him singing and playing the "Can you take me back where you came from, can you take me back?" snippet that appears on *The White Album* between "Cry Baby Cry" and "Revolution 9.") Also, Take 35 featured a brief and impromptu version of "Step Inside Love," a song Paul had written for Cilla Black. Other ad libs during this day's recording included "Los Paranoias" and "The Way You Look Tonight" (not the Sinatra song, but an original short number whose lyric was derived from "I Will"). "Step Inside Love" and "Los Paranoias" are on *Anthology 3*, as is Take 1 of "I Will." The sixty-seventh take of "I Will" was decided as the master. The four-track tape was copied to another for use as an eight-track.

September 17, 1968 – Only Paul was involved in overdubbing a backing vocal, a baritone "mouth bass" line, and a second acoustic guitar track.

September 26, 1968 – Mono mixing.

October 14, 1968 – Stereo mixing.

November 22, 1968 – First released on the U.K. LP *The Beatles*.

Players/Instruments:
- **Paul McCartney:** Acoustic guitar, vocal
- **Ringo Starr:** Drums, bongos, maracas
- **John Lennon:** Percussion (John tapped the rhythm by hitting metal on a piece of wood)

What we really like about this song

Steve: I like Paul's guitar work, and his innovative (and fun) "mouth bass" work. I like the fact that he dares to use one of the most clichéd chord progressions in rock (C–A minor–F–G) and yet makes it sound fresh. (And yes, I know "I Will" is in the key of F; I used C for illustrative purposes.) I like the fact the Paul can create a beautiful song, complete with a beginning, middle, and end, in the short space of one minute, forty-five seconds. Some songs five times as long don't come close to the excellence of "I Will."

Mike: I wish I could have been a fly on the wall in the studio during the recording of this song. It's hard to imagine the oft-impatient John tapping insistently on a block of wood, sitting through sixty-seven takes of the song, with Paul fiddling ever-so-slightly with the tune on each. (Listening to Take 1 on *Anthology 3*, it's not very different from *The White Album* version. But I digress.) This is a sweet, nonthreatening, simple song, in which Paul professes his love for his long-haired lady, Linda. I like the sparse instrumentation, especially the "mouth bass." I have read commentary from other writers comparing this to "I'll Follow the Sun," but I don't really see that much similarity. I get the same feeling from "I Will" as I do from "Put It There" from Paul's *Flowers in the Dirt*: Both would have benefited from another verse, or a repeat of the middle eight. I overdubbed "I Will" onto my wedding video, so it will always hold a special place in my heart.

31
Eight Days A Week

John and I were always looking for titles. Once you've got a good title, if someone says, "What's your new song?" and you have a title that interests people, you are halfway there. Of course the song has to be good. If you've called it, "I Am On My Way To A Party With You Babe," they might say, "OK..." But if you've called it "Eight Days A Week," they say, "Oh yes, that's good!"

—Paul McCartney
The Beatles Anthology

"Eight Days a Week" was never released as a single in the United Kingdom. That happened with Beatles singles sometimes. The song was available on the 1964 U.K. album *Beatles for Sale*, but only America was offered the single of "Eight Days," which was backed with "I Don't Want to Spoil the Party" (which did not make this ranking).

What was the Beatles' competition when the "Eight Days a Week" single was released in America in February, more than two months after the U.K. LP release? The Righteous Brothers' "You've Lost That Lovin' Feeling," Gary Lewis and the Playboys' "This Diamond Ring," Petula Clark's "Downtown," and, ironically, the Beatles' own "I Feel Fine."

None of this mattered, though, and within a week of its release "Eight Days a Week" was solidly perched at the top of the charts. It was the Beatles's second Number One single in America in 1965. "I Feel Fine" had owned the charts in January.

Why it made the top 100

"Eight Days a Week" is a classic Beatles track, an example of the kind of rocker they could—and did—churn out almost automatically. But it is also an example of the effort and craft that went into every Beatles recording. The attention the Fabs put into recording handclaps alone might have rivaled the total effort of many other releases of the times.

How good is "Eight Days a Week"? So good that even people who claim not to be Beatles fans can sing along with the song.

Those Beatles sure did write some catchy numbers, didn't they?

What the song is about

The message of "Eight Days a Week" is as blatant as can be: The singer is so in love with his girlfriend that there aren't enough days in the week for him to show he cares.

That is pretty much it.

He needs her love and he hopes she needs his love as much; she's always on his mind, he loves her every day, he "ain't got nothin' but love"; and he pleads with her to "hold me, love me."

We get it. Like we said: blatant, and one of the most unambiguous love songs ever written.

There is some question as to where the title "Eight Days a Week" came from. In *The Beatles Anthology*, Paul said, "I remember writing that with John, at his place in Weybridge, from something said by the chauffeur who drove me out there. John had moved out of London, to the suburbs. I usually drove myself there, but the chauffeur drove me out that day and I said, 'How've you been?'—'Oh, working hard,' he said, 'working eight days a week.' I had never heard anyone use that expression, so when I arrived at John's house I said, 'Hey, this fella just said 'eight days a week.' John said, 'Right—"Oooh I need your love, babe…"' and we wrote it." In a 1984 *Playboy* interview, however, Paul said the song title was a Ringoism: "He said it as though he were an overworked chauffeur: [heavy accent] 'Eight days a week.' When we heard it, we said, 'Really? Bling! Got it!'"

- On the *Cash Box* U.S. chart for 1965, "Eight Days a Week" was Number One for three weeks. It was kicked out of the top spot by the Supremes' "Stop in the Name of Love." Subsequent Beatles Number One singles that year were "Ticket to Ride," "Help!," and "Yesterday."

- "Eight Days a Week" is one of six Beatles songs with a number in its title. (The others are "One After 909," "Two of Us," "When I'm Sixty-Four," "Revolution 1," and "Revolution 9." You may also want to count "Not a Second Time" and "12-Bar Original.")

The recording

Location: **Abbey Road Studios, London.**

Dates: **October 6, 1964,** 3:00–6:45 p.m., 7:00–10:00 p.m. – These two sessions were the first time the Beatles took an unfinished idea into the studio and worked through how it should be recorded. Thirteen takes were recorded (a few of these versions appear on *Anthology 1*). By Take 6, the song started to resemble the final version, and they began overdubbing onto it. The last take was considered the best.

October 12, 1964 – Mono mixing.

October 18, 1964 – Intro and outro pieces were recorded, but ultimately only the dramatic fade-in would be used.

October 27, 1964 – Mono mixing, editing, stereo mixing, editing.

December 4, 1964 – First released on the U.K. LP *Beatles for Sale.*

Players/Instruments:

- **John Lennon:** Rhythm guitar, acoustic guitar, lead vocal
- **Paul McCartney:** Bass, harmony vocal
- **George Harrison:** Lead guitar
- **Ringo Starr:** Drums

What we really like about this song

Steve: I love Paul's bass during the fade-in and, for that matter, I love the fact that a rock single fades *in*, surely one of the first times that had ever happened on a Beatles-era pop record. (Chuck Berry's "Downbound Train" used a fade-in, but that track was released in the fifties.) I love Paul and John's harmony on the bridge, and John's irrepressible, gut-wrenching wail at the end of the third verse (technically known as a "melisma" and harking back to Gregorian chanting) that wordlessly expresses his depth of love for his girl. I also greatly admire the writing, especially the way the second part of the bridge suggests a key change to E, but then they smoothly and naturally swing it all back to the home key of D with nothing more than a transitional G chord.

Mike: Okay, so it's not the deepest song on the list, but it is among my wife's favorites. I admit, it is catchy. I like the intro—it always sneaks up on you. And I never get tired of Ringoisms—he was to the Beatles what Yogi Berra is to the Yankees. I can see, though, why John didn't speak very highly of the song: It's simplistic and somewhat trivial. At this time in their songwriting careers, John and Paul were venturing out into more challenging and meaningful territory; it's almost as if "Eight Days" were a leftover from 1963.

Day Tripper

32

That's mine. Including the lick, the guitar break and the whole bit. It's just a rock 'n' roll song. Day trippers are people who go on a day trip, right? Usually on a ferryboat or something. But it was kind of—you know, you're just a weekend hippie. Get it?

—*John Lennon*
Playboy

The buildup is classic Beatles. The opening guitar riff plays five times before Paul comes in with an almost shouted "Got a good reason."

First, it's only a double-tracked guitar. Then the bass comes in, mirroring the guitar riff. The third and fourth repetitions add an excitement-inducing tambourine and rhythm guitar, all of which leads to Ringo's just-plain-fantastic drumroll and metronome-like, rock-solid cadence for the fifth iteration.

The bloody song is only seventeen seconds old and we're already tapping our feet and in love with what we're hearing.

Why it made the top 100

The Beatles were on a roll in 1964 and '65, and "Day Tripper" was one of several brilliant rock singles that immediately shot to the top of the charts; it could be counted as the last release of their middle period. (Their first 1966 single, "Paperback Writer," served as an intro to their later period, the *Magical Mystery Tour*/*Pepper*, et cetera, years.)

Before "Day Tripper," the Fabs had released a series of incredible songs, including "I Feel Fine," "She's a Woman," "Ticket to Ride," and "Help!"; "Day Tripper," for all its apparent rush-to-record and rush-to-release, admirably continued (and perhaps concluded) their middle-years streak.

What the song is about

According to John, "That was a drug song. I've always needed a drug to survive. The [other Beatles], too, but I always had *more*, I always took more pills and more of everything, because I'm *more* crazy."

The lyrics are rather cryptic and don't blatantly support this assertion. In fact, the words suggest that the singer was taken for a ride, so to speak, by a girl—a day tripper who used him, teased him, and then dumped him.

The opening line is a bit puzzling: The narrator immediately tells us that he had a good reason for taking the easy way out. What was that reason? That he was horny and the girl who "only played one-night stands" was available? And what was the "easy way out"? Accepting the favors of this girl? Would seem so.

The revealed irony lies in the fact that he tried to please her, but she was a big tease, and his well-laid plans for sex fell apart.

Can the song be interpreted as a drug song simply because of the "tripper/trip" connotation?

Eye of the beholder, as it were.

• • • • 🎵 • • • •

- According to John's friend Pete Shotton, John's original lyric was "She's a prick teaser." Obviously no record company was going to release a single with the word *prick* on it, so it was ultimately recorded as "she's a *big* teaser."
- "Day Tripper" is one of the few Beatles tracks on which an obvious mistake was left in for the final release. At 1:55, there is a dropout of the second guitar and tambourine from the right channel. It comes back by 1:59, and is today assumed to have been an engineering mistake: A few seconds were accidentally erased, and it wasn't fixed. This theory can be supported by John's comment in *The Beatles Anthology* that "Day Tripper" "was written under complete pressure...and it sounds it."

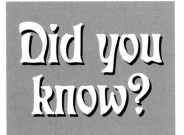

- On September 28, 1974, John guested on NYC's WNEW-FM and played records with a DJ. During his appearance, he played "Watch Your Step" by Bobby Parker and said it was the inspiration for his memorable "Day Tripper" riff.
- "Day Tripper" has been covered by Ramsey Lewis, Otis Redding, Nancy Sinatra, Sergio Mendes and Brasil '66, Electric Light Orchestra, Anne Murray, James Taylor, Whitesnake, Cheap Trick, Julian Lennon (live performance only), Jimi Hendrix, 10CC, Lulu, Mongo Santamaria, the Flamin' Groovies, and Mae West (God help us).

The recording

Location: **Abbey Road Studios, London.**

Dates: **October 16, 1965,** 2:30–7:00 p.m. – Rehearsing and recording of the rhythm track. The Fabs recorded three takes, but only the last one was complete. They overdubbed the vocals during the evening session.

October 25, 1965 – Mono mixing.

October 26, 1965 – Stereo mixing.

October 29, 1965 – Mono mixing—one for the record, and one for TV playback on November 1–2, 1965.

November 10, 1966 – Stereo mixing for *The Beatles 1962–1966* (The Red Album).

December 3, 1965 – First released as U.K. single. (On this day, the *Rubber Soul* album was also released in the United Kingdom. It did not include "Day Tripper" or "We Can Work It Out." Back then, including a single on an album was thought to be a gyp.)

Players/Instruments:

- **John Lennon:** Lead vocal, rhythm guitar, tambourine
- **Paul McCartney:** Bass, lead vocal
- **George Harrison:** Lead guitar
- **Ringo Starr:** Drums

What we really like about this song

Steve: "Day Tripper" holds a special place in my heart because its opening riff was the first thing I ever learned to play on the guitar. Tommy D'Agostino taught it to me at Marty Buonfiglio's house on Poplar Street in Fair Haven. (After "Day Tripper," I went on to learn "Hang on Sloopy" and "I'm Down.") The song is really a primer for budding rock stars. Every element of the tune—the guitars, the bass, the drums, the harmonies—is basic Rock 101, and learning it note for note can teach more than all the lessons in the world. One thing I especially like is how the signature riff is played throughout the song—lesser musicians would have been content to just strum E and A chords after the riff opened the song. Not the Beatles, though. The ostinato is continued throughout the verses, providing a tasty foundation for what is, in the end, a kickass rocker that still sounds as good today as when it was first unleashed on the world.

Mike: Give John credit for writing one of the catchiest, most enduring riffs in rock music—the Beatles' answer to the Rolling Stones' "Satisfaction." True, there's not much of a message to the song, but who cares? Its jubilant melody builds and the vocals rise to a crescendo, reaching Ringo's midsong rave-up drumroll. I like the way the bass follows along in step with the guitar—I guess even Paul agreed it was a killer riff. This is a classic pop song you can listen to over and over again and never get sick of.

33 Come Together

It's John's song, but when he just played it with him singing and guitar, it wasn't all that distinguished a song… It's another example of how the two of them triggered each other off with good ideas.

—George Martin
Rolling Stone, *March 2001*

"Come Together" did not sound very much like anything the Beatles had done prior to *Abbey Road*, and to say some listeners were a tad surprised when the first song on the first side of the album began is a bit of an understatement.

What is John saying there? "Shoot"? "Shoot *me*"? Mercy.

And what is it with that weird piano and Ringo's odd-sounding drumrolls?

And for that matter, where the hell are all the instruments? All we heard were bass and drums, with a bluesy guitar buried in the mix until it power-chords its way through the (very brief) chorus.

And *these* reactions all took place before we listened carefully to the words.

It was then that many of us surrendered to the moment and just listened to the song, somehow intuitively understanding that someday all would be made clear.

Many of us are still waiting for that day.

Why it made the top 100

"Come Together" is a seminal moment in the Beatles'—and John Lennon's—recording history. The song kicks off a brilliant album, and it is a classic John composition, subtly tempered by him still being in, and recording with, the Fabs.

Anyone studying John's evolution from being one-quarter of a group to being a solo artist could perhaps look at "Come Together" as the bridge between those two epochs.

What the song is about

The surrealistic imagery and odd use of language in "Come Together" make it, in a sense, a musical version of John's *A Spaniard in the Works* or *In His Own Write*.

It would seem that the main character in the song is something of a degenerate. Old Flat-Top, with his long hair ("hair down to his knee"), unshined shoes ("he wear no shoeshine"; "walrus gumboots"), stinking hands ("he got monkey finger"), and dirty feet ("he got toe-jam football")[1] wanders around town ("groovin' up slowly"), preaching ("he one holy roller") and apparently trying to lure the unsuspecting into a sordid embrace ("hold you in his armchair you can feel his disease").

Old Flat-Top rants and raves to whomever he comes across. "I know you, you know me," he tells his victims; along with "you got to be free," and, of course, "one and one and one is three."

Old Flat-Top, in addition to being a reprobate, also has all the characteristics of a suicidal paranoid schizophrenic. He manifests mood swings ("he roller coaster"); is fearful and paranoid ("he got early warning"); and apparently believes he needs to protect himself from magic and curses ("he got joo-joo eyeball"; "he one mojo filter").

And throughout the song, he repeatedly encourages someone to "shoot me."

In the end, however, after all this armchair (sorry) psychoanalysis, we are left with one key question: Is the character in the song John?

Some of the lyrics are especially Lennonesque. "Got to be a joker he just do what he please" is evocative of John the irreverent comedian. "He bag production" specifically references John and Yoko's company Bag Productions. "Walrus," of course, immediately brings to mind one of John's finest—and most arcane—songs, "I Am the Walrus." "He got Ono sideboard" names Yoko; and "he want spinal cracker" we know refers to Yoko's practice of walking barefoot on John's back to "crack" his spine.

And then there is the "One and one and one is three" line, which was one of the most compelling "Paul is Dead" clues, although in hindsight we can ask the question, Could John have been referring to himself, Yoko, and the soon-to-be-born third being of their trinity, Lenono, created by the union of their two souls? (Lenono was the name of their production company, but John also frequently referred to himself and Yoko as a new being created by their union.) Or could he have been referring to himself, Yoko, and Julian? Or himself, Yoko, and Kyoko?

Then again, maybe all this interpretation is nonsense and the song, as John said in *The Beatles Anthology*, is nothing but lyrical gobbledygook:

> The thing was created in the studio. It's gobbledygook. "Come Together" was an expression that Tim Leary had come up with for his attempt at being president or whatever, and he asked me to write him a campaign song. I tried and tried, but I couldn't come up with one. But I came up with "Come Together," which would have been no good to him—you couldn't have a campaign song like *that*.

> Leary attacked me years later, saying I ripped him off. I didn't. It's just that it turned into "Come Together." What am I going to do, give it to *him*? It was a funky record—it's one of my favorite Beatles tracks (or one of my favorite Lennon tracks, let's say that). It's funky, it's bluesy and I'm singing it pretty well. I like the sound of the record.

Nothing you can know that isn't known. So on that note, we'll let it be.

• • • 🐛 • • •

- When John started composing "Come Together," he worked off an old Chuck Berry tune called "You Can't Catch Me." That song contained the line "Here come old flat-top," which John used in his own lyrics. A few years after the song came out, John was sued because he admitted the influence, even though "Come Together" sounded nothing like the Chuck Berry tune. He settled out of court and, as part of the agreement, had to record three Big Seven Music songs (which was the publisher of the Berry song).

Did you know?

On his 1975 *Rock 'n' Roll* album, John performed "Angel Baby," "You Can't Catch Me," "Ya-Ya," and "Sweet Little Sixteen." Paul spoke about the Berry influence in *The Beatles Anthology*: "John came in with an up-tempo song that sounded exactly like Chuck Berry's 'You Can't Catch Me,' even down to the 'flat-top' lyric. I said, 'Let's slow it down with a swampy bass-and-drums vibe.' I came up with a bass line and it flowed from there. Great record."

- "Come Together" was banned from airplay by the BBC

when it was first released because of the mention of "Coca-Cola" in the lyrics. This violated the BBC's anti-advertising rules.

- "Come Together" has been covered by Aerosmith (on the *Sgt. Pepper* movie soundtrack), the Brothers Johnson, Diana Ross, Ike and Tina Turner, Soundgarden, the Neville Brothers, Blues Traveler, Howard Jones, Michael Jackson, Butthole Surfers, Paul Weller, Charlie Byrd, Dionne Warwick, and Barbara Feldon. (*Agent 99?* Yes.)

The recording

Location: **Abbey Road Studios, London.**

Dates: **July 21, 1969**, 2:30–10:00 p.m. – "Come Together" was the first song John had brought to the band since "The Ballad of John and Yoko" on **April 14, 1969** (although John had separately recorded "Give Peace a Chance" by this time). They recorded eight takes. The basic track was recorded on the four-track machine. The best take (Take 6) was then brought across to the eight-track machine. (Take 1 is on *Anthology 3*.)

July 22, 1969 – Overdubbing of a new lead vocal, electric piano, rhythm guitar, and maracas.

July 2, 1969 – Overdubbing.

July 25, 1969 – Overdubbing of vocal harmonies.

July 29, 1969 – Overdubbing of guitar for the middle part.

July 30, 1969 – Overdubbing of guitars.

August 7, 1969 – Stereo mixing.

September 26, 1969 – First released on the U.K. LP *Abbey Road*.

Players/Instruments:

- **John Lennon:** Lead guitar, electric piano, lead vocal
- **Paul McCartney:** Bass, piano, harmony vocal
- **George Harrison:** Lead guitar
- **Ringo Starr:** Drums, maracas

What we really like about this song

Steve: I like the sound of this song, perhaps more than the song itself. I've never been a big fan of one- or two-chord songs, but in the case of "Come Together," the production of the track wins me over. I like Paul's bass work, Ringo's drumming, and George's tasty guitar licks (especially what he does in the fade-out).

Mike: "*Shoot me…*" Considering what happened to him, it still disturbs me to hear John sing that. But I heard the song many, many times before I knew what John was really quietly singing/mumbling. As a kid, I tried to make sense of mojo filters and walrus gumboots, but I've grown to realize that "Come Together" is more about vibe than message. In that sense, it's kind of a funky version of "I Am the Walrus." This is one of my *Abbey Road* favorites—no mean feat, considering how many great songs are on the disc. Ringo's tribal beat and minimal use of the high hat, the interplay with the electric piano and the guitars… it's a wonder George Clinton never recorded a cover version of this one.

---

[1] It seems that toe jam is an idiom for that disgusting buildup of effluvia between the toes of the nonbathing. Toe-jam football has been interpreted to refer to the equally disgusting pastime of balling up this ordure and flicking it like a little football. Yuck.

I'll Be Back

An early favorite that I wrote.

—John Lennon
The Beatles *by Hunter Davies*

When Billy Joel finished writing the classical piano compositions that appear on his album *Fantasies & Delusions: Music for Solo Piano* (2001), he enlisted the renowned classical pianist Richard Joo to play them for the recording. Why? Because even though he *composed* them, he said they were too difficult for him to play in their entirety without mistakes.

We couldn't help but be reminded of this upon hearing Take 2 of "I'll Be Back" on *Anthology 1*. This version of the song is played in 3/4 time and, during the second bridge ("I thought that you would realize…"), John, almost out of breath, breaks out of his performance to exclaim, "It's too hard to sing!"

Imagine. John Lennon wrote something he himself had difficulty singing properly.

He couldn't very well give the song away to someone who might be able to sing it in 3/4, so John changed it to the time signature it probably should have been in all along: 4/4. The undeniable "rightness" of the song in the new meter is obvious.

Why it made the top 100

"I'll Be Back" is a unique song in the Beatles canon, because it is purely acoustic and because it has two fully realized bridges ("I love you so…" and "I thought that you would realize…"), instead of the traditional single bridge.

It is a really interesting song to close out the *A Hard Day's Night* album, and boasts an excellent John vocal. Once he found the right tempo, he hit a home run with his singing!

Also worth noting is John's deft manipulation of major and minor key changes, a bit of songwriting expertise that seemed to come naturally to Mr. Lennon.

What the song is about

The story told in "I'll Be Back" is odd, to say the least.

The first line has our young man telling his significant other that she knows that if she breaks his heart, he'll go. But he'll be back.

He loves her so, and he assures her and us that he is the one who wants her, but there is an obvious sense that the relationship is a tad one-sided.

The next verse scolds her, telling her she could find better things to do than to break his heart *again*. How many times has this happened? This is followed by a truly cryptic line: "This time I will try to show that I'm not trying to pretend." *Pardon?*

Then comes the scary part. He tells her that he thought she'd realize that if he ran away from her, she would want him back. The logical next line would be, *but I got a big surprise*. Instead, he sings, "but *I've* got a big surprise." *He's* got a surprise for *her*. Uh-oh.

Then he admits that he wants to go, but he hates to leave her.

Was John just stringing together words that rhymed and fit, or is there a message buried in the lyrics?

Can you say "delusional schizophrenia"? The character John chose to write about in "I'll Be Back" is, without question, one of his most enigmatic.

- According to John, "I'll Be Back" was his variation on the chords from a Del Shannon song, which has been speculated to be "Runaway." The Beatles had played the song in their early shows, and its similarities to "I'll Be Back" include beginning with a minor chord, and a descending bass line. The Beatles had played the Royal Albert Hall with Del Shannon on

April 18, 1963, and Shannon had suggested that he cover a Beatles song to help expose them to America. He wound up covering "From Me to You," which reached only Number Seventy-seven on the chart, but was the first Lennon/McCartney cover song to chart.

The recording

Location: **Abbey Road Studios, London.**

Dates: **June 1, 1964,** 7:00–10:00 p.m. – Sixteen takes were recorded; the first nine were of the rhythm track, while the last seven were vocals, double-tracked, with an acoustic guitar overdub. Takes 2 and 3 are on *Anthology 1*, where we can hear how the song started out in 3/4 time as a waltz (Take 2). It was an interesting idea that never seemed quite right and broke down as John began to sing "I thought that you would realize…" Take 3, also on *Anthology 1*, is a very appealing electric version of the song, with the meter changed from 3/4 to 4/4 time. Note that there is some discrepancy as to the numbering of the takes. In *The Beatles Recording Sessions*, Lewisohn says that the first nine takes were only of the rhythm track, yet on *Anthology 1* we're told that the two versions we hear are Takes 2 and 3. (One explanation is that he may have been referring to Takes 2 and 3 of the seven vocal takes recorded after the rhythm track was recorded.)

June 10, 1964 – Mono mixing (never used).

June 22, 1964 – Mono mixing, remixing; stereo mixing.

July 10, 1964: First released on the U.K. LP *A Hard Day's Night*.

Players/Instruments:
- **John Lennon:** Acoustic guitar, lead vocal
- **Paul McCartney:** Bass, acoustic guitar, harmony vocal
- **George Harrison:** Acoustic guitar (some sources say he also sang background vocals, but we don't hear him)
- **Ringo Starr:** Drums

What we really like about this song

Steve: I love the all-acoustic sound; the nonstop major/minor changes; the tight harmonies, with Paul on top instead of John; the double bridges; and the fade-out, which suggests a hesitancy and an uncertainty. (Considering the lyrics, this makes sense.) I should also state that I really love the electric version of the song on *Anthology 1* and would have been just as happy if that was the performance that made it onto *A Hard Day's Night*.

Mike: It's a love song where the love borders on obsession. There's nary an electric instrument in sight, and yet there's a lot to love about the song—the opening four-note guitar riff that can then be heard throughout the song, the perfect harmonies, the lovely three-part acoustic guitar playing. (On a personal note, I remember hearing this song in a whole new way just after John was murdered. I automatically interpreted John's promise that he would be back within the context of the promise of another messiah figure whom John once, uh, mentioned, and for which he got in a whole heap of trouble.)

Getting Better

John contributed the legendary line "It couldn't get much worse," [sic] which I thought was very good. Against the spirit of that song, which was all super-optimistic—then there's that lovely little sardonic line. Typical John.

—Paul McCartney
Playboy, 1984

"Getting Better" comes after "Lucy in the Sky with Diamonds" (see song number 12) on *Sgt. Pepper*, and its clipped guitar intro serves as a somewhat startling wake-up from the spacey zone we're in following the mantra-like repetition of the "Lucy" chorus in that song's fade-out.

Why it made the top 100

We're tempted yet again to say "Getting Better" made the top 100 because it's on *Pepper* (which we're sure Beatlefans would accept without question), but we'll go a step farther than that. "Getting Better" is not only a classic Beatles song, it is a classic rock song. It is a bright, entertaining, and appealing song, with insightful lyrics and strong production.

Not to mention a *tamboura*.

What the song is about

"Getting Better" is, in a nutshell, about the power of love.

The narrator of the song is—was—a mess. He hated school, he hated his teachers, he felt suffocated by the rigid rules of the establishment (school, probably his parents), and he was withdrawn, in denial ("hiding me head in the sand"), and, most assuredly, asocial.

This detachment and alienation bred (as it often does) violence. The narrator (whom John admits was his young persona for the verse in question) was cruel to his woman, he beat her, and he kept her away from friends, family, and the things she loved. Nasty boy.

But the song is called "Getting Better," so what happened to turn him around?

He met someone who showed him the error of his ways; someone who gave him "the word." Was it a girl? Could be.

And what was that "word"? There were probably *several* words, and the sum total of them was more than likely a variation on the message of "Get your act together or we're through."

So he "finally heard" and started doing his best.

And guess what? He had to admit things were getting better.

Like we said… the power of love.

(Which is, as we know, all you need.)

• • • 🦋 • • •

Did you know?

- Beatles biographer Hunter Davies related the story of Paul telling him how "Getting Better" was written: "I was walking around Primrose Hill with Paul and his dog Martha. It was bright and sunny—the first spring-like morning we'd had that year. Thinking about the weather, Paul said, 'It's getting better.' He was meaning that spring was here but he started laughing and, when I asked him why, he told me that it reminded him of something." Actually, it reminded Paul of Jimmy Nicol, the drummer who filled in for Ringo briefly in 1964 when Ringo was sick. Davies continued: "After every concert, John and Paul would go up to Jimmy Nicol and ask him how he was getting on. All that Jimmy would ever say was, 'It's getting better.' That was the only comment they could get out of him. It ended up becoming a joke phrase and whenever the boys thought of Jimmy they thought of "it's getting better."

- A cover version of "Getting Better" is now used in a commercial. We think it's for an electronics company but we don't really pay much attention to anything but the song when the commercial airs. (That's money well spent by the sponsor, eh? Thank you, Michael Jackson!)

- "Getting Better" has been covered by Bon Scott, the Hawaiian Style Band, Robbie Nevil, Steve Hillage, and Status Quo.

What we really like about this song

Steve: I *love* this song and it ranks at Number Two on my list of personal favorite Beatles songs. What is it that I love? The guitars; the rhythm; the fact that Paul's bass is in dead-on perfect tune; George's simply great tamboura playing, which is perfectly accompanied by Ringo's bongo playing. The tamboura-and-bongo combination lasts about twenty seconds but, like the perfect seasoning in the perfect proportion, the segment makes the song. I also love the harmonies and Paul's vocal, which interestingly, sounds like a vocal more suited for John. Imagine: John singing the lead on "Getting Better." He would have turned that mother out, yes?

Mike: I like it because it's the only real love song on *Pepper*. It reflects the optimism of 1967, and it stands Paul's "Good Day Sunshine"–type mantra side by side with John's jaded cynicism. It has an almost march-like beat, thanks to the clipped guitar. I also love Ringo's jazzy drumming. All these elements, combined with George Martin's hammering of the piano strings, the drone of the tamboura, and Paul's bass cascading up and down the scales, illustrate the amazing varieties of sounds and the richness of production they were able to coax from four-track equipment.

[1] A tamboura is an unfretted lute, a huge Indian instrument with four strings that produce a droning resonant note.

[2] George struck the strings instead of the keys.

The recording

Location: **Abbey Road Studios, London.**

Dates: **March 9, 1967** – Recording was scheduled from 7:00 p.m. until 3:30 a.m., but the boys apparently didn't file in until around eleven. They then recorded seven takes of the basic rhythm track with guitars, bass, drums, and George Martin hitting the piano strings. A reduction mix took everything down to one track.

March 10, 1967 – Bass, drums, and George playing tamboura were overdubbed onto the three remaining tracks.

March 21, 1967 – Lead and backing vocals were overdubbed. Beatles biographer Hunter Davies was there, and in *The Beatles Recording Sessions* he recalled, "The Beatles had already done the backing track and now they were doing the vocals. They could hear the backing through their headphones while they were singing but all I could hear was their voices: flat, grainy, hoarse, and awfully disembodied." Ringo was not needed for this vocal recording, so he had the night off. After repeatedly hearing the track, however, Paul summoned Ringo to the studio to re-record the drums. But then they readjusted some knobs and, upon further listening, decided that Ringo's drums were fine. They then called Ringo back and told him there was no need for him to come to the studio after all. (This was the night John unknowingly took an acid trip and George Martin unwittingly brought him to the roof to get some air. He thought John was ill.)

March 23, 1967 – A vocal overdub was re-recorded. The bongos were overdubbed. Three mono remixes were made.

April 17, 1967 – Stereo remixing.

June 1, 1967 – First released on the U.K. LP *Sgt. Pepper's Lonely Heart's Club Band.*

Players/Instruments:
- **Paul McCartney:** Bass, lead and backing vocal
- **John Lennon:** Lead guitar, backing vocal
- **George Harrison:** Lead guitar, tamboura,[1] backing vocal
- **Ringo Starr:** Drums, bongos
- **George Martin:** Piano[2]

The Abbey Road Medley[1]

consisting of…

"Because," "You Never Give Me Your Money," "Sun King," "Mean Mr. Mustard," "Polythene Pam," "She Came in Through the Bathroom Window," "Golden Slumbers," "Carry That Weight," "The End," "Her Majesty"

I love the second side of Abbey Road, where it's all connected and disconnected. No one wanted to finish those songs, so we put them all together and it worked. I think that piece of that album is some of our finest work.

—Ringo Starr
The Big Beat

I liked the A side, but I never liked that sort of pop opera on the other side. I think it's just junk because it was just bits of songs thrown together.

—John Lennon
The Beatles in Their Own Words

It was Goethe who said, "Be bold and mighty forces will come to your aid." (We actually got the quote from the movie *Almost Famous,* but we always liked it. We never came across it in our voracious reading of Goethe, though.)

Consider this: An almost-twenty-minute medley of unfinished songs, in different keys and styles, by different composers, all seamlessly woven together to cover almost the entire B side of an album. That, to us, sounds like the definition of *bold.*

And yet the Beatles pulled it off, with the mighty forces of talent, creativity, and heart coming to their aid.

Why it made the top 100

Even though the Fabs put this medley together to "use up" a bunch of incomplete songs, they did it in such a way that the finished product seems as though it had been conceived that way from the start.

The songs that make up this beloved collection range from soft ballads to hard rockers, and they are united by the aura of finality that pervades Side Two of *Abbey Road.* This handful of songs comprises the last recordings by the Beatles. Beatlefans know that the *Let It Be* album was still to come, but we also know that that LP was recorded before *Abbey Road* and during a time of acrimony.

The *Abbey Road* medley is the Beatles' *true* swan song and, fittingly, it boasts some of their finest work as a group.

What the songs are about

- **"Because":** John's poetic lyrics for this song offer a simple message: *My love for you makes everything wonderful.* He begins by telling us that something as simple as the fact that the world is round turns him on. This is followed by an even more pedestrian event—the wind blowing—having an equally profound effect on him. The bridge then explains everything: Love is all, new, and "you." As we know, this song was inspired by John hearing Yoko playing Beethoven's heartbreaking *Moonlight Sonata* (Sonata no. 14, op. 27, no. 2, written in 1801 when Beethoven was thirty-one). John asked Yoko to play the chords backward, he wrote some accompanying poetic lyrics and a melody, and the song was complete.

- **"You Never Give Me Your Money":** Paul told Beatles biographer Hunter Davies, "I wrote this when we were going through all our financial difficulties at Apple." The three sections of the song tell of financial "issues." The first "funny paper" section bemoans the Beatles' business dealings, which seemed to grow increasingly complex as the years passed and the boys grew successful beyond anyone's expectations. The second section takes us back to a time when there did not seem to be a future for a young, out-of-college lad who wanted to make music, and these lyrics ("see no future," "all the money's gone," "nowhere to go," et cetera) serve to emphasize the contrast between what the Fabs were *before* they were Fab, and what they later became. The third section ("one sweet dream...") has our hero imagining jumping into the limo and fleeing ..."soon we'll be away from here," he sings, and he concludes this musing with the phrase "one sweet dream came true today... ," which can mean a million different things within the context of being a Beatle at the end of an era.

- **"Sun King":** The Sun King is coming and, apparently, everybody's happy about this. This proclamation is followed by three lines of Italian/Spanish gibberish (mostly) in which the words "how much," "my love," "paparazzi," "parasol," and "carousel" can be discerned. In *The Beatles Anthology,* John talked about the genesis of the non-English lyrics: "When we came to sing it, to make them different we started joking, saying 'cuando para mucho.' We just made it up. Paul knew a few Spanish words from school, so we just strung any Spanish words that sounded vaguely like something. And of course we go 'chicka ferdi'—that's a Liverpool expression; it doesn't mean anything, just like 'ha ha ha.' One we missed: We could have had 'para noia,' but we forgot all about it. We used to call ourselves Los Para Noias."

- **"Mean Mr. Mustard":** Joining John's memorable character Old Flat-Top from "Come Together" is another odd denizen of Lennon Land, Mr. Mustard. He's homeless, and he keeps money up his nose. We also learn about his sister Pam, who is a go-getter, and once took him to Buckingham Palace to look at the queen. He said something obscene and embarrassed Pam. Mr. Mustard is a mean, dirty old man.

- **"Polythene Pam":** Is Polythene Pam Mr. Mustard's sister? Since an early version of "Mean Mr. Mustard" named his sister Shirley, we have to assume the switch was intentional and that Polythene Pam and Mr. Mustard are, indeed, sibs. And what of this lass? Well, she's attractive in a masculine sort of way ("she looks like a man"), she dresses in plastic, wears jackboots, a kilt, and has a nice body underneath it all. No doubt about it: The Mustard family are a peculiar lot.

- **"She Came in Through the Bathroom Window":** A retired cop tells the story of a privileged young girl ("protected by a silver spoon") who strayed from the straight and narrow and started robbing houses before sinking into mindlessness and despair. She may or may not have resorted to turning tricks ("Tuesday's on the phone with me…"). It seems that our former Mr. City P'liceman started acting as her pimp to help her out, but the grip of whatever vices she was ensnared in prevented her from being as "productive" as he might have liked: "And though she tried her best to help me/She could steal but she could not rob…" The chorus twice laments her sad state of affairs and wonders why no one helped: "Didn't anybody tell her?/Didn't anybody see?" (An Apple scruff named Diane Ashley once broke into Paul's house and took clothes, pictures, and other items. This may have had something to do with Paul's initial idea for the song.)

- **"Golden Slumbers":** Inspired by a poem by Thomas Dekker (a contemporary of Shakespeare's), the lyrics to this song tell of a young girl who is away from home and crying about it. The singer quiets the child by singing a lullaby, and it isn't long before "golden slumbers fill [her] eyes." The line "smiles awake you when you rise" suggests that our hero will find one of those ways to get back the girl back homeward so he won't have to contend with another night of sobs and sadness.

- **"Carry That Weight":** The message of "Carry That Weight" is simple: *Boy, you're going to be working a long time, so you better get used to it.* The middle section of the song, though, is a new verse of "You Never Give Me Your Money." Our hero tells the boy that he never gives

him a pillow (to cushion the weight?), but sends him an invitation. To what? A celebration of a resolution between the two? Maybe, but the final line of this section is an admission that nothing has been resolved: "and in the middle of the celebration, I break down." A reference to more Apple problems? Probably.

- **"The End":** After all the contentiousness and strange characters and sorrowful lasses, our singer has but one question: "are you gonna be in my dreams tonight?" This is followed by a drum solo, a metaphorical pause as our hero awaits an answer. The answer does not come, so he offers one final bit of encouragement/advice to his young lady (and, by extension, everyone else he's dealt with in this suite): "And in the end, the love you take is equal to the love you make."

- **"Her Majesty":** For a song that's supposed to be a tribute to the queen of England, it comes off as a tad cheeky and disrespectful. We're told she's a pretty nice girl, "but she doesn't have a lot to say." So far so good, as there really isn't anything wrong with being taciturn (as Queen Elizabeth is known to be). But then we learn that "she changes from day to day." Is this a commentary on British governmental policy, or a personal observation about the queen herself? The bridge is even more puzzling. Our balladeer wants to tell her that he loves her "a lot" but he's got to get drunk to pull it off and then, as suddenly as it begins, the ditty ends with him proclaiming that "someday I'm going to make her mine." Say what? We cannot help but suspect that the title may have been a sly jab at a woman most assuredly not the queen herself, because then the lyrics makes sense. For years, though, the song has been interpreted as being about the queen, and Paul has not denied it. (Talk about cheeky! He even sent complimentary copies of *Abbey Road* to Buckingham Palace.)

"Because"

- Paul suspected that Yoko "was in on" the writing of "Because": "It's rather her kind of writing... Wind, sky and earth are recurring, it's straight out of *Grapefruit.*"
- John wrote the lyrics for "Because" on the back of a business letter to the Beatles from John Eastman in July 1969.
- A piece of this song was first heard on John and Yoko's *Wedding Album.*
- On the *Fly on the Wall* disc of *Let It Be... Naked,* the Beatles can be heard working on "Because," but they've added the "Don't Let Me Down" guitar lick to it!
- The three-part harmony in this song was overlaid three times, making nine-part harmony. George Harrison considered the harmony on this song the best of the Beatles' career. ("Because" was Paul's and George's favorite song on *Abbey Road.*)
- The song has been covered by Diana Ross and the Supremes, Percy Faith, Mike Marshall, the Nylons, and Stanley Jordan.

"You Never Give Me Your Money"

- This is the longest song of the medley, clocking in at 4:02.
- It's one of five Fabs songs that mention the color yellow. (See song number 12, "Lucy in the Sky with Diamonds," for the complete list.)
- In *The Beatles Anthology,* Paul talked about the motivation behind this song: "We used to ask, 'Am I a millionaire yet?' and they used to say cryptic things like, 'On paper you are.' And we'd say, 'Well, what does that mean? Am I or aren't I? Are there more than a million of those green things in my bank yet?'"

"Sun King"

- John said that "Sun King" came to him in a dream. (Shades of "Yesterday"!)
- *Sun King* was the nickname of France's King Louis XIV. Louis adopted the sun as his emblem.
- The song begins with the identical words as George's "Here Comes the Sun": "Here comes the Sun (King)."
- In a November 1987 interview in *Musician* magazine, George talked about the genesis of the song's sound: "At the time, [Fleetwood Mac's] *Albatross* was out, with all the reverb on guitar. So we said, 'Let's be Fleetwood Mac doing *Albatross*' just to get it going. It never really sounded like Fleetwood Mac... but [it was] the point of origin." ("Albatross" was an instrumental that hit the top 10 early in 1969.)

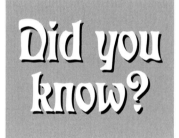

- "Sun King" is one of seventeen Beatles songs that mention the sun. (See song number 62, "Mother Nature's Son," for the complete list.)

"Mean Mr. Mustard"

- A demo of "Mean Mr. Mustard" was recorded during *The White Album* days, and was rehearsed during the *Let It Be* sessions.
- John told *Playboy* about the inspiration for the Mr. Mustard character: "I'd read somewhere in the newspaper about this mean guy who hid five-pound notes, not up his nose but somewhere else. No, it had nothing to do with cocaine."

"Polythene Pam"

- This song was based on two people. One was a Beatles fan from the Cavern Club days who used to tie polythene into knots and eat it. (Yes, *eat it.*) Her name was Pat Hodgett (now Dawson), and she was known as Polythene Pat. The other was a girl John met in 1963 through the British poet Royston Ellis. John spent the night at Ellis's place and they all slept in the same bed, wearing polythene bags.
- John wrote "Polythene Pam" while in India.
- John deliberately used a thick Liverpool accent when recording the song.
- The song was originally intended for *The White Album* but was left uncompleted.

"She Came in Through the Bathroom Window"

- The song's original title was "Bathroom Window."
- Paul wrote this song in June 1968 while in the United States doing business with Capitol Records. The line "And so I quit the police department" was inspired by New York City police officer Eugene Quits, who was assigned to protect him.
- A bootleg exists on which John sings lead.
- The song has been covered by Joe Cocker, Ray Stevens, and Ike and Tina Turner.

"Golden Slumbers"

- The original poem by Thomas Dekker that inspired this song contained the lyrics: "Golden slumbers kiss your eyes/Smiles awake you when you rise/Sleep pretty wantons do not cry/And I will sing a lullaby/Rock them, rock them, lullaby."
- "Golden Slumbers" has been covered by George Benson, James Galway, Lou Rawls, the Mystic Moods Orchestra, and Jackson Browne.

"Carry That Weight"

- All four Beatles sing the chorus of "Carry That Weight." The only other time they did this was the "la la" chorus of "Flying." (All but Ringo sing the "I never give you my pillow" verse.)
- Paul later admitted he was under a great deal of stress when he wrote this song.
- The "Golden Slumbers"/"Carry That Weight" medley has been covered by Billy Joel, Mary Hart, and Neil Diamond.

"The End"

- The much-anticipated "surprise" on *Anthology 3* was described in the accompanying booklet simply as "final chord," with a note that it had been recorded February 22, 1967, two years before the recording of *Abbey Road*. What was this "final chord"? It's the legendary final chord from "A Day in the Life"—first played *backward* from its fade-out to its strike, and then *forward* to its fade-out. (And February 22, 1967, was that historic day during the recording of the *Sgt. Pepper* album when that *original* "final chord" was committed to tape.)
- The working title of the song was "Ending."
- Paul, George, and John—in that order—take turns playing the guitar lead solo during the song, each taking three turns.
- In *The Beatles Anthology*, Ringo talked about his ultra-rare drum solo in the song: "Solos have never interested me. That drum solo is still the only one I've done. There's the guitar section where the three of them take in the solos and then they thought, 'We'll have a drum solo as well.' I was opposed to it: 'I don't want to do no bloody solo!' George Martin convinced me."

"Her Majesty"

- At twenty-three seconds, this is the shortest recorded Beatles song.
- "Her Majesty" was originally intended to go in the middle of the medley, between "Mean Mr. Mustard" and "Polythene Pam." When the rough edit of the medley was put together on July 30, 1969, Paul changed his mind and decided to leave it out. But memories of its original placement remain: You can still hear the last chord of "Mustard" at the opening of "Her Majesty," and its last sounds were once the opening for "Polythene Pam."
- "Her Majesty" is one of four Beatles songs that mention wine. (See song number 42, "Norwegian Wood," for the complete list.)

The recording

Locations: **Abbey Road Studios; Olympic Studios, London.** All recording sessions were at Abbey Road except for May 6, 1969. Also, it's interesting to note that the *Abbey Road* medley songs were recorded out of sequence.

Dates: **January 22, 1969** – "She Came in Through the Bathroom Window" was rehearsed during the *Let It Be* sessions. Billy Preston was on hand to help with chord structure at the end of a busy day of recording. This version sounds pretty similar to the LP version, albeit a little slower tempoed, and with wah-wah on guitar and no overdubs. (It can be heard on *Anthology 3*.)

May 6, 1969, 3:00 p.m.– 4:00 a.m. – Thirty-six takes of the basic track of "You Never Give Me Your Money" were recorded, consisting of Paul's piano and guide vocal, Ringo's drums, John's distorted electric guitar, and George's chiming electric guitar put through the Leslie. Rough stereo mix.

July 1, 1969, 3:00–7:30 p.m. – Overdubbing of Paul's lead vocal for "You Never Give Your Money." (He was the only Beatle in attendance at this session.)

July 2, 1969, 3:00–9:30 p.m. – Three takes of "Her Majesty" were recorded, two of which were complete. Fifteen takes of "Golden Slumbers" and "Carry That Weight" were recorded after George and Ringo arrived, with Paul on piano and singing a guide vocal, Ringo on drums, and George (!) on bass. The songs were recorded together as one song.

July 3, 1969, 3:00–8:30 p.m. – Takes 13 and 15 of the previous day's recording of "Golden Slumbers" and "Carry That Weight" were edited together, and then overdubbed with Paul's rhythm guitar and two lead vocals. Then, in unison, they all sang the "Carry that weight" chorus. Tape reduction.

July 4, 1969, 2:45–5:30 p.m. – First overdubs for "Golden Slumbers" and "Carry That Weight" were recorded. (The logs do not give specifics.)

July 11, 1969 – Overdubbing of bass guitar track for "You Never Give Me Your Money."

July 15, 1969, 2:30–11:00 p.m. – Overdubbing of vocals and chimes for end of song for "You Never Give Me Your Money." Six stereo remixes.

July 23, 1969 – Seven takes were recorded of "The End." Ringo's drum solo changed with each take, the last one being sixteen seconds long. Take 7 was considered best, and the solo was spread over two available tracks (a technological recording breakthrough). In the final version, any instruments overdubbed alongside Ringo's solo—the two lead guitars and tambourine—were removed so that the solo would remain solo. So far, the song was only 1:20. The final version would include lengthy guitar solos, more drums, an orchestra, vocals, and piano, and the song would grow to more than two minutes in length. (The guitar solos are even longer on the *Anthology 3* track.)

July 24, 1969, 3:30–10:30 p.m. – "Sun King" and "Mean Mr. Mustard" were recorded together as one song and known today as "Here Comes the Sun-King." Thirty-five takes were recorded of the basic track, consisting of bass, drums, electric and rhythm guitars, and John's guide vocal.

July 25, 1969 – Overdubbing of vocals, piano, and organ onto the previous day's Take 35 of "Sun King" and "Mean Mr. Mustard." Also, thirty-nine takes of "Polythene Pam" and "She Came in Through the Bathroom Window" were recorded together as one song. "Polythene Pam" started with John sharply jabbing a twelve-string acoustic guitar, and "She Came in Through the Bathroom Window" ended with Paul's vocal line "on the phone to me, oh yeah." The basic track included Paul on bass, Ringo on drums, George on lead guitar, and John on acoustic. They also recorded off-mike guide vocals by Paul and John. Then, in a 10:30 p.m.–2:30 a.m. session, lead vocal, bass guitar, and drums were overdubbed onto Take 39.

July 28, 1969, 2:30–8:30 p.m. – Overdubbing of another lead vocal, acoustic and electric guitars, tambourine, miscellaneous percussion, electric piano, and ordinary piano onto "Polythene Pam" and "She Came in Through the Bathroom Window." Reduction mix.

July 29, 1969 – "Sun King" and "Mean Mr. Mustard" were now known by their individual song names. Vocal, piano, organ, and percussion overdubs.

July 30, 1969 – Reduction mix, and then overdubbing of vocals for "You Never Give Me Your Money." Overdubbing of vocals, percussion, and guitar for "Polythene Pam" and "She Came in Through the Bathroom Window." Overdubbing of vocals for "Golden Slumbers" and "Carry That Weight."

Stereo mixing of the medley in the following order ("Because" had not yet been recorded):
"You Never Give Me Your Money"
"Sun King"
"Mean Mr. Mustard"
"Her Majesty"
"Polythene Pam"
"She Came in Through the Bathroom Window"
"Golden Slumbers"
"Carry That Weight"
"The End"

Second engineer John Kurlander recalled the "Her Majesty" incident: "We did all the remixes and crossfades to overlap the songs, Paul was there, and we heard it together for the first time. He said, 'I don't like "Her Majesty," throw it away,' so I cut it out—but I accidentally left in the last note. He said 'It's only a rough mix, it doesn't matter,' in other words, don't bother about making a clean edit because it's only a rough mix. I said to Paul, 'What shall I do with it?' 'Throw it away,' he replied. I've been told never to throw anything away, so after he left I picked it up off the floor, put about 20 seconds of leader tape before it, and stuck it onto the end of the edit tape. The next day, down at Apple, Malcolm Davies cut a playback lacquer of the whole sequence and, even though I'd written on the box that 'Her Majesty' was unwanted, he too thought, 'Well, mustn't throw anything away, I'll put it on at the end.' I'm only assuming this, but when Paul got that lacquer he must have liked hearing 'Her Majesty' tacked on the end. The Beatles always picked up on accidental things. It came as a nice little surprise there at the end, and he didn't mind. We never remixed 'Her Majesty' again, that was the mix which ended up on the finished LP."

Medley editing and crossfading were also done. The most problematic crossfade was between "You Never Give Me Your Money" and "Sun King."

They decided to merge the songs on an organ note. (For now. A better alternative came on August 5.)

July 31, 1969 – Overdubbing of the bass and piano tracks of "You Never Give Me Your Money," the version before the previous day's reduction mix. Overdubbing of drums, timpani, and vocal for "Golden Slumbers" and "Carry That Weight."

August 1, 1969, 2:30–10:30 p.m. – Twenty-three takes of the basic track for "Because" were recorded, with George Martin playing harpsichord, John playing the repeated electric guitar riff, and Paul playing bass. Ringo tapped on the high hat, but in the musicians' headphones only, to give them a beat.

August 4, 1969, 2:30–9:00 p.m. – Overdubbing of two more vocal tracks for "Because." George Martin recalled, "Having done the backing track, John, Paul and George sang the song in harmony. Then we overlaid it twice more, making nine-part harmony altogether, three voices recorded three times. I was literally telling them what notes to sing."[2] (This harmonizing, sans instrumentation, can be heard on *Anthology 3*.)

August 5, 1969 – Paul came up with the solution for the crossfade between "Sun King" and "You Never Give Me Your Money": He brought in loose strands of tapes and added sound effects from tape loops of birds, crickets, and the like. Also, Moog overdubs by George were recorded twice for "Because." Overdubbing of vocals for "The End."

August 7, 1969, 6:00 p.m.–midnight – Overdubbing of vocals and electric guitar for "The End."

August 8, 1969 – Overdubbing of drums and bass for "The End."

August 12, 1969 – Stereo mixing of "Because."

August 13, 1969 – Stereo mixing of "You Never Give Me Your Money."

August 14, 1969 – Stereo mixing of "Polythene Pam" and "She Came in Through the Bathroom Window." They were then joined with "Sun King" and "Mean Mr. Mustard." Stereo mixing of the crossfade between "You Never Give Me Your Money" and "Sun King."

August 15, 1969, 2:30–5:30 p.m. – Orchestral overdubs made for "Golden Slumbers," "Carry That Weight," and "The End." Alan Brown recalled the session: "The orchestral overdub for 'The End' was the most elaborate I have ever heard: one 30-piece playing for not too many seconds—and mixed about 40 dBs down. It cost a lot of money: all the musicians have to be paid, fed and watered; I screw every pound note out of it whenever I play the record!"[3]

August 18, 1969 – Stereo mixing of "Golden Slumbers" and "Carry That Weight." Overdubbing of the brief piano track (played by Paul) that preceded the "love you make" line in "The End."

August 19, 1969 – Stereo mixing of "Golden Slumbers" and "Carry That Weight."

August 21, 1969 – A new stereo mix of the crossfade between "You Never Give Me Your Money" and "Sun King." Editing and stereo mixing of "The End."

August 25, 1969 – Editing of "The End" (still known as "Ending").

September 26, 1969 – First released on the U.K. LP *Abbey Road*.

Players/Instruments:

"Because" (2:44):
- **John Lennon:** Lead guitar, harpsichord, harmony/lead vocal
- **Paul McCartney:** Bass, harmony/lead vocal
- **George Harrison:** Moog synthesizer, harmony/lead vocal

"You Never Give Me Your Money" (4:02):
- **Paul McCartney:** Bass, piano, lead and backing vocal
- **John Lennon:** Lead guitar, backing vocal
- **George Harrison:** Rhythm guitar
- **Ringo Starr:** Drums, tambourine

"Sun King" (2:32):
- **John Lennon:** Lead guitar, maracas, multitracked vocal
- **Paul McCartney:** Bass, harmonium
- **George Harrison:** Lead guitar
- **Ringo Starr:** Drums, bongos
- **George Martin:** Organ

"Mean Mr. Mustard" (1:06):
- **John Lennon:** Piano, lead vocal
- **Paul McCartney:** Fuzz bass, harmony vocal
- **George Harrison:** Lead guitar
- **Ringo Starr:** Drums, tambourine

"Polythene Pam" (1:18):
- **John Lennon:** Acoustic guitar, lead guitar, vocal
- **Paul McCartney:** Bass, lead guitar, harmony vocal
- **George Harrison:** Rhythm guitar, tambourine
- **Ringo Starr:** Drums, maracas

"She Came in Through the Bathroom Window" (1:52):
- **Paul McCartney:** Lead guitar, lead and backing vocal
- **John Lennon:** Acoustic guitar, backing vocal
- **George Harrison:** Bass, tambourine
- **Ringo Starr:** Drums, maracas

"Golden Slumbers" (1:31):
- **Paul McCartney:** Piano, vocal
- **George Harrison:** Bass
- **Ringo Starr:** Drums
- **Session musicians:** Twelve violins, four violas, four cellos, a string bass, four horns, three trumpets, a trombone, and a bass trombone

"Carry That Weight" (1:37):
- **Paul McCartney:** Piano, lead and chorus vocal
- **John Lennon:** Bass, chorus vocal
- **George Harrison:** Lead guitar, chorus vocal
- **Ringo Starr:** Drums, chorus vocal
- **Session musicians:** Twelve violins, four violas, four cellos, a string bass, four horns, three trumpets, a trombone, a bass trombone, and a bass

"The End" (2:04):
- **Paul McCartney:** Bass, piano, lead guitar, lead and backing vocal
- **John Lennon:** Lead guitar, backing vocal
- **George Harrison:** Rhythm guitar, lead guitar, backing vocal
- **Ringo Starr:** Drums
- **Session musicians:** Twelve violins, four violas, four cellos, a string bass, four horns, three trumpets, a trombone, and a bass trombone

"Her Majesty" (0:23):
- **Paul McCartney:** Acoustic guitar, vocal

Total time of all ten tracks: 19:09

What we really like about these songs

Steve: In order: The harpsichord arpeggios that open "Because," along with the song's heavenly harmonies; the piano part of "You Never Give Me Your Money"; the harmonies of "Sun King" (I'm not a big fan of the song itself, though); everything about John's rollicking duet of "Mean Mr. Mustard" and "Polythene Pam"; the chorus of "She Came in Through the Bathroom Window" (the "didn't anybody tell her" part); the piano part of "Golden Slumbers"; the horns in "Carry That Weight"; and absolutely everything about "The End," especially the dueling guitars and Ringo's drum solo.

Mike: The *Abbey Road* medley is the definition of the whole being greater than the sum of its parts. Some of these songs can stand on their own, but they just sound *so good together*. I like the harmonies, harpsichord, and Moog sounds on "Because"; the guitar riff that starts "Sun King," and its Spanglish lyrics; the chugging percussion on "Polythene Pam"; the lyrics of "Golden Slumbers" (thanks, Tom Dekker!); and every bit of "The End" (*especially* the guitar sparring). I could have done without the anticlimactic "Her Majesty," but knowing why that happened, I can accept it as a happy accident, and we know how the Beatles loved those. The medley perfectly brought the Beatles' recording career to a close, allowing them each to showcase their talents (even Ringo!).

[1] Most references to the *Abbey Road* "medley" begin the series with "You Never Give Me Your Money" and conclude with "The End," for a total of eight individual songs/song fragments. We have expanded the definition of the medley somewhat for this chapter, beginning it with "Because," and ending it with "Her Majesty." The pensive, anticipatory chord with which "Because" ends has always seemed to us to segue neatly into the piano intro of "You Never Give Me Your Money," and, for the sake of completeness, we have included the twenty-three-second acoustic ditty "Her Majesty" as well. We also had an ulterior motive by adding the two songs—we saved a ranking slot, allowing us to cover more songs!

[2] *The Beatles Recording Sessions.*

[3] Ibid.

Sexy Sadie

37

I like that tune. The words, that was John's concept of what happened to him...But even John was wrong some of the time.

—*George Harrison*
Entertainment Weekly, *1987*

Appearing as it does on *The White Album* between the manic and clanging "Everybody's Got Something to Hide Except Me and My Monkey," and the furious "Helter Skelter," "Sexy Sadie," for all its lyrical vitriol and bitterness, serves the listener as musical balm; a pleasant, melodic break from its bookends' ferocious intensity.

Why it made the top 100

"Sexy Sadie" made the top 100 because it's one of John's best songs, and one of the Beatles' best recordings. The song foreshadowed later Lennon solo works in sound and content (especially "How Do You Sleep?"), but unlike John's solo recordings "Sexy Sadie" benefited from, and was enhanced by, the collaborations of Paul, George, and Ringo.

Yes, it has become a cliché to state that *The White Album* consists of thirty solo songs, with the other Beatles constituting a backup band.

But damn: Has there ever been a more stellar assembly of "backup musicians" on any record, *ever*?

What the song is about

It would be a waste of time to discuss the *supposed* meaning of the lyrics of "Sexy Sadie"—that is, to talk about the singer addressing a woman named Sadie.

The working title of the song was "Maharishi." In *Playboy*, John said, "That was inspired by Maharishi. I wrote it when we had our bags packed and we were leaving. It was the last piece I wrote before I left India. I just called him 'Sexy Sadie.' Instead of [*singing*] 'Maharishi, what have you done, you made a fool of...' I was just using the situation to write a song, rather calculatingly, but also to express what I felt. I was leaving Maharishi with a bad taste. You know, it seems that my partings are always not as nice as I'd like them to be."

That's John being diplomatic.

There exists a tape in the EMI vaults in which John sings lyrics that express his *true* feelings about the guru: "You little tw*t/Who the f**k do you think you are?/Who the f**k do you think you are?/Oh, you c**t."

So what actually happened in Rishikesh that soured John on the Maharishi? Two things.

The first was the fact that the Beatles did not get what they had hoped they would from their sessions with the Maharishi.

Flautist Tom Horn (who was in Rishikesh during this time) said in *A Hard Day's Write* that the Fabs were taking courses with the guru designed for those who wanted to go on to become teachers of Transcendental Meditation themselves. The problem was that the four Beatles were not experienced enough in meditation and other enlightenment techniques to get much benefit from his teachings. Thus, they were disappointed. John especially felt cheated.

The second factor souring things was a rumor spread around the enclave that the Maharishi had made sexual advances toward an American girl with short blond hair. (This was not Mia Farrow, as many had presumed, but some schoolteacher from New York.) The rumor apparently wasn't true, but these two things inspired the Fabs to get back to where they once belonged.

John wrote "Sexy Sadie" immediately before leaving India, and its original version (as heard on *Anthology 3*) was slower and, well, *meaner*.

In the end, though, John felt that his time in India was worthwhile. In *The Beatles Anthology*, he said, "India was good for me and I met Yoko just before I went to India and had a lot of time to think things through out there. Three months just meditating and thinking, and I came home and fell in love with Yoko and that was the end of it. And it's beautiful."

• • • ❦ • • •

Did you know?

- "Sexy Sadie" is one of Julian Lennon's favorite songs of his father's. (His other favorites include "A Day in the Life," "Dear Prudence," and the Plastic Ono Band track "Isolation," which is his favorite John Lennon song.)
- At exactly 2:30 and 2:53, you can hear John whisper "Sexy Sadie" very softly.
- "Sexy Sadie" is the only Beatles song that includes the word *sex*—in any form—in the lyrics.
- Upon leaving Rishikesh, Paul commented to the press about the Maharishi: "He's a nice fellow. We're just not going out with him anymore."
- The song has been covered by Ramsey Lewis and Paul Weller (both instrumental versions).

The recording

Location: **Abbey Road Studios, London.**

Dates: **July 19, 1968,** 7:30 p.m.–4:00 a.m. – The Beatles recorded a rehearsal of the song in twenty-one takes, with lengths varying between 5:36 and 8:00. (The *White Album* track is 3:15.) The song's style varied, and included expletive-filled versions, bluesy versions, soporific, plodding-type ballads, and so forth. At the end of this session, John is heard on tape saying, "I don't like the sound very much for a kickoff. Does anybody?" The answer is not on the tape, but it must have been no, since they re-recorded the song on July 24.

July 24, 1968 – The song was remade, with twenty-three takes recorded, and the last one labeled the best. John was still not happy with the sound, though, and it would be back to the drawing board.

August 13, 1968 – Another remake, with eight takes recorded of the basic track—drums, piano, fuzz guitar, and lead vocal. The last take was called the best, and then given four reduction mixdowns.

August 21, 1968, 7:30 p.m.–7:15 a.m. – Three reduction mixes and overdubbing of another lead vocal, organ, bass guitar, two backing vocals, and tambourine. Five mono remixes.

October 14, 1968 – Mono and stereo mixing.

November 22, 1968 – First released on the U.K. LP *The Beatles* (The *White Album*).

Players/Instruments:

- **John Lennon:** Rhythm guitar, acoustic guitar, organ, lead and backing vocal
- **Paul McCartney:** Bass, piano, backing vocal
- **George Harrison:** Lead guitar, backing vocal
- **Ringo Starr:** Drums, tambourine

What we really like about this song

Steve: I get the sense that if John had lived and gone on to record "Free as a Bird" himself, it might have a sound similar to "Sexy Sadie." This is a quintessential "John Lennon" song that has always been one of my favorites. I love John's vocal, Paul's reverbed piano, and George's understated chromatic guitar riffs in the outro. I also really like the rapid-fire background vocal before the outro, "Sexy Sadie, she's the latest and the greatest of them all" (not to mention the switch from background "wah-wah"s to "see-see"s for the second verse). All in all, a great tune.

Mike: Before I ever knew what this song was about, or who the Maharishi was, I liked the song. Once I found out its meaning, I liked it even more. Much more than a not-so-thinly veiled attack on the Maharishi (who may or may not have done anything—I think John was just anxious to go back home to Yoko), I see this as a condemnation of any iconographic figure. John was particularly adept at knocking the establishment down a peg. The piano's at the front of the mix, John's in fine voice, and I especially like the somewhat comical background vocals. A nice midtempo musical interlude between "Monkey" and "Helter."

We Can Work It Out

In "We Can Work It Out," Paul did the first half, I did the middle eight. But you've got Paul writing, "We can work it out/We can work it out"—real optimistic, y'know, and me, impatient: "Life is very short and there's no time/ For fussing and fighting, my friend…"

—*John Lennon*
Playboy, January 1981

Beatle fans everywhere should be grateful that Jane Asher received a job offer in 1965 from the Bristol Old Vic Company in western England. At the time, she and Paul were dating and Paul was living in an upstairs room in the Asher family home in London. When Jane received the job offer, Paul became upset because it would have meant her having to move away. He wrote "We Can Work It Out," one of the Beatles' all-time most popular songs, as a plea to Jane to "think of what I'm saying."

Why it made the top 100

"We Can Work It Out," like "A Day in the Life," "I Want to Hold Your Hand," and the other definitive collaborative John/Paul songs, stands as a classic example of the best that could happen when John and Paul *truly* worked together. The song is simplicity itself—a guitar, a harmonium, bass, drums, and a tambourine. The harmonies are basic: two-part for the middle eight, and Paul's solo vocal for the rest of the song. The lyrics are conversational, and yet they are propelled by a sophisticated meter that transforms the words into poetry.

What the song is about

"We Can Work It Out" is about Paul's dismay over Jane leaving his side. The song is his attempt to stop the arguing and "work it out."

Other couples shout and argue when they have a problem; Paul McCartney writes a Number One song. (That recalls something John once said about their propensity for turning out hit after hit. "Let's write a swimming pool," he used to say to Paul.)

In the lyric, Paul is asking Jane to choose between their love and the new job. The first verse is somewhat threatening, in that he warns her that she's risking their relationship if she continues to see things her own way. The chorus resolves his frustration and, yes, anger, with the affirmation that "we can work it out."

For all its pleading and Paul's professed willingness to discuss their problems, though, Jane did, indeed, take the job some distance from London. And, ultimately, as we know, Jane and Paul broke up.

• • • ❧ • • •

- Paul performed "We Can Work It Out" during his appearance on a 1991 *MTV Unplugged* (which was later released as the CD *MTV Unplugged Official Bootleg*). Time took its toll on his memory, though, and he flubbed the lyrics, singing the verses out of order. Rather than continue, he stopped the band midsong, exclaiming, "Hang on, hang on, hang on. I only got the words wrong, didn't I? It's been a long time. But this is so informal, we'll start again!" And he did. And sang it flawlessly.

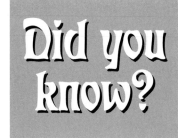

- The harmonium "wash" was added in the studio as an afterthought. George Harrison was the one who suggested changing the tempo to waltz (3/4) time (although it's done with half and quarter notes within the 4/4 tempo).

- "We Can Work It Out" was released as a double-A-sided single with "Day Tripper." But "We Can Work It Out" received more airplay in the United States. The week "We Can Work It Out" was Number One on the *Billboard* chart, "Day Tripper" was Number Ten. And yet they were on the same record! (Other songs in the *Billboard* Top Ten

Paul with Jane Asher.

that week included Simon and Garfunkel's "The Sounds of Silence" and the Byrds' "Turn, Turn, Turn.")

- A promotional clip was made for the "Day Tripper"/"We Can Work It Out" single.
- In addition to "We Can Work It Out," Jane Asher inspired other Paul songs, including "She Loves You" (which was written in the Asher home), "And I Love Her," "Every Little Thing," "You Won't See Me," "I'm Looking Through You," and the song that John considered his favorite of Paul's, "Here, There and Everywhere."
- There have been some interesting covers of "We Can Work It Out," including versions by Stevie Wonder, the Dillards, the Aranbee Pop Symphony directed by Keith Richards, Chaka Khan, Tesla, Exile, Frankie Valli and the 4 Seasons, Petula Clark, Hank Williams Jr., Deep Purple, Leslie Uggams, Mr. Fingers, Chucklehead, Disclocation Dance, Valerie Simpson, Killer Watts, Richard Anthony, and Dionne Warwick.

The recording

Location: **Abbey Road Studios, London.**

Dates: **October 20, 1965** – Two entire sessions (2:30–6:30 p.m. and 7:00–11:45 p.m.) of recording (two takes, second considered the best); vocal overdubs took the entire evening session.

October 28, 1965 – Rough mono mix. (This mix was made for the group to lip-synch to during the videotaping of the TV show *The Music of Lennon and McCartney*, which was scheduled to air in December 1965.) After hearing the playback, they realized the vocals needed more work.

October 29, 1965 – Vocal overdubs added, mono remixing.

November 10, 1965 – Stereo mixing.

November 10, 1966 – Stereo remixing for *The Beatles 1962–1966* (The Red Album).

Players/Instruments:
- **Paul McCartney:** Bass, lead vocal
- **John Lennon:** Acoustic guitar, harmonium, harmony vocal
- **George Harrison:** Tambourine
- **Ringo Starr:** Drums

What we really like about this song

Steve: I love the way Ringo just wails away on the drums, pounding a steady 4/4 rhythm, and George keeps up with him on the tambourine. I love the two-part harmony in the middle eight ("life is very short"). I love the sound of the harmonium, which foreshadows their later use of similar-sounding keyboards in "Being for the Benefit of Mr. Kite" and "Strawberry Fields Forever." I love the fact that Paul McCartney can write a long line like "run the risk of knowing that our love may soon be gone" and make it fit *perfectly* with his melody. And I love the fact that Paul uses the title of the song in both the lyrics ("We can work it out and get it straight, or say good night") *and* the chorus.

Mike: I like Paul's hopeful message in the verses and John's attempt to bring us back to reality with the trademark pessimism and doubt of his middle eight. I think this song is a classic example of how the Beatles were masters at creating pop music. It's a dialogue between John and Paul, accented by simple, clean instrumentation. (The harmonium adds a nice touch—it sounds almost like an accordion, an unusual sound on a rock song.) It was released during the group's songwriting heyday, a time when Paul and John were yinging and yanging with each other, playing off each other's strengths, and enhancing each other's songs. We can almost imagine them each keeping a notebook of snippets of lyrics, and stacks of reel-to-reel tapes and acetates filled with their unused pieces of music—just waiting to match them with something of their collaborator's… and the magic they made when the pieces matched.

39 Tomorrow Never Knows

Go far into the Void and there rest in quietness.

—*Tao Te Ching*

In "Tomorrow Never Knows,"

John offers departed souls two choices. The first is to become one with the void and escape the cycle of death and rebirth; the second, to continue on, be reborn, and "play the game 'existence' to the end."

John's lyrics were inspired by the Tibetan Book of the Dead. The music (and the overall vibe of the song) owed a debt to John's reading of Timothy Leary and Richard Alpert's *The Psychedelic Experience*, which discussed the Tibetan Book of the Dead, and, of course, to George Martin's and Geoff Emerick's willingness to experiment.

And ultimately, the disparate influences and elements of the song came together owing a debt to the mind-expanding properties of LSD.

Why it made the top 100

In October 2001, at the Concert for New York after the September 11 attacks, Paul McCartney (who performed at the concert) was overheard teasing a Beatles tribute band backstage, "Bet you don't do 'Tomorrow Never Knows'!" We bet Paul would have won that bet. (Although this is not to say that there aren't some Beatles tribute bands that tackle the daunting number. We found a review on the Internet of a band called the Australian Beatals that does a killer "Tomorrow Never Knows" as the encore at its shows—complete with a didgeridoo!)

Illustration from the Tibetan Book of the Dead.

"Tomorrow Never Knows" heralded—and, in a sense, defined—the era of musical psychedelia. The whirling, swirling tape loops fly and wreathe through the soundscape/landscape/wordscape of the song; Ringo's tribal drumming (of which he is justifiably proud) is hypnotic; George's sitar is otherworldly; John's "Leslied" voice somehow fulfills his wish that we would hear his words but not his voice.

"Tomorrow Never Knows" is, perhaps, even more awe inspiring when we consider that it was not only the fountainhead of the *Revolver* sessions, but also a confabulation of firsts:

- It was the first *Revolver* track recorded (although it is the last song on the album);
- It was the first recording session with engineer Geoff Emerick;
- It was the first time the Leslie speaker was used for something other than an organ;
- It was the first time the Fabs created tape loops individually and brought them in for assimilation into a track;
- It was the first time the Fabs had stayed out of the studio for a lengthy period (four months) and then returned to record new material, songs that had had time to "come of age";
- It was—by his admission[1]—John's first psychedelic song;

- It marked the first time an ancient religious book inspired a set of Beatles lyrics.

What the song is about

"Tomorrow Never Knows" is an instruction manual for the newly departed.

According to some religious philosophies and sacred texts (including the aforementioned Tibetan Book of the Dead), all souls are trapped in an endless cycle of death and rebirth. During the interim period between death and new life, however, the soul can apparently choose to eschew rebirth and "surrender to the void."

John's lyrics offer advice to the wandering soul ("turn off your mind," "lay down all thought," "surrender," "float," "listen to the color of your dreams," et cetera) and conclude with a summation of the consequences of the soul's ultimate decision: If you do choose to play the game of existence, the circular nature of the life cycle mandates that you will only play it "to the end of the beginning."

Life goes on. And "love is all."

• • • 🐢 • • •

- "Tomorrow Never Knows" was originally titled "The Void," then "Mark I."
- The title "Tomorrow Never Knows" came from a Ringo malapropism—he had intended to say "tomorrow never comes."
- The use of tape loops to add weird sounds may have been a first. George Martin, in *The Beatles Anthology*, recalled:

> "It was Paul, actually, who experimented with his tape machine at home, taking the erase-head off and putting on loops, saturating the tape with weird sounds. He explained to the other boys how he had done this, and Ringo and George would do the same and bring me different loops of sounds, and I would listen to them at various speeds, backwards and forwards, and select some…That was a weird track, because once we'd made it we could never reproduce it. Nobody else was doing records like that at the time—not as far as I knew."

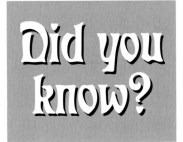

- The use of a Leslie for John's vocal (which begins at eighty-seven seconds into the song) surprised the hell out of everyone in the studio when it actually worked: Geoff Emerick, in *The Beatles Anthology*, recalled, "It

meant actually breaking into the circuitry. I remember the surprise on our faces when the voice came out of the speaker. It was just one of sheer amazement. After that they wanted everything shoved through the Leslie: pianos, guitars, drums, vocals, you name it." George Martin recalled John telling him "he wanted his voice to sound like the Dalai Lama chanting from a hilltop, and I said, 'It's a bit expensive going to Tibet. Can we make do with it here?'"

- At one point, John wanted to be hung upside down from a rope in the middle of the studio ceiling. He wanted a microphone placed on the floor below him and then to be pushed so that he swung around the mike in a circle while he sang. According to Geoff Emerick, "That was one idea that *didn't* come off although they were always said to be 'looking into it.'"[2]
- "Tomorrow Never Knows" has been covered by Phil Collins, Brian Eno (live recording), and Jimi Hendrix.

The recording

Location: **Abbey Road Studios, London.**

Dates:

April 6, 1966, 8:00 p.m.–1:15 a.m. – Three takes of the rhythm track were recorded (the second track was incomplete), with the third considered best. (This is the version on *Anthology 2.*) This was the first session with Geoff Emerick working as engineer.

April 7, 1966, 2:30–7:15 p.m. – Overdubbing, with a live mix of tape loops. (Some sources say as many as sixteen different loops were used.)

April 22, 1966 – Overdubbing of George on sitar and another Lennon vocal, this time put through the Leslie rotating speaker.

April 27, 1966 – Mono mixing of nine remixes, none of which was used on the finished album.

June 6, 1966 – The song was now officially known as "Tomorrow Never Knows." Mono mixing. At the eleventh hour, however, George Martin called Emerick and told him to go back to the *previous* best mono mix for the album.

June 22, 1966 – Stereo mixing.

August 5, 1966 – First released on the U.K. LP *Revolver.*

Players/Instruments:

- **John Lennon:** Vocal, tambourine
- **Paul McCartney:** Bass
- **George Harrison:** Lead guitar, sitar
- **Ringo Starr:** Drums
- **George Martin:** Piano

What we really like about this song

Steve: It has long been said that "Tomorrow Never Knows" is the Beatles song with one chord, specifically a droning C chord, typical of the type of Indian sitar music George had been listening to and playing for the other Fabs before the recording of *Revolver*. But this is a myth. Even a cursory listen to the song reveals a B-flat chord at the end of every verse. Granted, it's a processed overdub, and only played by the brass, but the movement to B-flat is definitely there. George Harrison discussed this in *The Beatles Anthology*: "Indian music doesn't modulate; it just stays. You pick what key you're in, and it stays in that key. I think 'Tomorrow Never Knows' was the first one that stayed there; the whole song was on one chord. But there is a chord that is superimposed on top that does change: It was in C, it changes down to B-flat. That was like an overdub, but the basic sound all hangs on the one drone."

Personally, I like this because it provides a sort of back-and-forth "rocking" of the melodic themes of the song, musically suggesting the rebirth/void choice espoused in the lyrics. "Tomorrow Never Knows" is, quite frankly, not all that easy to listen to, but that's irrelevant: This brilliant landmark song has been, and always will be, *must listening* for anyone seriously interested in twentieth-century music.

Mike: I remember early on, listening to *Revolver* and getting to the last song on Side One ("She Said She Said") and thinking it was strange. Maybe not so much the music, but the message. Even weirder was the last song on Side *Two*, "Tomorrow Never Knows." It was strange, but "strange creative" not "strange unlistenable"—and would we expect otherwise from the Beatles? It still commands attention, still carries tremendous weight. The song might as well be the theme song for Timothy Leary and his followers—it definitely promotes expanding one's consciousness. The fact that this was the first song recorded for *Revolver* really set the standard for the tracks that would follow. Many tape loops swirl in and out of the song, but give George Martin and Geoff Emerick credit: The loops don't overwhelm, but rather provide tasty spice to what otherwise might be an incessant drone. Ringo sounds like a human beatbox, banging away like a modern-day electronic drum machine, and Paul follows right along with him on bass. John's eerie, detached voice seems to take us to realms of metaphysical enlightenment, beyond the norm.

[1] *Hit Parader,* April 1972.

[2] *The Beatles Recording Sessions.*

Across the Universe

I was a bit more artsy-fartsy there.
—*John Lennon*
Playboy

One night John lay in bed with his first wife, Cynthia, and she irritated him by chattering on and on about something and then falling asleep. John couldn't stop hearing her words, and the first line of a song came to him and demanded to be written down—as did the remainder of the lyrics.

Interestingly, Cynthia does not mention this incident in her autobiography *A Twist of Lennon*, but she does include one of her own poems, the first two lines of which seem to have been influenced—in both meter and subject—by John's "Across the Universe": "Voices flit like shadows down the passage of my mind/They grow and fade in volume as the passing of the days."

Why it made the top 100

One of John's most important songs, "Across the Universe" tackles the universal themes he began to explore, albeit more narrowly, in "Because" and "All You Need Is Love." It is a pity that such a significant work was treated (according to John) with disdain, or at the very least apathy, by Paul.

It's a song in which John moved beyond personal relationships or nostalgic reminiscence into grander themes. It is righteous that a clean, *in-tune* version was finally released on the *Let It Be… Naked* CD.

What the song is about

The collection of nouns John chose for the lyrics of this song are a lovely combination of the *personal* (eyes, laughter, mind, thoughts, images, words); the *natural* (pools, rain, light, sounds, suns, waves, wind); and the *universal* (life, love, universe, world).

John was rightly proud of the meter and how the words flowed together. In *Playboy* he commented on the song's birth: "Such an extraordinary meter and I can never repeat it! It's not a matter of craftsmanship; it wrote itself. It *drove* me out of bed."

That said, though, what does the song *mean*? The precise meter of the poetry serves the narrative, which tells of the thoughts and experiences of a person meditating and achieving elevated consciousness and almost-perfect awareness. The key revelation comes in the second line of the second verse when he describes the joy and sorrow "drifting through [his] *opened* mind…" He then chants the mantra "*Jai guru deva…*" for the first time, which means, "thanks to the great teacher." Guru Deva was the Marahishi Mahesh Yogi's own personal guru, and his teachings obviously influenced John.

To us, though, the puzzling line in the song is "Nothing's gonna change my world," which, upon first consideration, seems to contradict the mandate of prayer and meditation: to change the world—and the self—for the better.

So, then, is "Across the Universe" a statement of defeat? Is John saying, *I am aware; I see all, but nothing's going to change the terrible real world in which I live?* Or is he saying, *I am one with the universe, and nothing dark or negative will change my world, which is the world of peace and love?* We opt for the latter interpretation, borne out by the line, "limitless, undying love… shines around me like a million suns…"

The singer of the song has achieved enlightenment and offers an account of his experience as an object lesson for those still mired in the negativity and pain of nonenlightened reality.

The recording

Location: **Abbey Road Studios, London.**

Dates: **February 4, 1968,** 2:30–5:30 p.m., 8:00 p.m.–2:00 a.m. – Six takes of the song were recorded. The first take was of the rhythm track, with John on acoustic guitar, Ringo on tom-toms, and George on tamboura, all of which was fed through the Leslie speaker. Take 2 included a flanged sitar intro by George, another acoustic guitar, and John's lead vocal. (This version can be heard on *Anthology 2*, although it's incorrectly cited as being recorded on February 3.) By Take 7 (there was no take numbered 3), the rhythm track was complete, and vocal dubs were added in the evening session. John retaped his vocal at slow speed so it would play back faster. John and Paul decided they wanted falsetto harmonies on the song, so they went to a group of fans gathered outside the studio and invited two in for a try. John was not pleased: "The original track was a real piece of shit. I was singing out of tune and instead of getting a decent choir, we got fans from outside…"[2] A tape reduction was made, followed by an overdub of backward bass and drums, which would be wiped and replaced by vocals during the February 8 session. They also experimented with several overdubs that didn't make it to the final version, including a fifteen-second take of humming that would be repeatedly overdubbed to fill the four-track tape, as well as a guitar sound effect and a harp-like sound, both of which were to be played backward. The tape was copied, and John took the copy home.

February 8, 1968 – An organ part by George Martin and a Mellotron part by John were recorded, but both overdubs were wiped in favor of John playing tone pedal guitar, George playing maracas, and Paul on piano. Engineer Geoff Emerick considered John's vocal "superb," but John was still unsure of his performance, as well as what else the song might need, so it was placed on the shelf. Mono mixing.

October 2, 1969, 9:30–11:00 a.m. – Sound effects of birds flying and chirping, along with children in a playground, were added from the EMI archives, and the song was speeded up. Stereo mixing.

December 12, 1969 – Released on a charity album for the World Wildlife Fund, *No One's Gonna Change Our World*.

January 5, 1970 – The song was remixed for the *Get Back* project to make it sound "less overdubbed." Glyn Johns mixed out the Apple scruffs, as well as the Beatles' backing vocals. Stereo mixing.

March 23, 1970 – Stereo mixing.

April 1, 1970 – Phil Spector removed selected sounds from the original tape, slowed it down, and overdubbed an orchestra and choir. Fifty musicians provided the overdubs, playing strings, brass, and choir. Tape reduction.

April 2, 1970 – Stereo mixing.

May 8, 1970 – Released in the United Kingdom on the *Let It Be* LP (this was released on May 18 in the United States).

November 18, 2003 – *Let It Be… Naked* was released worldwide.

Players/Instruments:

- **John Lennon:** Acoustic guitar, lead guitar, organ, vocal
- **Paul McCartney:** Piano
- **George Harrison:** Sitar
- **Ringo Starr:** Maracas
- **George Martin:** Organ
- **Session musicians:** Strings, brass, choir
- **Lizzie Bravo:** (a sixteen-year-old from Brazil who wanted to be an actress): Falsetto background vocals
- **Gayleen Pease:** (from London, studying for her A levels): Falsetto background vocals

What we really like about this song

Steve: I've always been a big fan of the sequence of chord changes John uses for the verses of this song. Yes, these changes are used in many other pop songs (including some Fabs tunes), but John employs them with skill and emotion for "Across the Universe" and avoids turning this popular pattern into a cliché. On the downside, I think the "Nothing's gonna change my world" refrain is twice as long as it needs to be.

Mike: Three producers, multiple overdubs recorded and discarded, four released versions, and none of them acceptable to its composer—"Across the Universe" deserved a better fate. I can imagine how frustrated John must have felt as the song he was hearing in his head just didn't seem to be coming to fruition in the studio. It's a lovely song, full of poetry concerning sustaining the purity of life. It's no wonder it wound up on a World Wildlife charity LP. (For the record, I prefer the version on *Past Masters*, although I'm not a big fan of John's speeded-up vocal.)

[1] *Playboy.*

[2] *Lennon.*

41 Lady Madonna

It's a bit sad when you have to wait for a ten-year-old record to come on the radio to turn it up.

—*Elvis Costello*
Crawdaddy, March 1978

It sounds like Elvis, doesn't it? No—no it doesn't sound like Elvis. It is Elvis—even those bits where he goes very high.

—*Ringo Starr*
The Beatles by Hunter Davies

According to Ringo, Paul does a jolly good Elvis impersonation in "Lady Madonna."

Later, Elvis himself covered "Lady Madonna," thus completing the bizarre, self-referential, nepotistic circle that is the World of Rock. Rock on.

Why it made the top 100

"Lady Madonna" is definitely a straight-on rocker, but it is also one of the Beatles' more interesting recordings, a track filled with odd sounds and swampy bass lines that can justifiably be described as "pure Beatles."

Paul admitted nicking the arrangement from an old song called "Bad Penny Blues," a George Martin–produced minor hit for Humphrey Lyttelton in 1956, but, as was *always* the case, the specific influences for the song were filtered through the unique artistic sensibilities of the Fab Four, and an innovative, yet foursquare kickass single was the result.

What the song is about

Paul was inspired to compose "Lady Madonna" by, of all things, a *National Geographic* photo caption.

While in New York to catch a Jimi Hendrix concert, the story goes, a woman asked Paul if "Lady Madonna" was about America. "No. As a matter of fact, it is not about America at all. I was reading *National Geographic* magazine when I saw a photo of an African woman with her baby, and the caption said 'Mountain Madonna,' and I said, 'She looks like a Lady Madonna.' That's really what started the song for me." Later, in a 1986 issue of *Musician* magazine, he said, "Lady Madonna's all women. How do they do it?—bless 'em—it's that one, you know. Baby at your breast—how do they get the time to feed them? Where do they get the money? How do you do this thing that women do?"

The lyrics, for the most part, bear out Paul's comments, with "Wonder how you manage to make ends meet" summing up the song's theme. But, as has been noted over the years, some of the lyrics are open to other interpretations. It has been suggested that the line "Friday night arrives without a suitcase," refers to our Madonna turning to prostitution to supplement her income. This theory is buttressed by the previous references to money and rent.

And what or who, specifically, is "creeping like a nun" on Sunday morning? Lady Madonna? Her Friday-night john? One of her many children?

These possible darker meanings do not detract from the song's main message, which is, in Paul's words, "How do you do this thing that women do?"

- In *The Beatles Recording Sessions*, engineer Geoff Emerick recalled, "We spent a lot of time getting the right piano sound for 'Lady Madonna.' We ended up using a cheaper type of microphone and heavy compression and limiting."
- The flip side of the "Lady Madonna" single was "The Inner Light," the first time a George song appeared on a Beatles single.
- At the last minute, "Lady Madonna" replaced the original version of "Across the Universe" as the single's A side.
- Saturday is the only day of the week not mentioned in the song's lyrics.

Did you know?

- During Ringo's remake of "Back Off Boogaloo" (on his *Stop and Smell the Roses* LP), Harry Nilsson sings lines from "Lady Madonna" (among other Fab songs, including "Help!" and "Baby You're a Rich Man").
- Paul's "Lady Madonna" is mentioned by name in one other Beatles song: "Glass Onion"—which was written by John.
- "Lady Madonna" was one of five Beatles songs Paul performed on his 1976 *Wings Over America* tour.
- The song has been covered by Apollo 100, Booker T. and the MG's, Elvis Presley, Eric Schoenberg, Fats Domino, James Last, Joan Osborne, José Feliciano, Little Junior Parker, Noel Redding, the Nylons, Ramsey Lewis, Rare Earth, Richie Havens, the Four Freshmen, and Union Gap.

The recording

Location: **Abbey Road Studios, London.**

Dates: **February 3, 1968,** 2:30–6:00 p.m., 7:00 p.m.–1:30 a.m. – The Fabs knew they were flying off to Rishikesh in a few days, so they wanted to finish a single for release while they were away. They recorded three takes of the rhythm track consisting of Paul on piano and Ringo drumming, using brushes, not sticks. In the evening session, overdubs were added to Take 3—Paul played bass, John and George played fuzzed guitars through the same amp, and another drum track was added. The first of two Paul lead vocals was also added. John and George added scat vocals while eating crackers. The cracker sounds were omitted in the remix stage.

February 6, 1968, 9:00 p.m.–2:00 a.m. – Overdub of second lead vocal, second piano, handclaps, "see how they run," and the middle eight in which John, Paul, and George imitated a brass section by cupping their hands over their mouths. (They later brought in a real brass section, but kept the vocals, too.) Mono mixing.

February 15, 1968, 4:30–6:00 p.m. – Mono remixing.

March 15, 1968 – First released as a single in the United Kingdom, backed with "The Inner Light."

December 2, 1969 – Stereo mixing for the *Hey Jude* album.

Players/Instruments:
- **Paul McCartney:** Piano, bass, lead vocal
- **John Lennon:** Backing vocal
- **George Harrison:** Lead guitar, backing vocal
- **Ringo Starr:** Drums
- **Session musicians:** Ronnie Scott (saxophone), Harry Klein (saxophone), Bill Povey (tenor saxophone), Bill Jackman (baritone saxophone)

What we really like about this song

Steve: I'm a big fan of Paul's vocal on this song, as well as his extraordinary bass playing. Also, the piano part is irresistible and the harmonies add a lot of fun to the recording's sound. Come to think of it, I like "Lady Madonna" more for its *sound* than its composition.

Mike: Just as the Beatles' music was becoming more and more complex, they released this single, which is, in a sense, them "getting back" to basic rock and roll. (Interestingly, this full-on rocker was backed by "The Inner Light," one of the group's most unusual yet quiet numbers.) "Lady Madonna" has a timeless quality, and it sounds as good today as it did thirty-five years ago. It has some nice touches, including Ringo's brushing, the fuzzed guitars, and the "real" brass layered on top of the "mouth brass" (glad they kept that part in). Listening to the stereo version with headphones, however, is not recommended. I found myself a little off kilter thanks to the piano playing so prominently in one ear!

Norwegian Wood (This Bird Has Flown)

When I first consciously heard Indian music, it was as if I already knew it. When I was a child we had a crystal radio with long and short wave bands and so it's possible I might have already heard some Indian classical music. There was something about it that was very familiar, but at the same time, intellectually, I didn't know what was happening at all. So I went and bought a sitar from a little shop at the top of Oxford Street called Indiacraft—it stocked little carvings and incense. It was a real crummy quality one, actually, but I bought it and mucked about with it a bit.

—George Harrison
The Beatles Anthology

John Lennon was open and honest about the writing of "Norwegian Wood (This Bird Has Flown)." When he was married to Cynthia, he was having an illicit, clandestine affair with what some say was a high-profile journalist, and he wanted the song to be about this relationship. He admitted, however, that he did not want Cynthia to find out about his affair (especially via a set of blatantly revealing lyrics), so he tried to couch the story in symbolism, metaphor, and vague language—and he did not completely succeed.

The lyrics of "Norwegian Wood (This Bird Has Flown)," when read with even a nominal attempt at understanding the true message, are not all that hard to get—the narrator did spend the night with a bird (whom he may or may not have been having an ongoing affair with), but he didn't actually sleep with her.

In hindsight, this is somewhat amusing. The legendary John Lennon, perhaps the premier musical artist of his time, the songwriter whose every utterance became the subject of study and deconstruction, was, at least briefly, nothing more than a paranoid husband afraid his wife would find out he was cheating on her.

We're sure John would today appreciate the irony.

139

Why it made the top 100

"Norwegian Wood (This Bird Has Flown)" was a groundbreaking song, both for the Beatles and for rock and pop music in general.

A sitar in a rock song? And no drums?

In the midsixties, the Beatles were experimenting with sounds and styles, and *Rubber Soul* was the album on which they manifested a more serious musicality after the unabashed more-or-less traditional pop rock of *A Hard Day's Night* and *Help!* (as well as the classic earlier stuff). The appearance of "Norwegian Wood (This Bird Has Flown)" was perhaps the most clear-cut evidence that the Beatles as artists had grown restless and were no longer content with what had been considered up until then to be traditional rock.

What the song is about

In an attempt to be obscure, John tells us in the opening lines of the song that he once had a girl, but wait: Actually, she had *him*.

What does this mean? A reading of the lyrics tells us what happened: He went to a girl's flat, she showed off her Norwegian wood furniture to him (but paradoxically, she didn't have a chair?), they sat on the floor, talked, drank wine, and then she said it was bedtime. She told him laughingly that she worked in the morning, suggesting he was not welcome in her bed, and the next line confirms this, as the narrator spends the night sleeping in the bathtub. So, does the line "she once had me" mean that she tricked him into thinking he was going to score with her, but in the end, she "got him" with her ruse? Had he been "had"?

He awakens the next morning alone—this bird has flown—so what does he do? He lights a fire. With her Norwegian wood furniture? Maybe. Paul McCartney has said that the last verse describes the narrator setting fire to the bird's house—although the earlier lyrics ("her room") suggest she lives in an apartment.

Was the narrator admitting he burned down her place out of spite for not sleeping with him? Or does the song actually end with this hapless soul sitting in front of a fireplace, looking around at his flown bird's good Norwegian wood furniture?

You tell us.

• • • ❧ • • •

- The original title was "This Bird Has Flown."
- Bob Dylan recorded a parody of the song, calling it "4th Time Around," and he included it on his *Blonde on Blonde* album. According to the November 23, 1968, issue of *Rolling Stone*, Dylan played the song for John in London and it made John uncomfortable, until he realized Dylan didn't mean any harm. Paul was the first to hear the Dylan song, on acetate. Al Kooper, the musical director on Dylan's album, told Dylan how much his song sounded like "Norwegian Wood," and Dylan said, "Well actually, 'Norwegian Wood' sounds a lot like this! I'm afraid they

Did you know?

took it from me, and I feel that I have to, y'know, record it."

- "Norwegian Wood (This Bird Has Flown)" has been covered by Acker Bilk, Cosmic Dilemma, the Kingston Trio, Buddy Rich, Hank Williams Jr., Herbie Hancock, Hourglass, Jan and Dean, Jazz Cafe, José Feliciano, the Mystic Moods Orchestra, Sergio Mendes and Brasil '66, the Spotnicks, Wayne Boyer, White Eisenstein, and the Ska Boys.
- It is one of only four Beatles songs that mention wine. The other three are "When I'm Sixty-Four," "Her Majesty," and "I Me Mine."

The recording

Location: **Abbey Road Studios, London.**

Dates: **October 12, 1965,** 7:00–11:30 p.m. – After much rehearsing, one take was recorded (the version heard on *Anthology 2*). This take was pretty similar to the final album version, but included more sitar. This take included a hokey "Good evening friends" sitar riff at the end.

October 21, 1965, 2:30–7:00 p.m. – The Beatles worked on a remake with three new takes recorded. The first take (Take 2 in the song's recording history) featured a heavy sitar intro, with no drums or bass; Take 3 started with an acoustic opening similar to the version on *Rubber Soul,* and was predominantly acoustic with two acoustic guitars, Paul's bass, and vocals from John and Paul. Take 4, with George's sitar returning, was ultimately decided upon as the album version. In Lewisohn's *The Beatles Recording Sessions,* session engineer Norman Smith remarked, "It [the sitar] is very hard to record because it has a lot of nasty peaks and a very complex wave form. My meter would be going right over into the red, into distortion, without us getting audible value for money. I could have used a limiter but that would mean losing the sonorous quality."

October 25, 1965 – Mono remixing.

October 26, 1965 – Stereo remixing.

Players/Instruments:
- **John Lennon:** Acoustic guitar, lead vocal
- **Paul McCartney:** Bass guitar, harmony vocal
- **George Harrison:** Sitar
- **Ringo Starr:** Finger cymbals, tambourine, maracas

What we really like about this song

Steve: I like the idea of combining a guitar and a sitar in the same song. (For some reason, it reminds me of the Clavioline and piano in "Baby You're a Rich Man"—the stark contrast between the two disparate instruments is quite compelling.) I like the two-part harmony and find it interesting that for the "she asked me to stay…" part, Paul takes over the main melody and John is relegated to singing harmony with him.

Mike: This song says so much yet so little. It's one of the more unusual Beatles songs, not only for the inclusion of the sitar. (Thank goodness it played a more "background" role in the finished song. George, admittedly, hadn't mastered it yet.) The song also has no chorus, no drums, and very few words. I love the ambiguity of the lyrics—was the "bird" a lesbian? Did they do anything? What happened when he lit a fire—was it pot, or did he burn the place down? And why was it good? I never get tired of this mature Beatles waltz.

This Boy

One of our 3-part harmony numbers. There were a lot of harmony songs around. Harmony in Western music is natural. Paul claimed that his father taught us 3-part harmony, but that's not the case from my memory. When you think back to early rock 'n' roll there was always stuff like Frankie Lymon and the Teenagers, the Everly Brothers, the Platters. Everybody had harmonies.

—George Harrison
The Beatles Anthology

Which came first: the scene or the song?

We all remember the sequence in *A Hard Day's Night* in which Ringo strolls around town, fooling with a camera and eating a stale sandwich as the melancholy strains of an instrumental "This Boy" play on the soundtrack. (Ringo once admitted that he was staggeringly hung over during this scene.)

"This Boy" was officially published with the subtitle "Ringo's Theme," so was it retitled after the scene, or was the scene shot to accompany the song?

Apparently the song was written first, and then George Martin arranged an instrumental version for the scene in the movie and subtitled it "Ringo's Theme."

Why it made the top 100

"This Boy" is one the Beatles' most memorable and recognizable ballads, and is one of the few honored songs that were given the full George Martin instrumental treatment. The song was an important part of the movie *A Hard Day's Night* and can rightfully be considered essential.

What the song is about

In "This Boy," our hero has been dumped by his lady love. Granted, the first line of the tune tells us that "that boy *took* my love away," suggesting some kind of hypnotic seduction of the young lady to which she had no resistance, but the reality is that it takes two to tango and his girlfriend did, indeed, agree to move on to "that boy."

The second line is a veiled threat: Someday, he'll regret what he did. The third line returns to the subject at hand, however: "but this boy wants you back again."

In the second verse, he attempts to reinforce his message by trashing the new guy: "that boy isn't good for you." He acknowledges that he may want her as much as our forlorn lover does, but too bad: I want you back and (the unspoken message proclaims) I *will* get you back.

The bridge begins with a simple declaration of his love for her, and then *really* slams the interloper by promising her that he will undoubtedly make her cry (and smile while he's doing it).

The final verse assures her that if she comes back to him, he will not throw it up to her, and that he will always feel the same toward her. He won't mind the pain, if he gets her back again.

"This Boy" is a tight, evocative rendering of a story many, *many* people experience at some point during their romantic lives.

- The song was written by John and Paul in a hotel bedroom as an exercise in three-part harmony, which they had never attempted before. It was inspired by Smokey Robinson and the Miracles. In the November 1987 issue of *Musician* magazine, George Harrison commented, "If you listen to the middle eight of 'This Boy,' it was John trying to *do* Smokey." John and Paul became familiar with three-part harmony from the Teddy Bears' Phil Spector–arranged song "To Know Him Is to Love Him," as well as from songs by the Everly Brothers.

- At precisely twenty seconds into the song, in the line "Though he'll regret it someday," John sings the word *though* all by himself. The harmonies don't come in until the word *he'll*. Since all the verses are sung in rich, three-part harmony, was this a mistake, or was it intended? The official sheet music for the song reads, "*Oh*, he'll regret it someday," although John definitely sings "though."

- The March 1, 2001, issue of *Rolling Stone* revealed that at one point George Harrison suggested having the bridge switch into waltz time.

- Kinks leader Ray Davies, in the March 1, 2001, issue of *Rolling Stone*, said about "This Boy": "You've got suspended chords—they suspend and pedal away. And that wonderful harmonium sound gives it a sort of religious quality." (For the record, there is no harmonium in the recording. We believe Davies is referring to the choir-like harmonies in the song.)

- In 1971, Stevie Wonder did a cover version that reached Number Thirteen on the charts.

Did you know?

The recording

Location: **Abbey Road Studios, London.**

Dates: **October 17, 1963** – This song was the first time the Fabs used Abbey Road's new four-track recording equipment. Technically, it is one of their superior songs. They recorded fifteen takes this day. Takes 16 and 17 were overdubs. There were some differences in the takes—the middle eight originally featured a guitar solo, and, like other Beatles songs of the time, it originally had a full ending. The final version was given a fade-out.

October 21, 1963 – Mono mixing, remixing, and editing.

November 10, 1963 – Remixing for the greatest hits LP.

November 29, 1963 – The song is first released as the B side of the "I Want to Hold Your Hand" single.

Players/Instruments:
- **John Lennon:** Acoustic guitar, lead vocal
- **Paul McCartney:** Bass, harmony vocal
- **George Harrison:** Lead guitar, harmony vocal
- **Ringo Starr:** Drums

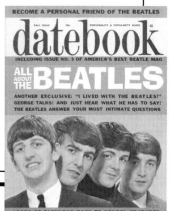

What we really like about this song

Steve: I am a big fan of the three-part harmony in this song, and I think it quite effectively foreshadows the harmonies that would come later in "Because" on *Abbey Road*. When the three singing Beatles (we'll respectfully exempt Ringo here) sing the kind of close harmonies they do in "This Boy" (and, later, in "Because"), their individual voices are a little difficult to make out, such is the perfect meshing of their tonality. They truly become greater than the sum of their parts. I also think that John's solo bridge in this song is one of his all-time best—filled with raw and powerful emotion that contrasts strikingly with the stately harmonies.

Mike: To me, the jangling guitar is reminiscent of the ubiquitous love ballads of the fifties. I also like the song's message—I may have lost you, but I treat you better than he does and I will get you back again (maybe because I was often jilted and heartbroken growing up, and yet I was always convinced that I was better than "the other guy"!). This song illustrates the Beatles' exemplary songwriting skills, even this early in their careers.

44

Sgt. Pepper's Lonely Hearts Club Band

*I started thinking about what we
would be with names like "Laughing
Joe and His Medicine Band" or
"Colonel Tucker's Medicinal Brew
and Compound"; all that old Western
going-round-on-wagons stuff, with
long rambling names. And so, in the
same way that in "I Am the Walrus"
John would throw together "choking
smokers" and "elementary penguin,"
I threw those words together: "Sgt.
Pepper's Lonely Hearts Club Band."*

—Paul McCartney
The Beatles Anthology

And so it began.
The unexpected sounds we
heard upon first placing needle to vinyl heralded the timeless
songs to come, beginning with this musical welcome to the
Sgt. Pepper concert. There were surprises aplenty in store,
in particular the first line—"it was twenty years ago today."
Excuse us? Considering the fact that John, Paul, George, and
Ringo were born in, respectively, 1940, 1942, 1943, and 1940,
we were puzzled, intrigued, and excited.

So what did we do?

We all sat back and let the evening go. And it did.

Why it made the top 100

This is the leadoff, title song of the album ranked the greatest
album of all time in many polls and by many critics and fans.
It is the *Pepper* fountainhead. It was not only necessary to
include it in this ranking, it was our sacred musical duty.

What the song is about

This is, perhaps, the most straightforward of all Beatles songs.
There can be no doubt about its meaning: The lyrics introduce
a band named Sgt. Pepper's Lonely Hearts Club Band. In
both the main song and the reprise, the words are obvious:
An announcer tells the audience a little about the group
("they've been going in and out of style...," et cetera), and
then the band members step up, introduce themselves, and
express their delight at being given the opportunity to play
for the "lovely audience" ("it's wonderful to be here...").

The reprise expresses the band's hope that the audience
enjoyed the show and thanks them for coming. They return
for an encore ("A Day in the Life"), and then the curtain
falls.

• • • ❦ • • •

- Paul and some of the others (Fabs and non-Fabs alike)
  went to see Jimi Hendrix in concert in London on
  Sunday, June 4, 1967. Jimi opened his show with a *smokin'*
  rendition of "Sgt. Pepper's Lonely Hearts Club Band."
  The *Sgt. Pepper* album had been released *the previous
  Thursday*—only three days before Jimi's concert—and
  Jimi had already learned the song and thought enough of
  the tune to open his show with it.

- John never considered *Sgt. Pepper* a "concept album":
  "*Sgt. Pepper* is called the first concept album, but it doesn't
  go anywhere. All my contributions to the album have
  absolutely nothing to do with this idea of Sgt. Pepper and
  his band; but it works 'cause we *said* it worked, and that's
  how the album appeared. But it was not as put together as
  it sounds, except for Sgt. Pepper introducing Billy Shears
  and the so-called reprise. Every other song could have
  been on any other album."[1]

- George—who did, after all, have only one song on the
  album—was not all that into Paul's concept: "I felt we
  were just in the studio to make the next record, and Paul
  was going on about this idea of some fictitious band. That
  side of it didn't really interest me, other than the title song
  and the album cover."[2]

- The origin of the *Sgt. Pepper* name is disputed. Mal
  Evans is sometimes cited as having created it as a jokey

substitute for *salt 'n' pepper*. Others say it was derived from the popular soda Dr Pepper, and that the Beatles would have used *Dr.* instead of *Sgt.* but were concerned about the possible legal issues.

- According to Derek Taylor (in his book *It Was 20 Years Ago Today*), it was Neil Aspinall's idea to segue the "Sgt. Pepper" reprise into "A Day in the Life."
- "Sgt. Pepper" is mentioned in the opening line of John's scathingly anti-Paul solo song "How Do You Sleep?"
- Two seconds into the beginning of the reprise, John can be heard saying, "Byeee."
- In an interview with *Playboy*, to give an example of the type of band name they were mimicking with *Sgt. Pepper*, John came up with "Fred and His Incredible Shrinking Grateful Airplanes."
- Paul, George, and Ringo performed "Sgt. Pepper" live at Eric Clapton and Patti Boyd's wedding reception on Saturday, May 19, 1979.
- The song has been covered by Jimi Hendrix and Bill Cosby.

The recording

Location: **Abbey Road Studios, London**.
Dates: **February 1, 1967,** 7:00 p.m.–2:30 a.m. – Nine takes (only two of them complete) of the rhythm track were recorded, consisting of echoed drums, bass, and George and Paul playing guitar. Paul's bass was played directly into the console, as opposed to through an amplifier. Geoff Emerick recalled, "John came up to the control room one day and asked if we could possibly inject his voice directly into the console. George [Martin] replied 'Yes, if you go and have an operation. It means sticking a jackplug into your neck!'"[3]

February 2, 1967, 7:00 p.m.–1:45 a.m. – Paul's lead vocal and the group's backing vocals were overdubbed onto Take 9 of previous day's work. A tape reduction was made, then a rough mono remix.

March 3, 1967 – Four French horn players overdubbed their parts based on what Paul hummed to them. Once the brass was finished, George recorded a heavily distorted guitar solo.

March 6, 1967, 7:00 p.m.–12:30 a.m. – To suggest a "live performance" atmosphere, they overdubbed sounds from Abbey Road's archives—Volume 6: *Applause and Laughter*, and Volume 28: *Audience Applause and Atmosphere, Royal Albert Hall and Queen Elizabeth Hall*—as well as the sound of the "A Day in the Life" orchestra warming up. They also added audience screams (for the reprise), taken from tapes of the Beatles' live performance at the Hollywood Bowl. Mono and stereo mixing.

April 1, 1967, 7:00 p.m.–6:00 a.m. (reprise) – This hurried session was to be Paul's last for the album. He was set to fly to the United States on April 3, and they had promised dates for the album. Nine takes were recorded of the rhythm track, with Paul providing a guide vocal. (Take 5, featuring Paul's rather "nonchalant" guide vocal, can be heard on *Anthology 2*.) The ninth take was considered best, and then all four Fabs shared lead vocals on an overdub. The track would ultimately include drums, guitar, organ, bass, various percussion instruments, vocals, and more audience sounds. Geoff Emerick commented, "I think the reprise version of the song is more exciting than the first cut of 'Sgt. Pepper.' There's a nice quality about it. We recorded the Beatles in the huge Abbey Road number one studio which was quite hard because of the acoustics of the place. It's difficult to capture the tightness of the rhythm section in there."[4] Mono mixing.

April 20, 1967 (reprise) – Stereo mixing.

June 1, 1967 – First released on the U.K. LP *Sgt. Pepper's Lonely Hearts Club Band*.

Players/Instruments:
- **Paul McCartney:** Bass, lead vocal
- **John Lennon:** Lead guitar, backing vocal
- **George Harrison:** Lead guitar, backing vocal
- **Ringo Starr:** Drums
- **George Martin:** Organ
- **Session musicians:** Four French horns

Reprise:
- **Paul McCartney:** Bass, lead vocal
- **John Lennon:** Lead guitar, maracas, lead vocal
- **George Harrison:** Lead guitar, lead vocal
- **Ringo Starr:** Drums

What we really like about this song

Steve: I have always loved songs that begin with a pounding backbeat. Both the main song and the reprise are downright *exciting*, and they do a terrific job of bookending the album's other classic songs. I also like the "extra added attractions": the French horns, the audience sounds, and the applause.

Mike: Could there have been a *Sgt. Pepper* concept *album* if there hadn't been a "Sgt. Pepper" song? Maybe, but it wouldn't have been as much fun, or as revolutionary. True, the song is just your typical rock song and, as John said, there wasn't much of a concept, but the opening song works as an opening of the curtain for the aural wonders that follow. Moreover, the faster-tempo reprise serves as the perfect intro to the Beatles' greatest song.

[1] *Playboy.*

[2] *The Beatles Anthology.*

[3] *The Beatles Recording Sessions.*

[4] *Ibid.*

Taxman

"Taxman" was when I first realized that even though we had started earning money, we were actually giving most of it away in taxes; it was and still is typical. Why should this be so? Are we being punished for something we have forgotten to do?

—George Harrison
I Me Mine

George Harrison never made the kind of money as a Beatle that John and Paul did. He earned performance fees and royalties on the albums, of course, but Paul and John also had publishing income coming in. All those Lennon/McCartney songs earned *huge*, and they continue to earn (and fatten Michael Jackson's pockets) today. Thus, it is completely understandable why, in "Taxman," George would rail against Britain's confiscatory 95.6 percent income tax rate. (They called it a "supertax." What was so super about it?)

Prior to "Taxman," George's songs were all about relationships: "If I Needed Someone," "I Need You," "You Like Me Too Much," and so forth. "Taxman" ushered in an era of more self-aware songs—and for George, this meant looking at living in the material world, as well at the committed search for enlightenment and higher consciousness.

Why it made the top 100

"Taxman" was George's best song to date when it was released on *Revolver*. His *Help!* songs were great fun, and quite competent in craft and production, but there was something immediately recognizable about "Taxman"; something that said George had become a better all-around songwriter. There is a new sheen of sophistication to the piece. (We do not feel similarly, however, about George's other contribution to that groundbreaking album, "Love You To.")

Unlike John's later call for a social revolution, however, George's was for a more practical type of rebellion: Don't take all our money, Mr. Wilson and Mr. Heath. As John said in *The Beatles Anthology*, "'Taxman' was an anti-Establishment tax song… At the time, we weren't aware of the whole tax scene. I'm still not really aware of what goes on with taxes. We believe that if you earn it, you may as well keep it, unless there's a communal or Communist or real Christian society. But while we're living in this, I protest against paying the Government what I have to pay them."

What the song is about

The meaning of "Taxman" is as plain as the ten-bob note up your nose: Taxes are too high. Americans gripe about a 33 percent tax rate, but we have never experienced anything close to the rates the Fabs were paying in the sixties. (No wonder so many British rock stars move to Monaco or California!)

George's lyrics are, at the same time, bitter and funny. The purported proclamations from the "Taxman" boast of taxing the street, your seat, the heat, and your feet. And if that doesn't get the point across, George advises us in the final verse to declare the pennies on our dead eyes, too.

- In the song's lyrics, British prime minister Harold Wilson and Edward Heath, leader of the opposition, are mentioned, the first living people (other than the Beatles themselves) to be named in a Beatles song.
- In *I Me Mine*, George reproduced some handwritten, unused lines: "You may work hard trying to get some bread/You won't make out before your [sic] dead/cos I'm the tax-man/so give in to conformity." Also: "Now what I let you keep for free/ Won't take long to get back to me."
- Money Matters: When Brian Epstein was alive and managing the group, he would keep whatever funds they earned and pay the lads wages. When the boys started earning serious money, Brian offered them a deal whereby they would each receive fifty pounds a week for life, and he would keep the rest. George said, "We thought, 'No, we'll risk it, Brian. We'll risk everything a bit more than fifty pounds a week.'"[1]

Did you know?

- John helped George with the lyrics to "Taxman," and he was upset that George never acknowledged him in *I Me Mine*.
- When George toured Japan December 1–18, 1991, backed by Eric Clapton and his band, he performed an extended version of "Taxman" that was twice as long as the original. He added extra warnings from the Taxman: "If you get ahead, I'll tax your hat/If you get a pet, I'll tax your cat/If you wipe your feet, I'll tax your mat/If you're overweight, I'll tax your fat." George also mentioned the names of more contemporary politicians such as Mr. Yeltsin, Mr. Major, and Mr. Bush.
- The song has been covered by Black Oak Arkansas and Stevie Ray Vaughn. Also, Tom Petty and the Heartbreakers performed "Taxman" live at the 2002 "Concert for George."

Location: **Abbey Road Studios, London.**

Dates: **April 20, 1966** – Four takes of the rhythm track were recorded, but only two were complete. After the fourth take, the group had a discussion (on tape) as to how the song could be better structured. The song was remade the next day.

April 21, 1966, 2:30 p.m.–12:50 a.m. – Eleven takes were recorded—the first ten of the rhythm track, with vocals introduced on Take 11. (This is the version on *Anthology 2*. It is different from the *Revolver* version. Instead of the Wilson/Heath lines, John and Paul sing, three times, a rapid-fire "Anybody gotta bit of money?" It also had a "stop" ending consisting of three guitar strums rather than a repeated guitar solo and a fade.)

April 22, 1966 – Reduction mix. Overdub of a cowbell and the Wilson/Heath line.

April 27, 1966 – Mono mixing. This mix was never used.

May 16, 1966 – Overdub of the "One-two-three-four" count-in. Mono mixing.

August 5, 1966 – First released on the U.K. LP *Revolver*.

Players/Instruments:
- **George Harrison:** Lead guitar, lead vocal
- **Paul McCartney:** Bass, lead guitar solo, backing vocal
- **John Lennon:** Tambourine, backing vocal
- **Ringo Starr:** Drums

Note: The logs do not tell who played the cowbell. It was probably either John or Ringo.

What we really like about this song

Steve: Yes, this is George's song, but it is Paul who truly shines here. (In fact, if you listen carefully to George's count-off at the beginning of the song, you'll hear Paul in the background doing the *real* count-off!) Paul's bass part here is an integral part of the song. His bouncy riff moves things along, and I can't imagine the track without it. His blistering guitar solo, with its Indian-inspired phrases and bent string accents, was as surprising to many of us as the Fabs opening an album with a faux live song start. I also love the harmonies throughout the song. George may not have been given many slots on Beatles albums, but when he came in with something worthy, the other Fabs treated it with the same care and attention they gave Lennon/McCartney tunes.

Mike: Nice to see a George song lead off *Revolver*. It deserved prominent placement: It's a scorcher with a seething message. There's a lot to like about "Taxman": the comic count-in, the distorted rhythm guitar sounds, and the way Paul taps out the notes on his bass, making it sound like another percussion instrument. Not to mention Paul stepping in to deliver a brief but explosive guitar solo. I always loved the lines warning how everything is subject to tax: "If you try to sit, I'll tax your seat; if you take a walk, I'll tax your feet!" All due respect to George, but I have to believe that those sarcastic lines came about with a little help from John

[1] *The Beatles Anthology.*

If I Fell

That's my first attempt at a ballad proper.

—John Lennon
Playboy

This was our close-harmony period.
—Paul McCartney
Playboy, *December 1984*

The movie

A *Hard Day's Night* has a great soundtrack, consisting mainly of classic Beatles rockers, but the movie and the album also boasted two ballads that are among John and Paul's finest work: "And I Love Her" and "If I Fell"—two songs that were released as the A and B sides of a single. Imagine! Two ballads on the same 45! In 1964, the Fabs were so hot, it never occurred to anyone that there wasn't a balancing "fast" song on either side of the single.

And it didn't matter one bit, either.

Why it made the top 100

Although released as a B side, "If I Fell" is the superior song of the "And I Love Her"/"If I Fell" dyad and is, thus, rated (slightly) higher. (See song number 48.)

The song is quite the piece of work, and John's songwriting is musically sophisticated. The introduction is a tour de force of chord changes that, on first glance, would seem to be the essence of discord and disharmony. The song is in the key of D and yet the first chord is an E-flat minor? Yep. One wonders how long it took John to work out the melody and chord changes for the seemingly simply eight-bar opening. The home key doesn't show up until the first verse, but by then we're sucked in and wide-eyed at John's intricate changes.

The song proper, as John acknowledged, is a sequence of simple chord changes, but even within such a traditional form, he injects surprising melodic nuances, including diminished and ninth chords.

"If I Fell" is a superb ballad with superb harmonies and a sublime production that epitomizes the notion of artists being so good that they make it look easy.

What the song is about

The strummed and drumless introduction to "If I Fell" is an admission of doubt.

The singer obviously wants to embark on a new romance, but he's not sure that he won't get hurt. In the intro, he explains his concerns: "I've been in love before…," suggesting that he knows and understands the pitfalls of relationships, but has been so wounded that he feels the need to bluntly ask her: "Would you *promise* to be true?"

He concludes the intro with the declaration that he now knows that love is more than just holding hands—a quantum leap of emotional growth from the previous year's "I Want to Hold Your Hand."

The first verse continues the "negotiations." He insists on being sure "from the very start" that this new object of his attention will "love me more than her," admitting for the first time in the song that if she meets his terms, he will leave someone else for her.

The next verse reveals trouble in paradise: He begs her not to "hurt my pride like her," honestly admitting that he wouldn't be able to take the pain. How did the one he's currently with hurt his pride? We're not told.

The song wraps up with the wistful wish that he hopes their new love won't be "in vain," along with a comment that has more than a touch of gloating in it: She will be sad "when she learns we are two." *That'll show her,* the subtext whispers gleefully.

Musically, John felt that "If I Fell" foreshadowed "In My Life." Even if that's true, there can be no denying that thematically, it's closer in spirit to "Norwegian Wood" (see song number 42).

- John considered "If I Fell" the precursor to "In My Life." (See song number 7.) In *Playboy*, he explained his thinking: "It has the same chord sequences as 'In My Life': D and B minor and E minor, those kind of things. And it's semiautobiographical, but not consciously. It shows that I wrote sentimental love ballads, silly love songs, way back when."
- "If I Fell" is a love song, but there is no love interest in *A Hard Day's Night*; in order to get the song into the movie, then, John sang it to Ringo. In 1964, Paul explained how it happened: "We're in the television studio and Ringo is supposed to be sulking a bit. John starts joking with him and then sings the song as though we're singing it to him. We got fits of the giggles just doing it."
- John's manuscript of the lyrics was auctioned at Sotheby's in London in early April 1988 for seventy-eight hundred pounds (about twelve thousand dollars these days).
- In a scene in the 1986 horror film *Poltergeist II*, Steven Freeling (played by Craig T. Nelson) and his wife, Diane (JoBeth Williams), sing a verse and a chorus of "If I Fell."
- "If I Fell" has been covered by Peter and Gordon, Adrian Belew, Keely Smith, Sonny Curtis, the Essentials, Lou Christie, and Gerry Mulligan.

The recording

Location: **Abbey Road Studios, London.**

Dates: **February 27, 1964** – Fifteen takes were recorded, with the song evolving as it went along. John and Paul sang on one microphone. A heavier drum sound from Take 3 was introduced at the suggestion of George Martin. John's acoustic opening first appears at Take 11, as does George's plucked lead guitar end piece.

March 3, 1964 – Mono mixing.

June 22, 1964 – Stereo mixing. Mono tape copying for the *A Hard Day's Night* soundtrack.

June 26, 1964 – First released on the U.S. LP *A Hard Day's Night*.

Players/Instruments:

- **John Lennon:** Lead vocal, acoustic rhythm guitar
- **Paul McCartney:** Backing vocal, bass
- **George Harrison:** Lead guitar
- **Ringo Starr:** Drums

What we really like about this song

Steve: The first time I heard "If I Fell" (through the screaming of a million teenage girls) was when I saw *A Hard Day's Night* at the Paramount Theater in New Haven, Connecticut, the week the movie was released. I was eleven years old, and I sat in the balcony with a couple of friends. I remember thinking, *Wow, that doesn't sound like "I Want to Hold Your Hand!" But man, is it beautiful!* Four decades later, I think the exact same thing.

Mike: I can't think of one John ballad that I don't like. Here, he shows his soft side, but with a hint of anxiety. This song has an interesting message—I'm considering leaving my wife for you, but you'd better swear your allegiance to me and be true. There's a sense of romantic angst, of hopefulness mingling with an undercurrent of trepidation. The melody is simple and elegant, yet boasts unique chord changes. I remember trying to nail the John harmony vocal when I was a kid. I could never seem to get it right. I still can't.

47 I Need You

We find George at his absolutely most vulnerable in this song… "I Need You" scores uniquely for its bittersweetly mixed tone of plaintive, terminal desperation.

—Musicologist Alan Pollack
Notes on *"I Need You"*

"I Need You" was an enormously important musical milestone for George Harrison.

What had he recorded before this *Help!* song? Only the *With the Beatles* song, "Don't Bother Me," his first recorded song.

Nothing of George's made it into *A Hard Day's Night*, although Paul and John did write "I'm Happy Just to Dance with You" specifically for him to sing in the movie. (In a September 1980 interview with *Playboy*, John said of "Happy," "That was written *for* George to give him a piece of the action… I couldn'ta sung it." See song number 87.)

Then came *Help!* and—surprise!—"I Need You," and suddenly George Harrison was seen not just as a backup guitarist for Paul and John, but as an accomplished songwriter.

"I Need You" is ranked below George's incredible classics "Something," "Here Comes the Sun," and "While My Guitar Gently Weeps," but only because those three songs are significantly more mature and skilled compositions.

As Hal Erickson acknowledged in the *All-Movie Guide*, "Harrison broke the Lennon-McCartney stranglehold… by writing the song 'I Need You.'"

Why it made the top 100

"I Need You" is a beautiful pop/rock/folk song that was notable for its use of a wah-wah pedal on George's lead guitar. The quality of the lyrics comes close to much of what Paul and John had come out with to this point; the music and melody are accomplished, and George's vocal is mellow and assured.

What the song is about

"I Need You" is told by a truly distraught guy to the woman who recently broke up with him.

The lyrics are quite blatant, and the singer is nakedly vulnerable as he addresses his ex in the first verse, telling her she simply doesn't realize how much he needs her. (Notice that there's a touch of hubris here: The very first line of the song piles on the guilt, the underlying message being, Because *I* need you, *you* should not have broken up with *me*.)

The second verse is a recap of the breakup. Apparently, he had no idea she was planning on breaking up with him. "How was I to know you would upset me?" he asks, in unmistakable pain. By now, we know that he was clueless to the difficulties in the relationship. It is also interesting that his main concern is himself—I did not know that you would upset *me*.

After she tells him that she "don't want my lovin' anymore," our hero is utterly devastated. He admits he can't go on anymore and, in the next verse, he tells us he can't live without her. No doubt about it: This young man is *depressed*. Is he suicidal? The language is pretty strong, but the focus remains on pleading with her to come back to him. He begs her to come back, he promises that she will see what she means to him, and the songs wraps up with a plaintive repeat of his present state of affairs in those three words: *I need you*.

What might happen if she says no? We don't know, because the song concludes as a plea for reconciliation, rather than a "postgame" suicide note.

• • • ❦ • • •

- "I Need You" was the first Beatles track to feature a guitar played with a foot-controlled wah-wah pedal.
- "I Need You" was written for Patti Boyd, from whom George was separated while filming *Help!* in the Bahamas. Contrary to many published sources, the song could not have been written *in* the Bahamas, since it was recorded on February 15, 1965, and the *Help!* Bahamas scenes weren't shot until a week later. It was the only George song featured in the film. (It is heard in the Salisbury Plain sequence.)
- On the Web site www.breakup-songs.com, "I Need You" was voted one of the 250 best breakup songs of all time.
- At the November 29, 2002, musical tribute to George at the Royal Albert Hall, Tom Petty and the Heartbreakers performed a stellar cover of "I Need You."

The recording

Location: **Abbey Road Studios, London.**
Dates: **February 15, 1965** – Five takes of the song were recorded in an evening session. The fifth take was considered best. The song was almost completely acoustic at this point.
February 16, 1965 – The Fabs overdubbed George's double-tracked lead vocal, a cowbell, and George's lead electric guitar played with a wah-wah pedal.
February 18, 1965 – Mono mixing.
February 23, 1965 – Stereo mixing.
August 6, 1965 – First released on the U.K. album *Help!*

Players/Instruments:
- **George Harrison**: Lead guitar with wah-wah pedal, lead vocal
- **John Lennon**: Acoustic guitar, backing vocal
- **Paul McCartney**: Bass, backing vocal
- **Ringo Starr**: Drums

What we really like about this song

Steve: This is one of George's finest compositions, and I've always been a little surprised that it never appeared anywhere but on *Help!* and that George didn't talk about it much in *I Me Mine*. John's acoustic work is excellent, Paul's bass equally so; the harmonies are classic Beatles; the wah-wah gives a signature sound to the song. With "I Need You," George proved he definitely had some game.

Mike: This is a quiet, understated George song. Interestingly (and somewhat puzzlingly), there's not a lot of scholarly commentary or recording information available on the classic Harrison track. The instrumentation is peaceful, almost soothing. It's a straightforward "lost love" song. George's singing is unstrained, as always, yet just as sincere as a Lennon rocker or a Paul ballad.

And I Love Her

"And I Love Her" is Paul again. I consider it his first "Yesterday." You know, the big ballad in Hard Day's Night. The middle eight, I helped with that.

—John Lennon
Playboy

The first song I ever impressed myself with.

—Paul McCartney

What's the difference between a mediocre, or even *good*, song and recording, and an unquestionably *great* song and recording?

Persistence.

On *Anthology 1*, we can hear an electric version of "And I Love Her," complete with a just-not-fitting drum part, a rushed meter, and an overbearing musical atmosphere. It just *wasn't right*, and the Fabs knew it. So they tried it again. And again. And again. Twenty agains, in fact, until they arrived at the perfect "less is more" version of the song.

Why it made the top 100

Was John right when he described "And I Love Her" as Paul's first "Yesterday"? We think yes, in that it is pretty close to a perfect ballad, and it boasts a level of musical sophistication heads above many of the moon/June/spoon love songs unleashed upon the music-loving public in any given year.

What a surprise it was upon first hearing the key change for George's guitar solo! The song could have easily continued on in the key of E (mostly C-sharp minor, actually); George's solo would have been a nice musical interlude. But instead, Paul moves gracefully up a half step to the key of F for the solo, thus highlighting it and grabbing our attention in a way that remaining "steady state" in the key of E could never have done.

Hell, if the song impressed Paul McCartney himself, how could we *all* not unhesitatingly concur?

What the song is about

There is nothing opaque about the lyrics of "And I Love Her." Our paramour is head over heels in love, and the song's lyrics are unequivocal: "I give her all my love"; "a love like ours could never die"; et cetera.

Our boy also seizes the opportunity to do a little innocent bragging: "And if you saw my love, you'd love her too." Wow. His young lady is so incredible that he is *guaranteeing* that anyone would fall in love with her at first sight.

Almost the entire song is a candid statement of love; the only detour into imagery is in the last verse, where the singer briefly waxes poetic: "Bright are the stars that shine, dark is the sky." (We cannot help but wonder if Paul veered into poesy simply to get the sky/die rhyme he needed for the last couplet.)

"And I Love Her" is a simple, beautiful, and evocative declaration of one man's love for his woman.

• • • ❦ • • •

- "And I Love Her" is 99 percent acoustic—the only electric instrument in the mix is Paul's Hoffner bass.
- Over the years, there was some speculation that "And I Love Her" was written about Jane Asher. This is not true, according to Paul. In 1984, in a *Playboy* interview, Paul said, "It's just a love song; no, it wasn't for anyone. Having the title start in midsentence, I thought that was clever. Well, Perry Como did 'And I Love You So' many years later. Tried to nick the idea. I like that—it was a nice tune, that one. I still like it."
- At precisely 2:10 into the song, we can hear someone "Dah Dah Dah" the guitar line. It sounds like Paul sort of unconsciously humming along, but there has also been speculation that it's George.
- The point of view of "And I Love Her" oddly changes during the song. For the verses, Paul is singing to someone else—"if *you* saw my love." But for the bridge—"A love

like ours…"—he is singing directly to his woman. This kind of shift is relatively uncommon for a ballad. Usually the point of view remains steady: Either he sings to someone else, or he sings to his lover. Rarely do the POV twains meet as they do in "And I Love Her."

- The song has been covered upward of four hundred times, including versions by Bob Marley and the Wailers, Bobby Womack, Chet Atkins, Christopher Clause, Connie Francis, Detroit Emeralds, Di Scherling, Esther Phillips, Gary McFarland, Georgie Fame, Jack Jones, José Feliciano, Julie London, Julio Iglesias, Keely Smith, Ken Dodd, Lena Horne, Michèle Torr, Nancy Wilson, Obo, Peter Nero, Pucho and His Latin Soul Brothers, Rahsaan Roland Kirk, Ramsey Lewis, Roger Williams, Ron San Filippo, Santo and Johnny, Shirley Horn, Smokey Robinson and the Miracles, Sonny Curtis, the Boston Pops, the Count Basie Orchestra, the Friends of Distinction, the London Film Orchestra, the Sandpipers, White Eisenstein, and Xavier Cugat.

The recording

Location: **Abbey Road Studios, London.**

Dates: **February 25, 1964** – Two takes were recorded, but only Take 2 was complete. (You can hear this take on *Anthology 1.*) The track featured drums, electric guitars, and a lead guitar solo in the middle eight.

February 26, 1964 – The Fabs remade the song, recording seventeen more takes. It was not easy going – Ringo traded his drums for bongos and claves (small wooden blocks), but they all ended up frustrated because they couldn't get the sound they wanted. When engineer Norman Smith announced Take 14, Paul replied, "Ha, Take 50!"

February 27, 1964 – They did another remake (Takes 20 and 21), with Take 21 considered the best. Ironically, later that day they were able to start and finish two complete songs—"Tell Me Why" and "If I Fell."

March 3, 1964 – Mono mixing, remix.

June 9, 1964 – Mono tape copying.

June 22, 1964 – Mono and stereo mixing.

Players/Instruments:
- **Paul McCartney:** Bass, lead vocal
- **John Lennon:** Acoustic rhythm guitar
- **George Harrison:** Acoustic lead guitar
- **Ringo Starr:** Bongos, claves

What we really like about this song

Steve: I love the all-acoustic, all-the-time sound; I like Ringo's bongo-ing and clave knocking; I like George's mellow guitar solo; and I especially like the fact that they did not gussy up the song with multiple harmonies, drums, or keyboards.

Mike: This sounds like a simple song, but it took them many tries to get the sound just right. It's nice to hear the early electric version on *Anthology 1*, but I'm glad they went with the pure acoustic version, which has a more distinctive and unusual sound than the typical Beatles rocker. You can imagine the pressure the boys were under to finish songs before they could begin film production on *A Hard Day's Night*. Listening to this song's classical guitar, understated percussion, and four-note riff, I'm glad they worked through the challenges.

A Hard Day's Night

I came up with the phrase "a hard day's night." It just came out. We went to do a job and we worked all day and then we happened to work all night. I came out, still thinking it was day and said, "It's been a hard day..." looked around, saw that it was dark and added..."'s night."

—Ringo Starr
A Hard Day's Write

There was no reason for Michael to be sad that morning, (the little wretch); everyone liked him, (the scab). He'd had a hard days night that day...

—John Lennon
"Sad Michael" from In His Own Write

There is some question as to the genesis of the title "A Hard Day's Night." It has long been accepted that the title was a Ringo malapropism, but it seems that John had previously used the phrase in his "Sad Michael" short story.

Our conclusion? It's Ringo's. Why? Because his story sounds quite credible, and it is unlikely that, even if he had read John's *In His Own Write*, that particular phrase would have stuck with him.

Coincidence? Probably closer to synchronicity, yet more undeniable evidence of Beatle minds thinking alike.

Why it made the top 100

"Based on… music and exuberant mood alone… the song 'A Hard Day's Night' arguably holds a place within the uppermost echelon of the Beatles catalog." So says musicologist Alan Pollack in his *Notes on* A Hard Day's Night. And he's right.

From the startling opening chord to Paul's soaring "when I'm home…" bridge, the song erupts with the excitement only the Beatles can inspire—and which we all first experienced with "I Want to Hold Your Hand" and "She Loves You." By the time the cowbell comes in, we're done for: We're all drowning in Beatle bliss.

Now, if we could only play that G7 sustained fourth chord that opens the song so that it sounds like it does on the record…

What the song is about

"A Hard Day's Night" opens with the singer musing that he's so tired from working his butt off that he should be sleeping. But the "things" that the love of his life does makes him feel all right and so, for now, he's going to remain awake.

In the second verse, he goes off on a bit of a complaining, chauvinistic rant: "You know I work all day to get you money, to buy you things." He then softens his tone and admits that it's worth it, because she's going to give him "everything." The key line "So why on earth should I moan?" is evidence of this man's realization that everything comes with a price.

The remainder of the song consists of him extolling the glories of his lover and proclaiming how wonderful he feels when he's home.

The equation is simple: Hard work equals domestic and romantic bliss.

Fast-forward six years. The Beatles are no more, and John and Yoko release their *Plastic Ono Band* album, with its incredibly bitter track, "Working Class Hero."

Being a Beatle obviously changed John Lennon in extraordinary ways. His evolution is conspicuous in the direct line from "A Hard Day's Night," through "I'm Only Sleeping" (*Revolver*), to "I'm So Tired" (*The White Album*), to "Working Class Hero": The glory of work is followed by inescapable exhaustion and laziness, and it all concludes with the horror of the class structure and the *meaninglessness* of work.

But in 1964, all John had to say was, "You know I feel all right." And he probably did.

• • •   • • •

- "A Hard Day's Night" was the last song written for the movie. Rejected titles for the film included *On the Move*, *Let's Go*, and *Beatlemania*.
- *Evening Standard* journalist Maureen Cleave was one of the first London journalists to write about the Beatles. She recalled John coming into the studio on April 16, 1964, with the "Hard Day's Night" lyrics written on the back of a card to his son Julian, who had just had his first birthday (Julian was born April 8, 1963). Initially, the lyrics were: "But when I get home to you, I find my tiredness is through, and I feel alright." Cleave told John she thought the "tiredness" line was weak. John took out his pen, crossed out the line, and wrote in the final version. Just like that.

- An instrumental version of the song, called "Another Hard Day's Night," is included on the Capitol Records soundtrack *Help!* Onscreen, the song is played by Clang's henchmen, who have abducted the "house musicians" in the Indian restaurant.
- The song has been covered by Peter Sellers (he speaks the lyrics, as if delivering a Shakespearean soliloquy), the Ramsey Lewis Trio, Otis Redding, Billy Joel, Chet Atkins, Count Basie, the Boston Pops, Henry Mancini, Johnny Rivers, Ella Fitzgerald, Quincy Jones, John Mayall and the Bluesbreakers, Billy Preston, Al Caiola, Keely Smith, Diana Ross and the Supremes, Dionne Warwick, and the Chipmunks.

The recording

Location: **Abbey Road Studios, London.**

Dates: **April 16, 1964,** 7:00–10:00 p.m. – Earlier in day, the Beatles filmed scenes from the *Hard Day's Night* movie (the chase scenes, complete with mock policemen). Nine takes were recorded; only five managed to make it to completion. The ninth take was considered best. (Take 1 is on *Anthology 1*.) The Beatles used four-track "technology" to the fullest for this song. They recorded the basic rhythm on Track 1, John's first lead vocal on Track 2, John's second vocal and Paul's backing vocal, along with bongos, drums, and acoustic guitar, on Track 3, and the jangling ending guitar and George Martin's piano on Track 4. George Martin, in *The Beatles Recording Sessions*, recalled, "We knew it would open both the film and the soundtrack LP, so we wanted a particularly strong and effective beginning. The strident guitar chord was the perfect launch."

April 20, 1964, 2:00–3:15 p.m. – Mono and stereo mixing. This tape was taken by the movie studio for the soundtrack.

April 23, 1964, 4:30–5:45 p.m. – Another mono remix, this time for the LP.

June 9, 1964 – Mono tape copying (for the soundtrack), and mono mixing, during which the song was given an extended ending.

June 22, 1964 – Stereo mixing.

June 26, 1964 – First released on the U.S. soundtrack *A Hard Day's Night* on the United Artists label.

Players/Instruments:
- **John Lennon:** Rhythm guitar, lead vocal
- **Paul McCartney:** Bass, harmony vocal
- **George Harrison:** Lead guitar
- **Ringo Starr:** Drums
- **George Martin:** Piano

Note: There is some dispute over whether George Harrison sang backing vocal. We don't hear him. (And while we're on the subject, we can't hear George Martin's piano, either. Is it buried so deep in the mix that it's essentially inaudible?)

What we really like about this song

Steve: I love how the Beatles can play one thing, and have it sound like something else. I've been listening to " A Hard Day's Night" for forty years now and its structure still befuddles me. The sheet music for the song has the first line sung under back-and-forth G and C9 chords. But if you play it that way, the accompaniment doesn't sound anything like the record. This is because John's melody line doesn't veer off a D note, so you feel like you never leave the home-key major chord—until you get to the F6 chord for "sleeping like a log." This is musical texture at its most arresting, making the song as fresh and interesting today as when it was first released. (And I do love that cowbell.)

Mike: This song is so familiar to me: I had four older siblings, so I was born listening to it. It always gets me from the opening chord, which is one of the most recognizable openings in rock music history. (Incidentally, I'm glad they edited out John's count-in to the song. Leaving it in would have been much less dramatic.) The song really has simple instrumentation, and is not very "extravagant," aside from the piano and guitar in the middle eight. The melody is in the vocal, kind of like Rod Stewart's "Maggie May." In the case of "A Hard Day's Night," what could be better than a song about coming home to the arms of one's lover after a hard day at the office? Always does wonders for me!

50 You've Got to Hide Your Love Away

That's me in my Dylan period again. I am like a chameleon, influenced by whatever is going on.

—John Lennon
Playboy

Paul's broken a glass, broken a glass, Paul's broken a glass, a glass, a glass, he's broke today.

—John Lennon
Anthology 2, *Take 5 of "You've Got to Hide Your Love Away"*

This is a rather sad song, and although the Beatles' performance of it in *Help!* is straightforward and (mostly) serious, one cannot help but find a bit of humor in the segment. The Alpine guy who plays the flute solo in the movie is the same bloke who had previously mowed the grass floor in George's area of the Beatles' apartment with two sets of toy windup teeth. And George's bemused expression while whistling the song's ending is anything *but* serious or sad.

Why it made the top 100

This ballad is one of the highlights of the *Help!* soundtrack and is John at his most acoustic (prior to "Norwegian Wood," which can be considered this song's descendant).

It's simple, yet well crafted, and the lyrics are some of John's most poetic. Plus the track boasts alto and tenor flutes—two instruments rarely heard outside a symphony orchestra, yet they fit beautifully in this elegant, elegiac tone poem.

What the song is about

The lad in this song is obviously depressed. The tune opens with him staring at the wall, mournfully moping, and fretting over the possibility that the departure of his lady love is imminent.

The second verse is our boy at his most paranoid. He sees (imagines?) people staring at him and laughing at him, and he hears them scolding him to hide his love away. Why? Are he and the woman he loves so obviously mismatched that even *strangers* advise him to restrain himself?

The third verse consists of more self-criticism. In the first line ("How could I even try?"), he questions the very notion of her loving him in return. The next line is Mr. Defeatist carping about his lot—"I can never win"—followed by an admission of his embarrassment at being so blatant about his passion for the unnamed object of his affection that others see "the state [he's] in."

The fourth verse is puzzling. He tells us that she has told him that "love will find a way." He himself is flabbergasted by this—"How could she say [this] to me?" Does this mean that she has rejected him and is trying to placate him by assuring him he'll find someone else? Or does it mean that he's so upset about everybody else's criticism of his love for her that she has to remind him that they're in love and, again, that their "love will find a way" (to get through this)? The last two lines, in which he calls the "mockers" clowns, is borderline masochistic: "Let me hear you say… ," he goads them. *Go ahead, rub it in,* he seems to be telling them.

There is no resolution in this plainspoken yet complex tale. The song ends with us not knowing if our lad is together with his love, nor what state of mind he is in.

Two of them riding nowhere?

- This song marked the first time the Beatles called in outside musicians to play an instrument that they didn't know how to play—in this case, flutes. (Andy White of "Love Me Do" doesn't count, because the group didn't call him in; George Martin did.)
- Longtime Lennon friend Pete Shotton recalled in *The Beatles Anthology* that "You've Got to Hide Your Love Away" was the first Beatles song composed in his presence. He remembered contributing the sustained "hey"s that introduce the main chorus. Also, he told the story of the lyric "feeling two foot small" instead of *tall*. "[W]hen he first performed it for Paul McCartney, however, John accidentally sang 'two foot small.' He paused to correct himself, then burst into laughter. 'Let's leave that in, actually,' he exclaimed.

Did you know?

'All those pseuds will really love it.'"
- "You've Got to Hide Your Love Away" was covered by the Silkie, a folk group managed by Brian Epstein. The Silkie version was recorded in early August 1965, and on it Paul played rhythm guitar, George played tambourine; the session was produced by Lennon and McCartney. The record hit Number Twenty-nine on the NME chart.
- The song has been covered by Oasis, the Beach Boys, Gary Lewis and the Playboys, Joe Cocker, Elvis Costello, Dino, Desi and Billy, Percy Faith, Jan and Dean, Barry McGuire, the Grass Roots, the Kentucky Headhunters, and Blue Rubies.

The recording

Location: **Abbey Road Studios, London.**

Dates: **February 18, 1965,** 3:30–5:15 p.m. – Nine takes of the song were recorded, but only two were complete. (The other complete rendition of the song, Take 5, is on *Anthology 2*, but it doesn't have the flute solos.) To Take 9, they added the flute parts, which were played by Johnnie Scott. In *The Beatles Recording Sessions*, Scott recalled the gig: "They told me roughly what they wanted… and the best way of fulfilling their needs was to play both tenor flute and alto flute, the second as an overdub. As I recall, all four of them were there and Ringo was full of marital joys, he'd just come back from his honeymoon." Scott was paid a six-pound session fee and did not receive sleeve credit.

February 20, 1965 – Mono mixing.

February 23, 1965 – Stereo mixing.

August 6, 1965 – First released on the U.K. LP *Help!*

Players/Instruments:
- **John Lennon:** Acoustic guitar, vocal
- **Paul McCartney:** Acoustic guitar, bass
- **George Harrison:** Acoustic guitar
- **Ringo Starr:** Tambourine, maracas
- **Johnnie Scott:** Alto and tenor flutes

What we really like about this song

Steve: The acoustic foundation of this song summons up for me an image of dozens of hands strumming dozens of acoustic guitars, seen through a fish-eye lens. This is a beautiful Beatle ballad, and one of my fondest memories of the song is watching a father-and-daughter team perform it live at a Beatles convention. The daughter just sat there on a stool on stage as her father played guitar and sang… until the very end of the song, when she reached down into her bag, pulled out a flute, and played the final solo note-perfect. The crowd, as they say, went wild.

Mike: Another Beatles "lost classic," one you don't often hear on the radio. It's a quiet, unassuming acoustic work, but what makes it stand out from other largely acoustic numbers (like "And I Love Her" and "If I Fell") is John's passionate vocal performance, accented by his admonition of "Hey!" before the chorus. I like its sparse instrumentation: The only percussion is Ringo's tambourine and maracas, and the flutes at the end wrap things up nicely. (Compare the *Help!* version to the flute-free version on *Anthology 2* and you'll hear what I mean.) My one fault with the song is that it could be a little longer, which is my one complaint with most of the Beatles songs I like.

Julia

One of the more surprising moments upon first listening to *The White Album* was the transition from Paul's upbeat, folk-rock "I Will" (see song number 30) to John's ethereal "Julia," which began, as did Paul's "I Will," without a musical introduction.

Paul started with "Who knows…" and John followed with "Half of what I say…"

It is a stunning moment of parallel musical messages: Paul is singing to a woman he has loved forever, telling her he'll wait a lifetime for her reciprocal love; John follows with a sad lament that he, too, loves the woman he is singing to, but he cannot reach her. "Julia" takes on even deeper meaning when interpreted vis-à-vis Paul's song, and when we consider the fact that the character of Julia is both John's mother and his wife Yoko (whom he routinely addressed and referred to as "Mother").

Why it made the top 100

"Julia" is a gorgeous acoustic number performed solely by John, which stands as one of his more heartfelt and honest compositions. It is beautifully performed and sung, and is powerful evidence of how independent each of the Beatles was becoming during the recording of *The White Album*. "Julia" is a solo John Lennon song, yet credited to Lennon and McCartney and released as a Beatles song.

Yes, the final days of the Fabs got strange.

What the song is about

"Julia" could rightfully be considered part one of a two-part message from John to his mother. Written when John was in India with the Maharishi, the song incorporates imagistic poetry ("seashell eyes," "sleeping sand," "floating sky") with heartfelt expressions of longing and sadness. He jabbers on meaninglessly to capture his mother's attention (as many children do); he cries out to her by trying to "sing my heart," but in the end all he can do is speak his mind. "Julia" is, in John's words, a "song of love" for his mother, Julia. He is the yearning son, wanting desperately to "reach" his mother, resorting to desperately spouting "meaningless" words half the time, in a futile attempt to break through to the woman who gave him away when he was five, to be raised by his aunt Mimi after Julia had another man's child.

There is no anger in "Julia." That would come later in "Mother." In that wrenching song from John's *Plastic Ono Band* album, he shrieks, "Mama don't go…" and tells Julia that he wanted her, "but you didn't want me."

For all its surreal, arcane imagery, "Julia" is one of John's most important autobiographical works.

- "Julia" has been covered by John's son Sean Lennon (performed live at the post-9/11 concert "Come Together: A Night for John Lennon's Words and Music"), Charlie Byrd, Raffi, Ramsey Lewis, Bongwater, Javier Solis, Los Muecas, Richard Dworsky, and Sting.
- According to Donovan, he taught John how to do the guitar fingering he used in "Julia." From *A Hard Day's Write:* "John would take particular interest in the finger-style guitar parts I was playing in my songs. He wanted to know the patterns I was using and I told him I would teach him. John was a diligent student and mastered the complex pattern in a few days. In common with most songwriters, learning a new style meant composing in a different way. In his deep meditation sessions, John had opened up feelings for his mother. He found release for these emotions in 'Julia,' the tune he had learned with the new finger style."

- In the *Playboy* interview, John explained the impact his mother's death had on him: "My mother was alive and lived a 15-minute walk away from me all the time. I just didn't live with her… She got killed by an off-duty cop who was drunk. She was just at the bus stop and he ran her down in a car. So that was another big trauma for me. I lost her twice. The underlying chip on my shoulder that I had as a youth got *really* big then. Being a teen-ager *and* a rock 'n' roller *and* an art student *and* my mother being killed just when I was reestablishing a relationship with her. It was very traumatic for me."
- Julia was more of a friend than a mother to John while growing up. She taught him the banjo, then the guitar, and encouraged him to play. The first time he heard "Rock Around the Clock" was during a visit to her house.

The recording

Location: **Abbey Road Studios, London.**

Dates: **October 13, 1968** – With a delivery date looming, this was the thirty-second and last song recorded and intended for *The White Album.* The was the first Sunday session since February 11, 1968, at which the Beatles had recorded "Hey Bulldog." The song was recorded simply on a four-track machine. The acoustic guitar and vocal were taped twice over. A total of three takes were recorded, with Take 3 being the master. The second take, which can be heard on *Anthology 3,* is mostly instrumental, as John tries to nail the guitar part. The song was immediately mixed for both mono and stereo. John was not alone at Abbey Road while recording "Julia." Paul was in the control room, communicating with him through the talkback key and offering advice. (Paul can be heard talking to John on the *Anthology 3* track.)

November 22, 1968 – First released on the U.K. LP *The Beatles.*

Players/Instruments:
- **John Lennon:** Guitar (double-tracked); vocal (occasionally double-tracked). This is the only song John Lennon recorded completely on his own while he was with the Beatles.

What we really like about this song

Steve: I like John's guitar work and his breathy vocal; I like the two-word haiku-like imagery; I like very much the double-tracking of both guitar and voice; and I like the mostly acoustic version of this song on *Anthology 3.* One gets a sense of just how much effort John put into making sure he played this song perfectly—and the final version is proof positive that he did, indeed, perfect it.

Mike: Knowing the events in John's life that inspired this song, it always touched me. Relistening to it while writing this book, its emotional pain struck closer to home for me. Having lost my own mother just as I was preparing to write this book, I feel a kinship with John in this loss we both shared. In this dream-like, often fragile, simple, and gentle song, John mourns his loss and celebrates a life. It contains the raw energy found in the best of John's songs.

Being for the Benefit of Mr. Kite

The whole song is from a Victorian poster, which I bought in a junk shop. It is so cosmically beautiful. It's a poster for a fair that must have happened in the 1800s.

—John Lennon
Playboy

What a way to end Side One of *Sgt. Pepper!* After we were all blown away by such instant classics as "With a Little Help from My Friends" and "Lucy in the Sky with Diamonds," along comes John's visit to a nineteenth-century circus, complete with a swirling calliope and a waltzing horse. "Mr. Kite" can quickly transport you to another time and place, and it's easy to imagine John as the derbied barker with a garter on his shirtsleeve, pointing the way with his cane into a tent where we will see all manner of wonders and rarities!

Left: The poster that inspired the song.

The recording

Location: **Abbey Road Studios, London.**

Dates: **May 9, 1966,** 7:00–11:00 p.m. – Ten takes were recorded, with the first nine being rhythm tracks only. Paul played piano and Ringo played drums. The tenth take was considered best, and on that one, Paul overdubbed a clavichord while Ringo added additional cymbals and maracas. (The clavichord was brought in by George Martin. The Beatles rented it for five guineas from Martin's company, AIR.)

May 16, 1966 – Paul overdubbed the lead vocal, recorded at forty-seven cycles to make it sound faster on replay.

May 19, 1966, 7:00–11:00 p.m. – The French horn solo was overdubbed by Alan Civil, the principal horn player in the London Philharmonia. Civil, speaking in *The Beatles Recording Sessions*, recalled, "George Martin rang me up and said, 'We want a French horn obligato on a Beatles song, can you do it?'…It was rather difficult to actually understand exactly what they wanted so I made something up which was middle register, a baroque style solo. I played it several times, each take wiping out the previous attempt." He added, "My friends would ask 'What have you done this week?' The day would almost go into their diaries as being the day they met someone who'd played with the Beatles… For me it was just another day's work, the third session that day in fact, but it was very interesting."[2]

June 6, 1966 – Mono mixing.

June 21, 1966 – Mono and stereo mixing.

August 5, 1966 – First released on the U.K. LP *Revolver*.

Players/Instruments:
- **Paul McCartney:** Lead vocal, bass, piano, clavichord
- **Ringo Starr:** Drums, tambourine, maracas
- **Alan Civil:** French horn

What we really like about this song

Steve: In "For No One," Paul uses the same chord changes that John would later use in "A Day in the Life" and that Paul would revisit in "Let It Be." As I have previously admitted, I have always loved that descending bass line chord progression, and "For No One" is a classic example of this classically inspired riff. I also greatly admire Paul's bass playing on the track—it's so melodic, it almost becomes something akin to a cello or viola line in the piece.

Mike: Superb playing, great writing, stellar performances—by just half of the Beatles! This is one of my favorites of Paul's underrated songs. I look at it as Paul's answer to John songs like "No Reply" or "I'm a Loser." Contrary to Paul's frequent "sunny day" songwriting, its message is sobering, jarring—you feel sorry for the narrator, who is obviously clueless about how he has completely lost the love of his life. The addition of unusual instruments, the clavichord and French horn, was the perfect touch. The Beatles' dabbling in such instruments sparked my interest in classical music.

---

[1] *Things We Said Today*, page xli, crediting the John Cage "Notations" Collection at the Northwestern University Music Library.

[2] *The Beatles Recording Sessions*, page 79.

If I Needed Someone

"If I Needed Someone" is like a million other songs written around the D chord. If you move your finger about you get various little melodies (and sometimes you get various little maladies). That guitar line, or variations on it, is found in many a song and it amazes me that people still find new permutations of the same notes.

—George Harrison
I Me Mine

The first time

we heard a George tune on *Rubber Soul* was the song "Think for Yourself," which came after John's stunning "Nowhere Man."

Seven Lennon/McCartney songs followed, and then "If I Needed Someone" made its jangly guitar way into our hearts.

171

This second Harrisong on *Rubber Soul* immediately engaged us all, much more so than the rather bland and unfocused earlier George track.

Rubber Soul concluded with "Run for Your Life," a song even its composer didn't like. Maybe the last track on this landmark album should have been "If I Needed Someone"? Just asking.

Why it made the top 100

"If I Needed Someone" is one of George's better songs, and is a worthy precursor to the next Harrisong we would hear, the terrific "Taxman."

We don't think we would be off base to state with certainty that the song comes close to much of John and Paul's work at the time, and that it is evidence of George's maturation as a songwriter.

Interestingly, we can hear an early hint of George's Indian period in the pedal-point bass line that runs throughout the song. A D note can be played through most of the verse without discord, suggesting later Indian-inspired Harrisongs such as "Within You Without Out" and even (illustrating the influence the Fabs all had on each other) John's own "Tomorrow Never Knows."

What the song is about

"If I Needed Someone" was written to another girl, yet it is a tribute to Patti Harrison, who, at the time it was written and recorded, was still Patti Boyd.

Patti and George were married in January 1966, a few months after the song was recorded. In the lyrics, George tells some other bird that he is "too much in love" to consider a relationship. He tries to soften the blow by assuring her that *if* he needed someone, she'd be the one he'd think of, but he also makes it clear that there's simply no chance of that by specifically addressing her as "my *friend*."

In the bridge, he plays the game of telling her that things might have been different if he had met her first. But then, in the next verse, he throws salt in the wound by sarcastically telling her to carve her number on his wall. (*Carve*? What's with the violent imagery?) He callously teases her by suggesting that *maybe* he'll call her—if the relationship he's in falls apart and he ends up needing someone new. *Maybe* I'll come to you, he taunts—but only if something better doesn't come along. Not nice.

All in all, the commitment in the song to his relationship with Patti is admirable, but his rebuff of the "other woman" seems needlessly cruel.

• • • ❦ • • •

- In his autobiography *I Me Mine*, George talked about fooling around with the D chord to write "If I Needed Someone" (see the epigraph). He was accurate, of course, but the song is actually in the key of A. In the November 1987 issue of *Guitar* magazine, he explained that he used a capo: "It was written in D nut position (capoed at the 5th fret)." This allowed him to finger a D chord, but play the song in the key of A.
- "If I Needed Someone" was recorded on the same day that the Fabs recorded "Day Tripper." (Can you sense a similar musical sensibility in the two songs? We do.)

Did you know?

- When Derek Taylor moved to Los Angeles to work for the Byrds, George Harrison asked him to pass a message on to Byrds guitarist Roger McGuinn: The tune for "If I Needed Someone" was inspired by the Byrds songs "The Bells of Rhymney" and "She Don't Care About Time."[1]
- "If I Needed Someone" was one of four *Rubber Soul* tracks banned from airplay in the United States until the release in the States of the *Yesterday... and Today* album. (The others were "What Goes On," "Nowhere Man," and "Drive My Car.")
- The song has been covered by the Hollies, the Kingsmen, the Cryan' Shames, Hugh Masekela, and Michael Hedges.

The recording

Location: **Abbey Road Studios, London.**

Dates: **October 16, 1965** – Recording of the basic rhythm track, done in one take at the end of the day's recording session.

October 18, 1965 – Just as they ended their October 16 session by working on this song, the Beatles began this session (their next day in the studio—they were off on the seventeenth) by working on it. They overdubbed the lead and backing vocals, and Ringo played tambourine.

October 25, 1965 – Mono mixing.

October 26, 1965 – Stereo mixing.

December 3, 1965 – First released on the U.K. LP *Rubber Soul.*

Players/Instruments:
- **George Harrison:** Lead guitar, lead vocal
- **Paul McCartney:** Bass, backing vocal
- **John Lennon:** Tambourine, backing vocal (some sources say John also played rhythm guitar)
- **Ringo Starr:** Drums, tambourine
- **George Martin:** Harmonium

What we really like about this song

Steve: I love George's guitar work on this track. There is, indeed, good reason why many believe Mr. Harrison invented rock guitar. I am also enamored of the tight, three-part harmonies that are effortlessly continued throughout every verse (after a brief double-tracked George solo vocal line until the first appearance of the title in the lyrics). I also like the "ah" break—it adds a nice, elegant touch to the track, enhanced by Paul's stunning bass work. All in all, I consider this one of George's better songs.

Mike: Another George song, one of my Harrison faves, that's tucked away toward the end of *Rubber Soul* and kind of quietly sneaks up on you. I rather like his twelve-string guitar playing, even though, as George said, it's much like the playing in many other songs. Growing up, I was faced with the dilemma that George sings about here: having to choose between a current love or someone new. Thus, this song has personal significance for me.

[1] *A Hard Day's Write.*

I Should Have Known Better

55

That's me. Just a song; it doesn't mean a damn thing.

—John Lennon
Playboy

Admit it: You always thought the Fabs were really on a train when they lip-synched to "I Should Have Known Better" in *A Hard Day's Night*. Alas, they were in the studio, but this bit of commonplace moviemaking modus operandi in no way detracted from the excitement of the scene, as evidenced by the joyous expressions of the birds sitting and listening to John, Paul, George, and Ringo.

Why it made the top 100

There is something about the very *sound* of "I Should Have Known Better" that leaps out at us. It was bloody delightful from the first time we all heard it.

The opening passages, consisting of acoustic guitar, bass, drums, and harmonica, are immediately engaging, and the song becomes even more intriguing when John starts to sing: He holds a high D note for an entire measure (and then some) before the melody starts. In fact, the whole song is in quite a high register for John, who has to resort to falsetto for a few notes (especially the high B in "miii-iiine").

And there's no harmony! Paul and George remain silent while John sings his heart out.

The song works beautifully, and yet was not chosen to be the B side of the "A Hard Day's Night" single in the United Kingdom. That honor went to "Things We Said Today." Instead, the song was the B side for the U.S. single, and was also re-released in 1976.

What the song is about

He's in love with her, but he doesn't feel fine.

Not that he's worried about her love; far from it. He's confident in her feelings for him and assures her that when he tells her that he loves her, she will respond in kind. But there is a tone of self-scolding in the lyrics suggesting that the singer has been a bit guarded in the past, afraid to open up. Somehow, though, she managed to get through his defenses—even though he "should have known better."

He's delighted with the thrills of being in love, but, again, it appears that this is an alien state for him: "*If* this is love, you gotta give me more." If this is love? Clearly, he questions whether or not he has actually been in love before, and it appears as though this young lady has swept him off his feet and showed him precisely what it all means. All this is confirmed by the plaintive, "This could only happen to me," which hints at his frustration: I've spent so much time and energy protecting myself from love, and yet it won anyway.

"I Should Have Known Better" is about the power of love to consume and enthrall—and ultimately its ability to enable the realization that (Foreshadowing Alert) love is all you need.

• • • • ☙ • • • •

- "I Should Have Known Better" was the first song sequence to be filmed for *A Hard Day's Night*—the scene in which they're "locked" in the mail car of the train. Screenwriter Alun Owen commented, "It just seemed the natural place to have the first number."[1] The segment was actually filmed in a van in Twickenham Film Studios, with crew members rocking the vehicle to fake the action of a train in motion.

- "I Should Have Known Better" is another song in which the official title does not exactly match the sung words. John clearly sings, "I shoulda known better…" (See the Did You Know? section for song number 67, "You're Going to Lose That Girl," for more on the written/sung differences in Beatles songs.)

Did you know?

- "I Should Have Known Better" is notable for being the first time George Harrison played a twelve-string Rickenbacker on record.

- A George Martin–orchestrated instrumental version of the song appears on the U.S. soundtrack.

- In March 1976, the first "new" Beatles single since the band's breakup was released in the United Kingdom. The A side was "Yesterday"; the B side was "I Should Have Known Better."

- The song has been covered by the Naturals, the Beach Boys, Jan and Dean, Brinsley Schwarz, Wire, Phil Ochs, and Johnny Rivers.

The recording

Location: **Abbey Road Studios, London.**

Dates: **February 25, 1964** – Three takes were recorded, but only one was complete. On Take 2, John broke into laughter over his harmonica playing, causing the other Beatles to also crack up. The song at this stage was very different from the final version. It opened with a Dylan-like harmonica solo and ended with George's lead guitar. It was re-recorded the next day.

February 26, 1964 – The Abbey Road recording log shows that nineteen takes were recorded, but very few got beyond the middle-eight section of the song. Take 9 was the final version, with John singing without the harmonica. This was then overdubbed, adding a double-tracked vocal and harmonica.

March 3, 1964 – Mono mixing.

June 9, 1964 – Mono tape copying for the soundtrack.

June 22, 1964 – Stereo mixing.

June 26, 1964 – First released in the United States on the United Artists soundtrack LP *A Hard Day's Night.*

Players/Instruments:

- **John Lennon:** Acoustic guitar, harmonica, vocal
- **Paul McCartney:** Bass
- **George Harrison:** Lead guitar
- **Ringo Starr:** Drums

What we really like about this song

Steve: This is a great song, and it's the little touches that emphasize and illustrate what magicians the Fabs were in the studio, as well as their powerful sense of group musical aesthetics. As we've learned, this is the first song on which George played a twelve-string Rickenbacker, but does he wail away on it, using the debut of the instrument as an opportunity to grandstand? Hardly. He plays one single chord on the first beat of every measure. Dominating the track is John's acoustic guitar (and the come-and-go harmonica, of course). George's guitar solo is nothing but a vamping on the main melody. No fret pyrotechnics that could have easily overpowered the song's steady serenity. Less is more, indeed. I also really like John's vocal, one of his best, which is double-tracked except for the second bridge.

Mike: Just one look is all it took—John has fallen head over heels for this girl, and it's a feeling he's never felt before (and a theme he would continue in his solo song "How"—now that we're in love like never before, what do we do?). When I hear John enthusiastically playing harmonica on this song, it makes me wish he had played more of the instrument on Beatles records. It's a shame John didn't think very highly of this song, but I guess when you've written countless classic songs, you prefer some over others.

[1] *A Hard Day's Write.*

56

Glass Onion

*With "Glass Onion," I was just
having a laugh because there'd been so
much gobbledygook written about Sgt.
Pepper. People were saying, "Play
it backwards while standing on your
head, and you'll get a secret message,
etc."*

—John Lennon
The Beatles: A Celebration

The Beatles were apparently bemused,
puzzled, and angered (and apparently all at the same time)
by the feverish and fanatic deconstruction of their songs by
those fans looking for "clues." Clues to what? Paul's "death,"
of course, but also the identity of the walrus (and the eggman,
we suppose), and whether or not the lyrics of "Helter Skelter"
were *really* calling for a global race war culminating in a fiery
Armageddon. "Glass Onion" was John's caustic response to
this bizarre Beatlesong pecking frenzy.

Why it made the top 100

"Glass Onion" is one of John's best songs on *The White Album*, and the care the Fabs put into the production is obvious. George Martin's suggestion to add strings literally *made* the track, and it's to John and company's credit that they realized when a better idea was presented to them.

What the song is about

"Glass Onion" may be one of the few times when John was telling the whole truth and nothing but the truth when he said the song's lyrics were mostly gibberish or, at the very least, nothing more than a collection of surrealistic images.

Is there a hidden meaning in "Glass Onion"? Some arcane message that lies beneath the seemingly random cataloging of imagery? We *could* make the case that the subtext of the song is a plea to make an effort to achieve higher consciousness. By looking through the glass onion, a symbol for the "tool" of choice—meditation, prayer, drugs, sex, what have you—we can see "how the other half lives."

The problem with this is that the obvious, well-known, and repeated Beatles images screw up the reception, so to speak. It's hard to ascribe deeper meaning to a song when the scribe himself has cheekily admitted the whole thing was a bit of a goof.

• • • • 🎵 • • • •

- Both John and Paul were the walrus. In 1997, Paul told journalist Robert Yates, "In the stills we had taken, I was the one with the Walrus head on—in the film it's [John]. So John then immortalized it in 'Glass Onion.'"
- In Bill Harry's *Ultimate Beatles Encyclopedia*, Paul discussed the genesis of the song. "John wrote the tune…but I helped him on it, and when we were writing it we were thinking specifically of this whole idea of all these kind of people who write in and say 'Who was the walrus, John? Were you the walrus?' or 'Is Paul the walrus?' So John… happened to have a line go 'Oh yeah, the walrus was Paul' and we had a great giggle to say 'Yeah, let's do that,' let's put this line in 'cause everybody's gonna read into it and go crackers…he said, 'Let's do this joke tune 'Glass Onion' where all kinds of answers to the universe are…' we [intended it as] a joke." In John's 1980 *Playboy* interview, he said the animal reference was irrelevant: "It could've been 'the fox terrier is Paul,' you know. I mean, it's just a bit of poetry."
- On the *Anthology 3* version of the song (Track 20), John sings, "Well here's another place you can go/Where everything *glows*." This was changed to "flows" for the final version, but his initial choice of "glows" is interesting, yes?
- According to Derek Taylor, "bent-backed tulips" referred to a particular flower arrangement in Parkes, a London restaurant of the sixties. The arrangement had tulips with their petals bent all the way back so you could see the obverse side of the petals and also each flower's stamen. Apparently, this is what John meant about seeing "how

the other half lives," although the phrase had a double meaning, since Parkes was an expensive restaurant that only the well-to-do "other half" could afford to visit. Taylor added that "cast iron shore" referred to a beach in Liverpool, and "dove-tail joint" to a wood joint using wedge-shaped tenons (not marijuana, as is widely believed).

- "Glass Onion" is one of five songs in which an individual Beatle (Paul) is mentioned by name. The other four are "The Ballad of John and Yoko," "For You Blue," and "I'm Down" (John); and "You Know My Name (Look Up the Number)" (Ringo). The only George mention in the canon is in "Dig It," but the line is "That was 'Can You Dig It' by Georgie Wood," so we don't consider it a Harrison mention.
- "Glass Onion" refers to five specific Beatles songs (two John songs, three Paul songs): "Strawberry Fields Forever," "I Am the Walrus," "Lady Madonna," "The Fool on the Hill," and "Fixing a Hole." (The latter three are the only ones referred to by their full names—although some report that if you listen carefully, you can hear someone say "for-evuh" after John sings the opening line "I told you 'bout strawberry fields…" We don't hear it, though.)
- "Glass Onion" was one of George Harrison's favorite songs on *The White Album*.
- "Glass Onion" was the name John intended to use for the Apple-signed group that ultimately became known as Badfinger (which had formerly been known as the Iveys).
- The song has been covered by Arif Mardin.

The recording

Location: **Abbey Road Studios, London.**

Dates:

September 11, 1968, 7:00 p.m.–3:30 a.m. – Thirty-four takes of the song were recorded, consisting of drums, bass, and lead and acoustic guitars, with Take 33 considered the best. All versions were around 1:50 in length, except for Take 15, which evolved into a six-minute jam.

September 12, 1968, 8:30 p.m.–1:30 a.m. – Overdubbing of John's lead vocal and Ringo's tambourine.

September 13, 1968, 8:00 p.m.–1:45 a.m. – Overdubbing of an additional drum track and piano.

September 16, 1968 – Two overdubs of the recorder riff, played by Paul, were added to the "Fool on the Hill" line.

September 26, 1968 – Mono mixing. John decided to add sound effects: a window (or a glass onion, perhaps?) being smashed, a ringing alarm clock, an announcer repeating "It's a goal!" (This version can be heard on *Anthology*.)

George Martin, just back from vacation and hearing the song for the first time, suggested to John that a string section be added instead. John liked the idea, and it was agreed that Martin would score it. This day's mixes and sound effects were now unusable.

October 10, 1968 – Overdubbing of strings, both for "Piggies" and "Glass Onion." (At the same time, Paul was off elsewhere finishing up "Why Don't We Do It in the Road?") Mono and stereo mixing.

November 22, 1968 – First released on the U.K. LP *The Beatles* (*The White Album*).

Players/Instruments:

- **John Lennon:** Acoustic guitar, vocal
- **Paul McCartney:** Bass, piano, recorder
- **George Harrison:** Lead guitar
- **Ringo Starr:** Drums, tambourine
- **Session musicians:** Four violins, two cellos, two violas

What we really like about this song

Steve: This song took some getting used to, but now I love it. Paul's bass has an extraordinary sound on this track, and the strings at the end—those bizarro, slowing-down descending seventh chords—are somewhat unsettling. Maybe that's why they selected the good-natured, nonsensical "Ob-La-Di, Ob-La-Da" to follow it? I think this is one of John's better songs, and I love the arrangement.

Mike: This is one of my favorite songs on *The White Album*. I like the fact that John is giving the finger (or at least chucking a moon) to all who tried to find clues in the Fabs' songs. (The only thing missing is some backward singing!) The song features some of Paul's most aggressive fuzz bass playing, as well as what, to me, sounds like some intentionally sloppy drumming by Ringo. I'm glad they scrapped the sound effects overdubs in favor of the string arrangement (even though it's relegated to little more than ambience in the background of the mix).

57

I'm Only Sleeping

In order to record the backward guitar on a track like "I'm Only Sleeping," you work out what your chord sequence is and write down the reverse order of the chords—as they are going to come up—so you can recognize them. You then learn to boogie around on that chord sequence, but you don't really know what it's going to sound like until it comes out again. It's hit or miss, no doubt about it, but you do it a few times, and when you like what you hear, you keep it.

—George Martin
Musician, July 1987

Considering the amount of time and effort the Beatles put into perfecting the backward guitar sound on "I'm Only Sleeping," it's amazing that they used the weird effect so sparingly in the final version of the track.

By our reckoning, there are approximately seventeen seconds of backward guitar during the song proper, and another ten seconds in the fade-out, which is about 15 percent of the song's 2:57 running time. Some sources say the backward guitar took more than fourteen hours to record.

When the Fabs wanted an effect, they moved earth and sky to achieve it.

Why it made the top 100

"I'm Only Sleeping" is an amalgam of styles and sounds, all of which are commonplace today, yet they broke new ground when *Revolver* was first released.

Is it a folk song? Well, the acoustic guitars do sound very "folky."

Is it a psychedelic experiment? Well, all those weird sounds snaking through the song sure do sound acid-inspired.

Is it a Beatles ballad? Well, those gorgeous harmonies (foreshadowing "Because," "Sun King," and other choir-like singing by the boys) sure do sound like the traditional Beatles.

And, of course, the answer to all those questions is yes.

What the song is about

"I'm Only Sleeping" is an Argument (in the syllogistic sense) for inertia; it is a defense of torpor; it is a plea to those who consider idleness a prosecutable offense to look the other way.

John did not like physical activity, but how much of his laziness was inborn and how much was due to drugs?

John's childhood friend Pete Shotton, writing in *John Lennon in My Life,* said, "'I'm Only Sleeping' brilliantly evokes the state of chemically induced lethargy into which John had… drifted."

Perhaps. Yet we can read much more into the lyrics than John simply saying, "I'm high, I'm sleepy, sod off."

After the gritty reality of George's "Taxman" and the reflective lament of Paul's "Eleanor Rigby," John steps onto the *Revolver* stage and speaks of floating away ("float upstream") and sleeping away the world. George dealt with taxes realistically; Paul acknowledged death and loss; John, however, yearns to escape.

In the end, we don't think it's reaching to say that "I'm Only Sleeping" was one of John's first admissions (albeit told in metaphor) that he wanted out of the Beatles.

• • • • • • •

- John wrote the first draft of the "I'm Only Sleeping" lyric on the back of a letter from the post office. The letter was dated March 25, 1966, and it was a reminder that he owed them twelve pounds and three shillings for an outstanding radiophone bill.
- In John's "bigger than Jesus" interview with the *Evening Standard* in March 1966, he talked about his laziness: "[I'm] physically lazy. I don't mind writing or reading or watching or speaking, but sex is the only physical thing I can be bothered with anymore."
- If you listen very carefully, at 1:57 into the song you can hear a voice (John?) saying, "Yawn, Paul." Then, at 2:01, you can actually hear Paul yawn.
- "I'm Only Sleeping" has been covered by Rosanne Cash and Suggs (from the English New Wave group Madness). The Suggs version was voted one of the ten worst Beatles covers of all time in a poll taken in May 2003 for the digital TV channel Music Choice.

Did you know?

The recording

Location: **Abbey Road Studios, London.**

Dates:

April 27, 1966, 11:30 p.m.–3:00 a.m. – Eleven takes were recorded, all of which focused on the rhythm track, which was mostly acoustic at this stage. Take 11 was considered the best.

April 29, 1966 – Overdubbing on John's lead vocal. The tape was run at forty-five cycles instead of fifty so the vocal would be sped up. The rhythm track onto which they were overdubbing John's vocal was taped at fifty-six cycles and played back at forty-seven and a quarter. (Some of the results of this day's work can be heard on *Anthology 2*.)

May 5, 1966, 9:30 p.m.–3:00 a.m. – Backward guitars were added. They could have chosen the easy way to get this effect (record the guitar playing and then play the tape backward), but, of course, they didn't. They added difficulty to the process by recording both a "regular" guitar and a fuzz guitar played by George Harrison, which were superimposed on top of each other.

May 6, 1966, 2:30 p.m.–2:15 a.m. – Vocal harmonies were overdubbed. Mono mixing.

May 12, 1966 – Mono mixing.

May 20, 1966 – Stereo mixing. (The boys were out of the studio busy filming clips for "Paperback Writer" and "Rain.")

June 6, 1966 – Tape copying and mono mixing.

June 15, 1966 – First released on the U.S. album *Yesterday…and Today*. (This is the release date of the infamous "butcher" cover version of *Yesterday…and Today*, which was quickly withdrawn after fans reacted with shock and awe. The album was re-released on June 20, 1966, with a new cover. Today, an original butcher cover *Yesterday…and Today* is worth a small fortune.)

Players/Instruments:

- **John Lennon:** Acoustic guitar, lead vocal
- **Paul McCartney:** Bass, backing vocal
- **George Harrison:** Lead guitar, backing vocal
- **Ringo Starr:** Drums

What we really like about this song

Steve: I like the sound of the acoustic guitars, and I especially like the background harmonies. I think it's one of John's cleanest and most well-written lyrics. I also like very much the backward guitar sounds. (Interestingly, the rehearsal version of this song on *Anthology 2* had a vibraphone on the track, which sounded great. I think it would have added a lot to the final track if they had decided to use it.)

Mike: This is one of the band's drowsiest, most lethargic songs—or is it? John does sound like he's singing the song from under the covers, but that's all a studio creation. As you listen to the *Anthology 2* version of the song, you can hear it was "peppier" in its earlier life. Thanks to production high jinks, they fiddled with tape speeds to make it appear that the song is drifting and shuffling lazily along. Unlike the similarly themed number "I'm So Tired" from *The White Album*, this one's much more intricate and complex. My favorite part of song is the backward guitar playing at the end—they almost sound like sitars run through fuzz boxes!

58

With a Little Help from My Friends

You know I'm not very good at singing because I haven't got a great range. So they write songs for me that are pretty low and not too hard.

—*Ringo Starr*
The Beatles *by Hunter Davies*

"I'd like to return this, please."

"Sgt. Pepper? That's the hottest album this summer!"

"Yeah, but it's not a Beatles album."

"What are you talking about, man?"

"Dude. Last I heard, the Beatles were John, Paul, George, and Ringo. Who the hell is Billy Shears?"

Why it made the top 100

When did you realize that you knew every single word to this song and could sing along with it from any point in the recording?

This is one of those Beatles songs (like "Yesterday" and "She Loves You") that has a presence so enormous, it has become (almost) a cliché. "With a Little Help from My Friends" had a heavy mission: be the first complete, self-contained song on the *Sgt. Pepper* album (recently ranked the greatest rock album in the history of music, by the way). The leadoff song after the *Sgt. Pepper* intro had to be artistically nonthreatening and engaging enough to serve as a musical "welcome mat," so to speak.

"With a Little Help" delivered, and then some. It was the Beatles we knew and loved, the Beatles of "Good Day Sunshine" and "I Should Have Known Better" and, yes, even "Yellow Submarine." In the end, the song served as a gentle introduction to the spacier, more challenging songs that would come later.

What the song is about

The poor chap singing his tale of woe to us in this song is looking for love (in all the wrong places?). He begins by asking his friends if they would be upset with him if he "sang out of tune," a lovely metaphor for what, in essence, is, as we said, his tale of woe. Who really wants to listen to people complain about their lives? Our hero instinctively knows this, and would like some assurance that his friends will not "stand up and walk out" on him.

This is followed by the chorus, in which he acknowledges their help ("I get by with a little help from my friends"), expresses his gratitude to them ("I get high…"), and asserts his determination to get through this ("Gonna try…").

Once the ground rules have been established (*I'll talk, you'll try to help*), the dialogue begins. The second verse is a question-and-answer exchange in which our hero asks, first, what he should do when his love is away, to which his friends, in classic shrink mode, respond with a question: "Does it worry you to be alone?" This is followed by a rhetorical question about how he feels by the end of the day, which is similarly answered with a question: "Are you sad because you're on your own?"

After a repeat of the chorus, the bridge has the friends asking him if he "needs anybody" and "could it be anybody?" His response is blunt: I *need* somebody to love and I *want* somebody to love.

The final verse delves into the psyche of our lovelorn loser. His friends ask him if he'd consider believing in "a love at first sight?" Sure, it happens all the time, he tells them. This is followed by a question with a range of meanings: "What do you see when you turn out the light?" What, if anything, do you see in the dark; when you're *blind*, both literally and figuratively? Mr. Codependent is apparently not self-aware enough to know the answer to the question, but he does provide a response of sorts: "I can't tell you but I know it's mine." A suitably vague and innuendo-laden reply from a man who can only get by "with a little help from his friends."

- According to John, the song was originally conceived by Paul, but they completed it "pretty well fifty/fifty."[1] One specific line John remembered contributing was, "What do you see when you turn out the light / I can't tell you but I know it's mine."
- The crowd noise at the beginning of this song was from the Beatles August 23, 1964, concert at the Hollywood Bowl. George Martin recorded their performance, and it was released in 1977 as *The Beatles at Hollywood Bowl* LP (still not available on CD).
- The working title of the song was "Badfinger Boogie." (John had an injured finger while the boys were working on it.)
- The first line of the song was originally written as "What would you do if I sang out of tune, would you stand up and throw tomatoes at me?" Ringo refused to sing it because he had not-so-fond memories of fans throwing things at them when they performed live. The line was changed.

Did you know?

- Without question, the single most memorable cover of this song was by Joe Cocker, who slowed it down and performed it with such, er, "passionate spasticity" that it instantly became a modern classic. Adding to its legendary status was John Belushi's flawless impression of Cocker doing the song. (Belushi once performed the song with Joe Cocker on *Saturday Night Live*, imitating his every move. Cocker was an incredibly good sport and completely played along.)
- "With a Little Help from My Friends" was intentionally written to be for kids—a sing-along akin in spirit to "Yellow Submarine," and "All Together Now."
- The song has been covered by Joe Cocker (a Number One hit), Sergio Mendes and Brazil '66, Santana, Richie Havens, Ike and Tina Turner, Barbra Streisand, Herb Alpert and the Tijuana Brass, Steve Cropper, Kenny Rankin, David Peel and the Apple Band, Pandora, the Beach Boys, Jean-Luc Ponty, and Bon Jovi.

The recording

Location: **Abbey Road Studios, London.**

Dates: **March 29, 1967** – Ten takes of the song were recorded. From the first take, they began with what sounds like the ending of "Sgt. Pepper's Lonely Hearts Club Band": the "Billll-lyyyyy Shears!" introduction of Ringo's lead vocal. (They had decided early on that "Sgt. Pepper" would segue right into "With a Little Help from My Friends.") Underscoring the opening line was a Hammond organ piece played by George Martin. Then Paul added piano; George, guitar; Ringo; drums; and John, cowbell. The tenth take was considered best. They did a reduction mix down to one track, and then overdubbed Ringo's vocal onto Tracks 3 and 4.

March 30, 1967, 11:00 p.m.–7:30 a.m. (the reason for the late start was that the Fabs were posing for the now-famous Michael Cooper shots on the album cover and gatefold) – The song now had its final title, and they overdubbed guitar, tambourine, bass, backing vocals by John and Paul, and another guitar piece by George.

March 31, 1967 – Fifteen mono remixes, with a heavy dose of Artificial Double Tracking (ADT).

April 7, 1967 – Stereo remixing.

June 1, 1967 – First released on the U.K. LP *Sgt. Pepper's Lonely Hearts Club Band*.

Players/Instruments:
- **Ringo Starr:** Drums, lead vocal
- **Paul McCartney:** Bass, piano, backing vocal
- **John Lennon:** Cowbell, backing vocal
- **George Harrison:** Guitar, tambourine
- **George Martin:** Hammond organ

What we really like about this song

Steve: I love how, in the second verse, Ringo asks the questions and Paul and John answer him, but in the third verse, it's reversed. I also have always been impressed with the care put into this peppery *Pepper* song. Although it's a bit of a lightweight, the Fabs did not skimp on either the production or their performances. Paul's bass part is terrific; Ringo's drumming was obviously meticulously thought out ahead of time; plus there are lovely, subtle touches throughout, all of which combine to make it irresistible. After smiling through this song, we were all in good spirits and ready to go on an acid trip with John in the next song on the album, "Lucy in the Sky with Diamonds."

Mike: "We Will Rock You." "We Are the Champions." "Living Loving Maid." "Heartbreaker." Some songs are meant to be part of "a couple," so to speak, so it's hard for me to consider "With a Little Help from My Friends" by itself because I've always heard it as the song that followed "Sgt. Pepper's Lonely Hearts Club Band." Once the needle hit the vinyl, it stayed there. Okay, so Ringo's voice isn't much more than a drone (which he admits!); still, it's a fun song, and one of his best vocal performances. I defy anyone to try to skip past this song—if your kid knows it's there, you'd *better* play it! You might even find yourself joining the sing-along.

[1] *The Beatles Anthology.*

She Said She Said

That's mine. It's… an interesting track. The guitars are great on it. That was written after an acid trip in L.A. during a break in the Beatles tour [August 1965] where we were having fun with the Byrds and lots of girls. Some from Playboy, I believe. Peter Fonda came in when we were on acid and he kept coming up to me and sitting next to me and whispering, "I know what it's like to be dead." He was describing an acid trip he'd been on. We didn't want to hear about that!

—John Lennon
Playboy

"She Said She Said"

"She Said She Said" concluded Side One of the original *Revolver* disc, and by that point we were all exhausted from the sheer overload of musical brilliance we'd just experienced. And still to come was "Good Day Sunshine," "And Your Bird Can Sing," "For No One," and, of course, "Tomorrow Never Knows" (and others), which "She Said She Said" (*sort of*) prepared us for.

Why it made the top 100

An impressive ten of the fourteen tracks on *Revolver* made it onto this top 100 ranking, including "She Said She Said." Why? A progressive sound, odd and wonderful lyrics, amazingly creative drumming, searing guitars, and terrific John/George harmonies. John's genius is center stage on "She Said She Said"; Paul's contribution is limited to a great bass line that is simply a small part of a larger creation. The track is as fresh today as it was when it was first released.

What the song is about

The lyrics of "She Said She Said" have a reputation for being arcane and surrealistic, mostly because it's well known that John wrote the song after an acid trip. Yet, in our opinion, the lyrics can also be interpreted in a very straightforward, narrative manner.

The song opens mise-en-scène. After a rousing guitar intro, we are in the midst of the action—which is to be the "ear" for a puzzled pilgrim. An unnamed woman has told our hero that she knows what it's like to be dead, and he recounts the conversation for us. She also tells him she knows what it's like to be sad. His reaction? "[S]he's making me feel like I've never been born." (It takes one hell of a morbid conversationalist to raise the issues of death and existential nonexistence in the first few lines of a chat, eh?)

Never-been-born guy rebels against this onslaught of negative imagery by asking her (with obvious exasperation), "Who put all those things in your head?"—these things "that make me feel like I'm mad"?

Miss Depressing 1966 fires back that he just doesn't understand what she's saying, but he certainly *does* understand, and he tells her so—emphatically: "No, no, no, you're wrong."

Frustrated and anxious, our lad wanders off into a nostalgic reminiscence of a simpler time: "When I was a boy, everything was right…"

After this restorative reverie, he is now confident enough to fire back at Morticia, telling her sarcastically that, for all her cocky bravado ("even though you know what you know…"), he has had quite enough, thank you very much, and he is "ready to leave."

"She Said She Said" is a snapshot of a hapless lad corralled into a depressing, frustrating, and rather pointless conversation with a young woman who, in today's culture, would probably be a Goth.

• • • ❦ • • •

- An early demo of the song was angrier. Some of the unused lyrics were, "I said who put all that crap in your head/You know what it's like to be dead/And it's making me feel like my trousers are torn."
- During the break from their August 1965 tour (when John got the inspiration for this song), the Beatles stayed in a house in Los Angeles at 2850 Benedict Canyon. This house would later belong to Jimi Hendrix.
- George Harrison played a role in helping John finish writing this song. In *The Beatles Anthology*, George recalled, "He [John] had loads of bits, maybe three songs, that were unfinished, and I made suggestions and helped

Did you know?

him to work them together so that they became one finished song, 'She Said She Said.' The middle part of that record is a different song: 'She said, "I know what it's like to be dead," and I said, "Oh, no, no, you're wrong…"'

Then it goes into the other one, 'When I was a boy…' That was a real weld. So I did things like that. I would also play him, on occasion, songs I hadn't completed. I played him a tune one day, and he said, 'Oh, well, that's not too bad.' He didn't do anything at the time, but I noticed in the next song he wrote that he'd nicked the chords from it!"

- At the Benedict Canyon house, John and George decided that Paul and Ringo needed to take acid with them.

George talked about this day in *The Beatles Anthology:* "John and I decided that Paul and Ringo had to have acid, because we couldn't relate to them anymore. Not just on the one level—we couldn't relate to them on *any* level, because acid had changed us so much. It was such a mammoth experience that it was unexplainable: it was something that had to be *experienced*, because you could spend the rest of your life trying to explain what it made you feel and think. It was all too important to John and me… Paul wouldn't have LSD; he didn't want it. So Ringo and Neil took it, while Mal stayed straight in order to take care of everything."

- The song has been covered by Matthew Sweet and Nerdy Girl.

The recording

Location: **Abbey Road Studios, London.**

Dates: **June 21, 1966,** 7:00 p.m.–3:45 a.m. – Today was the last recording day for *Revolver.* John's "She Said She Said" was the only new song recorded; the rest of the session was spent remixing. The song was untitled at the beginning of session, but named at the end. They rehearsed the song through at least twenty-five takes. They then recorded three takes of the rhythm track consisting of drums, bass, and two guitars. Onto Take 3, they added John's lead vocal and John and George's backing vocals. They then did a reduction mix, and added another guitar and organ (played by John and barely discernible in the mix) to the vacated track. Three mono remixes.

June 22, 1966 – Mono and stereo mixing.

August 5, 1966 – First released on the U.K. LP *Revolver.*

Players/Instruments:
- **John Lennon:** Acoustic guitar, organ, vocal
- **Paul McCartney:** Bass
- **George Harrison:** Lead guitar, backing vocal
- **Ringo Starr:** Drums

What we really like about this song

Steve: I like the way John and the Fabs were able to integrate several influences to write and record this song. There is a strong Indian influence (thanks, of course, to George) in the pedal-point drone tone running throughout the track. Ringo's drumming is very tribal and disjointed, the perfect accompaniment to the neurotic, frenzied feel of the lyrics and the track's overall sound. Plus it's got great harmonies and some groovy guitar effects.

Mike: This is one of my favorites on a great album—to me it's like "Tomorrow Never Knows," although a little less weird. The lyrics are interesting but confusing, and I suspect the narrator is confused, too, either by the things "she" is saying, or by the distortion of the truth brought on by LSD. I like all the instrumentation: Ringo's drum fills and crashing cymbals, the guitar sounds, and Paul's bass trotting along with the melody. It's a song John admits to piecing together from fragments, but the pieces aren't quite as visible as they are in, say, "Happiness Is a Warm Gun."

All My Loving

I always liked it. I think it was the first song where I wrote the words on the tour bus during our tour with Roy Orbison. We did a lot of writing then. Then, when we got to the gig, I found a piano and worked out the music.

—Paul McCartney
The Beatles Recording Sessions

For a song that was never released as a single, "All My Loving" certainly is well known, wouldn't you say? This *With the Beatles* track was a favorite for the Fabs to perform live; the annals of rock are replete with venues where they kicked out the jams with this beloved, instantly recognizable song.

189

Why it made the top 100

"All My Loving" made the top 100 because, quite simply, it would have been a Musical Felony in the First Degree to omit it.

What the song is about

"All My Loving" has one of the simplest lyrics of any Beatles song, and its meaning is plain: I'm going away, I'll miss you, I won't cheat, I love you.

It opens with our traveler telling his lady love to close her eyes so he can kiss her good-bye. First he tells her he will miss her, and then he assures her that he'll "always be true." The first verse concludes with him promising to write her a love letter every day while he's away.

In the second verse he tells her that he will turn to fantasy ("I'll pretend that I'm kissing...") while he is away to keep her in his heart, and he includes the hope that someday his "dreams will come true." (What dreams? Marriage, kids, a house? He doesn't provide an inventory of his dreams, but we get the point anyway.) He again promises her a love letter every day, and the song ends with his repeated promise that he'll "be true."

We might doubt our hero's capacity to remain faithful to his love. He tells her twice that he will always be true. We can't help but wonder whom he's trying to convince: her or himself?

Is there a backstory we're not being told about? Is it possible that this young man cheated on his girlfriend in the past and, now that he's going away, she needs intense reassurance that he'll be true to her?

Perhaps. Or maybe he just wants to reinforce his love for her, because he knows women love to be told that they're the only one. In the end, let's all hope that he wrote the letters, enjoyed his fantasies, and kept his roaming eyes affixed on her return address.

• • • 🐞 • • •

- "All My Loving" was one of five songs the Fabs performed on the February 9, 1964, *Ed Sullivan Show*. (The others were "Till There Was You," "She Loves You," "I Saw Her Standing There," and "I Want to Hold Your Hand.") Also on the show that night was Davy Jones, later of the Monkees. (He acted out scenes from the Broadway musical *Oliver!*)
- Paul never thought of "All My Loving" as a single. In *The Beatles Recording Sessions*, he recalled, "That was on an album and the first person I heard single it out was the disc-jockey David Jacobs, who was pretty hip. Still is, actually—he knows pop music. He was always quite an expert, for one of the older generation. I remember him singling it out on his radio show and I think from that moment it did become a big favorite for people. And I heard it differently. Till then I'd heard it as an album track. But when he played it on his radio show, and it went over to however many million people on network BBC, it was like 'Woh! That is a good one.'"
- Some critics argued that the melody for "All My Loving"

Did you know?

was lifted from a work by Tchaikovsky. (We don't know what particular piece was being referred to, and neither of us is conversant enough in the Russian composer's work to hazard a guess. Any ideas from you Tchaikovsky aficionados out there?)

- It is believed that John got his rapid-fire strummed guitar part for this song from the Crystals' 1963 hit "Da-Doo Ron Ron."
- The song is heard in the 1983 film *Testament*, starring Jane Alexander and William Devane. It is sung by Mitch Weissman over a portable cassette player. Weissman performed as Paul in the Broadway show *Beatlemania*, and he also played with the Beatles tribute band Liverpool.
- The song has been covered by the Hollyridge Strings, Herb Alpert and the Tijuana Brass, Count Basie, Duke Ellington, Matt Monro, Frank Sinatra, Max Bygraves, Nick Heyward, the Chipmunks, Keely Smith, the Sandpipers, and Sonny Curtis.

The recording

Location: **Abbey Road Studios, London.**

Dates: **July 30, 1963** – Thirteen takes were recorded. (Abbey Road recording logs say they recorded fourteen takes, but there was no Take 5.) Takes numbered 12 through 14 were pure overdubs. The master version was an overdub, comprised of Take 14 onto Take 11. This was the last song recorded in a session that concluded at 11:00 p.m., an hour after the scheduled end time.

August 21, 1963 – Mono mixing.

October 29, 1963 – Stereo mixing.

November 22, 1963 – First released on the U.K. LP *With the Beatles*.

Players/Instruments:
- **Paul McCartney:** Bass, lead vocal
- **John Lennon:** Rhythm guitar, backing vocal
- **George Harrison:** Lead guitar, backing vocal
- **Ringo Starr:** Drums

What we really like about this song

Steve: I like that the song starts a cappella, and I especially love John's rhythm guitar part. Listen to what John does on this track and be impressed. It is *hard* to strum such a wide variety of chords as accurately and quickly as does Mr. Lennon. George's guitar solo is also notable because it's an integral part of the song—an improvised alternate guitar part would detract immensely from the cohesiveness of the track. It simply would not sound right. And you also have to love Paul's high C-sharp "Ooo!" in the choruses: a classic Beatles touch in a classic Beatles song.

Mike: Ho-hum, another classic Beatles hit, complete with all the Beatle bells and whistles. To say that, however, diminishes the power of this band: the ability to pump out hit after hit. Scores of bands would die for just one hit like this. The track boasts some of John's jangling guitar, some of Paul's best early bass playing, and the exuberant instrumental break at the middle eight. It's no wonder this is the first song they performed on *Ed Sullivan*. While John might write a love song with an underlying note of worry and paranoia at being separated from his love, Paul is confident that when they reunite, they will be closer than ever.

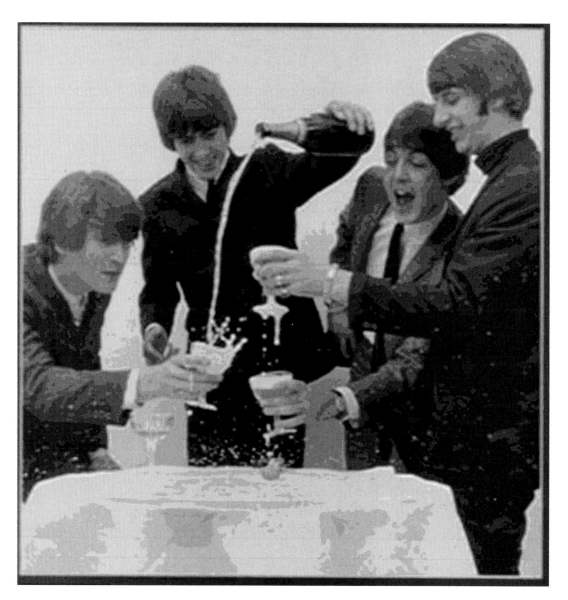

61
Baby You're A Rich Man

For a while we thought we were having some influence, and the idea was to show that we, being rich and famous and having all these experiences, had realized that there was a greater thing to be got out of life—and what's the point of having that on your own? You want all your friends and everybody else to do it, too.

—George Harrison
It Was 20 Years Ago Today

A song can capture the spirit of a time, reflecting it, commenting on it, and often thematically defining it.

When the "Baby You're a Rich Man" single (the B side of "All You Need Is Love") was released—a month after *Sgt. Pepper* had been unleashed on the world—we were all on a magical mystery tour through the final years of the sixties, a decade of upheaval that permeated every sector of society.

"Baby You're a Rich Man" captures the trippy feel of its day. There is a dreamy, laid-back vibe to the song, amplified and reinforced by the ultraweird sound of the Clavioline weaving throughout. Its message is multileveled, and its sound and production echo the eccentricity of the times.

Why it made the top 100

"Baby You're a Rich Man" was a bit of a departure for the Beatles. It is somewhat indefinable in terms of its sound—it is definitely rock, but it's *weird* rock—and that could be one of the reasons why it's one of the less played, less known, and less covered Beatles tunes.

Nonetheless, it's a terrific song and a great performance. Just John's singing on the line "What a thing to do!" would warrant inclusion in the top 100 ranking.

What the song is about

Some speculate that John and Paul are singing to Brian Epstein in "Baby You're a Rich Man." And does it really matter if they are?

Or are they singing to the hippie generation, asking them what it feels like to be one of the *beautiful people?*—an ironic question, since the appellation *beautiful people* was, of course, self-awarded.

The song works on two levels. The personal level is the Fabs singing to their manager, nonchalantly teasing him about becoming one of the beautiful people, thanks to the Beatles, and also rubbing his nose in the fact that now he is, indeed, a rich man, also thanks to them.

The universal level of meaning is the Beatles singing to an entire generation, sarcastically asking them what they want to be now that they know who they are. In this interpretation, the Beatles offer a scolding reminder that the beautiful people are "rich," suggesting that abundance and affluence are theirs—but they're not talking about money and material possessions. They're talking about spiritual growth and moral maturity, oft neglected by the beautiful. The lyric "what did you see when you were there?" is intended to serve as a reminder of what is truly important.

• • • ❦ • • •

Did you know?

- The song is a joining of two separate pieces—John's bit about the "beautiful people" and Paul's irresistible chorus.
- The official EMI title of "Baby You're a Rich Man" does not have a comma after "Baby." The song is often erroneously referred to with the comma in place, which *is* how Paul originally wrote it, but when he combined his fragment with John's to complete the song, they omitted the comma.

- In addition to being the B side of "All You Need Is Love," "Baby You're a Rich Man" was originally intended for the *Yellow Submarine* soundtrack. It was bumped, but the track was reinstated on the 1999 reissue of the soundtrack.
- The lyrics talk about people "tuned to a natural E," but the song is, in fact, in the key of G. The song also asks the beautiful people what they will do "now that you've found another key?" Could this new key be G?
- The mono version of the song is ten seconds longer than the stereo version.

The recording

Location: **Olympic Sound Studios, London.**

Dates: **May 11, 1967,** 9:00 p.m.–3:00 a.m. – The Beatles traveled to Olympic Studios for "Baby You're a Rich Man," and the song ended up being the first Beatles song recorded and mixed entirely outside Abbey Road Studios. (Two notes: "Fixing a Hole" had been recorded at London's Regent Studios in February of that year, but that song's final mix was completed at Abbey Road Studios. See song number 83. Also, a tape copy of the mono master of "Baby You're a Rich Man" was made at Abbey Road on August 22, 1968, and taken away that day by George Martin.)

Olympic engineer/studio manager Keith Grant, quoted in *The Beatles Recording Sessions*, said of the "Baby You're a Rich Man" session, "I'm a terrible pusher on sessions. I do a lot of orchestral work and you naturally push people along. The Beatles said this was the fastest record they'd ever made." Tape operator George Chkiantz later revealed that second engineer and future Jimi Hendrix producer Eddie Kramer and Grant were both amazed by John Lennon's voice. "They couldn't believe anyone could sing that well."[1] Twelve takes of the song were recorded. The last (Take 12) was considered the best.

Members of the Rolling Stones (frequent Olympic Studios users) were at the "Baby You're a Rich Man" session, and one of the tape boxes from that day has written on it "+ Mick Jagger?"—suggesting that Mick may have sung on one of the choruses at the end of the song. Other sources suggest that Stones guitarist Brian Jones played oboe on "Rich Man."

July 7, 1967 – First released as the B side of the "All You Need Is Love" single.

Players/Instruments:

- **John Lennon:** Piano, lead vocal, backing vocal, Clavioline[2]
- **Paul McCartney:** Bass, piano, harmony vocal
- **George Harrison:** Lead guitar, tambourine, backing vocal, handclaps
- **Ringo Starr:** Drums, maracas, tambourine, handclaps
- **Eddie Kramer:** Vibraphone

What we really like about this song

Steve: The eight-measure musical intro alone makes this song for me. The chug-chug rhythm and the ringing piano chords are immediately engaging, but then the song soars into the stratosphere when Paul's kickass bass comes in, immediately followed by… what the hell is that, a kazoo? No, it's a Clavioline, and its unique and odd sound takes "Baby You're a Rich Man" to another level. It's an unusual song in the Beatles canon, and John's falsetto contributes to its eccentricity. Curiouser and curiouser, indeed.

Mike: This is another one of those rarely played Beatles gems, and one of my favorites. For me, it perfectly captures the hippie vibe—you can almost picture a gal in a tie-dyed muumuu whirling in a stoned-out circle, on another plane, oblivious to any turmoil that may be around her. It's one of those songs in which you can just train your ear onto one instrument and still find enjoyment—be it Paul's trippy bass playing, John's stellar vocal, the chugging rhythm guitar, or the unusual sounds of the Clavioline. It's amazing how the Beatles could take many things—even parts of two disparate songs—and put them together in such an enjoyable way.

---

[1] *The Beatles Recording Sessions.*

[2] The Clavioline is a monophonic, portable, battery-powered amplified electronic keyboard that plays one note at time and can imitate tones of various instruments; it's heard at the beginning of the song. The Clavioline was designed by M. Constant Martin 1947 in Versailles, quickly became popular, and was used in the fifties and sixties by the Beatles, Sun Ra, and other musicians.

62 Mother Nature's Son

[Paul's "Mother Nature's Son"] was from a lecture of Maharishi where he was talking about nature.

—John Lennon
Playboy

Do you think John Denver would have had a career if Paul had not written "Mother Nature's Son"? We think it's a fair question, since with this simple, elegant tune, Paul essentially defined Denver's well-known "pastoral minstrel" persona.

Appearing as it does on *The White Album* between two of John's most blistering songs, "Yer Blues" and "Everybody's Got Something to Hide Except Me and My Monkey," it transports us to a serene place where we are treated to a comforting respite from bone-licking worms and high-flying simians.

Why it made the top 100

This superior ballad is more than just a man with a guitar. The bold addition of trumpets, trombones, and kettledrums adds consequence to the tune, elevating it from folky trifle to pastoral anthem.

Paul's ballads on *The White Album* are some of his finest, and "Mother Nature's Son" gave us all a preview of the countrified existence Paul would soon be living on his Scottish farm in his post-Beatles years.

What the song is about

A lad with a guitar sits in a mountain-ringed field beside a stream and serenades passersby. That is pretty much it. One point worth noting, though, is that the opening phrase—"Born a poor young country boy…"—is somewhat redundant. Sure, he could have been born poor, but born young? Well, duh.

Is there a deeper meaning to the lyrics of the song? Perhaps a hidden subtext in which Sir Paul rails against polluters, or anti-environmentalists? No, there isn't. But interestingly, some musicologists have interpreted the song as a slap against "Donovan-type" balladeers. In *Tell Me Why*, Tim Riley claimed that "Mother Nature's Son" "targets Donovan's foppishness." He described the song's main character as "pure beyond belief, a plastic pastoral," essentially negating the possibility that there is any sincerity whatsoever in Paul's words. Riley saw the song's final flatted seventh chord as "mocking the song's literal intentions like a deliberately satirical question mark."

This interpretation is open to discussion (and challenge), of course, and it's fair to say that many Fab fans choose to accept the song as an ode to nature, a paean to the pastoral, and one hell of an impressive guitar performance by Mr. McCartney.

• • • ❦ • • •

Did you know?

- The same lecture by the Maharishi that inspired this song also inspired John to write a song called "I'm Just a Child of Nature," which turned into "Jealous Guy" years later. (John's original song included a line about himself "on the road to Rishikesh." A brief snippet of John's song can be heard on the *Fly on the Wall* bonus disc of the 2003 *Let It Be… Naked* CD.)
- Paul once said that he remembered liking a song when he was a young boy called "Nature Boy." This 1948 Number

One song was written by Eden Ahbez and popularized by Nat King Cole.

- Things were tense among the Beatles in 1968. Ken Scott, one of the Beatles' engineers, described one particularly revealing moment: "Paul was downstairs going through the arrangement with George [Martin] and the brass players. Everything was great, everyone was in great spirits. It felt really good. Suddenly, halfway through, John and Ringo walked in and you could cut the atmosphere with a knife. An instant change. It was like that for ten minutes and then as soon as they left it felt great again. It was *very* bizarre."[1]
- "Mother Nature's Son" is one of seventeen Beatles songs in which the sun is mentioned.[2]
- The song has been covered by Sheryl Crow, Phish, the Grateful Dead, John Denver, Evan Marshall, Harry Nilsson, and Ramsey Lewis.

What we really like about this song

Steve: I like the second guitar part that was added for the final verse; I like that Paul did not hesitate to include verses without words; and I like the subtle tapping in the background of the song, a rhythmic drumming that can easily be overlooked but adds that little extra something to the song. I also *love* the timpani, especially the fancy fill thrown in at the end of the second bridge.

Mike: With this song, Paul takes his *White Album* acoustic numbers like "I Will" and "Blackbird" one step further by adding a dash of timpani and brass to the musical mix. "Mother Nature's Son" starts off quietly—is it a false start?—then builds a little, but not *too* much. It recalls Paul's longing for pastoral life, a theme he would revisit further in *Ram's* "Heart of the Country." (I bet the Beatles would have lasted another five to ten years if Paul had released a solo album during his Beatles tenure. He was always off working on something, to the exclusion of the other members. And, contrary to what all might say, I think at times they resented his soloing. But I digress…)

The recording

Location: **Abbey Road Studios, London.**

Dates: **August 9, 1968** – The day's regular recording session (during which the Beatles worked on "Not Guilty") ended around 10:00 p.m., but Paul stayed after the other Fabs went home. He then recorded twenty-five takes of "Mother Nature's Son," with the twenty-fourth considered best. As the song progressed, the guitar intro wound up being shortened to half Paul's original length.

August 20, 1968, 8:00 p.m.–4:00 a.m. – Alan Brown, the session's technical engineer, recalled in *The Beatles Recording Sessions*: "It was quite late at night, the whole building was quiet, and there was Paul playing this enchanting song. I love the phrase 'sitting in my field of grass.' It has a completeness about it. It isn't just any old field, it's a field of grass. We were all moved by it… Paul wanted an open effect on his drums [to give a bongos sound] and we ended up leaving the studio itself and putting the drums in the corridor, halfway down, with mikes at the far end. It wasn't carpeted then, and it gave an interesting staccato effect." Also that day, a tape reduction was carried out, along with overdubs of timpani, drums, a second acoustic guitar part, and brass (two trumpets, two trombones). George Martin was paid a twenty-five-pound fee for writing the brass arrangement. Mono mixing.

August 23, 1968 – Tape copying; the tapes were taken by Mal Evans.

October 12, 1968 – Stereo and mono mixing.

November 22, 1968 – First released on the U.K. LP *The Beatles* (*The White Album*).

Players/Instruments:

- **Paul McCartney:** Acoustic guitar, vocal, bongos, timpani
- **Session musicians:** Horns

---

[1] *The Beatles Recording Sessions.*

[2] The other sixteen are "Any Time at All," "Dear Prudence," "Good Day Sunshine," "Good Night," "Here Comes the Sun," "I Am the Walrus," "I'll Follow the Sun," "I've Got a Feeling," "It's All Too Much," "Julia," "Lucy in the Sky with Diamonds," "Rain," "Sun King," "The Fool on the Hill," "Two of Us," and "Yellow Submarine."

63
Everybody's Got Something To Hide Except Me And My Monkey

That was just a sort of nice line that I made into a song. It was about me and Yoko. Everybody seemed to be paranoid except for us two, who were in the glow of love. Everything is clear and open when you're in love. Everybody was, sort of, tense around us: You know, "What is she doing here at the session? Why is she with him?" All this sort of madness going around us just because we happened to want to be together all the time.

—John Lennon
Playboy

How fresh is this relentless *White Album* rocker?

Fresh enough that Paul Shaffer and the CBS orchestra play it *all the time* on *Late Night with David Letterman*. We, the stalwart home audience, never get to hear them play it beyond the instantly recognizable, kickass opening chords, but we're sure the studio audience is treated to a fierce cover of this frenetic John song during commercials.

64

Drive My Car

came up with that. Suddenly we were in LA, cars, chauffeurs, open-top Cadillacs, and it was a whole other thing.

—Paul McCartney
The Beatles Anthology

We couldn't get past one phrase that we had. "You can buy me golden rings." We struggled for hours; I think we struggled too long. Then we had a break and suddenly it came: "Wait a minute: 'Drive My Car!'" ... And then it became more ambiguous, which we liked, instead of golden rings, which was a bit poofy. "Golden rings" became "beep beep, yeah." We both

In late 1965 and early '66, many Beatlefans were a little puzzled by the title of the new Fabs album. *Rubber Soul?* You mean like *soul music*, à la the Temptations or James Brown? In the space of one album, did the Beatles metamorphose into a soul band?

But then we placed the disc on the turntable, waited in anticipation, and were treated to one of the hardest rockers the Beatles had released to date.

"Ah," went John, Paul, George, and Ringo lovers around the world. "Rubber *soul*. It's a *metaphor*."

Baby, it's understood.

Why it made the top 100

"Drive My Car" kicks off a milestone album, and is a meticulously written and produced piece of Beatlerock. It was the first song on the first album after the *Help!* soundtrack, and it signaled a shift in focus for the Fabs. It also heralded the beginning of the Beatles' astonishing creative surge that would soon include *Revolver* and all that followed.

What the song is about

A guy meets a full-of-herself, wannabe starlet who offers him a job as her chauffeur. He is quite enamored of her and, in return, she tells him that "*maybe* she'll love him" if he drives her car.

Perhaps to impress her, or simply to maintain some semblance of dignity, he assures her that he's got good prospects. She sees right through him, though, and tells him she knows he's "working for peanuts," and assures him that working for her is "a better time."

In a wry nod to the often frustrating dialogues men and women get themselves bogged down in, the verses of the song are sung by the hapless suitor; the chorus is sung by the object of his affection (lust?).

So, does the story resolve with the girl becoming a star and returning the guy's love?

Hardly. The punch line comes in the last verse, when we learn that after the guy accepts the job and tells her he can "start right away," she admits she doesn't even have a car, and it's breaking her heart (because she's broke and can't afford one? Or because she led him on?), but now she's got a driver "and that's a start."

"Drive My Car" is a clever look at ego, ambition, lust, deception, and delusional thinking, and it just might be one of the funniest songs the Beatles ever recorded.

• • • 🐛 • • •

- "Drive My Car" has a mistake in it that George Martin decided not to correct. In the last verse, Paul sings, "I told *the* girl I can start right away," while John sings "I told *that* girl…" George Martin talked about the difference in the July 1987 issue of *Musician* magazine: "That was never intended, but they did it that way. It was live, and things such as that slipped my attention. Once it went through and I saw it was there, I didn't think it was worthwhile calling them in again to replace a line; life's too short!"

- Stephen King used two lines from "Drive My Car" as an epigraph in his 1983 novel *Christine*.

Did you know?

- In early 1966, "Drive My Car" was one of four songs (the others were "What Goes On," "If I Needed Someone," and "Nowhere Man") that were restricted from airplay in the United States but could be played on the BBC, because they were not included on the U.S. version of *Rubber Soul.* "Drive My Car" came out in the U.S. on *Yesterday… and Today* on June 20, 1966.

- "Drive My Car" has been covered by Crosby, Stills, Nash and Young, Bobby McFerrin, the Breakfast Club, Bela Fleck, the McCoys, Cosmic Dilemma, and Sesame Street.

The recording

Location: **Abbey Road Studios, London.**

Dates: **October 13, 1965,** 7:00 p.m.–12:15 a.m. – The Beatles recorded four takes of the song, with the last one being the only complete run-through and the one determined to be the best. They also recorded many overdubs; by session's end, the song included Paul and John's lead vocal, George's backing vocal, tambourine, lead guitar, rhythm guitar, drums, piano, and cowbell. (This was the first time the Fabs had recorded past midnight.)

October 25, 1965 – Mono remixing.
October 26, 1965 – Stereo remixing.

Players/Instruments:
- **Paul McCartney:** Piano, bass, lead vocal
- **John Lennon:** Lead vocal, tambourine
- **George Harrison:** Lead guitar,[1] backing vocal
- **Ringo Starr:** Drums

What we really like about this song

Steve: One of the things I really like about "Drive My Car" is the beginning guitar, bass, and drums intro that utterly prevents the listener from zeroing in on the meter of the song until the "asked a girl what she wanted to be" line and, by that point, the familiarity of Ringo's steady drumming and John's accompanying tambourine. (Is John also playing the cowbell?) This brash intro sets the stage for a truly intricate piece of rock. I also like the dissonant harmony Paul and John sing fluidly for the last line of each verse. The addition of a piano for the chorus is also very tasty. And, of course, George's lead guitar sizzles, but even more impressive is the continual riffing George does under the verses. He lets the piano take center stage for the choruses and then jumps right back in with his sinuous licks for the verses. Nice.

Mike: I've got a soft spot for the songs sporting co-lead vocals by John and Paul—maybe it's the thought of them singing side by side at the mike? Hearing this song, my mind always flashes back to sitting on the floor of my mother's bedroom, age ten, listening to my sister's *Yesterday… and Today* album on Mom's self-contained record player/stereo. (I could swear the album had a butcher cover, but I couldn't figure out how to get the replacement cover sticker off, and Janet would have killed me if I started mangling it.) Of course, "Car" started the album, and I remember exactly where it always skipped at the guitar solo, and I would have to tap the player to help it over the skip. Much of the song's wit and ironic message was lost on me—I just liked the driving beat, the bass line, the "beep beep, mm, beep beep yeah"s. Flash forward about twenty-seven years, I'm playing the *Rubber Soul* CD in the next room while giving my oldest daughter, Sammy, a bath. She was about three and I was just starting to expose her to the Beatles. The song was unfamiliar to her, but she quickly latched on to the "beep beep mm, beep beep yeah"s. A new generation of Beatlefans was born!

[1] In The Beatles Anthology, George Harrison said, "I played the bassline on 'Drive My Car.' It was like the line from 'Respect' by Otis Redding." This does not mean George played bass on the track, though. In February 1977, in an interview with *Crawdaddy* magazine, George talked about playing the same bass line as Paul, but playing on the guitar: "I played that line on the guitar and Paul laid that with me on bass. We laid the track down like that."

It's the summer of 1967

and we're all listening to "Lovely Rita" pant to its orgasmic conclusion, when suddenly... hey! what is that, a rooster? A bloody *rooster?*

To say "Good Morning, Good Morning" was a surprise on first hearing is an understatement.

Why it made the top 100

"Good Morning, Good Morning" is, perhaps, one of the strongest pieces of evidence that the *Sgt. Pepper* album was a work of groundbreaking artistic significance.

No doubt about it: It's an odd piece of work. Yet, for all its strange meter, and bizarro world horns, and, yes, its zoo, "Good Morning, Good Morning" is still a *rock song*. It smokes with John's edgy vocal and Ringo's tasty, assured drumming; and Paul's guitar solo is *incendiary*. It speaks to the song's complexity and high musical caliber that it is one of the least covered Beatles songs. It's difficult to copy (or even imitate) perfection, eh?

Good Morning, Good Morning

What the song is about

A depressed guy goes to work (even though he doesn't want to) and, at the end of the day, he decides to walk home.

On his way, he starts to "roam" and he discovers that there's "nothing doing," that everything is closed and people are "half-asleep." But then his mood inexplicably improves, he starts to smile, and suddenly he sees things differently: Now there are people bustling around and everything is "full of

203

life." It's time for tea and a viewing of the popular British TV show *Meet the Wife*.

The message of "Good Morning, Good Morning" is optimistic. The passage of the song's working-class hero from doom and gloom to joy and the enjoyment of art is a metaphor for the creative process: John was coming up dry when, out of the blue, a line from a TV commercial inspired him.

Perhaps unconsciously, he then translated his experience of passing from creative vacuum to vibrant artist into the lyrics of the very song that was the result of the journey.

• • • 🦔 • • •

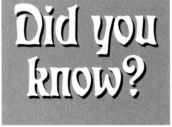

- The parade of animals on "Good Morning, Good Morning," in order, are: a rooster, cats, dogs, horses, sheep, lions, elephants, a fox being chased by bloodhounds, horses, a cow, and a hen. The sounds came from the sound effects archive at Apple, specifically Volume 35: *Animals and Bees* (for the lion, elephant, dog, sheep, cow, and cat) and Volume 57, for the foxhunt. Apparently, John was very specific about the order of the animals. Recording engineer Geoff Emerick, in *The Beatles Recording Sessions*, recalled, "John said to me during one of the breaks that they wanted to have the sound of animals escaping and that each successive animal should be capable of frightening or devouring its predecessor. So those are not just random effects, there was actually a lot of thought put into all that." (George Martin has discounted this story, calling it "fanciful.") Another story is that the animals are presented in order of size, although last time we looked, horses are usually bigger than sheep.
- "Good Morning, Good Morning" is one of two Beatles songs—both written by John—that repeat the title twice. (Can you name the other?[1])
- The final cluck in the song sounds remarkably like the opening guitar lick in the reprise of "Sgt. Pepper's Lonely Hearts Club Band." This was either intentional or it wasn't. According to George Martin, in *All You Need Is Ears*, it was an accident: "The way in which the record seemed to generate its own 'togetherness' became particularly apparent during the editing. A perfect example of that was 'Good Morning,' an up-tempo, fairly raucous song with a curious irregular metre to it. We normally faded out the music at the end of a song, but this time we decided to cover the fade with a host of sound-effects, particularly animals. We shoved everything in, from a pack of hounds in full cry to more basic farmyard noises. The order we had worked out for the album meant that that track was to be followed by a reprise of the 'Sgt. Pepper' song, and of course I was trying to make the whole thing flow. So imagine my delight when I discovered that the sound of a chicken clucking at the end of 'Good Morning' was remarkably like the guitar sound at the beginning of 'Sgt. Pepper.' I was able to cut and mix the two tracks in such a way that the one actually turned into the other. That was one of luckiest edits one could ever get." Geoff Emerick, in *The Beatles Recording Sessions*, disagreed: "No, no, that was no accident. We fully realized that the cluck matched the guitar. In fact, it wasn't a *perfect* match so we shifted the cluck up in time to match correctly. It was a fantastic little thing which will always stick in the mind."
- A snippet of "Good Morning, Good Morning" was played at the start of the fifty-eighth and final episode of *The Monkees* TV show, airing on March 25, 1968.

The recording

Location: **Abbey Road Studios, London.**
Dates: **February 8, 1967,** 7:00 p.m.–2:15 a.m. – Eight tracks were recorded of the basic rhythm track, but only four were complete.

February 16, 1967, 7:00 p.m.–1:45 a.m. – Overdubs of the vocals and bass guitar were recorded onto the rhythm track. ADT (Artificial Double Tracking) was applied to John's vocal, and a reduction mix was made. (This is the version on *Anthology 3*—the basic musical track with the vocal, but without the electric guitar solo, horns, or animal voices. The song ends with a cymbal crash.)

February 20, 1967 – Demo remix (mono).

March 13, 1967, 7:00 p.m.–2:30 a.m. – Today it was decided that brass instruments were needed for the track. They used Sounds Inc., a group Brian Epstein managed. Alan Holmes, sax player in the band, speaking in *The Beatles Recording Sessions*, recalled, "We were there for about six hours. The first three hours we had refreshments and the Beatles played us the complete song for the new LP." Richard Lush, the tape operator, also commenting in *The Beatles Recording Sessions*, said, "They spent a lot of time doing the overdub, about three hours or maybe longer, but John Lennon thought it sounded too straight. So we ended up flanging, limiting and compressing it, anything to make it sound unlike brass playing. It was typical John Lennon—he just wanted it to sound weird."

March 28, 1967 – John's lead vocal was overdubbed and the reduction mix was bumped down to two tracks. The lead guitar solo, played by Paul, was overdubbed, as were the backing vocals by John and Paul. The lead vocal was double-tracked (ADT) in remixing. The sound effects were assembled but not yet added to the song.

March 29, 1967 – More animal sounds were added and then all overdubbed onto the song.

April 6, 1967 – Mono and stereo mixing.

April 19, 1967 – Mono mixing. They went through fourteen mixes to get the cluck to match with the guitar, among other things they were trying to accomplish.

June 1, 1967 – First released on the U.K. LP *Sgt. Pepper's Lonely Hearts Club Band*.

Players/Instruments:
- **John Lennon:** Lead and backing vocal
- **Paul McCartney:** Bass, lead guitar and solo, backing vocal
- **George Harrison:** Lead vocal
- **Ringo Starr:** Drums
- **Sounds Incorporated:** Three saxophones, two trombones, and a French horn[2]

What we really like about this song

Steve: I like the wonky meter, the "Midnight Hour" horn riffs, John's vocal, and, of course, the menagerie. I also like the lyric—which, for all its serendipitous genesis, is one of John's best.

Mike: It has been said that by the time of *Sgt. Pepper*, John had grown lazy as a songwriter, drawing inspiration only from what was nearby. To that I say: *So what?* John repeatedly was able to take mundane elements of his life (here a TV commercial, for instance) and spin them into classic songs. Opening with a rooster's crow and ending with a chicken's cluck, this is one of my favorite *Sgt. Pepper* tunes, following beautifully after "Lovely Rita," at even a faster tempo. It's a straight-on rocker à la "Revolution," "Birthday," and "Back in the USSR." The lead guitar cuts into the song like a machete. It's interesting to compare the final version with the *Anthology* version and hear how the added solo added spice to the work. The song perfectly reflects the frenzied cacophony of everyday life, and it seems like every time I listen to it, I hear a new animal.

[1] "She Said She Said."

[2] Sounds Incorporated was a British band that appeared on the same bill as the Beatles on the '64 British fall tour, the '64 Christmas shows, and the '65 North American summer tour.

I'm a Loser

66

"I'm a Loser" is me in my Dylan period, because the word "clown" is in it. I objected to the word "clown," because that was always artsy-fartsy, but Dylan had used it so I thought it was all right, and it rhymed with whatever I was doing.

—John Lennon
The Beatles Anthology

Say it isn't so, Joe... er, John! A loser? You? But you're a Beatle!

Since "I'm a Loser" was never released as a single, the first time we heard it was on the *Beatles for Sale* album, right after "No Reply," a song in which John is unceremoniously ignored, lied to, and then dumped.

What in bloody hell, we all wondered, is going on in Beatleland? (We hadn't learned about Pepperland yet.)

All that aside, though, the song was Fab, and, as usual, the world went ballistic over another Fabs album, its pervasive lovelorn mojo notwithstanding.

Why it made the top 100

"I'm a Loser" is a great middle-period Beatles song, with a terrific chorus and displaying the early influences of Dylan and folk music that would soon blossom on *Rubber Soul*.

It has several Beatles trademarks, including beginning a cappella, beginning with the chorus, and the injection of a fun and unexpected harmonica solo from John (which we had not heard since "I Should Have Known Better").

What's with the sudden fade-out, though? Sounds early and rushed, doesn't it?

What the song is about

On the surface, "I'm a Loser" is a "love lost" song. But even a cursory examination of the lyrics makes it obvious that there is much more going on than a guy lamenting the loss of his love.

The opening chorus hints at the song's double meaning, with the singer telling us he's a loser, but then immediately cautioning us not to leap to conclusions with the line "And I'm not what I appear to be."

The first verse tells the story of him losing his girl—a one "in a million" lass, apparently.

The second verse is more generic: He tells us he's laughing and acting like a clown, but he's really frowning and crying. The self-analytical kicker comes in the last line: "Is it for her or myself that I cry?"

The last verse is pure introspection, and is perceived as John talking about the double-edged sword of fame and self-dissolution that came with being a Beatle. At first, he whines: "What have I done to deserve such a fate?" Then he admits that his pride played a role in his downfall, and he issues a cautionary warning to us all: "I'm telling you so you won't lose all," with the *all* meaning, of course, one's true identity.

Multileveled and complex, "I'm a Loser" is John's first oh-so-careful go at rattling the Beatle cage.

• • • ✿ • • •

- John considered "I'm a Loser" something of a breakthrough song in the sense that it was one of his first blatantly autobiographical works. In *The Beatles Anthology*, he said, "I had a sort of professional songwriter's attitude to writing pop songs; we would turn out a certain style of song for a single, and we would do a certain style of thing for this and the other thing. I'd have a separate songwriting John Lennon who wrote songs for the meat market, and I didn't consider them (the lyrics or anything) to have any depth at all, to express myself I would write *A Spaniard in the Works* or *In His Own Write*, the personal stories which were expressive of my personal emotions. Then I started being *me* about the songs, not writing them objectively, but subjectively."

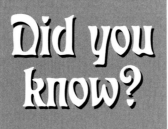

- Singer Jackie DeShannon was on the Beatles' summer 1964 North American tour and recalls John writing the song on the plane during the tour.
  - "I'm a Loser" is one of ten Beatles songs that mention the rain.[1]
  - "I'm a Loser" is one of eight Lennon/McCartney songs (of fourteen tracks) on *The Beatles for Sale* album. The Fabs had just released *A Hard Day's Night*, so not that many new songs had been written yet; thus they reverted to including covers on their albums, as they did with *Please Please Me* (six originals/eight covers), and *With the Beatles* (nine originals/five covers).
- The song has been covered by Marianne Faithfull and Vince Guaraldi.

The recording

Location: **Abbey Road Studios, London.**

Dates: **August 14, 1964,** 7:00–9:00 p.m. – Eight takes of the song were recorded, with four of them complete. A rough mono remix was made for John's personal use (presumably to take home and work on—as was his wont). Take 2 starts with John and Paul singing "I'm a loser," and Paul joining John on "not what I appear to be." It had a little faster tempo, no middle-eight harmonica or guitar solo, and they keep repeating "I'm a loser" together to the end.

October 26, 1964 – Remix from Take 8; mono mixing.
November 4, 1964 – Stereo remixing.

Players/Instruments:
- **John Lennon:** Acoustic guitar, harmonica, lead vocal
- **Paul McCartney:** Bass, harmony vocal
- **George Harrison:** Lead guitar
- **Ringo Starr:** Drums, tambourine

What we really like about this song

Steve: I state without hesitation that the choruses of "I'm a Loser" wouldn't be half as effective were it not for Paul's jazzy, walking bass line. He leaps into it excitedly after a standard two-notes-per-measure bass part in the verses. I also like the harmonies and George's lead guitar part. John's vocal is a tad odd, in that he never seems completely comfortable with the superlow notes in the last three words of the verses. One cannot help but wonder why he didn't raise the key to A (the song is in G) so that he wouldn't sound like he was rummaging around in the cellar trying to hit baritone notes almost out of his range.

Mike: Laugh, clown, laugh. The tears of a clown. I remember being slightly startled when I first heard it—why would John Lennon, leader of the Beatles, call himself a *loser*? Sacrilege! It's a revelation for John to admit that it's not so great, that he didn't always get the girl, and that he suffered loss and regret just like everyone else. You can definitely hear the Dylan influences in this song—the message, the harmonica, the rather stark and unaugmented John vocal. But I can also hear a touch of country, à la "Act Naturally," in the song.

---

[1] The other nine are "Across the Universe," "Fixing a Hole," "Hey Bulldog," "I Am the Walrus," "I'll Follow the Sun," "Penny Lane," "Please Please Me," "Rain," and "The Long and Winding Road."

You're Going to Lose That Girl

This is one of mine. I wasn't too keen on lyrics in those days. I didn't think they counted. Dylan used to come out with his latest acetate and say, "Listen to the words, man." And I'd say I don't listen to the words.

John Lennon
The Beatles *by Hunter Davies*

The "You're Going to Lose That Girl" sequence in the movie *Help!* is one of the greatest music videos ever made.

The Fabs (ostensibly) perform the song live in the studio, but it's staged with a wink and a grin, since Paul is seen playing bass *and* piano, Ringo is seen playing drums *and* then bongos, et cetera. All of which makes it clear that "we're not really live, but let's have fun anyway." (This scene is reminiscent of the train scene in *A Hard Day's Night* where the boys are in the cabin—then suddenly they're seen running alongside the train—and then they're back in the cabin.)

The "Lose That Girl" video is all smoky and hazy and some of the moments, like the one when Paul and George sing into one mike, if framed as a photograph, would undeniably be considered art. The fact that the background harmonies are classically Beatlesque (call/answer, call/answer) goes a long way toward making the scene memorable.

Why it made the top 100

This classic track from *Help!* is a straight-on rocker that does, indeed, fulfill John's intention of echoing girl groups like the Shirelles (see Did You Know?) while still maintaining the unique Beatles sound that could be imitated but never duplicated.

Especially nice here is the switch to a completely different key (G—the rest of the song is in E) for the bridge, followed by a smooth transition back to the home key.

Everything works on this track: John's vocal is quintessentially Lennonesque; Paul and George's tight, two-part harmonies are almost a song unto themselves; Ringo's drumming (not to mention his terrific bongo playing!) is understated yet provides the perfect bottom for the song.

What the song is about

Friend to friend, the singer makes his point: You *will* lose your girl, and it will be to me, if you don't get your act together and "treat her right."

In the first verse, the singer seems to be saying, *This is an easy fix*. All the guy has to do is take her out and treat her right, and if he doesn't, our hero will. (And he is specific and direct: He *will* take her out and he *will* treat her right.)

It's in the bridge that we learn that there might be more to the story. The singer's tone is harsher and more threatening. He'll "make a point" of taking her away from his friend. Where is the gentlemanly respect for an existing relationship? It has apparently been nullified by the way the guy treats his girl. And the singer isn't talking about simple disregard here. His "the way you treat her, what else can I do?" line comes off as though the girl is in desperate need of being rescued. Why? Perhaps the singer witnessed some behavior on the part of the existing boyfriend that appalled him?

The song concludes with a repeat of the title, and ends with one final, drawn-out "you're gonna loooose thaaat girl!"

The concerned and sympathetic friend of "She Loves You" has metamorphosed into a knight in shining armor—who happens to have an eye for the damsel he is promising to rescue.

• • • 🐞 • • •

- "You're Going to Lose That Girl" was written by John in a deliberate attempt to capture the spirit of one of his favorite girl groups, the Shirelles. (Some of their most famous hits were "I Met Him on a Sunday," "Soldier Boy," "Baby It's You," "Dedicated to the One I Love," and "Will You Love Me Tomorrow.") Do you think John succeeded?

- This is one of four Beatles songs in which the sung title does not perfectly match the official title. Even though it's "You're Going to Lose That Girl," John sings clearly, "You're gonna lose that girl." (The others are "I Want to Hold Your Hand," which is sung, "I wanna hold your hand"; "I Should Have Known Better," which is sung, "I shoulda known better…"; and "Everybody's Got Something to Hide Except Me and My Monkey," which is sung, "Everybody's got something to hide except for me and my monkey.")

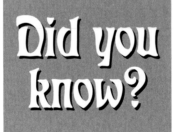

- "You're Going to Lose That Girl" is one of sixteen Beatles songs that begin a cappella (vocals only, without a musical accompaniment), if even for one syllable. This song is musicless for three syllables— "You're gonna…"

- On April 30, 1965, some two months after the song was actually recorded, the group filmed the memorable scene from *Help!* (at Twickenham Film Studios) of them recording the song. When they're done, they hear a buzzing sound and soon discover that the "bad guys" have been sawing a circular hole around Ringo and his drum set—and both proceed to fall through the floor!

The recording

Location: **Abbey Road Studios, London.**

Dates: **February 19, 1965**, 3:30–6:20 p.m. – Two takes were recorded. The first was a false start; the second was complete. Via overdubs, Paul added a piano and Ringo added bongos.

February 20, 1965 – Mono mixing.

February 23, 1965 – Stereo remixing (done twice, the second one ultimately preferred to the first).

March 30, 1965 – Overdubs of instruments (which were not specified on the studio documentation), none of which was ultimately used on the released version of the song.

April 2, 1965 – A third attempt at a stereo remix, using the material from the March 30 overdub, but they decided to stick with the second remix from February 23.

August 6, 1965 – First released on the U.K. LP *Help!*

Players/Instruments:

- **John Lennon:** Acoustic guitar, lead vocal
- **Paul McCartney:** Bass, piano, backing vocal
- **George Harrison:** Lead guitar, backing vocal
- **Ringo Starr:** Drums, bongos

What we really like about this song

Steve: In my younger years, I was in a band called Breakdown. (Don't blame me: Our manager came up with the name.) One song we did was "You're Going to Lose That Girl." I sang lead and my bandmates did the two-part harmony. We *loved* doing this song. The harmonies, the chord changes, the beat—all combined to make for a killer song to perform live. It always went over with the crowd, too. (It went over so well, in fact, that we often did it twice. Not that we minded.)

Mike: This song takes the theme only hinted at in "She Loves You" one step further. There's no beating around the bush this time—if you don't treat that girl right, I'm going to take her from you. The boys are in fine voice: The background vocals almost seem to be mocking and, while I'm not much of a fan of falsetto, John does a nice job with it. (I especially like when he sings "You're gonna looooooo!") Also, it's always nice when a little extra percussion is added, and I like the bongos that accent the music throughout.

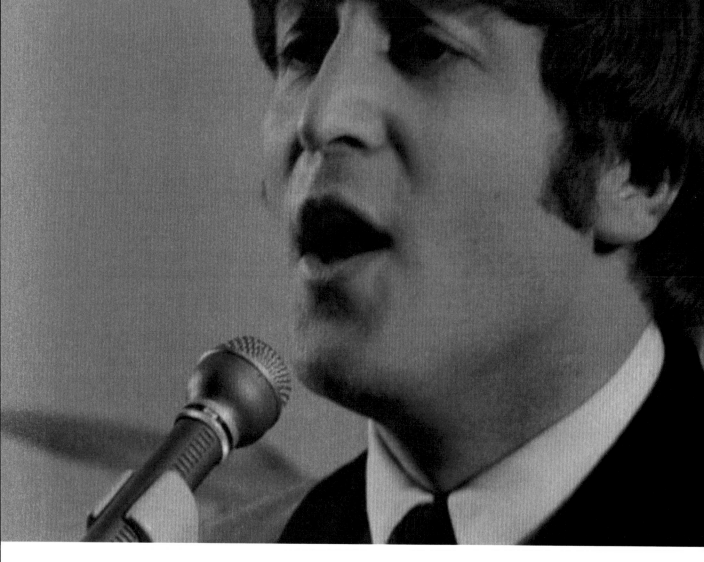

68 No Reply

That's my song. That's the one where Dick James, the publisher, said, "That's the first complete song you've written where it resolves itself." You know, with a complete story... I had that image of walking down the street and seeing her silhouetted in the window and not answering the phone, although I never called a girl on the phone in my life. Because phones weren't part of the English child's life.

John Lennon
Playboy, September 1980

An early version of this song can be heard on *Anthology 1* (Disc Two, Track 20), and what's notable about it is that the incredibly powerful chorus of "I saw the light, I saw the light" was truncated to only one phrase. The Fabs hit the first "I saw the light" like gangbusters, then go right back into the verse. Knowing the song as well as we all do now, the horrible "wrongness" of stopping at only one "I saw the light" stands out glaringly.

We find this version unsettling, and are delighted that John likewise knew something was missing and ultimately gave us the version we all know and love.

Why it made the top 100

This is a great rock ballad with a chorus that sells the song. It's an unusual composition in that the Fabs leap into the chorus after only two lines of the verse—their normal routine would have been to do another two. It's surprising to hear the chorus so quickly, and it emphasizes the neurotic urgency of the lyrics.

For all its acoustic instrumentation, this songs packs a powerful punch more akin to a fully electric production.

What the song is about

When the song begins, it is obvious that our hero has been dumped, and yet this has apparently not fully sunk in. He tells us in the very first line that he had previously been rebuffed after the breakup ("This happened once before…"), and yet he still stood outside her house and stared longingly up at her window.

In typical "ex" fashion, he calls her repeatedly, but she won't take his calls and her family runs interference for her by telling him she's not home. He knows they're lying, but he *doesn't get the message* and simply cannot accept that she wants nothing more to do with him.

The fourth verse is revealing: "I saw you walk in your door…" It's all too easy to conjure up an image of this pathetic lovelorn loser hiding in the bushes, watching her come home from a date with another guy. This could also come off as stalkerish, but he is so distraught ("I nearly died!") that we know he would never do anything to hurt Ms. Dream Girl, and what would make him truly happy is if she took him back.

He makes his case in the bridge, where he tells her that she should realize that he loves her more than any other guy. But then he makes a critical error. He tells her "I'll forgive the lies that I heard before…"—conveniently ignoring the fact that the only reason she's lying is that *he won't leave her alone.*

The song ends with this bereft ex-boyfriend lamenting he gets "no reply" from the woman he loves.

Yeah, the best way to win back a former lover is to knock on her door uninvited, ceaselessly call her, and spy on her. He's lucky all he's getting is "no reply." We know many women who would be singing "restraining order" if they were subjected to this kind of nonsense.

• • • 🐛 • • •

- The Fabs considered releasing "No Reply" as the follow-up single to "A Hard Day's Night"/ "Things We Said Today," but went with "I Feel Fine"/"She's a Woman" instead.
- John originally intended to give "No Reply" to British pop singer Tommy Quickly. If Quickly ever actually did record his version of the song, it was never released.

Did you know?

- The June 3, 1964, rough demo of "No Reply" has drumming on it, but no one—to this day—knows who was playing the drums on the track. Ringo was out sick and Jimmy Nicol had left for the day. Ah, nothing like an enduring Beatles mystery, eh?
- The song has been covered by the Buzzcocks and John Mayall and the Bluesbreakers.

The recording

Location: **Abbey Road Studios, London.**

Dates: **June 3, 1964** – On this day, John, Paul, and George rehearsed with drummer Jimmy Nicol, who was to be their touring drummer for the first few dates of an upcoming world tour after Ringo fell ill with tonsillitis and pharyngitis. After Nicol left, they recorded several demos in a 5:30–9:30 p.m. session. The only song the Beatles ever officially released from this last-minute session was "No Reply." Other tracks from this session included songs Cilla Black recorded, as well as ones that were never issued. The demo tapes were misfiled and rediscovered in 1993. Very little info about them exists on the official record, although two of the tracks were issued on *Anthology 1*: "No Reply" and George's second composition, "You Know What to Do" (which was never officially released).

September 30, 1964 – After a long day in the studio recording "Every Little Thing" and "What You're Doing," eight takes of "No Reply" were recorded. John's voice was blown out, however, so Paul handled the high-register harmonies. George Martin added a piano part. Take 5 experimented with making the song longer (3:17), but the final version clocked in at 2:14. Take 8 was considered the best, and echo was added to John's vocal at the remix stage.

October 16, 1964 – Mono mixing.

November 4, 1964 – Stereo mixing.

December 4, 1964 – First released on the U.K. LP *Beatles for Sale*.

Players/Instruments:
- **John Lennon:** Acoustic guitar, lead vocal
- **Paul McCartney:** Bass, harmony vocal
- **George Harrison:** Lead guitar, harmony vocal
- **Ringo Starr:** Drums
- **George Martin:** Piano

What we really like about this song

Steve: When I list my ten favorite Beatles songs, "No Reply" is usually number eleven. I love the sound of it, and I especially love the chord changes of the chorus—"I nearly died, I nearly died"—A minor to E minor, then F major 7 to E minor. It genuinely gives me goose bumps every time I hear it. I'm a little less enamored of the lyrics, though. The guy comes off like a loser who can't take no for an answer, and I have never liked people like that.

Mike: I feel bad for John, getting spurned by love yet again. He's trying to keep his self-confidence—"I love you more than any other guy"—but he doesn't sound very convincing, even to himself. I like the acoustic feel of the song, and Paul helping out on the high-register parts. Maybe there's just a little too much echo on John's vocal, though?

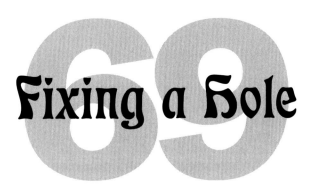

Fixing a Hole

The night we went to record ["Fixing a Hole"], a guy turned up at my house who announced himself as Jesus. So I took him to the session. You know, couldn't harm, I thought. Introduced Jesus to the guys. Quite reasonable about it. But that was it. Last we ever saw of Jesus.

Paul McCartney
Playboy, 1984

What an odd title for a song! many of us
thought upon first seeing the *Sgt. Pepper* track listing. "Fixing a Hole"? Like, uh, "Painting a Fence"? Or "Hammering a Nail"?

Well, sort of. And once we got past the title, we were off, experiencing and enjoying one of the Fabs' most offbeat yet ironically mainstream songs.

Why it made the top 100

With its jazzy syncopation and straight rock bridge, "Fixing a Hole" is one of the more innovative songs on *Sgt. Pepper*, an album that is *overflowing* with innovative tracks.

Paul's writing is sophisticated and confident here, evidenced by his assured and easy use of augmented and minor sixth chords, as well as his multileveled lyrics. The smooth production does the song justice, too, making wonderful use of a harpsichord, a sizzling guitar, and so-subtle-you-almost-don't-notice-them background vocals by John and George.

What the song is about

If the printed lyrics for this song had not been included with the original *Sgt. Pepper* LP (and later in a booklet with the CD), how many of us would have heard Paul sing "stops my mind from *wondering*..." instead of "wandering"? Both are verbs, and they are but one letter apart, but they hint at a different psychology, depending on which one you choose to hear. Stopping a mind from *wondering* where it will go suggests doubt, uncertainty, confusion, and a lack of focus about the *self*. On the other hand, stopping a mind from *wandering* where it will go suggests a censoring from *outside* the self, a deliberate shutting down of a mind that confidently wishes to... well, *wander*.

But the word Paul uses is definitely *wandering*, and thus we know that, in this song at least, he is feeling besieged by outside forces, which he quickly identifies as "the people standing there who disagree and never win," and the "silly people" who "run around," concluding with the unsettling admission, "they worry me."

A question comes to mind: Could the subconscious "wandering/wondering" wordplay affect our reaction to the song? This "hidden" ambiguity might very well have been intentional.

Paul continues the wordplay with the bridge, where he sings, "And it doesn't really matter if I'm wrong I'm right/Where I belong I'm right/Where I belong..."

Is he saying that even if he's wrong, he's right? Or is he saying that even if he's wrong, *he's right where he belongs?* Different parsing, different meanings.

The "home improvement" metaphors—fixing a hole, filling the cracks, painting a room—all lead toward the final image of him "taking the time for a number of things that weren't important yesterday."

Paul's own comments about the meaning of this song (from *The Beatles in Their Own Words*) are revealing: "This song is just... a good old analogy—the hole in your makeup which lets the rain in and stops your mind from going where it will. It's you interfering with things..."

After the confusion and doubt, the song concludes with the aforementioned "taking the time..." image, providing listeners with confirmation of newfound clarity and the ultimate message of the song, "free your mind." This nicely foreshadows *Pepper*'s Side Two opening song, "Within You Without You," in which George tells us, "When you've seen beyond yourself/ Then you may find/Peace of mind is waiting there..."

- Paul wrote "Fixing a Hole" after repairing the roof on his Scottish farmhouse (which he bought, along with four hundred acres of land, sight unseen in June 1966).
- Beatles road manager Mal Evans helped write this song. He was paid for his efforts, but not given official credit. (Tragically, Mal was shot to death by police in 1976 when he waved an air pistol at two policemen while in a depressed state.)

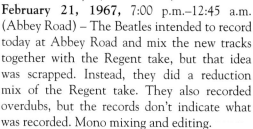

Did you know?

- "Fixing a Hole" is one of ten Beatles songs that mention rain. (See the complete list in song number 72, "Hey Bulldog.")
- The song was covered by George Burns (yes, that George Burns) for the *Sgt. Pepper* movie soundtrack.

The recording

Location: **Regent Sound Studios; Abbey Road Studios, London.**

Dates: **February 9, 1967** (Regent Sound Studios) – In their first session outside Abbey Road since being under contract with EMI, the Beatles recorded six unofficial rehearsal takes, followed by three takes of the full song, including lead vocal. (Usually the Fabs recorded the rhythm track first, and then added overdubbed vocals.) George Martin, in *The Beatles Recording Sessions*, recalled the Regent studio: "We couldn't get in to Abbey Road that night. But Regent Sound was a pretty awful little studio, very cramped and boxy." George Martin was no longer an EMI employee, so he was free to go with the Beatles, but Geoff Emerick and the other Abbey Road supporting staff could not work at Regent and so were spelled by Regent staff. The first two takes were complete, with Take 2 deemed the better. Interestingly, a Regent session tape shows that the harpsichord and bass were played on a single track at the same time. Could George Martin have played the harpsichord at Regent and Paul at Abbey Road, thus the conflicting recording

notes? (See Players/Instruments.)

February 21, 1967, 7:00 p.m.–12:45 a.m. (Abbey Road) – The Beatles intended to record today at Abbey Road and mix the new tracks together with the Regent take, but that idea was scrapped. Instead, they did a reduction mix of the Regent take. They also recorded overdubs, but the records don't indicate what was recorded. Mono mixing and editing.

April 7, 1967 – Stereo mixing.

June 1, 1967 – First released on the U.K. LP *Sgt. Pepper's Lonely Heart's Club Band.*

Players/Instruments:
- **Paul McCartney:** Bass, harpsichord, lead guitar, lead vocal
- **John Lennon:** Backing vocal, maracas
- **George Harrison:** Lead guitar and solo (double tracked), backing vocal
- **Ringo Starr:** Drums

Note: Some sources say George Martin played harpsichord on the track. Neil Aspinall, however, confirmed that it was Paul playing harpsichord on "Fixing a Hole."[1]

What we really like about this song

Steve: Listen to Paul's bass playing during the second half of George's double-tracked lead guitar solo: It echoes the little bass triplet he uses at the end of each line of the verse. This could not have been unplanned. I remember thinking the first few times I heard this song, *Well, now, this certainly is something different.* Coming on the heels of "Getting Better" and "Lucy," "Fixing a Hole" confirmed unequivocally (in case any of us had any lingering doubts) that *Sgt. Pepper* was, indeed, something quite extraordinary.

Mike: Never before has home improvement sounded so jazzy and cool. Like most songs on *Pepper*, the instrumental backing is unusual, but it all works together: A harpsichord is played throughout (not just as an accent, as in other songs); Ringo plays very little drum but lots of swingin' cymbal; Paul's bass, again, sounds like a tuba (!); George's distorted guitar adds spice before launching into a blistering solo. (Perhaps in his solo career, Paul should have made an entire concept album about home repair!)

[1] *Beatles Monthly.*

70 Lovely Rita

He makes them up like a novelist.
—*John Lennon*
Playboy, *January 1981*

Paul McCartney is a natural storyteller, and we cannot help but wonder what kind of short stories and novels he would have produced if he had gravitated toward fiction instead of songwriting. "Lovely Rita," like "Rocky Raccoon," "Back in the USSR," "Eleanor Rigby," "Lady Madonna," "Maxwell's Silver Hammer," "Ob-La-Di, Ob-La-Da," and others, is one of Paul's "story" songs. He can take a trifling event such as receiving a parking ticket and transform it into a classic rock song.

Why it made the top 100

We're tempted to say that "Lovely Rita" made the cut because it's on *Pepper*. Period. But even though almost every cut on *Pepper* made this ranking (sorry, Paul, but we agree that "When I'm Sixty-Four" should have been kicked in favor of "Strawberry Fields" and/or "Penny Lane"), "Rita" is here because it's a great tune, with great lyrics and superior production. It is, in a word, essential.

What the song is about

The opening verse sounds as if the singer and Rita are an item—"nothing can come between us"—but by the end of the song, we realize that his affection for Rita may be one-sided. In retrospect, the song has a slight "stalker" vibe to it.

The narrator does take Rita out and *tries* to win her, but it doesn't sound as if he succeeds. She allows him to come home with her (after independently paying the restaurant bill—no obligations of any kind for Rita), but he and Rita are chaperoned on the sofa by "a sister or two." We believe that the narrator apparently tried something because he "nearly" made it, but, in the end, he's begging her to at least give him a wink so he can think of her. It appears that he can only truly have Rita in his fantasies.

It is then that the line "when it gets *dark* I tow your heart away" makes a little more sense, eh? Sounds to us like a rejected suitor refusing to take no for an answer and waiting until it gets dark to go after what he wants.

• • • 🐛 • • •

- Years after the release of *Sgt. Pepper,* a female traffic warden named Meta Davies stepped forward and claimed that she was the inspiration for the song. In 1967, while on duty, she wrote a parking ticket for expired meter time for a "P. McCartney." "I'd just put it on the windscreen when Paul came along and took it off. He looked at it and read my signature which was in full, because there was another M. Davies on the same unit. As he was walking away, he turned to me and said, 'Oh, is your name really Meta?' I told him that it was. We chatted for a few minutes and he said, 'That would be a good name for a song. Would you mind if I use it?' And that was that. Off he went." She was twenty-two years older than Paul and was not a Beatlefan, although at the time her teenage daughter was.

- The almost immediate reaction to the line "When are you free to take some tea with me?" was that Paul was referring to marijuana. In *The Beatles in Their Own Words,* Paul set the record straight: "Tea, not pot. It's like saying, 'Come and cut the grass' and then realizing that could be pot, or

the old teapot could be something about pot. But I don't mind pot and I leave the words in. They're not consciously introduced just to say pot and be clever."

- It seems that Rita makes an appearance in the "Free as a Bird" video. A woman is seen crossing Abbey Road and walking toward the "28IF" Volkswagen. She is wearing a dress and a hat, but it is unclear whether or not it's a uniform. Since she also appears to be carrying a pad, this would seem to be Rita the meter maid. Just before she disappears out of frame, it looks as if she veers slightly toward the front of the Volkswagen.

- "Lovely Rita" played a role in the "Paul is Dead" hoax (uh, mystery). In the song, Paul tells us that he "caught a glimpse of Rita" and was so distracted that he "took her home" and "nearly made it." This leads to the line telling us that he "didn't notice that the light had changed," from "A Day in the Life." We are also told in "A Day in the Life" that "he blew his mind out in a car." Thus, Rita was apparently the cause of the fatal car accident that killed Paul McCartney.

- Fats Domino covered "Lovely Rita."

The recording

Location: **Abbey Road Studios, London**.

Dates: **February 23, 1967,** 7:00 p.m.–3:45 a.m. – The Fabs started recording "Rita" after finishing the stereo master of "A Day in the Life" (see song number 1). Takes 1–8 had George on acoustic guitar on Track 1, John playing acoustic guitar on Track 2, Ringo drumming on Track 3, and Paul playing piano, with tape echo, on Track 4. Take 8 was considered the best, and a reduction mix into Take 9 with all the instruments sharing one track was created. Paul's bass was then superimposed onto this track.

February 24, 1967, 7:00 p.m.–1:15 a.m. – Paul's lead vocal was recorded. (At this stage, the song had a longer piano intro than on the album.) Following further reduction mixes, Take 9 became Takes 10 and 11.

March 7, 1967, 7:00 p.m.–2:30 a.m – A reduction mix, now called Take 11, was recorded on which John sang backing vocal, heavily echoed. John got lost in the echo, riffing cha-chas, moaning, sighing, et cetera. They also recorded the sound of comb and toilet paper. Geoff Emerick, in *The Beatles Recording Sessions*, recalled, "John always wanted repeat echo in his headphones, it gave him more excitement. They'd finished doing the vocal on 'Lovely Rita' and he just started fooling around, using the echo as his inspiration."

March 21, 1967, 7:00 p.m.–2:45 a.m. – This was an infamous day at the Abbey Road Studios. John had dropped acid and George Martin took him up to the roof, thinking he'd fallen ill. After recording the backing vocals for "Getting Better" (see song number 35), they recorded the piano solo for "Rita," which was played by George Martin. They taped it at forty-one cycles per second so that it sounded very fast on replay. Geoff Emerick, in *The Beatles Recording Sessions*, said, "I used to try out funny things in odd moments and I discovered that by putting sticky tape over the capstan of a tape machine you could wobble the tape on the echo machine, because we used to delay the feed into the echo chamber by tape. So I suggested we did this using a piano sound. The Beatles themselves couldn't think what should go into the song's middle eight and they didn't really like my idea at first, but it turned out fine in the end because of the effect. It gave the piano a sort of honky-tonk feel. In fact, Paul asked me to play the solo when I made the suggestion but I was too embarrassed." Members of Pink Floyd were also at Abbey Road that night recording their first album, and they were brought in to meet the Beatles, including the tripping John.

Players/Instruments:
- **Paul McCartney:** Bass, piano, comb and paper, lead and backing vocal
- **John Lennon:** Acoustic guitar, comb and paper, backing vocal
- **George Harrison:** Acoustic guitar, comb and paper, backing vocal
- **Ringo Starr:** Drums
- **George Martin:** Honky-tonk piano

What we really like about this song

Steve: I love the piano intro, the harmonies, and the weird piano outro. Unlike my coauthor, I think the ending is just right for the song, and the glissando piano slide that sets the stage for the barnyard animals of John's "Good Morning, Good Morning" is just perfect.

Mike: As John said, "Lovely Rita" is just a pop song without any real depth or weight, but its catchy lyrics, unusual instrumentation, and stellar production carry it. Its imagery is vivid—we can almost see the whole song taking place. It's got a jaunty, lively vibe and follows perfectly after the old-time-sounding "When I'm Sixty-Four." I like Paul's trippy bass—he trots through arpeggios and he is brought to the "front" of the song. It also sounds like the acoustic guitar has been distorted somehow. It's continually amazing what sounds they were able to achieve with ancient production facilities. If I had a criticism of the song, I'd say that "Rita" sounds like it doesn't know how to end. It almost sounds as if someone pulled the plug or just slammed a door.

71

Please Please Me

"Please Please Me" is my song completely. It was my attempt at writing a Roy Orbison song, would you believe it?

John Lennon
Playboy

The year 1963 started the Beatles ball rolling. In January, the "Please Please Me" single was released, and it quickly became the first Beatles record to truly connect with the music-buying public. Also in 1963, Ringo bought a new set of Ludwig drums (gray/blue pearloid) and had "The Beatles" lettered on the bass for the first time, a momentous acknowledgment of the group's ambitious plans.

And in October, after the release of "She Loves You," the term *Beatlemania* was used for the first time, in press coverage of the Fabs' live appearance on *Val Parnell's Sunday Night at the London Palladium.*

Why it made the top 100

The Beatles' second single succeeded beyond the band's wildest expectations and was the seed from which grew their first album, *Please Please Me*.

John's songwriting may have been his best to date, and the performance on the record is tight and polished.

No wonder it went to Number One almost immediately, eh?

What the song is about

"Please Please Me" takes place the day after "the night before" ("Last night I said these words…"), and its message is easily summed up: *One hand washes the other.* Or at least it should.

The singer is complaining to his lady love that she doesn't even try to please him the way he pleases her. He scolds her for not even trying, reminds her that he doesn't need to draw her a picture ("You don't need me to show the way…"), and snipes that he always has to be the one to initiate romance ("Why do *I* always have to say 'love'?").

He apparently loves this girl, but her inability (refusal?) to reciprocate really bothers our hero. He uses the bridge to apologize reluctantly ("I don't wanna sound complainin'"), but again reminds her of how miserable he is ("there's always rain in my heart") and rails against her for being guarded and cold ("it's so hard to reason with you").

The last line of the song is a desperate question: "Why do you make me blue?" made all the more pathetic by the mantra-like pleading "Come on, come *on!*" throughout, voiced the way a child would beg a parent to let him have his way.

The Beatles' first single was "Love Me Do," a song with an almost identical message to "Please Please Me," their second single.

Even at an early age, all the Fabs needed was love.

- During the September 1962 recording of "Please Please Me," Ringo eccentrically played the bass drum with one hand, and shook maracas and a tambourine with the other. He believes this was why George Martin hired Andy White for the "Love Me Do" single.
- In the first year of the Beatles' career, George Martin had the final decision on what songs to release. In *The Beatles Anthology*, he recalled, "I didn't later, but I did then."
- "Please Please Me" was the Fabs' second Parlophone single, and it quickly went to Number One in the United Kingdom. This necessitated rush-recording their *Please Please Me* LP, which was captured in one marathon session on February 11, 1963— one month to the day after the single had been released.

- In *The Beatles Anthology*, Neil Aspinall talked about the boys signing away the rights to their songs: "Dick James got the rights to the single 'Please Please Me,' and all the subsequent songs, too. We were all pretty naïve back then and I think that the Beatles have all since regretted the deals they got into regarding song ownership." The Beatles lost control of their own copyrights in 1969 after selling part of their company for tax reasons.
- On May 18, 1963, the Beatles began the first tour on which they were the top-billed act. Also on the bill were Roy Orbison and Gerry and the Pacemakers.
- "Please Please Me" was on of the songs performed by the Beatles on their second appearance on the *Ed Sullivan Show* on February 16, 1964.
- The song has been covered by David Cassidy, the Flamin' Groovies, Sluts for Hire, and Gigi on the Beach.

The recording

Location: **Abbey Road Studios, London.**

Dates:

September 4, 1962 – The Beatles practiced but did not record "Please Please Me," one of six songs they rehearsed. (On this day they did record Mitch Murray's "How Do You Do It," then "Love Me Do.")

September 11, 1962 – A slower "Roy Orbison–inspired" version was recorded, but it didn't seem quite right. The recording logs do not reveal how many takes were recorded. (The tape was believed to have been erased. It resurfaced in 1994 and is on *Anthology 1*.) George Martin remarked, "We haven't quite got 'Please Please Me' right, but it's too good a song to throw away. We'll leave it for another time."[1]

November 26, 1962 – At first, George Martin wouldn't let them re-record "Please Please Me"; he wanted them to release "How Do You Do It?" They gave in, and did record "How Do You Do It?" (which is on *Anthology 1*), but then they tore into a faster version of "Please Please Me." They rehearsed for an hour and then recorded eighteen takes. Harmonica would be dubbed in later in the session because it was hard for John to sing, play guitar, and play harmonica all at the same time. Martin, in *All You Need Is Ears*, recalled the day: "The whole session was a joy. And the end of it, I pressed the intercom button in the control room and said, 'Gentlemen, you've just made your first No. 1 record.'"

November 30, 1962 – Mono mixing.

January 11, 1963 – First released as a single in the United Kingdom, backed with "Ask Me Why."

February 25, 1963 – Editing and stereo mixing for the *Please Please Me* LP.

Players/Instruments:
- **John Lennon:** Rhythm guitar, harmonica, lead vocal
- **Paul McCartney:** Bass, harmony vocal
- **George Harrison:** Lead guitar, harmony vocal
- **Ringo Starr:** Drums

What we really like about this song

Steve: "Please Please Me" intrigued me the very first time I heard it: I had never heard a descending harmony vocal line in a pop song before. You know the line I'm referring to: "Last night I said these words… ," et cetera. This sounded, well, *new*. And it was. There was an aura, a special something about the record that far exceeded the feeling we had gotten when we heard the Fabs' first single, "Love Me Do." The writing was better, the performance was more exciting, and truly, for the first time, the Beatles magic was real and irresistible. And still to come in 1963 *alone* was "From Me to You," "She Loves You," and "I Want to Hold Your Hand."

Mike: "Please Please Me" stands head and shoulders above any other song on the Beatles' debut album. It's so energetic, uptempo, and fun that it seems almost out of place on an LP replete with slower, more "pensive" songs (aside from "Twist and Shout" and "I Saw Her Standing There," of course). My favorite parts of the song are the guitars jangling up the scale after each verse, the call-and-response "c'mon"s, and the six-guitar-note riff played just before the "c'mon"s. I'm glad they decided to scrap the first draft of the song in favor of the more upbeat final recording. (Think about how cool it would have been to hear Roy Orbison do a cover version of the song he inspired!)

[1] *The Beatles Recording Sessions.*

The recording

Location: **Abbey Road Studios, London.**

Dates: **February 11, 1968, 4:00 p.m.–2:00 a.m.** – The Beatles were in the studio, making a promotional film for "Lady Madonna," and decided to try to complete and record a new song on the spot. They recorded ten takes of the basic rhythm track of piano, drums, tambourine, lead guitar, and bass on straight four-track, with no reduction mixes. They then overdubbed onto Take 10 fuzz bass, drums (deliberately off beat—you can hear it), the middle eight guitar solo, a double-tracked lead vocal, and a single-tracked backing vocal. Mono mixing was then completed. Geoff Emerick, speaking in *The Beatles Recording Sessions*, recalled, "That was a really fun song. We were all into sound texture in those days and during the mixing we put ADT [Artificial Double Tracking] on one of the 'What did he say? Woof woof' bits near the end of the song. It came out really well."

October 29, 1968 – Stereo mixing and remixing.

January 13, 1969 – First released on the U.S. LP *Yellow Submarine*.

Players/Instruments:
- **John Lennon**: Piano, lead vocal, lead guitar
- **Paul McCartney**: Bass, piano,[2] harmony vocal
- **George Harrison**: Lead guitar, tambourine
- **Ringo Starr**: Drums

What we really like about this song

Steve: There are several elements of this song that I have loved since I first heard it in the sixties. First, I had to immediately learn the opening piano riff (along with, I'll bet, every other Beatles-loving piano player on the planet). I also love (in order of delight) John's vocal (one of his best), Paul's bass (amazing), and John's surprising guitar solo (perfectly complemented by George riffing on the "Bulldog" riff). And I smile every time I hear Ringo saying, "Yeah?" after John sings "Big man." I'm still wondering how a wigwam can be frightened of the dark, though.

Mike: Freewheeling, playful, out of control, surreal. John dismisses the song and he's right—it really doesn't mean anything. But that doesn't make it a bad song. Paul was kicking butt with his bass (doing his best John Entwistle impression); I always liked the song's riff, played on both guitar and piano; and, for some reason, the song reminds me of the Monkees' "I'm Gonna Buy Me a Dog," which was obviously made up in the studio and includes the band members goofing around, chattering, howling, barking—just having a good time. The result, in both cases, was a memorable song.

---

[1] Ten Beatles songs mentioning rain: "Across the Universe," "Fixing a Hole," "Hey Bulldog," "I Am the Walrus," "I'll Follow the Sun," "I'm a Loser," "The Long and Winding Road," "Penny Lane," "Please Please Me," "Rain."

[2] There is some question over whether Paul or John played piano on the track, although many Beatles chroniclers assume it was Paul.

Doctor Robert

John Lennon: Another of mine. Mainly about drugs and pills. It was about myself. I was the one that carried all the pills on tour and always…

Playboy: Dispensed them?

JL: Yeah. Well, in the early days. Later on, the roadies did it. We just kept them in our pockets loose. In case of trouble.

—Playboy

Prior to *Revolver*, all the Beatles ever wrote about was romance and relationships (with the notable exception, of course, of *Rubber Soul*'s "Nowhere Man"). Suddenly, with one album, their focus changed. Confiscatory taxes, the alienated and lonely, laziness, consciousness, the afterlife, and, lest we forget, yellow submarines were all topics found on *Revolver*.

And then, on this same album, came "Doctor Robert," which was about (blimey!) recreational drug use.

The message was clear: *We've changed. Either get on board or get out of the way.*

Most of us happily went along for the ride.

Why it made the top 100

"Doctor Robert" is a great rocker with a completely unexpected interlude that sounds like a stoned celestial choir singing the praises of their drug supplier.

Coming, as it does, after the melancholic "For No One," it serves as a bracing musical tonic of sorts, a turn-up-the-heat and kick-out-the-jams ode to sex, drugs, and rock and roll (without the sex).

The song's hint of country, druggy lyrics, and its euphoria-tinged harmonies, contributed to making *Revolver* the landmark album that it was—and still is.

What the song is about

Yes, it's true. Our charming and lovable mop-tops were naughty boys during their Beatle days, and "Doctor Robert" is a tongue-in-cheek snapshot of one area of their recreational interests: prescription drugs, mainly amphetamines.

But who *is* Doctor Robert? As we know from the epigraph, John claimed that *he* was the good doctor, and that he had written the song about himself.

But Beatles lore and many expert sources all agree that the subject of the song was one Dr. Robert Freymann, a sixty-year-old (at the time) German-born physician who had a practice on East 78th Street in New York City. (The "Dr. Charles Roberts" cited in some Beatles books didn't exist. It was an alias used by Jean Stein, the biographer of Andy Warhol actress Edie Sedgwick, to conceal the identity of another "speed doctor in New York who was likewise prolific with his prescription pad at the time."[1])

Robert Freymann was known as Dr. Robert or the Great White Father, and was famous for his shock of white hair and his willingness to prescribe amphetamines for the asking. He signed jazz legend Charlie Parker's death certificate, and was very connected to New York's art scene. "I have a clientele that is remarkable, from every sphere of life," he once boasted. "'I could tell you in ten minutes probably 100 famous names who come here."[2]

John Lennon was one of his steady patients, and he wrote the song in the doctor's "honor." The lyrics are praising and grateful: He'll be there anytime you need him; "he helps you to understand"; "he's a man you must believe"; he's "helping anyone in need."

Interestingly, in his lyrics John revealed (perhaps unconsciously) his compulsive personality and his future addictions.[3] He specifically used the word *need* to describe what Dr. Robert fulfilled and satisfied. Not *want*. He made it clear that the people who saw Doctor Bob had a need. And he was one of those who kept Doctor Robert writing prescriptions.

But what about John's claim that *he* was Doctor Robert? Faulty memory? Dual meaning to the character?

We'll never really know.

Did you know?

The recording

Location: **Abbey Road Studios, London.**

Dates: **April 17, 1966,** 2:30–10:30 p.m. – All things considered, this is one of *Revolver's* most straightforward recordings. Seven takes of the backing track were recorded, comprising lead and rhythm guitars, bass, and drums, plus maracas (played by George). Also, John played harmonium, and, according to Lewisohn, Paul played piano (although a piano can most definitely not be heard in the final track). The last take was considered the best. The song ended up running 2:56, but would ultimately be edited down to 2:13.

April 19, 1966, 2:30 p.m.–midnight – All vocal overdubs were recorded, and three rough mono

mixes were made.

May 12, 1966 – Mono mixing for *Yesterday… and Today.*

May 20, 1966 – Stereo mixing.

June 20, 1966 – First released on U.S. LP *"Yesterday"… and Today.*

June 21, 1966 – Three mono remixes; editing.

Players/Instruments:
- **John Lennon:** Harmonium, maracas, lead vocal
- **Paul McCartney:** Bass, harmony
- **George Harrison:** Lead guitar
- **Ringo Starr:** Drums

What we really like about this song

Steve: I like the inverted word play on the two-line "well, well, well" interlude. The first line is very straightforward, stating, "well, [now] you're feeling fine." The second line is "Well, well, well, he'll make you… ," which translates to "he'll make you well." This is reminiscent of the Fabs' love of word play, as in "Please Please Me," where they use *please* as both an adverb and a verb. I like George's guitar work and John's vocal on this song. I also very much like the song's sarcastic, gleeful tone.

Mike: "Doctor Robert" sounds like it could be a trippy radio commercial for the Good Doctor, advertising his services (satisfaction guaranteed) to make you a "new and better man." As a matter of fact, when you hear the "Well, well, well…" line, it's as if the spaced-out doc himself is singing. It's one of *Revolver's* least complicated recordings, but is great fun nonetheless—regardless of who "Doctor Robert" really is, and whether some or all of the Beatles actually were his patients.

[1] *A Hard Day's Write.*

[2] *Ibid.*

[3] Most people, when they kick heroin, go into rehab and suffer through withdrawal. John suffered, but he also managed to write a hit song about it, "Cold Turkey."

Real Love

74

The thing for me that wasn't quite as much fun in the recording of "Real Love" was it was finished. It had all the words and the music. So I didn't really get to input, which the three of us had been able to input on "Free as a Bird." So it made it more like a Beatles session. This was more like we were side men to John which was joyful and it was good fun and I think we did a good job.

Paul McCartney
The Beatles Anthology

Could the Beatles do it again?

Could the Threetles take a John Lennon monaural cassette, add themselves to the mix (both playing and singing), and turn out a single that would not only serve John's memory, but be worthy of being called a Beatles single?

Yes, and yes.

Once again, Paul, George, Ringo, Jeff Lynne, and Geoff Emerick gathered at Paul's Sussex studio to make a new Beatles record, even though the Beatle named Lennon was no longer with them. At least not in the flesh.

Why it made the top 100

Listening to the final version of "Real Love"—a lavishly produced gem of a pop song—all we can think of is just *how damn good* the Beatles are as a group. (And the use of the present tense is intentional, mates.)

Paul and George obviously have a deep understanding of this bond. In *The Beatles Anthology*, Paul said, "We work well together. That's the truth of it, you know. We just work well together. And that's a very special thing. When you find someone you can *talk* to, it's a special thing. When you find someone you can *play music with* it's really… it's something."

George also weighed in: "I think we've had so much of the same background. You know, our musical background and where we came from and what we listened to, you know, in common. And then all those years we played together. Somehow it's made a deep groove in our memories. And it doesn't take much to lock in."

Locking in. That's what these guys do when they get together to make music, and on "Real Love," they even make it look easy.

What the song is about

"Real Love" is yet another Lennon love song for Yoko. The lyrics are reflective ("all my little plans and schemes…"), confident ("from this moment on I know/exactly where my life will go…"), and self-aware ("all I was really was doing was waiting for you…").

The chorus states the obvious: "It's *real* love… ," and John's choice of the adjective *real* instead of the perhaps more expected *true* tells us a great deal about his later-in-life perception of his previous tries at love: *They were all false.*

The bridges are similarly revealing in that he states he no longer needs to be alone or afraid. It is interesting that in the three bridges, he uses "alone" twice but only a single mention of "afraid." John seems to be happier that he is no longer *alone*, rather than *without fear*. The song's defining message is summed up in two lines near the end: "Thought I'd been in love before, but in my heart I wanted more…"

Once he found Yoko, he got what he wanted, and "Real Love" is his way of telling the world.

• • • • • • • •

- In early March 1996, the BBC declined to play the new Beatles single, "Real Love," by not adding it to their official Radio 1 FM playlist. At the time, it was speculated in the press that some of the younger staff at the BBC considered the Beatles too old for the station's target demographic. The parent company of Radio 1 denied these allegations.
- After Radio 1 refused to play "Real Love," Paul wrote an eight-hundred-word op-ed piece for the United Kingdom's *Daily Mirror* newspaper. Here is an excerpt, boasting some of his most trenchant comments: "The Beatles don't need our new single, 'Real Love,' to be a hit. It's not as if our careers depend on it. If Radio 1 feels that we should be banned now it's not exactly going to ruin us overnight. You can't put an age limit on good music. It's very heartening to know that, while the kindergarten kings of Radio 1 may think the Beatles are too old to come out to play, a lot of younger British bands don't seem to share that view. I'm forever reading how bands like Oasis are openly crediting the Beatles as inspiration, and I'm pleased that I can hear the Beatles in a lot of the music around today. As Ringo said to me about all this, who needs Radio 1 when you've got all the independent stations?"
- The surviving Beatles toyed with the idea of reuniting yet again for a third reunion single—"Now and Then"—but George Harrison was so uncomfortable with the reception of "Real Love" by Radio 1 that he didn't want to participate. Paul commented on this third single in an interview in the May 1996 issue of *Beatles Monthly*: "There was only one of us who didn't want to do it. It would have meant a lot of hard work, the song would have needed a lot of re-writing and people would have had to be very patient with us. We'd have to do a hatchet job on it. There are a couple of things that may surface at some point. You see, with the Beatles, there's always a surprise somewhere along the line. There are these one or two things lurking in the bushes. The Beatles might just raise their ugly little heads again…"
- "Real Love" began as a song called "Real Life," the verses of which later appeared in John's posthumous song "I'm Stepping Out."
- The upright bass Paul plays during "Real Love" was once played by Bill Black on Elvis's "Heartbreak Hotel."
- "Real Love," the Beatles' final single, entered the singles charts at Number Four, selling fifty thousand copies in its first week. "Free as a Bird" and "Real Love" were officially certified gold singles for 1996. They were the group's twenty-first and twenty-second gold singles.
- A version of "Real Love" had been used in the 1988 film *Imagine: John Lennon*, and was on the soundtrack.

Did you know?

The recording

Location: **The Dakota Arms, New York, New York; McCartney home studio, Sussex, England.**

Dates: **Fall 1980** – John Lennon records a demo of "Real Love" on a portable cassette tape recorder. Accompanying himself on the piano, he sings two lead vocal parts, and adds a drum machine.

January 1992 – Paul and Yoko discuss the possibility of the Beatles working on some of John's uncompleted songs.

January 1994 – Yoko sends Paul cassette tapes of "Free as a Bird" and "Real Love."

February 1995 – Paul, George, and Ringo record the Beatles version of "Real Love" at Paul's home studio.

November 1995 – *The Beatles Anthology* CDs are released. "Real Love" leads off Volume 2.

March 4, 1996 – "Real Love" backed with "Baby's in Black" is released as a single, entering the singles charts at Number Four.

March 11, 1996 – "Real Love" sells fifty thousand copies in its first week and is certified gold for 1996.

Players/Instruments:
- **John Lennon:** Piano, lead vocals, drum machine
- **Paul McCartney:** Acoustic guitar, electric bass, upright bass, lead vocal, backing vocal, percussion
- **George Harrison:** Acoustic guitar, lead guitar, backing vocals, percussion
- **Ringo Starr:** Drums, percussion
- **Producers:** Jeff Lynne, John Lennon, Paul McCartney, George Harrison, Ringo Starr
- **Engineers:** Geoff Emerick, Jon Jacobs

Note: At the end of the song, we hear what sounds like a ukulele or a banjo—although it could be a piano. Anyone know for certain? Paul? Jeff?

What we really like about this song

Steve: The "Free as a Bird" video is fun. *Let's pick out the Beatles references! Can we get them all?* But watching the "Real Love" video today is an absolutely heart-wrenching experience. It begins with John's white grand piano rising up to heaven; later, the Beatles' other instruments follow it. This could move even the most jaded Fab fan to tears. Also, to see Paul and now-gone George embracing like the brothers they always were, and then to see Paul sing along with John on a line from the song (giving a fallen mate a hand with the high parts), is both painful and beautiful. The melody and chorus of the song add to the poignancy of the video and, even though the final audio track is more Beatles than John (Paul, George, and Ringo added *a lot* to John's spare track), "Real Love" just might be the most Beatlesque Beatles single of all time.

Mike: Some days I like "Real Love" more than "Free as a Bird." They are vastly different, and they came to be recorded under much different circumstances. For "Real Love," there was much less creative input from the surviving Beatles, because the song had already been released (although I like the *Anthology* version better than the unfinished fragment on the Imagine soundtrack). "Real Love" is livelier, sounding more like a mid-era Beatles track (think: "And Your Bird Can Sing"–ish), but the message is more typical of John's post-Beatles work: The trappings of celebrity are irrelevant; what's important is love.

Why it made the top 100

"It's Only Love" is a lovely pop ballad with a charming sound—an amalgam of folky acoustic guitar and a subtle electric guitar accompaniment.

John's double-tracked vocal is slightly askew: It almost sounds as though two separate vocal tracks were recorded independently and then not perfectly aligned. Artificial Double Tracking (ADT), a favorite studio technique of the Beatles and George Martin, is *always* perfect—the vocals are in flawless sync. For this track, John's voice is not aligned—and whether this was intentional or a mistake, it adds an interesting element to the sound.

What the song is about

This song tells an odd story. The lyrics never answer the question of whether the singer and the girl are an official couple. It would seem so, yet the opening line of the second verse—"why am I so shy when I'm beside you?"—suggests a timidity somewhat anomalous for a happy twosome. In that light, then, the opening line thus suggests a moonstruck suitor watching the object of his affection *from afar*.

Throughout, the singer repeatedly reassures himself that "it's only love," trying to convince himself that he should not make as big a deal of his relationship as he obviously feels compelled to do. Trouble in paradise creeps into the lyrics with the line "it's so hard loving you," which is then amplified by the question, "Is it right that you and I should fight every night?" They fight every night, but the sight of her makes nighttime bright? Someone is confused in this scenario, but we don't know if it's our hero or the object of his affection (obsession?).

This mini drama concludes with him telling her (*twice*) "it's so hard loving you."

Can they work it out? Tomorrow never knows

It's Only Love

I always thought it was a lousy song. The lyrics were abysmal. I always hated that song.

—John Lennon
Playboy

"It's Only Love" was on the *Help!* soundtrack, but not in the movie. Nonmovie Beatles songs were added to fill out the album, along with one non-Beatles cover—"Dizzy Miss Lizzie." (And speaking of that, we've always wondered about the spelling of Lizzie's name. On the *Help!* soundtrack, it's spelled *Lizzie*. Yet other sources spell it *Lizzy*, which makes more sense from a compositional standpoint—that way, it echoes the y ending of *Dizzy*. Was it a typo on *Help!?*)

- The working title of the song was "That's a Nice Hat" (alternately reported as "That's a Nice Cap").
- It has long been reported that George Martin and his orchestra recorded "It's Only Love" as an instrumental, under the original working title "That's a Nice Hat." If this is true (and we could not confirm that it is), the track did not appear on any of Martin's orchestral albums, including the most commonly cited, *Off the Beatle Track*. It also does not appear on *George Martin Plays Help!* and, in fact, we could not find any documentation whatsoever that Martin ever released an instrumental version of the song. It may be on a bootleg somewhere, but it cannot be found in the standard sources (particularly www.allmusicguide.com, one of the best and most exhaustive databases).

Did you know?

- John wrote an additional verse for the song that he decided (wisely, wouldn't you say?) not to use:
  Can't explain or name I think it's pain
  I'm ashamed the flame of love is maimed
  Now and then I'll complain in vain
  And I'll still love you.

- At 1:55, this is one of the Beatles' shortest records; it's even shorter (by two seconds) than "I'm Happy Just to Dance with You."
- John adds an odd vibrato trill to the *b* in the word *bright* in the song, and it sounds to us like he was goofing around. Supporting this theory is the version of the song heard on *Anthology 2* (Take 2), in which he sings the *bright* straight on, without any elaborations.
- The song has been covered by Bryan Ferry, Gary U.S. Bonds, Eddy Arnold, Tommy James and the Shondells, Ray Price, the Stowaways, and Ella Fitzgerald.

The recording

Location: **Abbey Road Studios, London.**
Dates: **June 15, 1965,** 2:30–5:30 p.m. – Six takes were recorded, one of which was a false start, and one of which broke down when Ringo made an uncharacteristic drumming error. George played tone pedal guitar. Take 6 was the version released on the nonsoundtrack side of *Help!*; Takes 2 and 3 (the false start) can be heard on *Anthology 2.*

June 18, 1965 – Mono and stereo mixing.
August 6, 1965 – First released on the U.K. LP *Help!*

Players/Instruments:
- **John Lennon:** Acoustic guitar, lead vocal, tambourine
- **Paul McCartney:** Bass
- **George Harrison:** Lead guitar
- **Ringo Starr:** Drums

What we really like about this song

Steve: This is one of those songs that, once you hear it, you can't get it out of your head. It reminds me of the comment Smashing Pumpkin Billy Corgan made about the Beatles making everything the chorus (see song number 20). Every little bit of business in "It's Only Love" is a legitimate hook, from the opening four-note ostinato (which reprises discreetly throughout the song) to the melody of the instantly memorable three-word chorus. Interestingly, John's vitriol toward this song notwithstanding, for all its pop sensibility the melody and construction have a "classicalesque" quality. Imagine John's vocal line being plucked out by violins with a swirling piano accompaniment and you'll get a sense of what the song could *also* sound like.

Mike: John abhorred this song, but I think he was being a little harsh. Okay, so the lyrics are somewhat trite and contrived, but John set the bar higher for himself than many songwriters did. Since the complete tune clocks in at less than two minutes, we can indulge him that long, can't we? I like the song more for its overall message than for its line-by-line lyrics—the narrator (John) being disappointed in himself for allowing a woman to affect him so. (Revealingly, he would soon become much more aloof and distant—see "Norwegian Wood" for a particularly potent example.) Also worth noting is George's electric guitar "garnish," which adds a nice diversion throughout the track.

76

Hello, Goodbye

The answer to everything is simple. It's a song about everything and nothing. If you have black you have to have white. That's the amazing thing about life.

—Paul McCartney
Disc *magazine*, 1967

"Hello, Goodbye" (and yes, there is a comma in the title) is a better track than its reputation. Throughout the years, the song has garnered a somewhat deserved, but mostly undeserved, rep as pop trash, disposable and irrelevant. Tim Riley, in his excellent critical study *Tell Me Why*, summed up the commonly accepted perception of the song when he wrote that "Hello, Goodbye" is the kind of song Paul McCartney could write in his sleep, "and probably did."[1]

But the production is impeccable, the lyrics are simple yet meaningful, and the performances are excellent. And since it is 100 percent a Paul song, his legendary attention to detail is very evident. Yes, it's simplistic, but try listening to it without tapping your foot or singing along. "Hello, Goodbye" is Paul writing a pop symphony but employing an artistic restraint he at times abandoned in his post-Beatles, Wings years.

Why it made the top 100

"Hello, Goodbye" is one of the most recognizable Beatles songs of all time. Even non-Fab fans have heard, and can probably sing along, with the tune. The song exudes Paul's sensibility, and that was part of the reason why John didn't like it much, but it is nonetheless a classic, and, for all its simplicity, stands up surprisingly well.

Some songs from the sixties by other artists just sound so dated when heard today (all the current retro fanaticism notwithstanding), but "Hello, Goodbye" is a fine, fresh, fun piece of pop.

What the song is about

"Hello, Goodbye" is a conversation between two lovers splitting up and, as evidenced by the key line, "You say goodbye and I say hello," it's clear that *she* is the one who wants to end it. Nowhere in the song does the *singer* say goodbye and, in fact, he plaintively cries out to her, "I don't know why you say goodbye, I say hello." He sounds desperate, and the lyrics detail the push/pull endgame of a doomed relationship: yes/no, stop/go, and why?/I don't know. There really isn't anything more profound in it than, I don't want to break up, why do you?

There is one last attempt to forestall the inevitable with the line "I can stay until it's time to go," suggesting that perhaps there is still hope, but in the end she says goodbye, ignoring the fact that he is still chanting "hello," apparently summoning absent Hawaiian gods with his "hela, heba hello-a" refrain. (A note: We have always heard the final chant as "hey-la, hey-a, hello-a," but the "official" version, published in the Hal Leonard sheet music for the song, has the lyric as "hey-la, heba hello-a." Plus, Paul says "heba" in his interview with Mark Lewisohn in *The Beatles Recording Sessions*. So, it must be "heba," hey?)

- In *Lennon Remembers,* John admitted that he always hated "Hello, Goodbye" and it bothered him that it was the A side of the single while his "I Am the Walrus" (an infinitely superior, more complex piece of work) was relegated to the B side.

- In his interview with Mark Lewisohn in *The Beatles Recording Sessions,* Paul talked about the writing and recording of "Hello, Goodbye": "It almost wrote itself because it was to be 'Hello, Goodbye.' I was thinking of that this morning. From the recording aspect I remember the end bit where there's the pause and it goes [sings] 'heba, heba hello.' We had those words and we had this whole thing recorded but it didn't sound quite right, and I remember asking Geoff Emerick if we could *really* whack up the echo on the tom-toms. And we put this echo full up on the

tom-toms and it just came *alive.* We Phil Spector'd it."[2]

- The Beatles recorded what was then called a "promotional film"—now known as a video—for "Hello, Goodbye," which Paul directed. "We'll just hire a theater and show up there one afternoon," Paul said. "And that's what we did: we took our *Sgt. Pepper* suits along and filmed at the Saville Theater in the West End."

- The "Hello, Goodbye" video was shown in the States on the *Ed Sullivan Show,* but it was banned by the BBC in the United Kingdom because the boys lip-synched the vocals, and this was forbidden by the British Musicians' Union. (Doesn't it seem that the BBC was always banning some Beatles song or video back then? Bloody uncivilized, if you ask us.)

The recording

Location: **Abbey Road Studios, London.**

Dates: **October 2, 1967** – The Beatles recorded fourteen takes to capture the basic rhythm track of piano, organ, drums, bongos, maracas, congas, and tambourine. From the outset, the song had the chanting reprise ending (nicknamed the "Maori finale")—although today it was just instrumental.

October 19, 1967 – Onto Take 14 they overdubbed two guitar parts, Paul's vocal, and John and George's backing vocals. This "working version" can be heard on *Anthology 2*. The final song would ultimately have more background vocals and less scale-like guitar lines woven throughout. The middle eight of this version was different from the final version, and the chanting was included at the end.

October 20, 1967 – Session musicians Ken Essex and Leo Birnbaum overdubbed violas. Essex and Birnbaum were originally paid for an 8:00–11:00 p.m. session, but their session ran over, ending at 2:30 a.m., for which they received double-time pay. Birnbaum, speaking in *The Beatles Recording Sessions*, recalled, "Paul McCartney was doodling at the piano, and George Martin was sitting next to him writing down what Paul was playing." Essex said, "All of the Beatles were there. One of them was sitting on the floor in what looked like a pyjama suit, drawing with crayons on a piece of paper."

October 25, 1967 – Bass guitar overdub.

November 1, 1967 – Reduction mixdowns.

November 2, 1967 – Another bass overdub; mono mixing and remixing.

November 6, 1967 – Stereo mixing.

November 15, 1967 – Mono mixing.

November 24, 1967 – First released in the United Kingdom as a single, backed with "I Am the Walrus."

Players/Instruments:
- **Paul McCartney**: Bass, piano, bongos, conga drum, lead and backing vocal
- **John Lennon**: Lead guitar, organ, backing vocal
- **George Harrison**: Lead guitar, tambourine, backing vocal
- **Ringo Starr**: Drums, maracas
- **Session musicians:** Two violas

What we really like about this song

Steve: I like "Hello, Goodbye" because it makes me feel good. The opening piano and organ intro, accompanied by Paul's soaring "You say yes… ," comes out of nowhere and immediately sucks you into its irresistible, good-natured, foot-tapping vibe. I also love the sound of the violas, and Paul's extraordinary bass line.

Mike: "Hello, Goodbye" is innocuous and infectious at best, vapid at worst. I suppose *whimsical* is a good word to describe it. It's pure pop—not that there's anything wrong with that! (Silly aside: When I think of this song, I can't help but think of that old song that goes, "You say potato, I say potata…")

[1] *Tell Me Why*, page 236.

[2] *The Beatles Recording Sessions*, page 15.

77 Michelle

[Paul] and I were staying somewhere and he walked in and hummed the first few bars, with the words… and he says, "Where do I go from here?" I had been listening to Nina Simone—I think it was "I Put a Spell On You." There was a line in it that went… "I love you, I love you, I love you." That's what made me think of the middle eight for "Michelle": 'I love you, I love you, I l-o-ove you."

John Lennon
Playboy

Paul couldn't play guitar or bass with his left hand, so he learned to play with his right hand. Paul couldn't write music notation, so he played what he composed and had somebody else transcribe it. Paul couldn't speak French, so he turned to a French teacher to translate into French the lyrics he wanted to include in a song, resulting in one of the Beatles' most beautiful ballads.

Amazing what you can do when you can't do something, eh?

Nothin' you can do that can't be done, indeed.

237

Why it made the top 100

"Michelle" was yet another *Rubber Soul* track that defied expectations and redefined rock music.

What the hell is that? *French?* The word *surprised* does not do justice to how Beatlefans felt upon first hearing this classic ballad.

"Michelle" is an impeccably produced ballad, with the perfect mix of electric and acoustic instruments. One can hear little touches of an acoustic chord here, an intriguing bass riff there, all of which is topped off by rich, sonorous harmonies that conjure up images of walking along the River Seine. At sunset, of course.

What the song is about

Paul's in love and it's a sunny (French) day.

The singer in "Michelle" is in love with a French girl named Michelle and he wants her to know it. Unfortunately, our hero no shpeaka da lingo, so he will repeat to her the only French phrase he knows. How long will this continue, we wonder? "Until I find a way." "I'll get to you somehow," he assures her (and himself).

Surprisingly, though, he hasn't learned the only French words that might, indeed, make his love for her clear: *Je t'aime* (I love you). *That* phrase he sings to her in English, the language she *cannot* understand. He goes about his pursuit of her in a somewhat skewed manner. He tells her that *Ma* and *Michelle* go together well. Why the obfuscation, Monsieur Paul?

There is an obvious sense of trepidation on the part of our young non-French-speaking suitor. He is clearly nervous that, first, someone will step in and snatch her away, and, second, she will not understand his message—"what you mean to me."

Does our binational couple end up living together happily ever after, spending summers in Britain and winters in France? We don't know. This charming love song ends with the singer again proclaiming that he will say the only words he knows that she will understand.

In the end, though, they may have been the wrong words.

• • • ❦ • • •

- The origin of "Michelle" goes back to Paul and John's Liverpool days. The lads often attended parties thrown by John's art tutors and, at one of them (thrown by Austin Mitchell), a goateed French beatnik in a striped shirt sat hunched over a guitar and sang a French ballad. This cracked Paul up, and he put together a comical impression of the guy—including a faux French art song—that he performed for friends. Years later, John suggested that he put words to the song, and "Michelle" was born.
- The French lyrics in the song were translated by Jan Vaughn, wife of Ivan Vaughn, former Quarry Men member and longtime friend of John and Paul.
- We ran the line "These are words that go together well" through the BabelFish translation service, and it came back with, "*Ce sont des mots qui vont ensemble bien.*" As you know, Paul's teacher friend Jan Vaughn translated the line as "*Sont des mots qui vont très bien ensemble.*"

Did you know?

- It seems that Bob Dylan may have had some slight resentment toward the Beatles in the sixties. In the Dylan biography *No Direction Home*, circa 1966, Dylan said, "It's the thing to do, to tell all the teenyboppers, 'I dig the Beatles,' and you sing a song like 'Yesterday' or 'Michelle.' Hey, God knows, it's such a cop-out, man, both of those songs. If you go into the Library of Congress, you can find a lot better than that. There are millions of songs like 'Michelle' and 'Yesterday' written in Tin Pan Alley."
- The song has been extensively covered, including versions by Andre Kostelanetz, Andy Williams, Anita Kerr, Bela Fleck and the Flecktones, Billy Vaughn, Bobby Goldsboro, Bobby Vinton, Booker T. and the MG's, Count Basie, Diana Ross and the Supremes, the Four Tops, Henry Mancini, Jack Jones, Jan and Dean, Laurindo Almeida, the Moscow Sax Quintet, Perry Como, the Sandpipers, Sarah Vaughan, Stan Getz, and Yusef Lateef.

The recording

Location: **Abbey Road Studios, London.**

Dates: **November 3, 1965,** 2:30–11:30 p.m. – The afternoon was spent filling four tracks with the rhythm track. Then, this was mixed down onto three tracks so they could fill the fourth track with overdubbed vocals and guitar. Occasional EMI tape operator Jerry Boys, on listening to playback of the song as they were working on it that night, said: "I stood there quite spellbound. It sounded lovely. George [Martin] asked me what I thought of the Beatles singing a song with French lyrics and I got the impression that with me being a young chap he was sounding me out, perhaps because they weren't too sure themselves. I said it sounded very pleasant, which it certainly did!"[1]

November 9, 1965 – Mono mixing (unused), stereo mixing.

November 15, 1965 – Mono mixing.

Players/Instruments:
- **Paul McCartney:** Bass, lead vocal
- **John Lennon:** Acoustic guitar, backing vocal
- **George Harrison:** Acoustic guitar, backing vocal
- **Ringo Starr:** Drums

What we really like about this song

Steve: This song could easily have been a joke—if Paul and his brethren didn't unquestionably *know what they were doing.* The arrangement is not over-the-top (as these type of cabaret art songs are wont to be); the deep and rich backing harmonies are some of the Fabs' most lovely, and Paul's vocal is restrained and (dare I say it) somewhat unemotional. Throughout the song there is a sense of discretion. In a word, "Michelle" is *subtle.* As it should be.

Mike: This is a lovely tune, and one I will surely sing to a French coquette should I ever have the opportunity to woo one. All kidding aside, this is the first rock song I ever heard that had French lyrics in it. When I finally took French in junior high, it was cool to finally learn what Paul was singing (which is, of course, a loose French translation of the English verses). A nice touch was adding the slightly distorted, more uptempo baritone electric guitar break after the "I need to" verse (and which is also repeated into the fade at the end).

[1] *The Beatles Recording Sessions.*

Can't Buy Me Love

The way they first sang "Can't Buy Me Love" was by starting on the verse, but I said: "We've got to have an introduction, something that catches the ear immediately, a hook. So let's start off with the chorus." It was all really a matter of tidying things up. But that record was the point of departure for something rather more sophisticated.

—George Martin
All You Need Is Ears

Paul wrote "Can't Buy Me Love" on a rented piano in a Paris hotel room in the winter of 1964 because the Beatles had to release a single in March of that year and there was no time to waste. John once commented that he thought he might have had something to do with the chorus, but that he actually considered the song "Paul's completely."[1]

Why it made the top 100

This is a quintessential Beatles song (and here we're using the word *Beatles* as an adjective to describe their inimitable style), and it was one of the small number of their songs that harked back to traditional twelve-bar blues. It's evidence of their brilliance that they could take an old style and create a wonderfully appealing amalgam of traditional I–IV–V chord changes and a pop-rock sensibility.

What the song is about

The lyrics are the words of an anxious, somewhat confused suitor who is desperate to win the love of a lady but, in the end, hopes he doesn't have to pay for it.

In the first verse, he's looking for any way into her heart. He offers to *buy* her and *get* her material things (a diamond ring and, in the end, *anything*) just to "make [her] feel all right." No mention of love. Yet.

In the second verse, he has moved from buying to giving. Now he'll *give* her everything/anything he's got… but she has to tell him she loves him. He admits he doesn't have a lot to give, which is a subtle way of saying "love me for myself."

The chorus (which opens the song, too) is the singer trying to shake some sense into himself, repeating over and over that he is not going to succeed if he tries to buy her love.

By the third verse, he has "woken up," so to speak. He's focusing on what will satisfy *him*. Now he's telling her that he wants to hear her say she "don't need no diamond ring." Then, using his new understanding, he implores her to tell him she wants the "kind of thing money just can't buy."

I know I can't buy your love, he seems to be telling her, but please tell me I don't have to. Does the singer win the girl with this heartfelt entreaty? We don't know. The song ends with him repeating the mantra that he can't buy love.

(Paul himself commented in *The Beatles Anthology*, "Personally, I think you can put any interpretation you want on anything, but when someone suggests that 'Can't Buy Me Love' is about a prostitute, I draw the line. That's going too far.")

- "Can't Buy Me Love" entered the charts at Number One. On the April 4, 1964, *Billboard* Hot 100 chart, the Beatles had a staggering twelve songs:

  1. "Can't Buy Me Love"
  2. "Twist and Shout"
  3. "She Loves You"
  4. "I Want to Hold Your Hand"
  5. "Please Please Me"
  31. "I Saw Her Standing There"
  41. "From Me to You"
  46. "Do You Want to Know a Secret"
  58. "All My Loving"
  65. "You Can't Do That"
  68. "Roll Over Beethoven"
  79. "Thank You Girl"

- "Can't Buy Me Love" was the only previously released song included on the *A Hard Day's Night* soundtrack. It replaced "I'll Cry Instead." Director Richard Lester didn't think "I'll Cry Instead" fit the scene in which the boys escape from the theater and run around like nuts in the field. (He was right—"Can't Buy Me Love" is much better for that raucous scene.)

- "Can't Buy Me Love" played over the opening and closing credits of the 1987 Touchstone comedy *Can't Buy Me Love*, starring Patrick Dempsey and Amanda Peterson. (The original title of the film was *Boy Rents Girl*.)

- The song was played by a British military band as the boys received their MBEs at Buckingham Palace on October 26, 1965.

- The song has been covered by Diana Ross and the Supremes, Ella Fitzgerald, Henry Mancini, Johnny Rivers, Peter Sellers, Dick James, Brenda Lee, the Chipmunks, the Chorallaries of MIT, and Keely Smith.

Did you know?

The recording

Locations: **Pathé Marconi Studios, Paris; Abbey Road Studios, London.**

Dates: **January 29, 1964** – EMI's Pathé Marconi Studios. The Beatles had just finished recording German versions of "She Loves You" and "I Want to Hold Your Hand" ahead of schedule, and then went on to record four takes of "Can't Buy Me Love." Takes 1 and 2 had a bluesy Paul lead vocal (intended only to be a guide vocal) similar to his singing in "She's a Woman." (Take 2 is on *Anthology 1*.) These takes include a little more guitar backing behind the verse (the single has only acoustic guitar strumming), and background vocals by John and George ("oooh, just can't buy;" "oooh, satisfied"). Take 3 was more like the final single version, although the song breaks down. Take 4 was considered best. In less than an hour, the Fabs had begun, reworked, and completed one of their biggest-selling songs.[2]

February 25, 1964 – Back at Abbey Road, the Beatles overdubbed Paul's new lead vocal and George's final lead guitar overdub. (Interestingly, the final version of the track has what originally was thought to be two mismatched George guitar solos at 1:16 to 1:25. This is now known to be leakage from George's less-than-stellar solos recorded in Paris that made it onto the final master tape. George commented on the double solo in *The Beatles Anthology*: "I once read something that tries to analyze 'Can't Buy Me Love,' talking about the double-track guitar—mine—and saying that it's not very good because you can hear the original one. What happened was that we recorded first in Paris and re-recorded in England. Obviously they'd tried to overdub it, but in those days they only had two tracks, so you can hear the version we put on in London, and in the background you can hear a quieter one.")

February 26, 1964 – Mono mixing.

March 10, 1964 – Stereo mixing.

March 16, 1964 – The single "Can't Buy Me Love"/"You Can't Do That" is rush-released in the United States. Advance orders for the single total two million copies.

June 9, 1964 – Mono tape copying/mixing for the *A Hard Day's Night* soundtrack.

June 22, 1964 – Stereo mixing.

Players/Instruments:
- **John Lennon:** Rhythm guitar (acoustic)
- **Paul McCartney:** Bass, vocal
- **George Harrison:** Lead guitar (twelve-string?)
- **Ringo Starr:** Drums

What we really like about this song

Steve: I love the fact that the song opens with the chorus (like "She Loves You" and, for that matter, "Don't Let Me Down"); I love Paul's bass, I love the hissing cymbals, and I love the fact that they knew they had a kickass rocker and decided to dump the fancy background harmonies that can be heard on *Anthology 1*. The Beatles not only knew what to *add*, but what to *lose*.

Mike: This is a lively, fun song that always makes me think of the scene from *A Hard Day's Night*, although I saw the movie long after I was familiar with the song. (Unlike my coauthor, I was too young to see the film in theaters.) It's one of the Beatles' fastest-tempo songs.

[1] *Playboy.*

[2] *The Beatles Recording Sessions.*

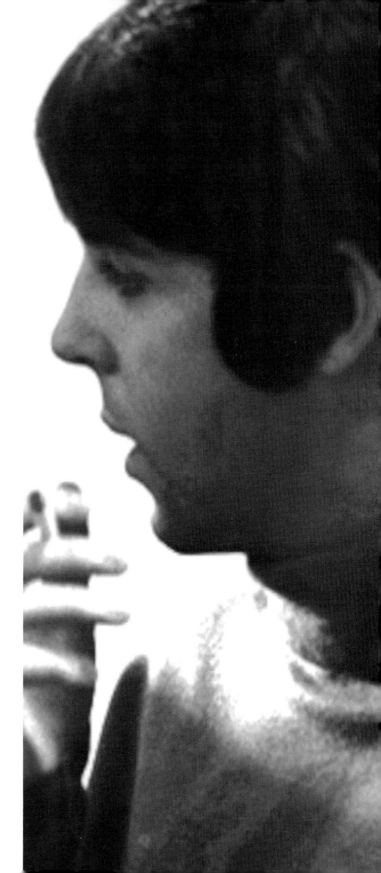

She's Leaving Home

The amazing thing about the song was how much it got right about my life. It quoted my parents as saying, "we gave her everything money could buy," which was true in my case. I had two diamond rings, a mink coat, hand-made clothes in silk and cashmere and even my own car. Then there was the line "after living alone for so many years," which really struck home to me because I was an only child and I always felt alone. I never communicated with either of my parents. It was a constant battle. I left because I couldn't face them any longer.

—Melanie Coe
A Hard Day's Write

In a creative process similar to that of
John's on "A Day in the Life" (see song number 1), Paul found his inspiration for "She's Leaving Home" from an article in the *Daily Mail.* A girl named Melanie Coe ran away from home. A reporter later interviewed her father, who said, "I cannot imagine why she would run away. She has everything here."

After learning that the song was inspired by her actions, Melanie Coe told the press, "If I had my life to live over again, I wouldn't choose to do it the same way. What I did was very dangerous but I was lucky. I suppose it is nice to be immortalized in a song but it would have been nicer if it had been for doing something else other than running away from home."[1]

Why it made the top 100

After "Yesterday" and "Eleanor Rigby," it wasn't all that surprising when we first heard "She's Leaving Home" on *Sgt. Pepper.* We were somewhat used to Paul's elaborate string arrangements for his ballads, but there was something different and quite special about "She's Leaving Home."

The song has since been described as "Schubertesque," and we happily defer to those who know Schubert well enough to make the comparison.

The song has also since been criticized as being Paul at his schmaltziest, but that's a judgment of taste. It cannot be denied that the song is beautifully written and performed, and actually quite sad.

What the song is about

A young girl runs away from home. She leaves the house at five in the morning, and we don't learn until the end of the first verse why she's leaving: She's been "living alone for so many years."

The father wakes up later, finds his daughter's "goodbye" note, and tells his wife. Her first reaction is self-involved—"how could she treat *us* so thoughtlessly?"; "How could she do this to *me?*" These reactions help us understand why she left in the first place.

The third and final verse takes place two days later, when she is "meeting a man from the motor trade." What is the "motor trade"? There have been several interpretations of this term, ranging from an abortionist to a used-car dealer. According to Paul, the phrase actually referred to Terry Doran, who was in the business selling premium vehicles with Brian Epstein. (Terry was later made head of Apple Music and, following that, personal assistant to George Harrison.)

Paul did not explain what kind of appointment the girl had with this "motor trade" man, but he did later say that the story in "She's Leaving Home" was "just fiction, like the sea captain in 'Yellow Submarine,' they weren't real people."

• • • 🐚 • • •

- The original mono version of "She's Leaving Home" is in the key of F major. For the 1967 stereo release of *Sgt. Pepper,* the song was slowed down just enough to drop it down a half step to E major. (Admit it: You've always thought Paul's voice sounded a little lower than usual. Apparently, the faster version was not as appealing to the Fabs and Mr. Martin as a slower, more stately version.)
- The string arrangement was written by Mike Leander because George Martin was busy with a Cilla Black session. (Paul had met Leander while producing a Marianne Faithfull recording session.) This is the only score written by someone other than George Martin during the entire period he worked with the Beatles. Martin later admitted

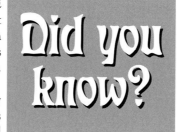

that he was hurt by Paul's decision (he called it "one of the biggest hurts of my life"), but did say that the song made him cry.
- Sheila Bromberg, harpist, was the first woman who ever performed on a Beatles record.
- Paul's video for his solo song "Pretty Little Head" opens with the final bars of "She's Leaving Home."
- "She's Leaving Home" has been covered by Harry Nilsson, Al Jarreau, Billy Bragg, and Richie Havens.

The recording

Location: **Abbey Road Studios, London**.

Dates:

March 17, 1967, 7:00 p.m.–12:45 a.m. – George Martin conducted the musicians and produced the session, even though he didn't write the score. Martin edited the score slightly—for instance, the cello was edited after each "bye bye." Six takes were recorded of the strings. (Paul was probably not there.)

March 20, 1967 – A tape reduction was made and Paul's vocal was overdubbed, as was John's backing vocal. Each vocal track was recorded twice so it sounded like four voices. Six mono remixes were made. An attempt was also made at adding Artificial Double Tracking (ADT) to the opening harp, but this was ultimately scrapped. (They probably didn't like the way it sounded.)

April 17, 1967 – Stereo mixing and editing. During the stereo remix, the tape was slowed down, making the stereo version eight seconds longer than the mono version.

June 1, 1967 – First released on the U.K. LP *Sgt. Pepper's Lonely Hearts Club Band*.

Players/Instruments:
- **Paul McCartney:** Lead and backing vocal
- **John Lennon:** Lead and backing vocal
- **Sheila Bromberg:** Harp
- **Session musicians:** String ensemble consisting of four violins, two violas, two cellos, and a double bass

What we really like about this song

Steve: I like the lyrics, the arrangement, and John's backing vocal. "She's Leaving Home" is one of the songs I cite to those less enlightened folk who still think the Beatles were nothing but "yeah, yeah, yeah."

Mike: This song can best be described as beautiful, poignant social commentary. It's hardly a rocker—but that's okay. It fits in nicely with the other groundbreaking songs on *Pepper*. It's a little melodramatic for my daily listening pleasure, but it perfectly sums up the growing generation gap between hippie children who were tuning in and dropping out, and their clueless parents.

[1] *A Hard Day's Write.*

80 Girl

"Girl" is real. There is no such thing as the girl, she was a dream, but the words are all right. It wasn't just a song, and it was about that girl—that turned out to be Yoko, in the end—the one that a lot of us were looking for.

It's about, "Was she taught when she was young that pain would lead to pleasure," did she understand it? Sort of philosophy quotes I was thinking about when I wrote it. I was trying to say something or other about Christianity, which I was opposed to at the time because I was brought up in the Church…

—*John Lennon*
The Beatles Anthology

Is that a cymbal in the chorus, that hissing sound that fills the space between the harmonized, multipart "Girl"?

Nope.

It's John breathing superclose to the mike and on maximum treble. Paul talked about this effect in the book *The Compleat Beatles*: "Listen to John's breath on 'Girl.' We asked the engineer to put it on treble, so you get this huge intake of breath and it sounds just like a percussion instrument."

Ringo could have simply brushed a wide cymbal to get the same effect, but instead, the Fabs went with a vocal effect that works on two levels—as sound, of course, but also as a metaphor for being breathless about this "girl." Her song not only *fills* the air, he is telling us, *it takes away* his air. Considering the last verse of the song (in which we learn that she puts him down), this can have many meanings, not all of which are positive.

Why it made the top 100

This song is a cornucopia of musical wonders. Let us count the ways:

First, John's vocal is one of his finest (including the aforementioned "intake of breath" trick). Also, the acoustic musical foundation of the song is disarming. A cursory listen does not reveal all that is going on. A careful listen uncovers an acoustic guitar that somehow sounds like a mandolin, and flawless harmonies that had to have been extremely difficult to sing in tempo. (Try singing the "tit-tit-tit" part along with the record and see how many times you lose your way when you simply *must* catch your breath!)

And then there's the stunningly accomplished musical break, consisting of George's sinuous sitar and a single-note acoustical variation on the melody played on the guitar—a leitmotif that had earlier been played under the previous verse.

Also worth noting is John's songwriting. The chord changes are sophisticated for a melancholy ballad; the lyrics (some of John's favorites) are among his best.

What the song is about

The girl in "Girl" is a handful.

She is preternaturally appealing and irresistibly seductive ("she's the kind of girl you want so much it makes you sorry…"), and her charms are such that "still, you don't regret a single day."

Our hero does have a semblance of understanding about the destructive nature of their relationship—he tells us in the first line of the second verse that he has tried many times to leave her, but all she has to do is turn on the waterworks and all his plans are abandoned.

We gain an even deeper understanding of this siren in the bridge when we learn that she insults him in front of his friends, and that she is so self-centered and vain that even when she is complimented, she can't find it in herself to express gratitude. Instead, "she acts as if it's understood…" that she's just *so* incredible.

The final verse is the man's last-ditch attempt to understand her. He wonders if she was taught that by being cruel, she would be rewarded: "Was she told when she was young that pain would lead to pleasure?" He also wonders if she realizes how hard he must work to satisfy her, and makes the point that he deserves his "day of leisure." (There is also in this line the secondary, exploded meaning in which John is talking about the state of man in general; the notion that life is work, life is suffering, life is *hard*.)

The last line of the verse is bitter and sardonic, asking if she'll appreciate him after he ends up working himself to death to win her heart.

"Girl" is a twisted little tale of a twisted relationship. What makes this all the more puzzling is that John is on record in *Playboy* with the following comment: "[I was] writing about that dream girl again—the one that hadn't come yet. It was Yoko."

Is Yoko "Girl"?

• • • • 🎸 • • • •

- John once talked about "Girl," and his words are notable for his particular emphasis on finding a girl who is *not* a fan: "I always had this dream of this particular woman coming into my life. I knew it wouldn't be someone buying Beatles' records. I was hoping for a woman who could give me what I get from a man intellectually. I wanted someone I could be myself with."
- Four months after the release of "Girl" on *Rubber Soul*, John gave his "we're more popular than Jesus" interview to journalist Maureen Cleave.
- The opening bars of "Girl" can be heard in the film *Mask* (starring Cher and Eric Stoltz) during a summer camp party scene.

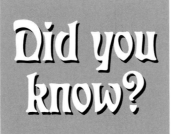

- John's first wife, Cynthia, thought "Girl" was about her. In the April 1995 issue of *Q* magazine, Cyn said, "I'm sure I was part of John's writing. In those days none of them would say, 'I'm writing this for so and so,' because it would be too embarrassing. But John actually wrote poetry to me quite a lot. The only song that I thought might be something to do with me was 'Girl,' but of course John isn't here to say anymore. But whatever they were writing at the time was about their lives anyway."
- The song has been covered by Charlie Byrd, St. Louis Union, Johnny Hallyday, Truth, and Tiny Tim and Brave Combo.

The recording

Location: **Abbey Road Studios, London.**

Dates: **November 11, 1965** – "Girl" was recorded in the final *Rubber Soul* recording session. The session included a fuzz guitar on the recording, played by George, which was deleted in the remix. Two takes were recorded, with the second considered the better.

November 15, 1965 – Mono and stereo mixing.

December 3, 1965 – First released on the U.K. LP *Rubber Soul.*

Players/Instruments:
- **John Lennon:** Acoustic guitar, lead vocal
- **Paul McCartney:** Bass, backing vocal
- **George Harrison:** Sitar, backing vocal
- **Ringo Starr:** Drums

What we really like about this song

Steve: Each time I listen to it, I find something new to like about "Girl." Particularly appealing to me is the lovely sitar/guitar counterpoint in the instrumental break of the song. George's sitar made its first appearance on *Rubber Soul* in "Norwegian Wood" (see song number 42), and it appears again here, but in this song its role is a much subtler one. Instead of being the center of attention, as it was on "Norwegian Wood," here George simply plucks notes that complement the guitar part, creating an odd but really sweet string duet. And once again, I am captivated by the Beatles' harmonies.

Mike: I can't think of any "Beatles Unplugged" song that I *don't* like. When I hear this song, I am transported to medieval times and envision strolling minstrels strumming lutes and mandolins, serenading the knights with tales of glory and lost loves. John, in fine voice, sings so dramatically here; his breath is literally taken away by the thought of this girl who "came to stay," but made a fool of him. I especially like the lyric of pain leading to pleasure, with its understated knock at the rites of Christianity. Finally—it's funny how the Beatles could get away with singing "tit-tit-tit," but not "had a smoke." Go figure.

What is the first song? Something called "Back in the USSR." The USSR? Russia? Say *what*? And then the confusion multiplies exponentially as we hear… wait—that's not music. It's the sound of a jet plane landing. Say, ahem, what? All was soon made clear when the band started playing and the song *really* began. And, yes, we were delighted to immediately hear, it kicked ass.

The White Album had begun.

Why it made the top 100

Yeah, right, we're going to rank the top 100 Beatles songs and not include the leadoff song on what may be the Beatles' greatest album. What do you think we are, barmy?

What the song is about

A young man sings about his delight at returning home to the USSR after spending some time in America. Why was he in the United States? We don't know. All we know is that he flew out of Miami, he got sick on the plane ("on the way the paper bag was on my knee"), and that as soon as he got back, he told his significant other to give him a day to unpack and to disconnect the phone. Apparently they had some "catching up" to do.

The chorus is a repetition of the sentiment that his comrades are lucky to be living in the USSR.

In the second half of the song, our returning son extols the virtues of his homeland and, since he sings the bridge about the Girls of Russia *twice*, we can assume that he wasn't thrilled with girls from the USA ("they leave the West behind…"). He does turn his attention from the ladies for a moment in the last verse, though, when he exalts the land's "snow-capped mountains" and the sounds of the balalaikas.

The song was interpreted by some (particularly the Reverend David A. Noebel, author of *Communism, Hypnotism and the Beatles*) as a condonation of Communism. Noebel wrote, "John Lennon and the Beatles were an integral part of the revolutionary milieu and received high marks from the Communist press, especially for *The White Album* which contained 'Back in the USSR' and 'Piggies'… The lyrics have left even the Reds speechless." Paul later commented, "'Back in the USSR' is a hands-across-the-water song. They like us out there. Even though the bosses in the Kremlin may not, the kids do. And that to me is very important for the future of the race."[1]

Back In The USSR

I wrote that as a kind of Beach Boys parody. And "Back in the U.S.A." was a Chuck Berry song, so it kinda took off from there. I just liked the idea of Georgia girls and talking about places like the Ukraine as if they were California, you know?

—Paul McCartney
Playboy, 1984

Today, we push a button. Back in
'68, however, when *The White Album* was first released, a tone arm with a ruby or diamond needle had to be placed gently onto the outside groove of a large disc of black vinyl spinning at the precise speed (if you had a decent turntable, that is) of thirty-three and one-third revolutions per minute. Never was this ritual more eagerly anticipated than when the spinning disc of black vinyl was a new Beatles record.

- Ringo left the Beatles on August 22, 1968, so Paul took over his drumming duties for "Back in the USSR." In the October 1986 issue of *Musician* magazine, Paul commented on the song: "I'm sure it pissed Ringo off when he couldn't quite get the drums to 'Back in the USSR,' and I sat in. It's very weird to know that you can do a thing someone else is having trouble with. If you go down and do it, just bluff right through it, you think, 'What the hell—at least I'm helping.' Then the paranoia comes in: 'But I'm going to show him up!' I was very sensitive to that."[2]

- "Back in the USSR" has been covered by the Beach Boys, Billy Joel, Chubby Checker, Cliff Bennett and the Rebel Rousers, Don Fardon, and John Fred and the Playboys.

The recording

Location: **Abbey Road Studios, London.**

Dates: **August 22, 1968** – Five takes of the rhythm track were recorded with Paul on drums, George on lead guitar, and John playing bass.

August 23, 1968 – Overdubbing of two more drum tracks (probably John and George), two more bass parts (by Paul and George), two more lead guitar parts (probably John and Paul), piano, lead vocal, George and John background vocals, and handclaps. They also overdubbed the opening airplane sound, which was a Viscount jet taken from EMI's effects library, Volume 17: *Jet and Piston Engine Aeroplane.* Mono mixing and tape copying were also done this day. (The mono and stereo versions of the song feature different jet overdubs.)

October 1, 1968 – Stereo mixing

November 22, 1968 – The song is first released on *The White Album* in the United Kingdom. (The recording log for this session is somewhat incomplete.)

Players/Instruments:

- **Paul McCartney:** Lead guitar, drums, piano, lead and backing vocal
- **John Lennon:** Six-string bass, backing vocal
- **George Harrison:** Jazz bass, backing vocal

What we really like about this song

Steve: I love the fact that the song is almost solely Paul, playing all the instruments. Paul had an amazing ability to write a song and then record a fully realized version of it without any help from anyone. (Listen to his version of "Come and Get It"—which he wrote for Badfinger—on *Anthology 3.* He recorded this by himself in a few hours.) "Back in the USSR" is classic evidence of Paul's multifaceted talents.

Mike: Can the right-wing wackos give it a rest? Ever heard of poetic license? So Paul writes about the pleasures of life in Russia—does that make him a Communist? If that's all they dwell on (and for many, it is—you know who you are), then the demagogues are missing one of the Beatles' most rollicking and energetic songs. You can clearly hear the Beach Boys and Chuck Berry influences, and even though Ringo was missing in action, it's one of the group's tightest numbers. A great way to start off a great album.

[1] Quoted in *A Hard Day's Write.*

[2] *Musician,* October 1986.

Dear Prudence

"Dear Prudence" is me. Written in India. A song about Mia Farrow's sister, who seemed to go slightly barmy, meditating too long, and couldn't come out of the little hut that we were livin' in. They selected me and George to try and bring her out because she would trust us. If she'd been in the West, they would have put her away.

—John Lennon
Playboy

What a scene

it must have been in Rishikesh, India! Longhaired adherents of the Maharishi mingling with real live Beatles and other celebs; the atmosphere a rich and heady *omnium gatherum* of meditation, creativity, and, of course, vegetarian food (which Ringo especially detested).

It was during this period that the Beatles wrote many of their most memorable songs, tunes that are universally considered classics today. "Dear Prudence" was one of them.

Why it made the top 100

"Dear Prudence" made the top 100 because it is one of John's simplest yet most engaging songs, and because it is a brilliant combination of influences—from Byrds-like folk to the drone of pedal-point Indian music. It echoed "Lucy in the Sky with Diamonds" and "Tomorrow Never Knows" but was determinedly more mainstream and accessible. (Not to mention that the song inspired what some consider Paul's greatest bass line.)

What the song is about

As is commonly known, John wrote "Dear Prudence" to lure Prudence Farrow out of meditation overload. She was locked away for three weeks, meditating constantly, and everyone began to get a tad concerned. In *Playboy*, John recalled, "She'd been... trying to reach God quicker than anybody else. That was the competition in Maharishi's camp: who was going to get cosmic first. What I didn't know was I was *already* cosmic."

The first verse is blatant and nonchallenging: Won't you come out to play? Come and greet the day; the sky is blue and, capping it off, *you* are beautiful. A nice message if you

happen to be on the receiving end of it. But since it was John Lennon (always the creative opportunist) writing this song, it didn't remain simple for long.

In the first line of the second verse, he enjoins Pru to "open up your eyes." He then instructs her to "see the sunny skies" and concludes his appeal with a reminder that she is "part of everything"—a statement of the "all is one" theme weaving through their time in India. The mantra-like bridge of the song is simple, yet profound: "Look around."

The final verse asks Prudence to smile for him, and suggests that if she does, "the clouds will be a daisy chain." *Nature itself* will respond to her return to a child-like sense of wonder… why, even the *clouds* will line up in delight.

A song that starts out as a simple plea to a friend to "snap out of it" evolves over a very short period into a joyous celebration of the connectedness of all life. John was right: He had been cosmic for quite some time!

• • • ❧ • • •

- John Lennon never played "Dear Prudence" for Prudence Farrow when they were in India. "George was the one who told me about it," she said later. "At the end of this course, just as they were leaving, he mentioned that they had written a song about me but I didn't hear it until it came out on the album. I was flattered. It was a beautiful thing to have done."[1] Today, Prudence teaches meditation in Florida.
- On June 27, 1987, Sotheby's in New York sold a page of "Dear Prudence" lyrics (fourteen lines of verse and notes and doodles around the border) to an unidentified bidder for $19,500.
- "Dear Prudence" is one of seventeen Beatles songs that mention the sun or sunshine.[2]
- It's one of Julian Lennon's favorite songs of his father's.
- The song has been covered by Siouxsie and the Banshees, the Jerry Garcia Band, the Jackson 5, Leslie West, and Ramsey Lewis.

Did you know?

The recording

Location: **Trident Studios, London.**

Dates: **August 28, 1968,** 5:00 p.m.–7:00 a.m. – Recording at Trident, an eight-track facility, meant that the Fabs could record track by track. The basic track of the song taped with George and John's guitars. (John's is the guitar that starts the song and picks away throughout.) *The Beatles Recording Sessions* says Paul played drums on the track. (When the Beatles recorded at Abbey Road, production costs were often covered up by creative accounting; this Trident session cost £431.)

August 29, 1968, 7:00 p.m.–6:00 a.m. – The boys added bass guitar, as well as a manually double-tracked lead vocal, backing vocals, handclaps, and tambourine. (Paul and George played tambourine but they were occasionally joined by Mal Evans, Paul's visiting cousin John McCartney, and Apple artist Jackie Lomax, but it wasn't logged who played what. On the original eight-track, mass applause was added by all who provided backing vocal/handclaps, but this was not included in the final master.)

August 30, 1968, 5:00–11:00 p.m. – Overdubbing of a piano track and a short blast of flügelhorn,[3] both played by Paul. Mono and stereo mixing.

October 5, 1968 – Mono mixing at Trident Studios.

October 13, 1968 – Mono and stereo mixing back at Abbey Road.

November 22, 1968 – First released on the U.K. LP *The Beatles* (*The White Album*).

Players/Instruments:
- **John Lennon:** Lead guitar, lead and backing vocal, tambourine
- **Paul McCartney:** Bass, piano, drums, flügelhorn, lead and backing vocal
- **George Harrison:** Acoustic guitar, backing vocal
- **Ringo Starr:** Drums? (Lewisohn says it was Paul hitting the skins)
- **Mal Evans:** Tambourine

What we really like about this song

Steve: Like my coauthor, I am blown away by Paul's bass playing in "Dear Prudence," but I take it one step further. I consider it his single best bass performance in the entire Beatles canon. I've been raving about Paul's bass in "Dear Prudence" for years; in fact, I dedicated my *Beatles Book of Lists* to my cousin Dan: "a totally devoted Beatlefan who completely understands why Paul's bass line in 'Dear Prudence' is a subject worthy of at least a half hour's discussion—even if the phone's ringing, the kids are screaming, and it's starting to rain with all the windows open." I also love the final "the sun is up" segment when the piano stops and Ringo (or Paul?) comes in with a steady drumbeat that resolves the unsettled rhythm of the prior verses.

Mike: As the flight back from the USSR reaches the horizon, we hear the opening strains of "Dear Prudence." The song comes in like a lamb, with John gently plucking away on the electric acoustic, slowly builds to a crescendo (taking care not to become too overpowering too quickly—wouldn't want to scare Prudence away!), and closes with John gently plucking away again. In between, you can really hear the "percussion" of the percussion—try turning up the bass on your stereo and tell me you can't *feel* Ringo tapping the bass drum pedal and Paul tapping at the bass strings. This is one of Paul's finest performances, and the rest of the band is in fine fettle as well.

[1] *A Hard Day's Write.*

[2] The other sixteen are "Any Time at All," "Good Day Sunshine," "Good Night," "Here Comes the Sun," "I Am the Walrus," "I'll Follow the Sun," "I've Got a Feeling," "It's All Too Much," "Julia," "Lucy in the Sky with Diamonds," "Mother Nature's Son," "Rain," "Sun King," "The Fool on the Hill," "Two of Us," and "Yellow Submarine."

3 A flügelhorn is a valved brass instrument similar to a cornet. And no, it's not what John is holding on Sgt. Pepper—he has a French horn in his hand.

Don't Let Me Down

That's me, singing about Yoko...
—*John Lennon*
Playboy

John was legendary for forgetting the lyrics to songs, even his own, and this is nowhere more evident than during the January 1969 rooftop Get Back concert. What the hell is our lad singing during some of the later verses?

When all else fails, Johnny, look to the gibberish!

And if possible, do so while wearing a woman's fur coat (accompanied, of course, by a drummer in a red lady's rain slicker).

Why it made the top 100

"Don't Let Me Down" is the Beatles as nature intended, to cop a phrase from an Apple ad of the time. This quirky ballad is one of John's most intense love songs, and the chords and tempo foreshadow his Abbey Road soother "Sun King" (as well as later solo Plastic Ono Band tracks that boast the kind of fierce singing John gives us in the chorus to this song).

"Don't Let Me Down" could be looked at as a bit of a breakthrough for John; it's the song in which he carries out a point/counterpoint type of dialogue consisting of an impassioned appeal for protection in the chorus, and a gleeful recitation of the ways his lover loves him in the verses.

It would have been interesting to see what would have happened if Apple had released "Don't Let Me Down"—clearly the superior work—as the A side of the "Get Back" single. It definitely warrants a slot in the ranking of the 100 best Beatles songs.

What the song is about

Whatever John got from Yoko, it was obviously something he never got from Cynthia. John's songs during the time he was married to Cynthia were not about her; they were generic love songs (or songs about cheating on his wife, like "Norwegian Wood"), or they were songs about himself (say, "Nowhere Man").

As soon as Ms. Ono arrived on the scene, though, John was writing heartfelt and insightful songs of love and introspection. All the mixed feelings about Yoko notwithstanding, there is no question whatsoever that she served as a muse for John and spurred him to grow as an artist. (Can we even begin to imagine, though, how hurt Cynthia must have felt when she heard John proclaim in the song, "I'm in love for the first time"?)

With that power, however, came what could be perceived as a downside. "Don't Let Me Down" is John Lennon at his most codependent. His heartfelt and borderline-desperate chorus (and title, of course) pleads with Yoko not to take from him all that she has given him—her love, her inspiration, her comfort, her sex, et cetera.

In the verses, John states his case by recapping how Yoko changed him and made him a better artist and a better man—all of which is summed up in the line "Nobody ever loved me like she does." All you need is love, after all, and with it you can move mountains.

"Don't Let Me Down" is John Lennon proclaiming his dependence on Yoko, acknowledging her importance to him, and recognizing the power she wields over him. Knowing all this, he reduced himself to begging her not to let him down.

Love can heal and inspire; love can also hurt and destroy. And, apparently, no one knew this better than John Lennon.

- Upon release of the "Get Back"/"Don't Let Me Down" single, Apple distributed to TV stations sixteen-millimeter color promotional clips utilizing Get Back footage. The clips for "Don't Let Me Down" were taken both from the Twickenham recording sessions and the Rooftop Concert.
- During the forty-two-minute lunch-hour concert on the roof of Apple, on January 30, 1969, the Fabs played "Don't Let Me Down" several times, along with "Get Back," "I've Got a Feeling," "One After 909," and "Dig a Pony."
- In "Don't Let Me Down," the Beatles once again play with

a song's meter (see "Happiness Is a Warm Gun" and "Good Morning, Good Morning"). The first measure of the verse ("Nobody ever loved me…") is in 5/4 time, and it then quickly switches to 4/4, and then back to 5/4 again for the verse. Odd, but interesting, and it makes for a somewhat exotic-sounding recording.
- The song has been covered by the Wallflowers, Ben E. King, the Hollies, Bobby Womack, Randy Crawford, Dillard and Clark, Phoebe Snow, and Annie Lennox.

The recording

Location: **Abbey Road Studios, London** (in the studio and on the building's roof).

Dates: **January 22, 1969** – This was the first day of recording back at the Abbey Road studio, after the Fabs wrapped up filming and recording at Twickenham Film Studios for the Get Back/Let It Be project. Billy Preston happened to be at EMI that day, and George literally begged him to sit in with the band to ease the tension (probably remembering how everyone had been on good behavior when guest musician Eric Clapton sat in with them for the "While My Guitar Gently Weeps" sessions). The Beatles had known Billy since their 1962 Hamburg days when he was in Little Richard's backing band. They also wanted Billy because they knew that a fifth instrument would add to the live sound, since there would be no overdubbing for the track. Before recording started, John asked Ringo to give him a good crash on the cymbals to "give me the courage to come screaming in." (John was always self-conscious about his singing, and was probably wishing they would double-track his vocal.)

January 28, 1969 – "Get Back" and "Don't Let Me Down" were recorded in succession.

January 30, 1969 – The Rooftop Concert. Two takes of "Don't Let Me Down" were recorded. One of the versions wound up in the Let It Be film.

February 5, 1969 – Stereo mixing of the rooftop recordings.

March 10, 1969 – Stereo mixing.

April 4, 1969 – Mono mixing.

Players/Instruments:
- **John Lennon:** Lead guitar, lead vocal
- **Paul McCartney:** Bass, harmony vocal
- **George Harrison:** Rhythm guitar
- **Ringo Starr:** Drums
- **Billy Preston:** Electric piano

What we really like about this song

Steve: One of the elements that appeals to me the most is the depth of emotion John communicates to us through his voice. His "don't let me down!" is raw and primal and, above all, honest. I also love the way the song begins, and I like the lovely interplay between the spacey guitars and Billy Preston's electric piano throughout the entire song.

Mike: This is a simple, straightforward, and hopeful—yet worried—song. I commiserate with John. Like many, I've experienced trusting someone, only to be, yes, let down. You can hear both John's hope and his fear in this song, as he's at once reveling in the only real love he's ever known, yet admitting he is afraid of the future. You can't blame him for being paranoid.

GEORGE HARRISON   PAUL McC

84

I Saw Her Standing There

That's Paul doing his usual good job of producing what George Martin used to call a "potboiler." I helped with a couple of the lyrics.

—John Lennon
Playboy

I wrote it with John in the front parlour of my house in 20 Forthlin Road, Allerton. We sagged off school and wrote it on guitars and a little bit on the piano that I had there.

—Paul McCartney
The Beatles Recording Sessions

Led Zeppelin usually did not do covers when performing live. The list of classic Zeppelin tunes was more than enough to fill out a set. But one song Zeppelin did cover was "I Saw Her Standing There." In September 1970, when Zeppelin was playing the Los Angeles Forum, the group did a medley of "Communication Breakdown" and "I Saw Her Standing There."

Our hearts went boom. (We're speaking metaphorically here—neither of your authors happened to have made it to that particular Zeppelin concert, but we both are certain our hearts would have gone boom had we been there.)

Why it made the top 100

"I Saw Her Standing There" was the first track of the Beatles' first album, and it announced their presence with energy and testosterone. The song is a kickass rocker that, at times, almost seems to be too fast for its own good, but in the end is at the perfect, foot-tapping tempo. The singing is vibrant; George's lead guitar work is fiery, Ringo's drumming, relentless.

The strength of "I Saw Her Standing There" is that even now, forty years after its release, it can still generate the same excitement and joy when it's performed live by a band, or played by a DJ at a club or dance.

It seems that musical freshness knows no expiration date when it comes to the Fabs.

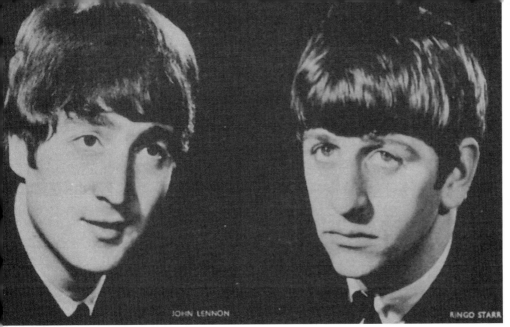

JOHN LENNON

RINGO STARR

What the song is about

Most hetero males would agree that there is something quite seductive about a young lady dancing with abandon, and the esteemed Sir Paul was no exception.

In December 1961, Paul saw Iris Caldwell dancing the Twist at the Tower Ballroom. Iris was Rory Storm's sister, and it wasn't long before she and Paul started dating. A few months later, as Paul was driving home one day, he came up with the idea of writing about a seventeen-year-old girl. Ostensibly, Paul was thinking like a businessman: He knew the Beatles needed songs to which the majority of their audience (teenage girls) could relate—but it's obvious that Iris was on his mind, and "I Saw Her Standing There" was born.

The song's lyrics re-create the moment Paul saw Iris dancing the Twist, yet the actual dancing does not occur until the third verse, when we're told they "danced through the night." At first, the narrator saw her simply "standing there," but that was enough for him to know that he'd never dance with another. (Such passionate commitment for a couple of teenagers!)

When he saw her, he knew he *could* fall in love with her; but it was only after they danced together that he *did* fall in love with her. The power of rock and roll.

• • • • • • •

- Paul's first try at the opening lyrics of this song went, "Well, she was just seventeen, she'd never been a beauty queen." John was apparently horrified at Paul's hokey use of *beauty queen* as a contrived rhyme and, in typical Lennon fashion, offered up "and you know what I mean…," which is as leering and suggestive—or as innocent and conversational—as the listener wants it to be.

- In an interview with *Beat Instrumental* magazine, Paul revealed that he had stolen the bass line for "I Saw Her Standing There" from Chuck Berry's 1961 song "I'm Talking About You." "I played exactly the same notes as he did and it fitted our number perfectly. Even now, when I tell people about it, I find few of them believe me."

Did you know?

- The original working title of "I Saw Her Standing There" was "Seventeen."
- Paul originally planned on giving away "I Saw Her Standing There" to Rory Storm for his band Rory Storm and the Hurricanes (he was, after all, dating Rory's sister, Iris) but he was overruled by Brian Epstein the moment Brian heard the song.
- Notable covers of "I Saw Her Standing There" include versions by Little Richard, Elton John, Jerry Garcia Band, Tiffany (as "I Saw Him Standing There"), the Pete Best Band, the Bar-Kays, the Crickets, Cliff Richard, the Grateful Dead, the Merseybeats, the Tubes, and Hank Williams Jr.

The recording

Location: **Abbey Road Studios, London.**

Dates: **February 11, 1963** – "I Saw Her Standing There" was the second song they recorded this day—it followed "There's a Place." Nine takes were recorded in the morning sessions, which took place from 10:00 a.m. to 1:00 p.m. During the 2:30–6:00 p.m. session, they recorded three more takes, and handclap overdubs were added to Take 1. In the ninety minutes between the two sessions, while George Martin and other production people went out to lunch, the lads stayed in the studio to continue rehearsing the song. The second engineer on the session, Richard Langham, quoted in *The Beatles Recording Sessions*, remarked, "We couldn't believe it. We had never seen a group work right through their lunch break before."

February 25, 1963 – Editing, mono and stereo mixing.

March 22, 1963 – First released on the *Please Please Me* LP in the United Kingdom.

Players/Instruments:
- **Paul McCartney:** Bass, lead vocal
- **John Lennon:** Rhythm guitar, harmony vocal
- **George Harrison:** Lead guitar
- **Ringo Starr:** Drums

What we really like about this song

Steve: I love the song's exuberance and excitement. John and Paul seem to be having a fantastic time playing and singing it, and on some of the live versions, their sheer joy is palpable. I also love how Paul's high E on "woo" comes across like an unstoppable expression of his pleasure with the song, while also serving to communicate an adolescent's unmitigated thrill at dancing through the night with his latest squeeze.

Mike: Coming from a marketing background, I can appreciate Paul's knowledge of his audience. He wrote a song perfectly tailored to the young teenage girls who made their live shows so successful—and their first album a hit. And, as always when they collaborated, John added his own memorable part. The beauty of the song is that it's innocent yet risky, confident yet innocent. As John says, it's still a "barn-burner."

85 Savoy Truffle

In the true White Album *spirit of masquerading in diverse musical styles, we find George here turning in a heavily syncopated, bluesy rock and roller that has a strong contemporary dance band undercurrent.*

—Musicologist Alan Pollack
Notes on "Savoy Truffle"

George Harrison's greatest musical achievements as a Beatle were "found" songs.

"While My Guitar Gently Weeps" came from two words picked randomly from a book. "Here Comes the Sun" burst into life thanks to perhaps the most mundane of all events: The sun came out. And our song for today, "Savoy Truffle," was born out of a box of chocolates.

In *I Me Mine*, George talked about the genesis of the tune: "'Savoy Truffle' is a funny one written whilst hanging out with Eric Clapton in the sixties. At that time he had a lot of cavities in his teeth and needed dental work. He always had a toothache but he ate a lot of chocolates—he couldn't resist them and once he saw a box, he *had* to eat them all… He was over at my house and I had a box of 'Good News' chocolates on the table and wrote the song from the names inside the lid…"

Why it made the top 100

Everything about "Savoy Truffle" works, in particular, the smoking brass section, which is made nasty as all get-out thanks to George's deliberate distortion of the four saxes' sound. Yes, the lyrics are a bit "ordinary," but the production more than makes up for it. Sizzling guitar work from George combines with an amazing bass part from Paul, both of which are enhanced by the kickass brass. Appearing as it does on *The White Album* after Paul's somewhat ridiculous "Honey Pie," "Savoy Truffle" does, indeed, (as George tells us) blow down those blues!

What the song is about

The "Savoy Truffle" lyrics are mostly about having to have all your teeth pulled out from eating too much chocolate.

The laundry list of individual chocolate candy names culminates with the line, "But you'll have to have them all pulled out after the Savoy truffle…" We must conclude that the Savoy truffle was the richest, most sugary, most tooth-rotting variety in the box!

There are three lines, though, that do not seem to "play along," as it were. The first is the second line of the second verse, "I feel your taste all the time we're apart." On the surface, this would seem to be a chocolate junkie's admission that the sensory delight of chocolate on his tongue stays with him, even when he's not eating chocolate. But it does not take a Larry Flynt to find an erotic subtext to the lyric. (And we are not the first Beatleologists to notice it.)

Was the anthropomorphizing of the chocolate—"when *we're* apart"—intentional? Could he be that obsessed with sweets? Or was George talking about a *person*? Was he being suggestive as, say, Paul was in "Penny Lane" ("fish and finger pie," "it's a clean machine," and so on), and John was in "Happiness Is a Warm Gun" ("I feel my finger on your trigger")? Without a definitive answer from George, these interpretations are "eye of the beholder," we suppose.

The other two intriguing lines are in the second bridge, which begins on message: "what is sweet now, turns so sour." Yes, if the sweet candy you were enjoying resulted in losing your teeth, then that would, indeed, be a "sour" state of affairs.

But the next two lines "We all know ob-la-di-bla-da/But can you show me, where you are?" are puzzling. Are they simply filler lines that George used to finish off the verse? Or do they have a meaning within the context of the song? Again, it's hard to know with certainty. That said, though, the song is blatant enough to, in a sense, blow off these lines as either illogical or simply convenient, and enjoy the rest of the lyrics for their fun and sense of humor.

• • • ❦ • • •

- In *I Me Mine*, George revealed, "I got stuck with the two bridges for a while and Derek Taylor wrote some of the words in the middle… *you know that what you eat you are…*" Taylor's line came from the 1968 American documentary *You Are What You Eat*, made by Alan Pariser and Barry Feinstein.
- Good News chocolates were made by a company called Mackintosh, and real flavors in the assortment were Savoy truffle, crème tangerine, montelimart, ginger sling, pineapple treat, and coffee dessert. George made up cherry cream, apple tart, and coconut fudge for the song.
- "Savoy Truffle" is one of the two songs on *The White Album* in which individual Beatles songs are mentioned by name. George mentions "Ob-La-Di, Ob-La-Da." ("Glass Onion" is the other—see song number 56.)
- "Savoy Truffle" has been covered by Ella Fitzgerald.

Did you know?

The recording

Locations: **Trident Studios; Abbey Road Studios, London.**

Dates: **October 3, 1968,** 4:00 p.m.–2:30 a.m. (Trident) – One take of the basic track was recorded, including drums, bass, and lead guitar.
October 5, 1968 (Trident) – An overdub of George's lead vocal.
October 11, 1968, 3:00–6:00 p.m. (Abbey Road) – Recording of the brass overdubs. Chris Thomas, in *The Beatles Recording Sessions*, recalled: "George Martin suggested that I score 'Savoy Truffle' for saxophone. I must say that I found it a real chore." Engineer Brian Gibson also commented: "The session men were playing really well—there's nothing like a good brass section letting rip—and it sounded fantastic. But having got this really nice sound George turned to Ken Scott and said 'Right, I want to distort it.' So I had to plug-up two high-gain amplifiers which overloaded and deliberately introduced a lot of distortion, completely tearing the sound to pieces and making it dirty.

The musicians came up to the control room to listen to a playback and George said to them 'Before you listen I've got to apologize for what I've done to your beautiful sound. Please forgive me—but it's the way I want it!' I don't think they particularly enjoyed hearing their magnificent sound screwed up quite so much until they realized that this was what George wanted, and that it was their job to provide it."

October 14, 1968 (Ringo absent) – Overdubs of a second electric guitar, organ, tambourine, and bongos. Mono and stereo mixing.

November 22, 1968 – First released on the U.K. LP *The Beatles* (*The White Album*).

Players/Instruments:
- **George Harrison:** Lead guitar, organ, vocal
- **Paul McCartney:** Bass
- **Ringo Starr:** Drums, tambourine
- **Session musicians:** Two baritone saxes, four tenor saxes
  Note: According to *The Beatles Recording Sessions*, John Lennon was not involved in any of the "Savoy Truffle" recording sessions.

What we really like about this song

Steve: The two things I like most about this song are the bass and the brass. Also, George's vocal is one of the toppermost of the poppermost of Harrison vocals. This *White Album* track has always impressed me because it is, essentially, the band Harrison. George handles almost all the elements of the song, he determined what the brass would sound like, and he eschewed Paul/John harmonies. The song sounds as fresh today as it did when it was first released.

Mike: A pop music confection… literally! George sings what's written on the inside of a box of chocolate, so the lyrics aren't all that meaningful, but the song works. I think it's the instrumentation—the organ, the prominent and distorted saxes, Paul's active bass. We're given little tastes of rhythm guitar throughout and a blistering (albeit brief) solo. I also like that the song ends strong with a blast of brass, instead of just fading into "Cry Baby Cry."

I'm So Tired

The one thing John hated more than going to bed at night was getting out of it the next day.

—Pete Shotton
John Lennon in My Life

"J'm So Tired" illustrates the adage:
Be careful what you wish for, for you may get it.

Meditation is a contemplative exercise that is intended to make a person more centered, more at peace, and, yes, more relaxed. When the Beatles were in India in February 1968, John spent most of his time meditating. All day long, he meditated, meditated, meditated, and the result was that he couldn't sleep at night. The meditating so screwed up John's sleep patterns that he spent the nights staring at the ceiling. (And writing songs, apparently.)

Be careful what you wish for, right?

Why it made the top 100

Does it mean anything that John's weary, hung-over, dragging-his-ass ballad "I'm So Tired" was placed on *The White Album* between two sunny, sparkling Paul songs, "Martha My Dear" and "Blackbird"? Was there a deliberate intent to highlight the differences between Paul's and John's tones—at least for these three songs?

Perhaps the more trenchant question would be, Did that much thought go into the lineup of songs, beyond the requirement that the John and Paul songs alternate? For the most part, that is—there are a few occasions on *The White Album* where two Paul songs ("Why Don't We Do It in the Road?" and "I Will") or two John songs ("Everybody's Got Something to Hide Except Me and My Monkey" and "Sexy Sadie") appear consecutively.

In any case, the placement works. John's world-weary gestalt is a stark shift in sensibility from Paul's piano-driven pop delight "Martha My Dear," and it powerfully highlights the personal and artistic divide between the two at the time. "I'm So Tired" is a John song through and through, and is one of his most personal songs on the record. It's also a terrific ballad that boasts some musical surprises (especially the organ glissandos!).

What the song is about

The song begins with our hero, Insomnia Man, lying in bed thinking confused thoughts and wondering if he should get up and make himself a drink. Why so tired, lad? So far, we don't know.

The second verse somewhat clears things up: He can't stop thinking about someone, perhaps a lady? Or maybe the Maharishi? "My mind is set on you," he moans, and he debates calling but, he tells us, he knows what would happen.

This brings us to the bridge, where he begins by telling us that this person would accuse him of deception: "you'd say I'm putting you on…" About what? That he can't sleep? Apparently.

He defends himself, though, proclaiming that his insomnia is "no joke" and that it's doing him harm. He can't sleep, he can't stop his brain from churning, and then we find out that this has been going on for three weeks. Three weeks without sleep? Yes, and thus there's no surprise in the admission, "I'm going insane."

Following all this comes the bartering: "I'd give you everything I've got for a little peace of mind." What could this person possibly say to Mr. Sleepy that would give him the "peace of mind" he so desperately craves? A clue as to where the sleeping pills are stashed? Perhaps some cosmic wisdom, if he is singing to the guru? We're not told.

We then arrive at the final verse, in which he reiterates his exhaustion and admits he's "so upset." About his insomnia or the problems that his friend might be able to resolve? Again, we're not told. The verse concludes with Tired Guy getting up to have a cigarette and cursing Walter Raleigh, the English colonizer who introduced tobacco to Europe in the sixteenth century. *As if I don't have enough problems,* he seems to be saying; *thanks to Sir Walter I also have a nicotine jones.*

The song ends with a refrain of the bridge, but this time he repeats the "give you everything I've got" line three times, underlining his desperation and pleading despairingly for the peace of mind that continues to elude his grasp.

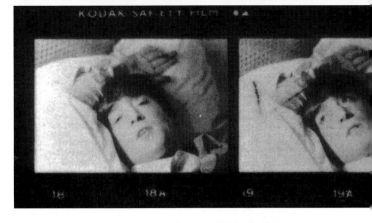

- Alcohol and drugs were not allowed at the Maharishi's compound, but some of John's friends smuggled in wine for him.
- It's believed that John's indecision about whether or not to leave his wife for Yoko contributed to his stress while in India.
- The "three weeks" reference in the lyrics is specific: John wrote the song after he had been in India for three weeks.
- The first two chords of "I'm So Tired" (A major–G-sharp major) are the same as those of "Sexy Sadie" (G major–F-sharp major), but one step higher.
- Many "Paul is Dead" disciples heard a clue at the end of "I'm So Tired" when John mutters something that was interpreted by the conspiracy-minded as "Paul is dead, miss him, miss him." This was later said to be "Monsieur Monsieur, how about another?" but even this is now known to be wrong. It is generally accepted that John was speaking gibberish. The verbatim, phonetic transcription (beginning at 1:58) of what he says is "Bliss'm bliss'ekimitzeh, habots-e-lone. Drsh, drsh, tidley." This is followed by what sounds like a child saying "pleh!"
- The song has been covered by Alex Chilton, and Willie Banks and the Messengers.

The recording

Location: **Abbey Road Studios, London.**
Dates: **October 8, 1968** – Fourteen takes and overdubs were recorded on eight-track tape. They recorded the bass, drums, guitars, lead vocal, backing vocals by John and Paul, drums, electric piano, and organ.
October 15, 1968 – Mono and stereo mixing.
November 22, 1968 – First released on the U.K. LP *The Beatles* (*The White Album*).

Players/Instruments:
- **John Lennon:** Acoustic and lead guitar, organ, lead vocal
- **Paul McCartney:** Bass, harmony vocal
- **George Harrison:** Lead and rhythm guitar
- **Ringo Starr:** Drums

What we really like about this song

Steve: John's life was his music was his life. He went through withdrawal, he wrote a song about it ("Cold Turkey"). He missed his mother, he wrote a song about it ("Julia"). He saw stuff during an acid trip (er, too many to list), he wrote a song about it. And he couldn't sleep, so he wrote this song about it. I like the "feel" of this song, and I give John props for beginning the song with a retro three-note climb that could have easily come off as corny—but didn't. I also like the organ swirling around in the background, and Ringo's understated drumming.

Mike: Another *White Album* sleeper (sorry, couldn't resist!). John's sleep ailments, first chronicled in "I'm Only Sleeping," seem to have gotten worse—first, he couldn't get out of bed; now he can't get to sleep. The band seems to shuffle drowsily through the song, then rally together and summon their strength to deliver the impassioned chorus. The song's time changes keep me from drifting off myself. The more I listen to these songs, the more I appreciate Ringo's drumming: He was not afraid to play the skins sparsely, and was creative enough to know the degree of drum required to set the tone of a song.

87

I'm Happy Just To Dance With You

I wrote this for George to sing. I'm always reading how Paul and I used to make him invisible or keep him out, but it isn't true. I encouraged him like mad.

—*John Lennon*
The Beatles by Hunter Davies

The "I'm Happy Just to Dance with You" sequence in *A Hard Day's Night* is great fun.

As the Fabs are extracted from the chorus-girl-abundant dressing room, we hear a jazzy piano version of the song, and then we see a dancing troupe tripping the light fantastic to the song on stage. Behind the dancers are, egads, giant (and disgusting) posters of beetles. (Yes, the insects.)

The Beatles walk onto the stage, and John immediately starts cavorting about in his, er, unique dancing style. The Fabs pick up their instruments, Ringo gets behind his drums and plays along with he piano for a bit, and then John exclaims, "Why don't we do the show right here!"

And then they perform the song, with Paul, John, and George standing in a semicircle *facing* Ringo.

When it's over, John compliments George on his performance.

Gear.

264

Why it made the top 100

"I'm Happy Just to Dance with You" is a classic *Hard Day's Night* track and video sequence, and a terrific Lennon composition. What impresses about this song is that John did not skimp while writing it—yes, it may seem a formula tune, but the chord changes and writing indicate that John did not consider it a throwaway just because he or Paul wouldn't be singing it. John was telling the truth when he said he always encouraged George. This song—a Lennon/McCartney song that George sang (how often did *that* happen?)—is evidence of his sincerity.

What the song is about

Our young man is helplessly smitten, and has concluded that by the time he finishes dancing with his lady love, his infatuation will unquestionably move into heartfelt, utterly delirious love. This guy is intense about how important it is to dance with his girl. He tells us that he doesn't "need or want" to hold her hand; he doesn't need to kiss her or hold her tight (hmmm, how does that jibe with his passionate desire to dance with her?); and he is, yes, happy *just* to dance with her.

The chorus reiterates his joy: "Just to dance with you is everything I need." (Doesn't take much to make our boy happy, eh?)

George sings the song directly to his dancing partner. In the third verse, he enlists her assistance in shutting out the world: He asks her to ignore anybody who tries to cut in on them. (What kind of cad would attempt to intrude on such a romantic moment anyway?) Then once again, he proclaims how important is simply dancing with her: "In this world there's nothing I would rather do…" Wow. This guy sure does love to cut a rug, wouldn't you say?

The second-to-last line is intriguing: He tells her he "discovered" he was in love with her. When did this happen? When they were dancing? The inevitable conclusion we must all reach is that, man oh man, this young lady must be one hell of a dancer!

(Did you notice how we tastefully ignored the lascivious, all-too-easy, dancing = sex metaphor? Yes, sometimes we make our mums proud.)

Did you know?

- John once remarked that he considered the word *just* an empty, useless word for song lyrics, and yet he uses it eleven times in this song, as well as in the title itself.
- At the very end of the song, at precisely 1:53 on the timer, a squeak is heard that somehow escaped the quick pulldown of the faders.
- Speaking of time, at 1:57 "I'm Happy Just to Dance with You" is one of the shortest of all Beatles songs.
- In this segment of the movie *A Hard Day's Night*, a couple of mistakes are obvious. At one point, George messes up his lip-synching—what he sings does not match the soundtrack. The other blatant error is the scene in which we hear Paul and John singing the backing "Oh-oh"s and the camera is on John, who has his mouth closed and is not singing along with the recording.
- "I'm Happy Just to Dance with You" was never released in the United Kingdom as a single. It was released as a single in the United States twice, however: in 1964 as the B side of "I'll Cry Instead," and in 1982 as the B side of "The Beatles Movie Medley" (which was Capitol USA's idea and which included short excerpts from "Magical Mystery Tour," "All You Need Is Love," "You've Got to Hide Your Love Away," "I Should Have Known Better," "A Hard Day's Night," "Ticket to Ride," and "Get Back." Initially, EMI did not consider the medley good enough to release in the U.K., but relented after tremendous demand for imported U.S. copies of the single.)
- "I'm Happy Just to Dance with You" has been covered by Maureen McGovern, Cyrkle, and Anne Murray.

The recording

Location: **Abbey Road Studios, London.**

Dates: **March 1, 1964** – Four takes were recorded. Takes 1 and 2 focused on the rhythm track, with 2 considered better. Take 3 was a breakdown, and Take 4 introduced the backing vocals, which were recorded with a slight tape echo.

March 3, 1964 – Mono mixing.

June 9, 1964 – Mono tape copying for movie soundtrack.

June 22, 1964 – Stereo mixing.

June 26, 1964 – First released on the U.S. LP *A Hard Day's Night*.

Players/Instruments:
- **George Harrison:** Lead guitar, lead vocal
- **John Lennon:** Rhythm guitar, backing vocal
- **Paul McCartney:** Bass, backing vocal
- **Ringo Starr:** Drums, Arabian bongos

What we really like about this song

Steve: Unlike my coauthor, and in clear disagreement with John and Paul (Paul called it a "formula song"— not that there's anything wrong with that!), I think this is a great Beatles song. I like John and George's guitar playing, Paul's bass, and the "Oh-oh" backing harmony part. I also think George's vocal is perfect for the song, and I love the simple, yet exciting production. There are no keyboards, no fancy guitar sounds, no weird effects, and yet from the opening ringing guitar chords, we're caught up in the song's unabashed *fun*.

Mike: This song is not among my Beatles favorites, but I recognize its importance. On the one hand, you can consider that John was being a nice guy and throwing George a song to include on the movie soundtrack (and subsequently on the B side of a single). On the other, you might see it as an insult to George, that his music just was not up to snuff and John was covering for him. It's a nice enough dance song, but George would eventually go on to write great songs in his own right.

265

Get Back

88

"Get Back" is Paul. That's a better version of "Lady Madonna." You know, a potboiler rewrite... I think there's some underlying thing about Yoko in there... You know, "Get back to where you once belonged." Every time he sang the line in the studio, he'd look at Yoko.

—John Lennon
Playboy

On December 18, 1968, about a month before the recording sessions for "Get Back" began, John and Yoko "appeared" inside a large white bag in the Royal Albert Hall in London.

On January 10, 1969, George announced he was quitting the Beatles because he couldn't take Paul's harassment anymore.

After the appearance of the January 1969 issue of *Disc and Music Echo* magazine, John and George came to blows over remarks John made in which he said that Apple was poorly managed from the start. George thought that such criticism was akin to airing the Fabs' dirty laundry in public.

Tension surrounded the Beatles like a fog upon LA, and it was in the midst of all this angst that they went into the studio (and then onto a roof) to record "Get Back" and the rest of the *Let It Be* album/film project.

Why it made the top 100

"Get Back" is not that great a Beatles song, but it might be one of their most important for its role in unifying four at-odds artists. Its raggedness, evident in the many versions of the song that exist, stand in stark contrast to the meticulousness of the *Abbey Road* sessions—which, incredibly, came *after* the less-than-stellar *Let It Be* songs and sessions.

No doubt about it. The Beatles could rally when they needed/wanted to.

What the song is about

The lyrics to "Get Back," many of which were apparently made up in the studio, are a classic example of abstract meaninglessness put to music.

Let's look at the two verses that tell the "story" of the song.

First, we meet Jo Jo, who "thought he was a loner." Jo Jo was wrong about that, so he moved to California, after which the narrator sings, "Get back to where you once belonged." But is he singing to Jo Jo? If so, what does "where you once belonged" mean? California? Arizona? Somewhere else? The song is only one verse old and we're already confused.

The second verse introduces us to Loretta Martin. Apparently Loretta was as confused about her identity as Jo Jo, because we are told that she "thought she was a woman," but she was *another* man. What does *that* mean? Our bewilderment is compounded as we're told that the girls around her "say she's got it coming." She's got what coming? Some sort of punishment or retribution? We don't know, but we are then informed that "she gets it while she can." Gets what while she can? Is this a sexual double entendre? And is Loretta a man or a woman? We still don't know.

The spoken outro does nothing to clear up this confusion. It seems that Loretta's mother, wearing high heels and a low-neck sweater, is waiting for her back home.

"Get Back" can be interpreted in many ways and the ultimate meaning, we suppose, if there even is one, is in the ear of the listener.

• • • • 🐨 • • • •

- "Get Back" was to be the theme song for the next Beatles project. The companion film would show them getting back to their roots, working on songs together from scratch, and then performing them live. There was actually talk of the Fabs putting on a concert in a desert in Tunisia, among other places. John, quoted in *The Beatles, A Celebration*, commented, "Someone mentioned the Coliseum in Rome, and I think originally Paul might have even suggested a bloody boat in the middle of the ocean. As for me, I was rapidly warming up to the idea of an asylum!"

- The Apple newspaper ad announcing the release of the "Get Back" single read, "The Beatles as nature intended. 'Get Back' is the Beatles' new single. It's the first Beatles' record which is as live as can be, in this electronic age.

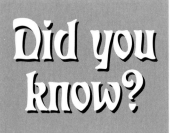

There's no electronic watchamacallit. 'Get Back' is a pure spring-time rock number."

- "Get Back" is one of only four Beatles songs in which cities in the United States are mentioned: Tucson, Arizona (in "Get Back"), Los Angeles (in "Blue Jay Way"), Miami Beach (in "Back in the USSR"), and Hollywood (in "Honey Pie").

- "Get Back" has been covered by Paul Mauriat, Al Green, Ike and Tina Turner, Elvis Presley, Veruca Salt, Mongo Santamaria, Billy Preston, the Grateful Dead, Mott the Hoople, Rod Stewart, Kenny Rogers, and Elton John. (Elton performed "Get Back" as part of the finale at his "11-17-70" concert. He started with his own "Burn Down the Mission," went into Elvis's "My Baby Left Me," and then into "Get Back.")

The recording

Locations: **Abbey Road Studios, London; Olympic Studios, London.**

Dates: **January 23, 1969** – Ten takes were recorded, with the last one considered best (although it ultimately would not be used). Alan Parsons debuted this day as tape operator.

January 27, 1969 – Today, the Beatles recorded at least fourteen different takes. Paul and John can be heard on the tapes agreeing that progress was being made. They finally recorded the version that closes the *Let It Be* album, with the "Loretta Fart" comical verse. This differed from the single version, which had not yet been recorded. Phil Spector added to the album track the "Thanks Mo" and "passed the audition" lines that were actually recorded at the rooftop concert.

January 28, 1969 – The splintered four seemed to function as a group on this day, and they recorded the version that was to be the single. They faded out for the disc, though, as the session continued for a "considerable time." (This end section, with the forced "ho-ho-hos" from Paul, was included as the last part of the unreleased *Get Back* LP, and was also used over the end titles of the *Let It Be* film.)

January 30, 1969 – The rooftop concert. The Fabs started with two takes of "Get Back." The two were pretty similar, and they were edited together for the *Let It Be* film. (The film also includes the arrival of the police.) The third take was also the last song of the ten-song concert. On this take, Paul can be heard ad-libbing the lyrics, "You've been playing on the roofs again, and your mommy doesn't like that, she's gonna have you arrested!" The band was understandably distracted as the police made it to the roof to shut them down, but they were determined to finish. It's here where Paul thanks Mo, and John says they hoped they passed the audition. (This take is on *Anthology 3*.)

February 5, 1969 – Stereo mixing (two versions).

March 10, 1969 – Stereo mixing.

March 26, 1969 – Mono mixing.

April 4, 1969 – Stereo and mono mixing.

April 7, 1969 – Remixing, mono mixing. British DJs John Peel and Alan Freeman had gotten hold of an acetate version of the song and played it on the air. (Paul happened to hear it broadcast and thought it needed some work.)

April 11, 1969 – First released as a U.K. single, backed with "Don't Let Me Down."

March 26, 1970 – Stereo mixing, remixing for *Let It Be* LP. (Spector edited in the "Loretta Fart" and "Thanks Mo/audition" chatter.)

Players/Instruments:
- **Paul McCartney:** Bass, lead vocal
- **John Lennon:** Lead guitar, backing vocal
- **George Harrison:** Rhythm guitar
- **Ringo Starr:** Drums
- **Billy Preston:** Electric piano[1]

What we really like about this song

Steve: I think my favorite elements of "Get Back" are Ringo's relentless military marching-style drumming and Billy Preston's piano solo. It's a straight-on rocker that is probably more fondly remembered by fans for its significance in the breakup than for its somewhat primitive musicality.

Mike: What a scene: The Beatles thrashing away on their instruments, bobby storm troopers at the door, bewildered people on Saville Row looking up to catch a glimpse of what all the commotion is about. I know the released versions of "Get Back" were not the live versions, but I love the thought of the rooftop concert (which U2 paid homage to on their video for "Where the Streets Have No Name"). A few facts learned when relistening to "Get Back": John plays a kickass lead (making me wish he did more of this sort of inspired playing); Billy Preston adds some sparkling keyboards; Ringo chugs along with an insistent beat, even while wearing his wife's red slicker. And finally: The Beatles *are* a great little live band.

[1] Billy was the first guest artist to be credited on a Beatles single.

I Want You (She's So Heavy)

The ground bass figure used here has a distinctive arch shape and portentous melodic character reminiscent of the themes of some of J. S. Bach's own pieces... such as the Passacaglia and Fugue for Organ in [C minor], or the Chaconne for Solo Violin in [D minor]."

—Musicologist Allan Pollack
Notes on "I Want You (She's So Heavy)"

This extremely heavy musical blitzkrieg bookended the other four songs on Side One of *Abbey Road* ("Something," "Maxwell's Silver Hammer," "Oh! Darling," and "Octopus's Garden") and was as different to our ears (and to its neighboring songs) as was John's opening song of the side, "Come Together."

Why it made the top 100

This song is one of the denser, more intense productions of the Beatles' career, and it's a landmark for them in its use of an odd amalgam of sounds, shifting tempos (and musical moods), and almost no words at all. (Not to mention an ending that makes you think somebody pulled the plug out of the stereo.) John was often able to make us *hear* what he was *feeling*, and "I Want You (She's So Heavy)" is one of the best examples of this gift.

What the song is about

This song consists of a mere thirteen words (and one of them is "yeah," so maybe it's only twelve words?—half the lyrics are in the title!) and is, without a doubt, John's bluntest, most in-your-face song.

The song is about Yoko, and after its release John said that her artistic minimalism probably influenced him and had something to do with its composition and style. (One of Yoko's 1964 poems consists of the single word "water.") John commented on the lyrics to Beatles biographer Hunter Davies, "This is about Yoko. She's very heavy, and there was nothing else I could say about her other than I want you, she's so heavy. Someone said the lyrics weren't very good. But there was nothing more I wanted to say."[1]

All that aside, though, we cannot help but be intrigued by the structure of the lyrics. The heart of the song is the jazzy main verse in which John sings "I want you" and "I want you so bad." Here, he is singing to Yoko, and he uses a gentle, almost caressing voice to do so.

269

But then, when the song shifts into megaheaviness with the "she's so heavy" line, John shifts his point of view to second person. Now he is talking *about* Yoko, and it's obviously not accidental that at the point in the song where John decides to announce his thoughts about her to the world, he uses sonic bombardment to do so.

Even with only thirteen words, John was able to communicate a heartfelt, almost painful depth of emotion, and then compose the perfectly intense music to accompany his words.

• • • 🐛 • • •

- According to George Martin, John was getting "disenchanted" with elaborate studio production: "He didn't really approve of what I'd done or was doing. He didn't like 'messing about,' as he called it, and he didn't like the pretentiousness, if you like. I could see his point. He wanted good, old-fashioned plain solid rock. 'The hell with it—let's blast the living daylights out!' Or, if it was a soft ballad: 'Let's do it just the way it comes.' He wanted authenticity."[2]
- There has long been a pervasive rumor that on the February 22, 1969, track there is a muffled shout of disapproval (at 4:32) from the control room after John screams "Yeah!" (at 4:28) and causes some audible distortion. *Was* someone instructing John to keep his voice down? No one would ever have interfered with a Beatles' performance that way. Mark Lewisohn closely scrutinized the Trident tapes; the shout (which sounds like "turn it down, man") belongs to one of the

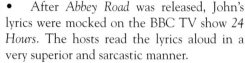

other Beatles (probably Paul), off-mike, and he was more than likely shouting to one of the engineers to turn down the gain so as to limit the distortion. As we know from "Helter Skelter," Paul had no problem with screaming per se.
- After *Abbey Road* was released, John's lyrics were mocked on the BBC TV show *24 Hours*. The hosts read the lyrics aloud in a very superior and sarcastic manner.
- At 7:44, this is the second longest Beatles song. Only "Revolution 9" at 8:12 (on *The White Album*) is longer. ("Hey Jude" is third, at 7:04.) (All times are from the digital readout of the original Beatles track on a CD player. Many books have different times for certain songs; we decided to use the time shown when the CD player changes to the next song on the disc.)
- The song has been covered by Soundgarden, Alvin Lee, the Eric Gales Band, and Coroner.

The recording

Locations: **Abbey Road Studios; Trident Studios, London.**

Dates: **January 29, 1969** (Abbey Road) – During the *Get Back* sessions, the boys rehearsed the song with the tape running. The song was now known simply as "I Want You."

February 22, 1969 (Trident Studios; Abbey Road was being remodeled to add new equipment) – "I Want You" was the first *Abbey Road* song committed to tape. Thirty-five takes of the basic track, along with John's guide vocal, were recorded. (They experimented on one take with Paul singing the lead vocal.) According to *The Beatles Recording Sessions*, Billy Preston was involved somehow in the session, but there are no specific details as to who played what.

February 23, 1969 – Mixing and editing of three different takes of the song recorded thus far.

April 18, 1969, 1:00–4:30 a.m. (Abbey Road) – Overdub of guitars, with only John, George, and producers/engineers involved. Engineer Jeff Jarratt recalled, "John and George went into the far left-hand corner of number two [studio] to overdub those guitars. They wanted a massive sound so they kept tracking and tracking, over and over."[3] A reduction mixdown was done, followed by more overdubs, and then the making of a rough stereo remix.

April 20, 1969 – Overdub of a Hammond organ, along with conga drums brought in by Mal Evans.

August 8, 1969 – Earlier on this day, the Beatles had gathered in front of Abbey Road Studios to take the now-famous "crossing" picture pix for the album cover. In the studio, they overdubbed John's Moog synthesizer sounds and effects, and Ringo's drums. (Paul was in the other studio adding overdubs to "Oh! Darling.")

August 11, 1969 – "(She's So Heavy)" was added to the title. Overdub and re-recording of John, Paul, and George repeatedly singing the "she's so heavy" line. John wasn't sure if he preferred the original Trident master with its overdubs, or the April 18 reduction mix of the same material with different overdubs, so this day's vocal inserts were added to *both* versions.

August 20, 1969 – This was the last time all four Beatles were in the studio together. "I Want You (She's So Heavy)," begun more than six months earlier, was the final song to be mixed for the *Abbey Road* album. They remixed both versions and then edited them together. John wanted both halves used because he had introduced the Moog and white-noise sounds only to the August 8 tape. The first half of the finished song (four minutes, thirty-seven

seconds) is the first Abbey Road session; the remaining three minutes, seven seconds is from the original Trident tape (for a total of 7:44). The track could have gone on until 8:04, but John decided on a "sudden" ending. Engineer Alan Parsons recalled, "We were putting the final touches to that side of the LP, and we were listening to the mix. John said 'There! Cut the tape there.' Geoff [Emerick] cut the tape and that was it. End of side one!"

September 26, 1969 – First released on the U.K. LP *Abbey Road*.

Players/Instruments:
- **John Lennon:** Lead guitar, lead vocal, organ, Moog synthesizer, white-noise maker
- **Paul McCartney:** Bass, harmony vocal
- **George Harrison:** Rhythm guitar, Moog synthesizer, white-noise maker
- **Ringo Starr:** Drums

What we really like about this song

Steve: This song has grown on me over the years. Initially, the ending seemed a little overdone, but now I see how it all works together to create a mind-numbing, trance-like mood that's perfect for the attitude and message of the song. John essentially created an aural rendering of obsessive love, and all the sounds and noises conspire to paint a dark soundscape of passion and fixation.

Mike: John sometimes wrote songs more for their vibe than their meaning, and the vibe of this song is *heavy*. (Heck, maybe the vibe *is* the meaning?) At the time he wrote it, he never knew he was defining grunge and heavy metal. I can hear a band like Tool doing this song—I'm surprised they haven't already. I like the time and mood changes throughout. I can hear a bit of bossa nova styling, and wonder if this song was an inspiration for Sean Lennon's album *Into the Sun*. Just when you find yourself hypnotized by the three-minute-long outro riff, the abrupt ending hits you like a shovel between the eyes.

[1] *The Beatles.*

[2] *The Beatles Anthology.*

[3] *The Beatles Recording Sessions.*

Long, Long, Long

I think all of love is part of a universal love. When you love a woman, it's the God in her that you see. The only complete love is for God.

—*George Harrison*
Rolling Stone

George Harrison worked his entire

life to achieve God-consciousness. He strove diligently to attain enlightenment and, whenever possible, to do it through his music. Within this context, "Long, Long, Long" may be George's most important *personal* song, his favorite prayer put to music.

Why it made the top 100

George had four songs on *The White Album*, three of which made this ranking. ("While My Guitar Gently Weeps" and "Savoy Truffle" were the other two—and yes, we did strongly consider "Piggies.") Of this trilogy, "Long, Long, Long" is his quietest and loveliest composition. Plus, its sound is a beautiful blend of flute-like organ, acoustic guitar, sitar, heavenly harmonies, and apocalyptic drums. It is a stripped-down production that, ironically, results in a rich, almost liturgical effect.

What the song is about

The lyrics to this song came to George Harrison in one of those moments of inspiration in which the words simply must be written down—such is the power of their message.

George scribbled the words to "Long, Long, Long" on a page of a calendar and, when we look at the first verse, it becomes clear that at this moment George experienced a profound revelation about his relationship with God and knew he had to express his feelings.

It's been a long time, he prays, and then berates himself for drifting: "How could I ever have lost you?" He further admits his newfound understanding by the phrase "when I loved you." *Loved.* Past tense. He goes on to explain that it took a long time for him to realize his errors, and he then expresses his joy at being back in the fold: "Now I'm so happy I found you."

The bridge is an evocative account of his desolate withdrawal from God. Interestingly, for the first line, instead of the expected "so many *years* I was searching," he sings "tears." The second line repeats the juxtaposition, "so many *tears* I was wasting," even though it would have been completely in order at this point in the lyric for him to lament the years he spent searching, the years he wasted. The choice of "tears" underscores the sorrow at being separated from God—a state that some religions believe is the definition of Hell.

The final verse completes our pilgrim's redemption. "Now I can see you," he begins, followed immediately by "*be* you." Now that his eyes are open, he can become one with God. He then asks himself, thinking out loud, "How can I ever replace you?" But this is, in the end, pointless hypothesizing, and his next lines—"How I want you" and "You know that I need you"—reaffirm his total embrace of the higher power.

"Long, Long, Long" is a stunning hymn of reconciliation. Yes, the lyrics can be interpreted as though he were singing to a lost lover, but the subtext is much too blatant to take that message seriously for very long.

- George admitted nicking the chords for "Long, Long, Long" from Bob Dylan's "Sad-Eyed Lady of the Low Land." To be fair to George, and acknowledging his forthright willingness to attribute an influence, the chords of the main verse of the song (F–E minor–D minor–C) have appeared in too many pop and rock songs to count. One wonders where Dylan got his from? At least George admits his source.
- At the end of the song, Paul hit a note on the Hammond organ that resulted in an unexpected sound effect. George talked about this moment in *I Me Mine*: "There was a bottle of Blue Nun wine on top of the Leslie speaker during the recording and when our Paul hit some organ note the Leslie started vibrating and the bottle rattling. You can hear it on the record—at the very end." In *The Beatles Recording Sessions*, engineer Chris Thomas (who also played piano on the track) recalled, "We thought it was so good that we set the mikes up and did it again. The Beatles always took advantage of accidents." Ringo then recorded an extra burst of fast drumming for the rattling passage.
- The working title of the song was "It's Been a Long Long Long Time."

Did you know?

The recording

Location: **Abbey Road Studios, London.**

Dates:
October 7, 1968 – Sixty-seven takes of the basic rhythm track were recorded, with George on acoustic guitar and vocal, Paul on organ, and Ringo on drums.

October 8, 1968 – Recording and overdub of a second acoustic guitar played by George, a second lead vocal, manually double-tracked, and a bass track, played by Paul.

October 9, 1968 – Overdubs of sporadic Paul backing vocal pieces, and piano played by Chris Thomas. The song was now known as "Long, Long, Long."

October 10, 1968 – Stereo mixing.
October 12, 1968 – Mono mixing.
October 14, 1968 – Mono mixing.
November 22, 1968 – First released on the U.K. LP *The Beatles* (*The White Album*).

Players/Instruments:
- **George Harrison:** Acoustic guitar, lead vocal
- **Paul McCartney:** Bass, piano, Hammond organ
- **Ringo Starr:** Drums
- **Chris Thomas:** Piano

What we really like about this song

Steve: The intro and first verse of this song may be some of the most beautiful music the Beatles ever recorded. In fact, until Ringo's drums come slamming into the mix, the song could fit nicely into almost any church service you could imagine. Interestingly, for such a serene and relatively unadorned song, it took sixty-seven takes for the Fabs (sans John) to be satisfied with the basic rhythm track. Simplicity can be deceptively labor-intensive.

Mike: This is George's softest, most understated song, and it is slipped in right after the manic "Helter Skelter" to conclude the third side of *The White Album*. It shuffles dreamily along, with a few smacks of Ringo's drums here and there, nudging us to see if we're still awake. (I think the cacophony at the end, which sounds like popcorn kernels about to pop—and of course the rattling wine bottle—was just a way to end the song because they had no other ideas.) Like a number of George's songs, you're not sure if he's singing about a longing for God or for a lady friend.

Good Day Sunshine

One of the wonderful things the Beatles had going for them is that they were so original that when they did cop an idea from somebody else it never occurred to you. I thought there were one or two of their songs which were Spoonful-oid but it wasn't until Paul mentioned it in a Playboy interview that I specifically realized we'd inspired "Good Day Sunshine."

—John Sebastian, founder of the Lovin' Spoonful
Quoted in A Hard Day's Write

"Good Day Sunshine" reminds us of a statement by Dick Rowe of Decca Records to Brian Epstein that "Guitar groups are on their way out." Why? Because, other than some deep strumming in the four-measure intro to "Good Day Sunshine" (which we still believe is Paul plucking a two-note chord on his bass), listeners will be hard-pressed to find any guitar at all on the recording.

"Good Day Sunshine" is a British music hall toe-tapper, an obvious forerunner to future Paul compositions. Songs like "Good Day Sunshine" can easily veer off into campy excess (as in some Wings tracks), but it's apparent that the "Beatles sensibility" (read that as "John's influence and judgment") kept a lid on Paul's tendency to transform the song into an obnoxious, unlistenable "oom-pah" musical abomination. The steady hand (on both the production sliders and the piano keys) of George Martin no doubt had a lot to do with that achievement as well.

Why it made the top 100

"Good Day Sunshine" made the top 100 because (here we go again) it's on *Revolver* and is a creative, infinitely appealing recording that stands in stark contrast to the hard-core Beatles rockers that had been playing on every radio in the world when the album was released. It lacks some of the profound poetry of other Paul songs, but the words fit the mood, fit the sound, fit the times.

The song's placement on *Revolver*—opening Side Two like a sunrise, right after the eerie and surreal "She Said She Said"—is the perfect counterpoint to the "out there" vibe of John's acid-inspired meditation, and brings the album back to earth.

Revolver broke new ground. Some of the songs on the album were probably somewhat unsettling for fans in the sixties, and tracks like "Good Day Sunshine" provided a solid, accessible anchor around which the Beatles could revolutionize popular music.

What the song is about

A young man is in love and a sunny day adds to his euphoria.

He and his lady love take a walk. Apparently they're barefoot ("burns my feet as they touch the ground"), and eventually they meander to a shady tree, beneath which they either do or do not have sex, depending on how you interpret the line "I love her and she's loving me."

The young lady "feels good" but, again, the interpretation is up to the listener. Does this mean she herself feels well? Or that she feels good to the singer, in a physical sense?

The song concludes with the narrator saying that he is proud to know that she is his. A sunny, happy ending to a sunny, happy song.

• • • ❦ • • •

- On October 8, 1990, in honor of John Lennon's birthday, Paul McCartney released in the United Kingdom a live single of "Birthday," backed with "Good Day Sunshine." This was the first time a new version of a Beatles song was released by a Beatle after the breakup.
- The title of the song was originally "A Good Day's Sunshine."
- "Good Day Sunshine" is one of seventeen Beatles songs in which the sun is mentioned.
- The song has been covered by Claudine Longet, Don

and the Goodtimes, Eddie Murphy, Joanie Bartels, Roy Redmond, Slowdive, and the Tremeloes.
- On Ringo's 1981 remake of "Back off Boogaloo," Harry Nilsson can be heard in the background singing snippets of "Good Day Sunshine," (as well as bits of "Help," "Lady Madonna," "With a Little from My Friends," and "Baby You're a Rich Man.")
- A recording of a Beatles soundalike group singing "Good Day Sunshine" was once used in a Mercury Topaz commercial.

Did you know?

275

The recording

Location: **Abbey Road Studios, London.**

Dates: **June 8, 1966,** 2:30 p.m.–2:30 a.m. – "Good Day Sunshine" was one of *Revolver*'s quickest recordings. After a long period of taped rehearsals, three takes of the rhythm track were recorded, consisting of bass, piano, and drums. Take 1 was considered the best. It was then rewound and Paul overdubbed his lead vocal, with George and John handling the backing vocals.

June 9, 1966, 2:30–8:00 p.m. – Overdubbing. More drums were added by Ringo, particularly the sound of cymbals. George Martin played a honky-tonk-sounding piano break for the middle eight, with the tape machine running at fifty-six cycles per second. All four Beatles added handclaps, with John, Paul, and George adding extra harmonies (which can be heard nine seconds before the song ends). Six remixes were made—the first was of the end vocal overdub, the other five of the complete song. The sixth was deemed best, but the version that ended up on the record was a new mix done on June 22, erroneously numbered Remix 2. The Beatles actually finished recording two hours ahead of the planned 10:00 p.m. end time.

June 22, 1966, 7:00 p.m.–1:30 a.m. – Mono and stereo mixing, done with the Beatles' involvement (which was usually not the case).

August 5, 1966 – First released on the U.K. LP *Revolver.*

Players/Instruments:
- **Paul McCartney:** Bass, lead vocal, handclaps
- **John Lennon:** Harmony vocal, guitar?, handclaps
- **George Harrison:** Harmony vocal, handclaps
- **Ringo Starr:** Drums, handclaps
- **George Martin:** Piano

What we really like about this song

Steve: I like the fact that the song is in 4/4 and yet it sounds like it's constantly changing tempo, thanks to the innovative phrasing and Ringo's drumming. I also like the harmonies and George Martin's terrific piano break.

Mike: I like the song's exuberant vocal, which sounds to me as if he's excitedly singing the song for the first time. We almost can't help but skip down the street when hearing it. The Beatles always seemed to know just the right sound for each song, just the right instrument to fit in and capture the mood of the song. Here, a distorted piano is added to the recording, a touch that gives it almost a ragtime feel, perfect for use as accompaniment for soft-shoe!

It Won't Be Long

"It Won't Be Long" is mine. It was my attempt at writing another single. It never quite made it.

—John Lennon
Playboy

Pop quiz: What group released two brand-new albums in the same year, within eight months of each other, each one a huge success?

Yes, it was the Beatles.

The Fabs released *Please Please Me* in March 1963 and *With the Beatles* in November of the same year. *Please Please Me* whetted the world's appetite for this new Liverpool band, with "I Saw Her Standing There," "Love Me Do," and the title song. We weren't prepared, though, for the excitement that flooded through us on hearing the first notes of the first song of *With the Beatles*. We placed the needle on the disk and—*bang!*—there was John crying out (with the first three words sung a cappella), "It won't be long!"

Nineteen sixty-three was a hell of a year for music lovers.

Why it made the top 100

"It Won't Be Long" made it into the top 100 because it is a classic early-period Beatles song and one of John's most heartfelt expressions of longing and reconciliation. Plus it's got a kickass arrangement that makes the track impossible to dislike.

(To those of you who reply to this, "*I don't like it*," we don't believe you.)

93 Rain

On the end of "Rain" you hear me singing backwards. We'd done the main thing at EMI and the habit was then to take the song home and see what you thought a little extra gimmick or what the guitar piece would be. So I got home about five in the morning, stoned out of my head, I staggered up to my tape recorder and I put it on, but it came out backwards, and I was in a trance in the earphones, what is it, what is it. It's too much, you know, and I really wanted the whole song backwards almost, and that was it. So we tagged it on the end. I just happened to have the tape on the wrong way round, it just came out backwards, it just blew me mind. The voice sounds like an old Indian.

—John Lennon
The Rolling Stone Interviews

"Rain" is one of those lesser-known Fab faves that never appeared on an album (other than the "greatest hits" compilations *Past Masters Volume 2* and *Hey Jude*); it was released only as the B side of the "Paperback Writer" single.

Nonetheless it's one of their most important recordings, and it is no coincidence that a little over a week prior to working on this Lennon song, the Fabs had recorded the groundbreaking Lennon *Revolver* track, "Tomorrow Never Knows."

Why it made the top 100

"Rain" is a superior example of everything that made the Beatles great: insightful lyrics, stunning bass playing by Paul, some of Ringo's finest drumming, and George's perfectly seasoned guitar flavoring. (Not to mention backward singing!) All these elements resulted in a record that was, conservatively, twenty years ahead of its time.

What the song is about

Ironically (or perhaps appropriately?), the last word in a song about rain is the word *sunshine*—sung *backward*. Is backward sunshine rain? Better question: Is the *opposite* of sunshine the rain?

"Rain" is one of John's most blatantly metaphorical songs. In *The Beatles Anthology*, he called it "a song I wrote about people moaning about the weather all the time," and the lyrics bear this out. But there's much more to the song than that seemingly purely empirical observation.

If we substitute "hard times" for rain, and "good times" for sun, then the song is elevated to a treatise on determination, self-reliance, and faith. And John's underlying message, then? *When it rains and shines, it's just a state of mind.*

Put another way? John is telling us we're all playing those mind games.

Together.

Did you know?

- John got the idea for the backward singing on "Rain" when he was herbally inebriated. From *The Beatles Anthology*: "That one was a gift of God—of Jah, actually, the god of marijuana. Jah gave me that one. The first backwards tape on any record anywhere. Before Hendrix, before The Who, before any fucker. Maybe there was that record about 'They're coming to take me away, ha ha,' maybe that came out before 'Rain,' but it's not the same thing."
- Ringo considered his drumming in "Rain" his best ever. In the book *The Big Beat*, he said, "My favorite piece of me is what I did on 'Rain.' I think I just played amazing. I was into the snare and hi-hat. I think it was the first time I used this trick of starting a break by hitting the hi-hat first instead of going directly to a drum off the hi-hat… I think it's the best out of all the records I've ever made."
- Promotional videos, in both color and black and white, were shot of this song on May 19, 1966, the same day that the Fabs filmed the "Paperback Writer" video. (You can see it on *The Beatles Anthology* DVD.) In the *Beatles Anthology* book, Ringo talked about the making of the video: "It was really exciting with 'Rain'—with Klaus Voormann, who did that whole set-up. It was a lot of fun."
- "Rain" is one of ten Beatles songs that mention the rain.[1]
- The song has been covered by Bongwater, Dan Fogelberg, Dragon, Gregg Allman, José Feliciano, Petula Clark, Randy California, Sam Bennett, Spirit, the Ancients, the Grateful Dead, Todd Rundgren, and Todd Rundgren and Utopia.

The recording

Location: **Abbey Road Studios, London.**

Dates: **April 14, 1966,** 8:30 p.m.–1:30 a.m. – Five takes were recorded, and the last one was the first to include a vocal. To give a slower "texture" to his voice, John was recorded at forty-two cycles per second instead of fifty. For this track, the Fabs used all the bells and whistles of the *Revolver* era, including limiters, compressors, the Leslie, et cetera. Geoff Emerick, in *The Beatles Recording Sessions*, recalled, "An offshoot of ADT [Artificial Double Tracking] was that we had a big audio oscillator to alter the frequency of the tape machines. We would drive it through a power amp and the power amp would drive the capstan wheel and would enable you to speed up or slow down the machine at will. John—or George if it was his song—used to sit in the control room on mixes and actually play the oscillator."

April 16, 1966, 2:30 p.m.–1:30 a.m. – First, they overdubbed the tambourine, bass, and backing vocals. They then did a tape reduction to add more overdubs; also mono mixing.

May 30, 1966 – The song is first released in the United States as a single, as the B side to "Paperback Writer." (This was the first Beatles single released in 1966.)

December 2, 1969 – Stereo remixing for the *Hey Jude* LP.

Players/Instruments:

- **John Lennon:** Rhythm guitar, lead vocal
- **Paul McCartney:** Bass, backing vocal
- **George Harrison:** Lead guitar, backing vocal
- **Ringo Starr:** Drums, tambourine

What we really like about this song

Steve: I love the *sound* of this record. From the moment it starts, I am ensorcelled. The feeling I get from the opening of this track is the same as when I hear "Baby You're A Rich Man." Usually I am not a big fan of songs that don't contain any minor chords. I make an exception in the case of "Rain," which is in the key of G, but was recorded faster and in a higher key and then slowed down. The whole song, for all its droning Indian feel, is actually jolly well traditional, consisting of nothing but rock's cliché I–IV–V chord progression. Also worth mentioning is Paul's amazing bass line and Ringo's superior drumming.

Mike: Although I'm not ensorcelled by it, I've always liked this song, probably because it just seems so… *different.* Paul's killer bass lick trips throughout the song, Ringo's drums are far out front—as a matter of fact, *everything* seems "out front." (I especially like the bottom-of-the-fret-board guitar bit that's played just before John's backward vocal.) It would have been cool if the *Anthology* CDs included the rhythm track at the fast speed at which it was initially recorded, but it's noteworthy that the instruments don't *sound* slowed down. That's a testament to the Beatles and their efforts. They were anxious to experiment, but they never opted for pure experimentation over a pleasing and melodic track. Personally, I strive to live by John's message that we should rise beyond our circumstances, and that the trials and tribulations we face are "just a state of mind." (After all, the weather's fine!)

---

[1] The other nine are "Across the Universe," "Fixing a Hole," "Hey Bulldog," "I Am the Walrus," "I'll Follow the Sun," "I'm a Loser," "Penny Lane," "Please Please Me," and "The Long and Winding Road."

Another Girl

94

You find here a song that is a veritable cross-section of the tricks and trademarks of the Beatles to this point of their career... We also find in this song yet another example of John's cross-influence on Paul.

—Musicologist Alan Pollack
Notes on "Another Girl"

"Another Girl" has been called

the Beatles' most sexist song (due, in large part to the "Another Girl" segment in *Help!*), and yet it's still a lot of fun, and one of the few instances where Paul (apparently) played both lead guitar *and* bass on a Beatles track.

The "questionable taste" segment of *Help!* has the Fab Four lip-synching this song on a rocky beach, frolicking and vamping (mostly John, of course), and generally just being Beatles. About a minute into the segment, though, suddenly Paul is not playing his bass but cradling a bikini-clad girl in his arms, rocking her back and forth as though she were an instrument. This is followed by her standing up in front of him with her right arm outstretched (as the neck) and forming a circle with her left arm (the strings). Paul "plays" her for a few seconds and then it's over.

This segment probably could never be shot in today's PC world, what with its objectification of women and macho bravado. But it *was* shot, and guess what? It comes off as nothing but good-natured fun. It simply *radiates* innocent humor.

283

Why it made the top 100

This infectious, bouncy pop song is one of the better of the seven original Beatles songs from *Help!* It's got a classic beginning, with Paul vocally sliding down the scale in half notes for the "For I have got…" a cappella beginning; it's got a smooth acoustic foundation for what is definitely an "electric" (amplified) song; and it's got those superfab Beatles harmonies, often imitated, but never duplicated. Add to all that the beguiling (*both* definitions of the word) lyrics, and you've got yourself a winner.

What the song is about

"Another Girl" comes off as a subtly *mean* song.

It begins with our coldhearted alpha cad insensitively announcing to his current girlfriend that he now has another girl. This probably comes as a complete surprise to her, since he tells us that she makes him say that she's the only one for him. (Do the words *one-sided relationship* come to mind?) He tells her, "as from *today*, well, I've got somebody that's new." Talk about short notice, eh?

He then justifies his behavior by telling her that he "ain't no fool" and he refuses to take what he doesn't want, meaning her.

These opening passages are bad enough, but then he rubs salt in the wound by telling her that this new girl is "sweeter than all the girls," and then reminds her that he's "met quite a few." ("Met." Yeah, right.) He twists the knife a little bit more by leeringly telling her that "Nobody in all the world can do what she can do."

Oddly, he then takes a defensive stance by telling her that "This time you'd better stop." Does this open up a possible new dimension to their story? Is it possible that our heroine is a harridan whom he truly wants to stay with, yet she is making it very difficult by being, well, very difficult? Could all of his glorification of his new girl simply be a tactic to put his current lady love off balance? Or perhaps to win back her affection by making her jealous?

He tells her that he now has another girl who will love him till the end, who will stay by his side "through thick and thin," and will always be his friend. "Friend"? Curioser and curioser. If "Another Girl" is one man's way of dumping his girlfriend, it is, in fact, a mean song. If it's a collection of shrewdly veiled threats to keep his girl in line, it may not be mean, but it could justifiably be considered duplicitous.

• • • ❧ • • •

- "Another Girl" was written by Paul during a ten-day holiday in Tunisia in mid-January 1965.
- In the two-minute "Another Girl" sequence in the movie *Help!*, the Fabs riff off the idea of "another": John is seen playing "another instrument"—the drums; Ringo is seen playing acoustic guitar; and George is seen playing Paul's bass. Paul, on the other hand, is seen playing a girl, specifically a supermodel-type blonde in a white bikini.
- In the *Help!* segment, George is seen playing the lead guitar fills heard on the record, even though it was believed to be Paul who played lead (along with his Hoffner bass) on the track. At the February 16 recording session, the Abbey Road studio logs state that Paul overdubbed lead guitar. We know that he played the fancy-schmancy riff at the conclusion of the song, but since the logs do not specify that the February 16 session was to record that particular

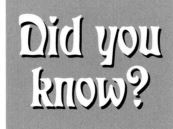

bit, it is possible that he overdubbed random guitar fills for the whole song. (Fans have long had mixed feelings about these seemingly scattershot bits and pieces. Personally, we think the guitar fills throughout the song aren't good enough to have been played by George. And they do, indeed, sound like someone playing along with the tape, inserting riffs here and there as whimsy might inspire.)

- On November 12, 1965, George Martin, the Beatles' producer, released a single in the United Kingdom consisting of instrumental versions of "Yesterday" and "Another Girl."
- "Another Girl" is one of sixteen Beatles songs that begin a cappella (vocal only, without a musical accompaniment, if even for one syllable).[1]
- The song has been covered by George Martin, the Kingsmen, the Queers, and Silver Convention.

The recording

Location: **Abbey Road Studios, London.**

Dates:

February 15, 1965 – The song was recorded in one take, although there were many unnumbered takes of the edit piece, with George attempting to perfect the guitar flourish at the end of song, and using a tremolo bar. The seventh take was considered best, but the tremolo idea was dropped in remixing.

February 16, 1965 – Overdubbing of lead guitar by Paul.

February 18, 1965 – Mono mixing.

February 23, 1965 – Stereo mixing.

August 6, 1965 – First issued on the U.K. LP *Help!*

Players/Instruments:

- **Paul McCartney:** Bass, lead guitar (solo at end, fills throughout?), lead vocal
- **John Lennon:** Acoustic guitar, backing vocal
- **George Harrison:** Lead guitar, backing vocal
- **Ringo Starr:** Drums

What we really like about this song

Steve: In my 2000 Beatles cookbook, *She Came in Through the Kitchen Window* (Kensington), I featured a delicious barbecue sauce recipe called "Another Grille." (I apologize for the seemingly self-serving reference, but I just love that pun and couldn't help myself.) "Another Girl" has the classic Beatles sound, including an interesting musical construct that, amazingly, uses only major chords. (As I've indicated elsewhere in this volume, I usually do not cotton to songs without any minor chords, but this one rings my bell.) The harmonies are terrific, as is Paul's vocal and bass. I am not as big a fan of the omnipresent guitar fills in this track as is my coauthor, but that's a small point; overall I'm a fan of this groovy *Help!* track.

Mike: Another hidden Beatles chestnut—one you won't hear too often on classic rock stations. The song has a pleasing, unthreatening melody, and the boys are in fine voice. But what gets my attention every time is the lead guitar that runs throughout the song, and seems to be running amok. It is as if George (or is it Paul? It's unclear from production notes who's playing it) is wrestling a wild guitar, like a bull rider corralling a stallion. The guitar is trying to leap away as he's trying to squeeze a few more notes out of it. Musical magic.

---

[1] The other fifteen are "All My Loving," "Can't Buy Me Love," "Girl," "Happiness Is a Warm Gun," "Hey Jude," "I Will," "I'm Down," "I'm a Loser," "If I Fell," "It Won't Be Long," "No Reply," "Nowhere Man," "Oh! Darling," "Paperback Writer," and "You're Gonna Lose That Girl."

95

It's All Too Much

"It's All Too Much" was written in a childlike manner from realizations that appeared during and after some LSD experiences and which were later confirmed in meditation.

—George Harrison
I Me Mine

Is it only us or does the opening riff of Michael Jackson's "Black or White" sound like a blatant, uh, homage to George's "It's All Too Much"?

"It's All Too Much" is one of the strongest tracks on the original *Yellow Submarine* soundtrack. ("Hey Bulldog" and, of course, "All You Need Is Love" are the other standouts on the original release.) The song has not gotten much notice and has only appeared on the two *Yellow Submarine* soundtrack albums.

Why it made the top 100

Of the half dozen or so George songs in this ranking, "It's All Too Much" deserved a slot if only for its "ahead of its time" mojo. Perhaps inspired by John's "Tomorrow Never Knows," the song stands as an example of what can be done with almost no chord changes and a very narrow melodic range.

What the song is about

The lyrics espouse George's standard message: Time is a stream, we move from life to life, love is all you need. He personalizes this universal message, though, by immediately introducing us to a woman we know is his wife, Patti, telling us that her love for him is a microcosm of the love permeating us all.

The most revealing line in the song is "The more I am, the less I know." George the teacher is, in essence, George the student.

And so it goes. It's all too much, isn't it?

The recording

Location: **De Lane Lea Studios, London.**

Dates: **May 25, 1967** – After much rehearsing, the Beatles recorded four takes of the rhythm track (organ, lead guitar, bass, drums) at London's De Lane Lea Studios (in the basement of an office building). George Martin was not in attendance.

May 31, 1967 – A reduction mixdown of Take 4 was completed, with overdubbing of additional percussion, George's lead vocal, John and Paul's backing vocals, and handclaps. (Paul and John chanting "too much" at the end degenerated into them shouting "tuba" and "Cuba.")

June 2, 1967 – Still at De Lane. Four trumpets and one bass clarinet were overdubbed in a session that was originally scheduled for 8:00–11:00 p.m. but ran on until 2:00 a.m. David Mason, one of the session trumpeters, speaking in *The Beatles Recording Sessions*, recalled, "George Harrison was in charge of that session. I don't think he really knew what he wanted."

October 12, 1967 – Mono mixing.

November 15, 1967 – A mono tape copy was made for the producers of the *Yellow Submarine* movie.

October 16–17, 1968 – Mono and stereo mixing for the *Yellow Submarine* soundtrack.

January 13, 1969 – First released on the U.S. LP *Yellow Submarine*.

Players/Instruments:
- **George Harrison:** Lead guitar, organ, lead vocal
- **Paul McCartney:** Bass,.harmony vocal
- **John Lennon:** Lead guitar, harmony vocal
- **Ringo Starr:** Drums, tambourine
- **Session musicians:** Two trumpets

What we really like about this song

Steve: I like the opening feedback and the kickass G to C introductory *ostinato*. I like George's lyrics, perhaps more so than any of his others. And I love the way he uses the trumpets like seasoning in an eclectic, colorful, vibrant musical stew.

Mike: I am a big fan of the more obscure/underplayed Beatles tunes, and "It's All Too Much" fits that bill. I appreciate the unique sounds they were able to get from such antiquated production facilities, I like their use of keyboards more than "traditional" Beatles guitars (although when you do hear a guitar on the track, it's blistering), and I like the droning/incessant groove, the feedback times ten. I also like the interesting lyrics that really make you think.

Stephen Teller tells

Stephen Teller is a composer and singer/songwriter with more than 350 pieces of music airing on TV, on radio, and in film. He was a founding member of the eighties Los Angeles melodic rock band Storyteller. His obsession is collecting vintage analog synthesizers; he currently has nearly fifty such instruments in his collection. When we asked him for his favorite Beatles song, we were quite surprised to learn that it is "It's All Too Much."

Considering the year this was recorded, it's very ahead of its time. How many tracks did they have? *Eight?* Definitely some improv going on also. George's vocal is double-tracked for a chorus effect. His first vocal line, "It's all too much," takes forty-six seconds to appear! Notice how the trumpet appears during the second instrumental break—tasty restraint indeed!

It's kind of like a drone with a backbeat. You definitely hear George's interest in all things Indian. The whole song basically pedals on Paul's G bass note. It's a classic Ringo groove. George Martin uses his signature heavy compression on Ringo's kit.

To me, it's always meant that whatever you think you need is probably right there in front of you—get out of your own way! I've always thought of George's songs as the hidden prize in a tasty box of Beatles cereal. With its swirly organ and trippy vocals, "It's All Too Much" is at once experimental and melodic Beatles heaven. It pays tribute to the art of doing music for the music. It's obvious the Beatles didn't give a shit if it was going to sell or get played on the radio.

96

The Ballad Of John And Yoko

I do hereby absolutely renounce and abandon the use of my former Christian name of Winston and in lieu thereof do assume as from that date hereof the additional Christian name Ono.

—John Lennon's official name change statement, April 22, 1969

John and Yoko were married

on Gibraltar near Spain on Thursday, March 20, 1969, and, a little over three weeks later, he and Paul (with Yoko as an onlooker) were in the studio recording "The Ballad Of John And Yoko." The song was recorded from start to finish in one day. A week later, on the twenty-second of April, John officially changed his middle name to Ono. As Derek Taylor said in *The Beatles Anthology*, "Yoko had taken the place of everybody in John's life. Since they had met she was his life, and he was hers, and they were co-dependent people. They had no life outside each other."

Why it made the top 100

This song deserves a ranking in the top 100 if only because it's a full-blown Beatles record on which only two Beatles show up for work. It's a superb example of what John and Paul could do in the studio when they had a game producer. Plus, it's one of the few times we get to hear Paul playing the drums on a Beatles record!

What the song is about

"Ballad" just might be John's most voluble set of lyrics ever and, the more nostalgic "In My Life" notwithstanding, his most specifically autobiographical song. Granted, it's about only one incident in his life—his marriage to Yoko—but he gives us an incredibly detailed accounting of the event, and manages to rhyme "Seine" with "Spain" and "France" with "chance" while doing so!

But since this is a John Lennon song, we should not be surprised that John uses it to touch on issues beyond the mundane logistics of getting from *here…* to *there*. Specifically, the bridge speaks of higher concerns in its key line—a third-person rendering of something Yoko said to John—"when you're dead, you don't take nothing with you but your soul…," which is then followed by the one-word punctuation, "Think!"

Suddenly, there are more important things to *think* about. It is revealing, and not all that unexpected, that the shift of focus that John unveils in the bridge was inspired by Yoko.

He always said she opened his eyes. Even in a rollicking travelogue like "The Ballad Of John And Yoko," we can see the results of her influence on him.

Interestingly, Yoko herself commented on the song, and also on the purported animosity between Paul and John in 1969. In the March 1, 2001, issue of *Rolling Stone*, she said, "It was reportage—but it was also the funny side of John coming out. Every song he'd written at the time was autobiographical. And actually we were having a very hard time, very heavy stuff going on. He just made it into a comedy, rather than a tragedy… It wasn't all dark and difficult then—people like the idea of John and Paul as two boxers, but it was not always like that. I think Paul knew about John's aggravation, about people being so nasty to him. And he just wanted to make it well for him. Paul has a very brotherly side to him."

• • • ❦ • • •

- John and Yoko couldn't get married in Southampton because Yoko was not a British citizen.
- John was pleased and proud that "The Ballad Of John And Yoko" was released as a Beatles single and that it reached Number One. The last Beatles single he had written had been "All You Need Is Love," which had been released on July 17, 1967. The four Fabs singles after that—"Hello Goodbye," "Lady Madonna," "Hey Jude," and "Get Back"—had all been Paul's.
- In return for Paul's recording help with "Ballad," John gave him coauthorship credit for "Give Peace A Chance."
- Prior to the single's release, the song had an official subtitle, the parenthetical "(They're Gonna Crucify Me)."
- John once jokingly described the songs as "Johnny B. Paperback Writer."
- "The Ballad Of John And Yoko" was the first Beatles single to appear in stereo, and it was the last song recorded specifically as a single by the Beatles. When "Ballad" was released, "Get Back" was still Number One on the charts.

Did you know?

- "The Ballad Of John And Yoko" was banned by the BBC and most U.S. radio stations for John's use of the name "Christ" in the refrain. Apple was pressured to bleep out the "Christ," but refused. Some radio stations edited the song themselves, and others played the flip side, "Old Brown Shoe." Its absence on the British airwaves notwithstanding, the single hit Number One on the U.K. charts on June 21, 1969.
- John did not do much to dissuade anybody of the idea that Yoko broke up the Beatles. Amazingly, some of the sleeves for the *Beatles* single of "The Ballad Of John And Yoko" showed the four Beatles *and* Yoko. Granted, John probably felt it was justifiable to include her on a Beatles jacket because the song was about her, but this "and suddenly there were five" attitude did nothing to endear Yoko to Beatlefans, and the dour expressions on Paul's, George's, and Ringo's faces in the photograph spoke volumes.
- The song has been covered by Percy Faith and Hootie and the Blowfish.

The recording

Location: **Abbey Road Studios, London.**

Dates: **April 14, 1969,** 2:30–11:00 p.m. – Eleven takes of the drums, acoustic guitar, and lead vocal were recorded. Five of the eleven takes broke down at the same point—when Paul added an extra snare drum fill before the line "Made a lightning trip to Vienna." Take 2 broke down because, as John said, "Un string avec kaput, Mal." On Take 4, John said, "Go a bit faster, Ringo!" and Paul answered "OK, George!" Take 10 was the best track, but they then tried one more take in a higher key (G major). Onto Take 10, they overdubbed bass, two lead guitars, piano, backing vocal, and maracas, as well as John tapping drum-like on the back of an acoustic guitar. The song was then mixed for stereo during the last two hours of the session. It became first stereo single in Britain and the first release not to be mixed for mono. Engineer Geoff Emerick, working on a new Beatles recording for the first time in nine months, recalled, "[It] was a very fast session. It was a really good record too, helped by Paul's great drumming and the speed in which they did it all."

May 30, 1969 – First released as a single in the United Kingdom, backed with "Old Brown Shoe."

Players/Instruments:
- **John Lennon:** Lead guitar, acoustic guitar, lead vocal
- **Paul McCartney:** Piano, bass, harmony vocal, maracas
  Note: The session notes also acknowledge John's "back of gtr thumps overdub."

What we really like about this song

Steve: I'll admit it: This song has grown on me over the years. At first, I didn't consider it anything beyond a novelty trifle, John's vanity piece to tell the world about the ridiculous hassles he and Yoko had to suffer through to get married. But then I listened to it more carefully, keeping in mind that all I was hearing was John and Paul, and suddenly the song came alive for me. It's a rocker of the first degree, and John's deft telling of a tale adds immeasurably to its appeal. I love how, as the story comes to its climax in the final verse and chorus, Paul's high harmony serves to impart a sense of urgency and excitement to the narrative. Yes, for all their internecine squabbles, the Nerk Twins could still rock the house when they wanted to.

Mike: I like the bass riff (is it out of tune?), the guitars (the chugging acoustic setting the rhythm, the electric guitar chirps, but especially the lead guitar piece closing out the song), and the piano played just before the "saving up your money" part. I especially like John's lead vocal. He certainly had the goolies (as the Brits are wont to say) to go with the crucify lyric, especially after all the flak he got for the "bigger than Jesus" quote. But most of all, I love the fact that John and Paul were working together on this song during a time of supposed contention between them… and having fun recording a great single.

Within You Without You

This was during the Sgt. Pepper period, and after I had been taking sitar lessons with Ravi Shankar for some time, so I was getting a bit better on the instrument… That's why around this time I couldn't help writing tunes like this which were based upon unusual scales.

—George Harrison
I Me Mine

If there is a single track on *Sgt. Pepper*

that unequivocally proved that the album was revolutionary for its time, it is "Within You Without You." No more flirting with a sitar here, a tamboura there: This song was pure Indian music, and the only connection it had with rock was the fact that a Beatle wrote it and performed it.

Why it made the top 100

The Fabs embraced musical experimentation with creative passion after they got into LSD and meditation. "Within You Without You" is, perhaps, the purest expression of the disparate influences the Beatles, both as a group and as individuals, were assimilating.

Opening Side Two of *Sgt. Pepper*, the song is surprising and unexpected, and if we were to be so bold as to proclaim a *signature* George Harrison song (romantic and cheery pleasures like "Something" and "Here Comes the Sun" notwithstanding) "Within You Without You" would probably be that song.

What the song is about

To understand this instructive song, we need to pay attention to the five things "talked about" in the lyrics—the subjects following the "we were talking…" phrases. They are:

1. *"The space between us all…"*
2. *"The people who hide themselves behind a wall of illusion…"*
3. *"The love we all could share…"*
4. *"The love that's gone so cold…"*
5. *"The people who gain the world and lose their soul…"*

292

What is George saying? Put simply, love is our (humankind's) salvation, as well as the path to God, as we conceive Him.

There is only *one* directive in all the lyrics, and these words are the key that unlocks the door to enlightenment: "Try to realize it's all within yourself and no one else can make you change."

Know thyself. And understand that, within the grand scheme of things, we are all "very small." This leads to the lyric embodying what might be the most brilliant wordplay of George's career (even though he got it from a book): "life flows on within you and without you." The "life flows on within you" passage is clear: It means within the person, within the *self*. The next phrase, though, is revelatory: "life flows on... without you." The double meaning here is simply, yet profoundly expressed: Life flows on *outside* the person, but also *without* (minus) the person.

The final message? Eternal life (God-consciousness) will *not* be yours unless you realize that love is *all*, love is *everywhere*, and love is, yes, all you need.

The lyrics to "Within You Without You" are plainly rendered, yet they express an elevated concept and provide sage counsel for all we pilgrims who hope to attain a life beyond the earthly.

• • • 🐢 • • •

Did you know?

- "Within You Without You" was written one night after dinner at Klaus Voormann's house in Hempstead, London, on Voormann's pedal harmonium. According to George, the tune came first.
- The line "Life goes on within you and without you" was relayed to George by Jenny Boyd, his former sister-in-law, who found it in a book she was reading at the time, *Karma and Rebirth* by the Buddhist scholar Christmas Humphreys.
- Musician Stephen Stills (of Crosby, Stills and Nash) was so impressed by the lyrics of the song that he had them carved on a stone monument in his yard.
- George Martin was paid thirty-three pounds to write the orchestral score for the song.

The recording

Location: **Abbey Road Studios, London.**

Dates: **March 15, 1967,** 7:00 p.m.–1:30 a.m. – One take of the still-untitled song was recorded, with Indian musicians from the Eastern Music Circle in north London. John recalled the night: "George has done a great Indian one. We came along one night and he had about 400 Indian fellas playing there, and it was a great swinging evening, as they say."[1] Mono mix.

March 22, 1967, 7:00 p.m.–2:15 a.m. – Overdubbing of two more dilrubas, taped at fifty-two cycles per second to sound slowed down on replay. Reduction mix and mono mixing.

April 3, 1967, 7:00 p.m.–6:30 a.m. (the last song completed for *Pepper*) – From 7:00 p.m. to 3:00 a.m., an unknown number of string parts were recorded, each subsequent take erasing the previous one. George also recorded his lead vocal and, according to Mark Lewisohn, added a dash of acoustic guitar to the track. The session musicians were all paid the Musicians' Union rate of nine pounds—except for the lead violinist, who received eleven pounds. George Martin recalled the session: "What was difficult... was writing a score for the cellos and violins that the English players would be able to play like the Indians. The dilruba player, for example, was doing all kinds of swoops and so I actually had to score that for strings and instruct the players to follow."[2] Mono mixing from 3:00 to 6:00 a.m., and for remix purposes the song was again divided into three parts.

April 4, 1967, 7:00 p.m.–12:45 a.m. –

Mono and stereo mixing, with heavy use of Artificial Double Tracking (ADT), and editing. A few seconds of laughter was edited onto the end of both mixes, courtesy of the Abbey Road sound effects collection, Volume 6: *Applause and Laughter*. George Martin remembered it differently: "The laugh at the very end of the track was George Harrison. He just thought it would be a good idea…"[3]

June 1, 1967 – First released on the U.K. LP *Sgt. Pepper's Lonely Hearts Club Band*.

Players/Instruments:
- **George Harrison:** Tamboura, swordmandel, lead vocal
- **Neil Aspinall:** Tamboura
- **Indian session musicians:** Dilruba (a bowed instrument), tamboura, tabla, swordmandel (a zither-like instrument)
- **Session musicians:** Eight violins, three cellos

What we really like about this song

Steve: Notre Dame High School, West Haven, Connecticut, 1969. I was taking a comparative religions class (which, for a Catholic high school, was pretty progressive at the time), and we all had to make a presentation to the class about a religion other than Roman Catholicism. (I did Buddhism.) One of my classmates brought in a portable record player and the *Sgt. Pepper* album and played "Within You Without You," after which he recited the lyrics and discussed them as they related to notions of cosmic consciousness. I have never been that big a fan of this song, but that day made me realize that it is, quite simply, more than a song. It is a *mission statement*. Plus, we must give George props for eschewing Western instruments for Indian instruments and having the moxie to insist that they appear in this odd song. (We both got an A, by the way.)

Mike: If you were listening to *Sgt. Pepper* for the first time, and if, by the end of "Mr. Kite," you didn't realize the Beatles were up to new and unusual things, then the first song on Side Two was your wake-up call. There were sounds we had never heard before, and a philosophy rarely heard in the West. Give George credit for sharing his love of exotic enlightenment with the rest of the world, and give George Martin credit for writing a score for Western instruments that blended nicely with their Indian counterparts. I especially like the instrumental break in the middle and the percussion played throughout.

[1] *The Beatles Anthology.*

[2] *A Hard Day's Write.*

[3] Ibid.

Love Me Do

If you think you're going to make your fortune with that, you've got another think coming.

—*John Lennon's aunt Mimi*

Aunt Mimi was not a big fan of this first single from her beloved nephew's new rock-and-roll band. And that begs the question: Was the Beatles magic present in this initial offering from the band that would change music for all time?

Today, with forty years of hindsight to look to, we would have to say yes. Granted, it's a simple song (with the same verse repeated a bordering-on-the-ridiculous four times!), but the Paul and John harmonies were instantly distinctive and memorable, and their sound was surprisingly polished for a band that had never before recorded.

What needs to be remembered, though, is that by the time the Beatles recorded "Love Me Do," John and Paul had collaborated on at least one hundred songs, and the boys had performed live countless times. This honed them, and explains their solid sound right out of the gate.

Why it made the top 100

The Beatles' first single *not* being on the list of their hundred greatest songs? What do you think we are? Barmy?

What the song is about

The meaning of "Love Me Do" is right in the title, which is interesting for its inverted syntax. It's not "Do Love Me"; it's "Love Me Do."

Our hero is singing to the girl he loves, and assuring her he'll always be true. The only revealing bit of info in the lyrics appears in the bridge when he sings, "Someone to love, somebody new," suggesting that he has just come off a relationship and now is seeking someone new, specifically the young lady to whom he is singing.

And that, as they say, is all she, er, *he* wrote.

• • • 🐛 • • •

- *Anthology 1* included the never-before-heard version of "Love Me Do" with Pete Best on drums, and it is noteworthy for a few things. First, Best fools around with the backbeat, mostly playing in a rather sloppy and distracting manner. He actually switches into some kind of weird salsa-like tempo for the harmonica instrumental bridge. Also, the song is much slower and, *most* noticeably, Paul and John sound incredibly hesitant and were obviously nervous wrecks for this, their first official recording session with George Martin. Comparing the overall vibe of this tentative recording with the final release that boasts Ringo on drums is a lesson in Rock Band Dynamics 101. The Fabs were, indeed, fast learners.
- The original title of the song was "Love, Love Me Do," which was shortened to "Love Me Do" by unanimous vote.
- Paul was sixteen in 1958 when he wrote "Love Me Do" for Iris Caldwell, Rory Storm's sister.
- George Harrison had a black eye at the "Love Me Do" recording sessions, a result of getting into a scuffle at the Cavern Club with loyal Peter Best fans who were quite upset that the Beatles had fired Pete and hired Ringo.
- During the recording session for the song, the boys suddenly realized that they had a problem with John's vocal and harmonica playing. There was no way John could sing the end of the verses with a harmonica in his mouth. (Multitracking was apparently not even an option for this brand-new band.) George Martin decided that Paul would sing the "love me do" line instead of John so the young Mr. Lennon could play his mouth organ. This made Paul very nervous, but he performed like a champ.

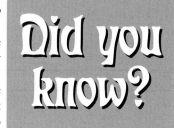

- "Love Me Do" hit the British music charts two days after its release.
- Capitol Records initially declined to release "Love Me Do" in America. It also passed on "Please Please Me" and "She Loves You."
- EMI ran a full-page ad for "Love Me Do" in *Record Retailer* a week before the single's release—the only time that year that the company did so for an artist.
- On *The Beatles 1* CD, the copyright for "Love Me Do" cites the 1962 copyright, which is in the name of EMI and Lenono Music. However, the copyright was renewed in 1990 and 1991 and, according to the 1995 Hal Leonard compilation of Beatles sheet music (*The Beatles: A Pocket Reference Guide to More Than 100 Songs!*), the copyright is in the name of MPL Communications (Paul's publishing company) and Julian Lennon, Sean Ono Lennon, and Yoko Ono Lennon. Of the songs published in the sheet music collection, John's sons also share in the copyright for "P.S. I Love You" and "Please Please Me" (as well as "Ask Me Why," which was not included in the sheet music book).
- In the song "Shooting Star," on their *Straight Shooter* LP, Bad Company refers to the song's title: "Johnny was a schoolboy when he heard his first Beatles song/'Love Me Do' I think it was…"
- The word *love* is repeated twenty-five times in the song. (The last one is during the fade-out, but it is audible.)
- The song has been covered by Badfinger, the Pete Best Band, the Cimarons, the Brady Bunch, Dick Hyman, Sandie Shaw, and Fats Domino.

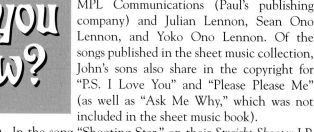

The recording

Location: **Abbey Road Studios, London.**

Dates: **June 6, 1962** – The Beatles audition. They perform and record "Love Me Do" with Pete Best on drums. In *The Beatles Recording Sessions*, Paul talked about what happened after the audition: "George [Martin] took us aside and said, 'I'm not happy about the drummer.' And we all went, 'Oh God, well I'm not telling him. You tell him… and it was quite a blow. He said, 'Can you change your drummer?' and we said 'Well, we're quite happy with him, he works great in the clubs.' And George said, 'Yes, but for recording he's got to be just a bit more accurate.'"

September 4, 1962 – After begrudgingly recording Mitch Murray's "How Do You Do It?" (which went on to become a Number One hit for Gerry and the Pacemakers), the Fabs recorded fifteen to seventeen takes of "Love Me Do." (The Abbey Road recording logs are incomplete on the exact number.) They first concentrated on the rhythm track (with Ringo on drums), and then spent considerable time on vocal overdubs. Mono mixing.

September 11, 1962 – The Beatles recorded eighteen takes of a remake of the song, with John playing a new Gibson J-160E acoustic guitar, special-ordered from Rushworth's Music in Liverpool, flown in from America, and delivered the day before. At George Martin's request, Andy White played drums and Ringo was relegated to tambourine. George Martin later spoke to the boys about the switch: "Ringo may be very good, but we're paying good money for this guy and I've already booked him, so tough. You sit out, Ringo. We're having Andy White." Ringo was devastated. (Earlier that day the Beatles had recorded "P.S. I Love You," for which Andy White also played drums. Ringo played the maracas.) Mono mixing.

October 5, 1962 – First released as a U.K. single, backed with "P.S. I Love You."

February 25, 1963 – Stereo mixing.

Players/Instruments:
- **John Lennon:** Lead vocal, harmonica, guitar
- **Paul McCartney:** Bass, lead vocal
- **George Harrison:** Acoustic guitar, harmony vocal
- **Ringo Starr:** Drums (on the single version); tambourine (on the album version)
- **Andy White:** Drums (album version only)
- **Pete Best:** *Anthology 1* unused version

Donovan's 5 Favorite Beatles Songs

1. "Love Me Do"
2. "Julia"
3. "Across The Universe"
4. "Within You Without You"
5. "Yellow Submarine"

What we really like about this song

Steve: I like how ballsy the Fabs were about simply repeating the verse four times. Write more lyrics? *Not bloody likely!* The song is simplicity itself, and it's great to hear the definitive version with Ringo on drums. It's a fun track from an earlier time, and is also notable that, for their first single, they went ahead and included a harmonica. A guitar solo? Nope. Keyboards? Nope. A bluesy harmonica part? Hell, yeah! Portents of things to come.

Mike: It's a simple little ditty, actually kind of primitive in many regards—especially if you were to put it up against something like "A Day in the Life" or "Nowhere Man." But on its own, it holds up as a catchy love song. And there's not one song on which John plays harmonica that I don't like.

99

Birthday

"Birthday" was written in the studio. Just made up on the spot. I think Paul wanted to write a song like "Happy Birthday Baby," the old Fifties hit. But it was sort of made up in the studio.

—*John Lennon*
Playboy

Do DJs play this song in clubs anymore?

If they don't, they should. As Paul has said, "It's a good one to dance to."

We think Sir Paul understates. The beat is so infectious, you literally cannot remain still during it. (And that is completely thanks to Ringo's metronome-like drumming. When Mr. Starr locked on to a tempo, he was like a machine.) Even if you're at a desk, you will find your foot tapping uncontrollably. As with some of the other gloriously loud tunes on *The White Album*, "Birthday" *brings it*, and we can only imagine the fun the Fabs must have had recording it.

298

Why it made the top 100

"Birthday" is a rocker of the first degree, complete with power chords, a drum solo, a pounding piano, and an attention to detail that belies its on-first-glance simplicity. A careful listen reveals wonders, especially the tasty connecting riffs between verses and the bridge, and how the bass and guitar play in sync throughout almost the entire song.

What is also notable is how we can clearly identify voices in the track, particularly Paul's in the verses; John's, in the "Yes, we're going to a party party…" line; and, yes, Yoko's in the background "birthday."

We've got a feeling that everybody had a good time. (And we're certain that everybody let their hair down.)

What the song is about

The song begins with our bard learning that it's his friend's birthday. ("You say it's your birthday.") But lo! It's also our hero's birthday! ("It's my birthday too, yeah.") What are the odds?

He assures his birthday buddy that they're "gonna have a good time" and tells her, "I'm glad it's your birthday." (How do we know he's addressing a "she"? During the bridge, he asks this person to dance, so it's a reasonable conclusion.)

The next thing Birthday Boy tells her is that they are going to a party. (Actually he tells her that they're "going to a party party." Must be a double-strength celebration, eh?)

At the party, he asks her to dance. She is hesitant, so he cajoles her to take a chance. (Specifically, he encourages her to "take a cha-cha-cha-chance." He is so excited he has developed a speech impediment.)

The song then wraps up with him repeating his sentiment that he's glad it's her birthday, and it concludes with the traditional salutation, "Happy birthday to you."

"Birthday" is a simple slice-of-life song that, while its intentions are good, will likely not replace the old-fashioned "Happy Birthday to You" you sang at your nephew's birthday party last year.

- Prior to writing "Birthday," Paul had been thinking about the song "Happy, Happy Birthday," a 1957 hit for the Tune Weavers.
- Some sources say the song was written for Patti Harrison, who celebrated her birthday while the Beatles were in Rishikesh. Another says that since Linda's twenty-sixth birthday would come in six days, it was probably written for her.
- George reportedly wore a glove during the recording of "Birthday" to prevent blisters.
- On October 8, 1990, in honor of John Lennon's birthday, Paul McCartney released in the United Kingdom a live single of "Birthday," backed with "Good Day Sunshine." This was the first time a new version of a Beatles song was released by a Beatle after the breakup.

- On June 14, 1991, Paul's promotional video for his live version of "Birthday" was released in Japan by EMI as the first-ever video single CD.
- "Birthday" is one of the two songs on *The White Album* on which Yoko sings. (The other is "The Continuing Story of Bungalow Bill.")
- In the 1984 film *Sixteen Candles*, über-geek Anthony Michael Hall sings Molly Ringwald a few lines from the beginning of "Birthday." (He also serenades her with "Hey Jude.")
- The song has been covered by Dan Baird, Rob Mullins, Saprize, Blur, Underground Sunshine, and John Smith.

The recording

Location: **Abbey Road Studios, London.**

Dates: **September 18, 1968,** 5:00 p.m.–4:30 a.m. – Engineer Chris Thomas commented in *The Beatles Recording Sessions* about the track: "Paul was the first one in, and he was playing the 'Birthday' riff. Eventually the others arrived, by which time Paul had literally written the song, right there in the studio." The Beatles recorded twenty takes. During the evening, the group took a break and went to Paul's house to watch the British TV premiere of the movie *The Girl Can't Help It*, which aired from 9:05 to 10:40. They returned to the studio around 11:00 p.m. to complete the vocals. The song was recorded on a four-track, but transferred to eight-track to accommodate all the overdubs and instruments. Mono mixing.

October 14, 1968 – Stereo mixing.
November 22, 1968 – First released on the U.K. LP *The Beatles* (*The White Album*).

Players/Instruments:
- **Paul McCartney:** Piano, lead vocal ,
- **John Lennon:** Lead guitar, backing and occasional lead vocal
- **George Harrison:** Bass, tambourine
- **Ringo Starr:** Drums
- **Yoko Ono:** Chorus vocals
- **Patti Harrison:** Chorus vocals

Note: Some sources say George played lead guitar; that Ringo and Mal Evans provided handclaps; and that Linda also sang in chorus.

What we really like about this song

Steve: I like how tight a jam can be when it's in the hands of the Beatles. I like Ringo's precision superdrumming. I like the guitar/bass interplay. And I like hearing Yoko singing on a Beatles track. I can picture the Fabs sweating away in the studio, with Yoko (and Patti) watching and singing along. The Beatles' later years were obviously not all contentious and unpleasant, and the good-natured fun of "Birthday" is, without question, a moment from the better times.

Mike: Here's the Beatles' answer to "Happy Birthday to You." Okay, so the song doesn't mean much and the message isn't too deep, but I still love its energy: The boys seem to be fueled by the pure joy of playing together. The song features an infectious riff (first conceived on the piano, interestingly), the hardest drums I've ever heard Ringo hit, and some interesting bass playing by Paul, as he seems to at once answer and echo George's guitar riff throughout.

100 Ḧelter Skelter

*I was in Scotland and I read in
Melody Maker that Pete Townshend
had said, "We've just made the
raunchiest, loudest, most ridiculous
rock 'n' roll record you've ever heard."
I never actually found out what track
it was that The Who had made, but
that got me going, just hearing him
talk about it. So I said to the guys, "I
think we should do a song like that;
something really wild." And I wrote
"Helter Skelter."*

—Paul McCartney
The Beatles Anthology

Js it overstatement to say that metal was
born in 1968 with "Helter Skelter"? Had there been anything
heavier than "Helter Skelter" before *The White Album*? The
Kinks' 1964 classic "You Really Got Me" is often spoken of
as the first heavy metal song, although its "heaviness" today
is perceived as rather tame. In 1965, Alice Cooper hit the
music scene with his band the Spiders and began delivering

a raw style of rock that garnered him the title of first heavy
metal artist. And what about Zeppelin? we hear you musing.
Zeppelin, the ancestral hallowed progenitors of metal as we
know it, were recording their legendary first album in London
in October 1968 as the Fabs were finishing up *The White
Album*. The following month, *The White Album* was released
in the United Kingdom; three days later, it hit the United
States. *Led Zeppelin* came out in January 1969. Was there any
inspirational crossover? Did Jimmy Page and Robert Plant
meet Paul and John for tea and discuss what each group was
working on?

It doesn't really matter who came first. The fact is that rock
got nasty in the late sixties. Peace, and love, and flowers, and
all that "Summer of Love" crap lost its allure; angry rock was
born, and "Helter Skelter" played an important role in its
launch.

Why it made the top 100

"Helter Skelter" is raw, intense, manic metal rock—and it's as fresh today as it was surprising and unexpected thirty years ago. Written solely by Paul, the original studio recording of the song lasted a staggering twenty-seven minutes. Picture the Beatles thrashing away at their instruments for almost half an hour, sweating to make them louder and raunchier and more... well, *metallic*. (No wonder blisters manifested, eh?)

The song begins with a bold, sliding guitar riff that is a perversion of John's similar opening riff for "Revolution"—something of a light side/dark side counterpoint. It was John from whom we expected the cynical, snarling musical mojo. In the case of "Revolution" and "Helter Skelter," however, we've got John espousing the optimistic "you know it's gonna be all right" message while Paul spits out a purgative, boiling-point caterwaul.

Paul has said that he often cites "Helter Skelter" when people dismiss him as nothing but a ballad writer. "Helter Skelter" rocks, and this *White Album* song, along with John's "Everybody's Got Something to Hide Except Me and My Monkey," showed that Paul and the Beatles could quite easily open up the whoop-ass can when they wanted to.

What the song is about

Today, "Helter Skelter" carries a lot of baggage, mostly because of a psychopath with a swastika tattooed on his forehead whose name will not sully this book.

Ostensibly about an amusement park ride, apparently what Paul was thinking about when he wrote the song (John said as much in his 1981 *Playboy* interview in which he described "Helter Skelter" as "Paul's song about an English fairground"), "Helter Skelter" is also a textbook example of a darkly obsessed lover haranguing the object of his affection for what he wants to hear.

"Do you, don't you want me to love you?" the singer shrieks, with more than a little threat in his question. The opening image of an adult sliding down an amusement park ride and then immediately climbing back to the top is classic obsessive-compulsive behavior.

The singer nags his lover and uses the odd phrase "don't let me break you," which could be interpreted a couple of ways. There is the suggested violence, of course, but also the sarcastic plea not to let his entreaties tax her state of mind.

Is this reading too much into the lyrics? Perhaps, since Paul claimed only to want to write something loud and manic, and he probably came up with words that fit the driving movement of the song.

But lyrics and meaning and intent can be misinterpreted, and there had never before been a Beatles song that incited violence. The Beatles were later concerned about what happened with "Helter Skelter" and, in some ways, felt responsible for the results. But they were also confused. At one point John wondered aloud what the words of "Helter Skelter" had to do with knifing someone. Yet the Fabs' production of the song was a deliberate and stark contrast to the theme: They are singing about a playground as industrial metal shrieks and slashes into our ears. Should they truly have been all that surprised that the song was misunderstood?

All art is subject to interpretation, and the possible underlying meanings of the song add more power to what is already a commanding recording.

• • • • ❦ • • • •

- Snippets of "Helter Skelter" can be heard on the Beatles' 1968 Christmas record.
- According to Brian Gibson, the recording engineer for the "Helter Skelter" sessions, "One of the versions developed into a jam which went into and then back out of a somewhat bizarre version of 'Blue Moon.'"[1]

Did you know?

- During the recording of "Helter Skelter," George Harrison lit a fire in an ashtray and ran around the studio holding it over his head, à la crazed British singer Arthur Brown.
- Notable covers of "Helter Skelter" have been recorded by Pat Benatar, U2, Aerosmith, Siouxsie and the Banshees, Mötley Crüe, and Hüsker Dü.

The recording

Location: **Abbey Road Studios, London.**

Dates: **July 18, 1968,** 10:30 p.m.–3:30 a.m. – Three takes were recorded, all of which were essentially rehearsals. Take 1 lasted 10:40, Take 2 lasted 12:35, Take 3 went on for twenty-seven minutes and eleven seconds. All three were similar, consisting of drums, bass, and lead and rhythm guitar played live, with no overdubs. The lyrics were similar to the album version. One of these "alternate" tracks is excerpted on *Anthology 3*.

September 9, 1968, 7:00 p.m.–2:30 a.m. – They liked the crazed song they recorded on July 18 but realized that a twenty-seven-minute song was too long. They decided to remake the song and recorded another eighteen takes. The last, Take 21, was considered the best. John played bass and sax; Mal Evans played trumpet. There were two lead guitars, as well as drums and piano; with backing vocals from John and George, Paul sang lead vocal.

September 10, 1968, 7:00 p.m.–3:00 a.m. – Overdubbing.

September 17, 1968 – Mono remixing. The song now clocked in at 3:36.

October 9, 1968 – Tape copying of the original twenty-seven-minute version. (Paul took this tape for his private collection.)

October 12, 1968 – Stereo remixing. The final song clocked in at 4:20. It had a fade-down and fade-up within the song, and Ringo's scream about the blisters on his fingers.

November 22, 1968 – First released on the U.K. LP *The Beatles*.

Players/Instruments:
- **Paul McCartney:** Bass, lead guitar, lead vocal
- **John Lennon:** Bass, lead guitar, saxophone, backing vocal
- **George Harrison:** Rhythm guitar, backing vocal
- **Ringo Starr:** Drums
- **Mal Evans:** Trumpet

What we really like about this song

Steve: I like that fact that the original version of the song lasted almost half an hour. I've been in jams that went on forever, and I can imagine the energy in the studio as they all just pounded away—on drums *and* guitars. I also like the fact that even though the song is a blistering (no pun intended) head-banger, the guitar work is as good as in any of their more sophisticated songs.

Mike: I like that the song is a full-on, startling, wrenching, determinedly harsh sonic assault. I like the staccato/machine-gun-like guitars, which are sometimes out of tune. I like the crashing cymbals and the insistent beat. I like that "Helter Skelter" is the closest thing to punk or alt rock the Beatles ever did, essentially setting the stage for those who followed. I can hear the Foo Fighters or Queens of the Stone Age doing this song—but the Beatles beat them to it.

[1] *The Beatles Recording Sessions.*

Fans' Faves

While working on this book, we also conducted an unscientific poll of fans' favorite Beatles songs. We asked people we know, celebrities, musicians, and many others to come up with their five favorite Beatles songs and this list is the result.

The picks are revealing (Donovan's favorite Beatles song is "Love Me Do"!) and illustrate the wide range of appeal the music has for people of all ages. Clearly, the band crosses generational lines. Ask a 75-year-old woman to name her favorite U2 song and she'll probably give you a blank stare. Ask this same lady to name her favorite Beatles song (as we did) and you'll get an immediate response: "Yesterday."

So, without further fan-fare (as it were), here are the results of our poll. These are the songs lodged most deeply in the hearts and minds of the fans we polled. Did we miss your favorite one? Sorry about that, but you weren't home when we called. The one thing that **all** of the fans we queried agreed upon unanimously was that choosing a favorite (or even five), is one of the hardest things they've ever done without breaking a sweat.

The Fans' Top 10

1.	"Let It Be"
2.	"In My Life"
3.	"Strawberry Fields Forever"
4. (tie)	"Eleanor Rigby"
	"Hey Jude"
5.	"Here Comes the Sun"
6.	"A Day in the Life"
7.	"I Want to Hold Your Hand"
8. (tie)	"Blackbird"
	"Yesterday"
9.	"Penny Lane"
10.(tie)	"Can't Buy Me Love"
	"Help!"
	"Nowhere Man"
	"Something"

The 206 Beatles Songs

Songs written by a Beatle and appearing on a Beatles album (followed by their Here, There and Everywhere *ranking, if any)*

A

The *Abbey Road* Medley[1] (36)
"Across The Universe" (40)
"All I've Got To Do"
"All My Loving" (60)
"All Things Must Pass"
"All Together Now"
"All You Need Is Love" (5)
"And I Love Her" (48)
"And Your Bird Can Sing" (22)
"Another Girl" (94)
"Any Time At All"
"Ask Me Why"

B

"Baby You're A Rich Man" (61)
"Baby's In Black"
"Back In The USSR" (81)
"The Ballad Of John And Yoko" (96)
"Because" (36)
"Being For The Benefit Of Mr. Kite!" (52)
"Birthday" (9)
"Blackbird" (17)

C

"Can't Buy Me Love" (78)
"Carry That Weight" (36)
"Cayenne"
"Come And Get It"
"Come Together" (33)
"The Continuing Story Of Bungalow Bill"
"Cry Baby Cry"
"Cry For A Shadow"

D

"A Day In The Life" (1)
"Day Tripper" (32)
"Dear Prudence" (82)
"Dig It"
"Do You Want To Know A Secret?"
"Doctor Robert" (73)
"Don't Bother Me"
"Don't Let Me Down" (83)
"Don't Pass Me By"
"Drive My Car" (64)

E

"Eight Days A Week" (31)
"Eleanor Rigby" 27)
"The End" (36)
"Everybody's Got Something To Hide
   Except Me And My Monkey" (63)
"Every Little Thing"

F

"Fixing A Hole" (69)
"Flying"
"The Fool On The Hill"
"For No One" (53)
"For You Blue"
"Free As A Bird" (25)
"From Me To You"

G

"Get Back" (88)
"Getting Better" (35)
"Girl" (80)
"Glass Onion" (56)
"Golden Slumbers" (36)
"Good Day Sunshine" (91)
"Good Morning, Good Morning" (65)
"Good Night"
"Got To Get You Into My Life"

H

"Happiness Is A Warm Gun" (24)
"A Hard Day's Night" (49)
"Hello Goodbye" (76)
"Hello Little Girl"
"Help!" (26)
"Helter Skelter" (100)
"Her Majesty" (36)
"Here Comes The Sun" 14)
"Here, There And Everywhere" (16)
"Hey Bulldog" (72)
"Hey Jude" (6)
"Hold Me Tight"
"Honey Pie"

I

"I Am The Walrus" (11)
"I Call Your Name"
"I Dig A Pony" (aka "Dig A Pony")
"I Don't Want To Spoil The Party"
"I Feel Fine" (19)
"I Me Mine"
"I Need You" (47)
"I Saw Her Standing There" (84)
"I Should Have Known Better" (55)
"I Wanna Be Your Man"
"I Want To Hold Your Hand" (20)
"I Want To Tell You"
"I Want You (She's So Heavy)" (89)
"I Will" (30)
"If I Fell" (46)
"If I Needed Someone" (54)
"If You've Got Trouble"
"I'll Be Back" (34)
"I'll Be On My Way"
"I'll Cry Instead"
"I'll Follow The Sun"
"I'll Get You"
"I'm A Loser" (66)
"I'm Down"
"I'm Happy Just To Dance With You" (87)
"I'm Looking Through You"
"I'm Only Sleeping" (57)
"I'm So Tired" (86)
"In My Life" (7)
"The Inner Light"
"In Spite Of All The Danger"
"It Won't Be Long"
"It's All Too Much" (95)
"It's Only Love" (75)
"I've Got A Feeling"
"I've Just Seen A Face"

J

"Julia" (51)
"Junk"

---

[1] Note that all of the songs in the medley are listed separately here, with their collective ranking of 36.

A Beatles Discography

This book celebrates individual Beatles *songs* based on their own merit, regardless of how they were initially released. We thought it would be interesting, however, to look at the entire list of "100 Best" songs as they were originally unleashed on the world. To avoid confusion, we're using the CD releases as our template since many of the U.K. and U.S. album releases differed in their playlists. After each song, we've listed their *Here, There and Everywhere* ranking.

1962

"Love Me Do"(98)/"P.S. I Love You"

1963

"Please Please Me" (71)/"Ask Me Why"

Please Please Me
* I Saw Her Standing There (84)
* Misery
* Anna (Go To Him)
* Chains
* Boys
* Ask Me Why
* Please Please Me (71)
* Love Me Do (98)
* I Love You
* Baby It's You
* Do You Want To Know A Secret
* A Taste Of Honey
* There's A Place
* Twist And Shout

"From Me To You"/"Thank You Girl"

"She Loves You"[1](15)/"I'll Get You"

With The Beatles
* It Won't Be Long (92)
* All I've Got To Do
* All My Loving (60)
* Don't Bother Me
* Little Child
* Till There Was You
* Please Mr. Postman
* Roll Over Beethoven
* Hold Me Tight
* You've Really Got A Hold On Me
* I Wanna Be Your Man
* Devil In Her Heart
* Not A Second Time
* Money (That's What I Want)

"I Want To Hold Your Hand"[1](20)/ "This Boy"[1](43)

1964

"Can't Buy Me Love"(78)/ "You Can't Do That"

Long Tall Sally EP
* Long Tall Sally
* I Call Your Name
* Slow Down
* Matchbox

"A Hard Day's Night"(49)/"Things We Said Today"

A Hard Day's Night
* A Hard Day's Night (49)
* I Should Have Known Better (55)
* If I Fell (46)
* I'm Happy Just To Dance With You (87)
* And I Love Her (48)
* Tell Me Why
* Can't Buy Me Love (78)
* Any Time At All
* I'll Cry Instead
* Things We Said Today
* When I Get Home
* You Can't Do That
* I'll Be Back (34)

"I Feel Fine"[1](19)/"She's A Woman"

Beatles For Sale
* No Reply (68)
* I'm a Loser (66)
* Baby's In Black
* Rock & Roll Music
* I'll Follow The Sun
* Mr. Moonlight
* Kansas City/Hey-Hey-Hey-Hey!
* Eight Days A Week (31)
* Words of Love
* Honey Don't
* Every Little Thing
* I Don't Want To Spoil The Party
* What You're Doing
* Everybody's Trying To Be My Baby

1965

"Ticket To Ride"(29)/"Yes It Is"

"Help!"(26)/"I'm Down"

Help!
* Help! (26)
* The Night Before
* You've Got To Hide Your Love Away (50)
* I Need You (47)
* Another Girl (94)
* You're Gonna Lose That Girl (67)
* Ticket To Ride (29)
* Act Naturally
* It's Only Love (75)
* You Like Me Too Much
* Tell Me What You See
* I've Just Seen A Face
* Yesterday (4)
* Dizzy Miss Lizzy

"We Can Work It Out"[2](38)/"Day Tripper"[2](32)

Rubber Soul
* Drive My Car (64)
* Norwegian Wood (This Bird Has Flown) (42)
* You Won't See Me
* Nowhere Man (13)
* Think For Yourself
* The Word
* Michelle (77)
* What Goes On
* Girl (80)
* I'm Looking Through You
* In My Life (7)
* Wait
* If I Needed Someone (54)
* Run For Your Life

> [1] Can be found on *Past Masters Vol 1*.
> [2] Can be found on *Past Masters Vol 2*.
> [3] Can be found on *Magical Mystery Tour*.

1966

"Paperback Writer"[2](23)/"Rain"[2](93)

Revolver

- Taxman (45)
- Eleanor Rigby (27)
- I'm Only Sleeping (57)
- Love You To
- Here, There And Everywhere (17)
- Yellow Submarine
- She Said She Said (59)
- Good Day Sunshine (91)
- And Your Bird Can Sing (22)
- For No One (53)
- Doctor Robert (73)
- I Want To Tell You
- Got To Get You Into My Life
- Tomorrow Never Knows (39)

"Yellow Submarine"/"Eleanor Rigby"(27)

1967

"Penny Lane"[3](2)/"Strawberry Fields Forever"[3](8)

Sgt. Pepper's Lonely Hearts Club Band

- Sgt. Pepper's Lonely Hearts Club Band (44)
- With A Little Help From My Friends (58)
- Lucy In The Sky With Diamonds (12)
- Getting Better (35)
- Fixing A Hole (69)
- She's Leaving Home (79)
- Being For The Benefit Of Mr. Kite! (52)
- Within You Without You (97)
- When I'm Sixty-Four
- Lovely Rita (70)
- Good Morning, Good Morning (65)
- Sgt. Pepper's Lonely Hearts Club Band (Reprise) (44)
- A Day In The Life (1)

"All You Need Is Love"[3](5)/"Baby You're A Rich Man"[3](61)

Magical Mystery Tour EP

- Magical Mystery Tour
- The Fool on The Hill
- Flying
- Blue Jay Way
- Your Mother Should Know
- I Am The Walrus (11)
- Hello Goodbye (76)

"Hello Goodbye"(76)/"I Am the Walrus"(11)

1968

"Lady Madonna"[2](41)/"The Inner Light"

"Hey Jude"[2](6)/"Revolution"[2](9)

The Beatles

- Back In The USSR (81)
- Dear Prudence (82)
- Glass Onion (56)
- Ob-La-Di, Ob-La-Da
- Wild Honey Pie
- The Continuing Story Of Bungalow Bill
- While My Guitar Gently Weeps (10)
- Happiness is a Warm Gun (24)
- Martha My Dear (18)
- I'm So Tired (86)
- Blackbird (17)
- Piggies
- Rocky Racoon
- Don't Pass Me By
- Why Don't We Do It In The Road?
- I Will (30)
- Julia (51)
- Birthday (99)
- Yer Blues
- Mother Nature's Son (62)
- Everybody's Got Something To Hide Except Me And My Monkey (63)
- Sexy Sadie (37)
- Helter Skelter (100)
- Long, Long, Long (90)
- Revolution 1 (9)
- Honey Pie
- Savoy Truffle (85)
- Cry Baby Cry
- Revolution 9
- Good Night

1969

Yellow Submarine

- Yellow Submarine
- Only A Northern Song
- All Together Now
- Hey Bulldog (72)
- It's All Too Much (95)
- All You Need Is Love (5)
- Pepperland
- Sea of Time & Sea of Holes
- Sea of Monsters
- March of the Meanies
- Pepperland Laid Waste
- Yellow Submarine in Pepperland

"Get Back"(88)/"Don't Let Me Down"[2](83)

"The Ballad Of John And Yoko"[2](96)/ "Old Brown Shoe"

Abbey Road

- Come Together (33)
- Something (28)
- Maxwell's Silver Hammer
- Oh! Darling
- Octopus's Garden
- I Want You (She's So Heavy) (89)
- Here Comes The Sun (14)
- Because (36)
- You Never Give Me Your Money (36)
- Sun King (36)
- Mean Mr. Mustard (36)
- Polythene Pam (36)
- She Came In Through The Bathroom Window (36)
- Golden Slumbers (36)
- Carry That Weight (36)
- The End (36)
- Her Majesty (36)

"Something"(28)/"Come Together"(33)

1970

"Let It Be"(3)/"You Know My Name (Look Up The Number)"

Let It Be

- Two Of Us
- Dig A Pony
- Across The Universe (40)
- I Me Mine
- Dig It
- Let It Be (3)
- Maggie Mae
- I've Got A Feeling
- One After 909
- The Long And Winding Road (21)
- For You Blue
- Get Back (88)

1996

Anthology 1

60 tracks, including "Free As A Bird" (26)

Anthology 2

45 tracks, including "Real Love" (74)

Index